Footprint Ca

Aleta Moriarty
4th edition

"If you are looking for gold lions, gold Buddhas, bronze elephants, bronze oxen, bronze horses, here is where you will find them."

Chou Ta-Juan, Chinese emissary to Angkor, 1296-1297

Cambodia Highlights

See colour map at back of book

❶ Royal Palace and Silver Pagoda, Phnom Penh
The capital's 19th-century concoction of temples, summerhouses and palaces

❷ Tuol Sleng Museum, Phnom Penh
To remember the dead and remind the living

❸ Choeung Ek
The infamous 'Killing Fields'

❹ Kep
Wonderful, small coastal town with beautiful blooming gardens. Quiet alternative to Sihanoukville

❺ Bokor Mountain National Park
Visit the colonial hill station, where French officers escaped from the heat of the plains

❻ Sihanoukville
Try this resort for an alternative beach holiday

❼ Kirirom National Park
A nifty day trip from Phnom Penh with walks and bathing pools

❽ Koh Kong Island
Laze on stunning white beaches

❾ Phnom Khieu Waterfalls
A seductive excursion from Pailin

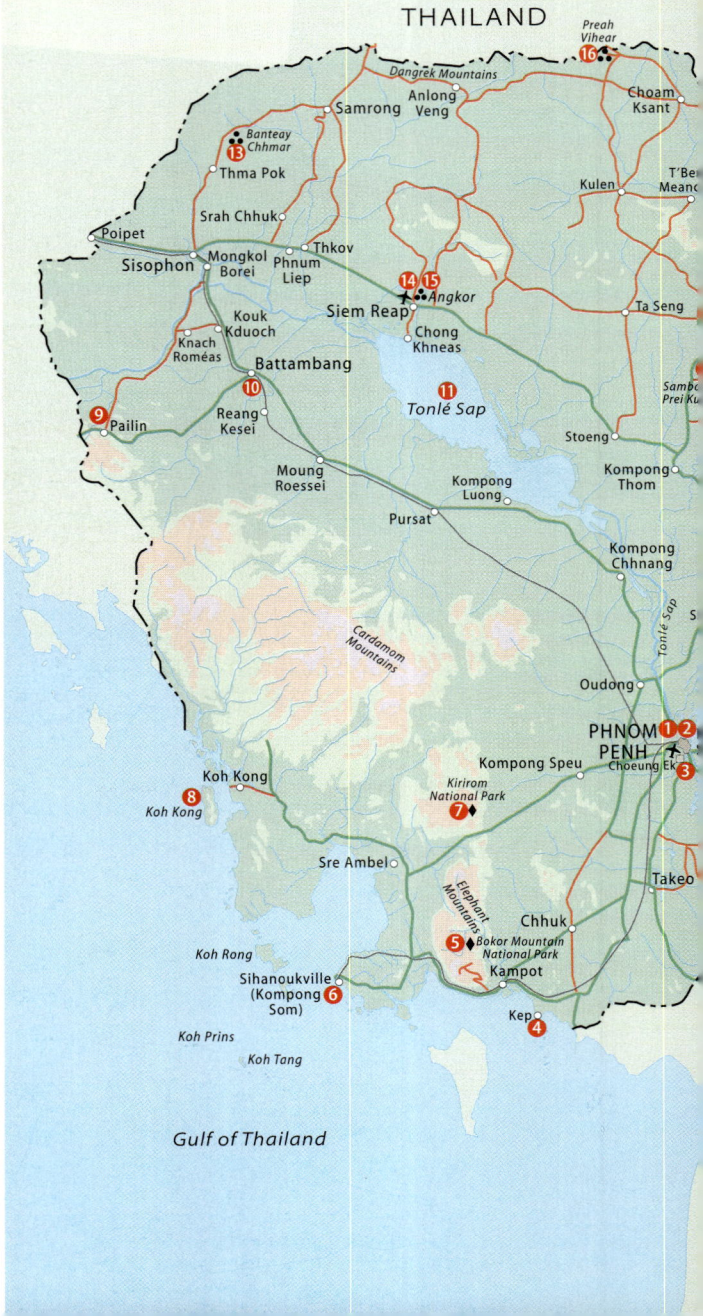

THAILAND

Preah Vihear
❶❻
Choam Ksant

Dangrek Mountains

Anlong Veng
Samrong

Banteay Chhmar ❶❸
Thma Pok

Kulen

T'Be Meanc

Srah Chhuk

Poipet

Mongkol Borei
Thkov

Sisophon
Phnum Liep

❶❹❶❺ Angkor
Siem Reap

Ta Seng

Kouk Kduoch
Chong Khneas

Knach Roméas
Battambang

Sambu Prei Ku

❿ ❶❶ Tonlé Sap

❾ Pailin
Reang Kesei
Stoeng

Moung Roessei
Kompong Luong
Kompong Thom

Pursat
Kompong Chhnang

Cardamom Mountains

Tonlé Sap

Oudong

PHNOM PENH ❶❷
❸ Choeung Ek

Koh Kong
Kompong Speu

❽ Koh Kong
Kirirom National Park
❼

Sre Ambel

Chhuk

Takeo

Koh Rong
Elephant Mountains

❺ Bokor Mountain National Park
Kampot

Sihanoukville (Kompong Som) ❻
Kep
❹

Koh Prins

Koh Tang

Gulf of Thailand

LAOS

Eastern Highlands

Ta Veng

Veng Xai

Ban Lung O Chum

Bokeo

17

Stung Treng

Lumphat

18
Kratie

19
Sen Monorom

Spoe Tbong *Mekong*

Chhlong

Kompong
Cham

Snuol

Prey Vang

VIETNAM

Kompong
Trabék

Svay
Rieng

Bavet

N

0 km — 30
0 miles — 30

10 Battambang
Beautifully situated provincial town. The nearby Bamboo train is Cambodia's most unlikely travel experience

11 Tonlé Sap
Largest freshwater lake in Southeast Asia, supporting numerous floating villages

12 Sambor Prei Kuk
Older than Angkor, the temples here date from the 7th century

13 Banteay Chhmar
One of the least visited of the major Khmer archaeological sites

14 Royal city of Angkor Thom and the Bayon
Simply awesome

15 Angkor Wat
The largest religious monument in the world

16 Preah Vihear
Breathtaking cliffside temple with spectacular views

17 Yaek Lom Lake
Crystal-clear volcanic lake, perfect for a dip

18 Irrawaddy dolphins
Use Kratie as a base to see these endangered mammals

19 Sen Monorom
Explore the area's jungles, local waterfalls and go elephant trekking

The Bayon
The multitude of giant carved faces around this complex at Angkor Thom have come to symbolize the magnificence of Angkor.

A foot in the door

Cambodia is perhaps the most beguiling of all the countries of the Orient. Long associated with the brutal Khmer Rouge, the country has risen above its blood-tinted history to finally take its place as one of the region's pre-eminent tourist destinations. Home to a truly rich mix of travel experiences from ancient monuments and powdery beaches to remote ethnic minority villages and city life, Cambodia never fails to excite the senses.

Ancient Cambodia produced one of world's greatest civilizations at Angkor. But Angkor Wat is merely one temple lying at the heart of a thousand others. The capital, Phnom Penh, retains the sort of skyline most travellers dream of: a sky punctuated by spires, turrets and pinnacles of royal and religious origin rather than by office blocks.

Further south is Sihanoukville, Cambodia's most popular beachside town, characterized by long, palm-fringed beaches, comfy deckchairs and gentle, lapping waters. More adventurous souls will be impressed by the outlying islands, which provide the perfect backdrop for snorkelling, diving or fishing trips. Decrepit colonial ruins scattered through a Garden of Eden landscape make Kep the real gem of the south, however. Infinitely more low key than Sihanoukville, the small town, with its blossoming flowers, burgeoning fruit trees and freshly cooked crab speciality is truly a slice of paradise.

In stark contrast to the laid-back beaches are the northeastern provinces. Here, tracts of red earth cut through hills, carpeted in jungle and speckled with the thatched huts that are home to a miscellany of minority groups. Elephant rides are the call of the day around Sen Monorom, while those looking for adventure in Ban Lung won't be disappointed by the waterfalls, boat rides and the stunning, bottle-green waters of Yaek Lom Lake.

6

1 *Spider cuisine. A lady sells oily arachnids to bus passengers on the Kompong Cham-Kompong Thom bus route.* ▶▶ *See page 35.*

2 *Villages, inhabited mainly by Vietnamese, float on the surface of the Tonlé Sap, the largest freshwater lake in Southeast Asia. Incredibly, it reverses its flow every year.* ▶▶ *See page 129.*

3 *Revered by the Phnong of northeastern Cambodia, elephants are believed to have existed in human form, until they ate some fish which transformed them into pachyderms.* ▶▶ *See page 185.*

4 *Fishing boats bob on the Gulf of Thailand at Sihanoukville on the south coast.* ▶▶ *See page 202.*

5 *The glass tower at Choeung Ek is a memorial to those that died during Cambodia's genocide. It contains skulls from 129 mass graves uncovered on the site, south of Phnom Penh.* ▶▶ *See page 61.*

6 *Cambodians parade during the Bon Om Tuk water festival, Phnom Penh, which celebrates the movement of the water in the Tonlé Sap .* ▶▶ *See page 39.*

7 *Traders do business at Siem Reap market.* ▶▶ *See page 138.*

8 *These five central sky-soaring towers lie at the heart of Angkor Wat.* ▶▶ *See page 101.*

9 *Despite the increase in beach resort facilities for tourists, fishing is still a way of life on the country's southern coast.* ▶▶ *See page 200.*

10 *These sandstone sanctuaries mark the top of the temple-mountain of Phnom Bakheng, Angkor.* ▶▶ *See page 114.*

11 *There are around 700 tigers known to be living in Cambodia.* ▶▶ *See page 208.*

12 *French colonial architecture can be seen in many of Phnom Penh's streets.* ▶▶ *See page 52.*

Historic heart
Monks wander past the gleaming Royal Palace and Silver Pagoda, which dominate the centre of Phnom Penh.

Contents

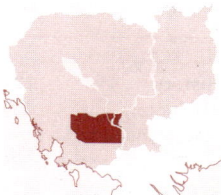

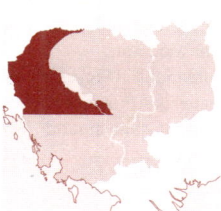

Central region

The Northeast

The South

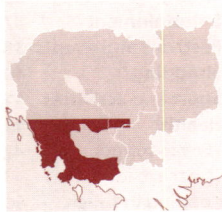

Background

Footnotes

Inside covers

Essentials

Footprint features

Planning your trip

Where to go

Particular highlights which any visitor to Cambodia should try to see include **Phnom Penh**. Sophisticated metropolis it is not, but charming, bustling town it is, with a good selection of early 20th-century architecture, a strong sense of latter 20th-century history and delightful restaurants and bars. The attractions of **Angkor** hardly need further amplification here but you should look beyond just Angkor Wat and the Bayon. Outlying temples, such as Banteay Srei and the Roluos Group, are quite easily accessible and even the less well known ones (for instance Sambor Prei Kuk and Banteay Chhmar) are worth trying to plan into an itinerary. **Cambodia's coastline** is pretty. Sihanoukville is yet to become the burgeoning seaside resort like its Thai counterpart, but still has some lovely beaches. The views on the road between Kampot and Kep (including Bokor Mountain National Park) are scenic highlights. **Kratie** is an idyllic riverside town, where one can rest to the slow ebb and flow of the **Mekong** and catch a glimpse of the rare Irrawaddy dolphins. The surrounding scenery is nothing short of stunning and the bright red sun that sets over the town is truly a highlight of any trip here. Despite the difficulties of getting there, almost all visitors rave about the simple and rustic charms of **northeast Cambodia**, particularly **Ratanakiri** with its hills, trees and tribal minorities. Colourful and remote, this area appeals enormously to the independent and hardened traveller. Otherwise, the remaining towns and areas of Cambodia, while imbued with typical Khmer charm and style, cannot be regarded as being so significantly different from the rest as to justify a major divers on. For most visitors Cambodia's tranquil and, dare one say it, timeless way of life is its greatest appeal – something which requires an unhurried schedule in order to be fully appreciated.

When to go

Those intending to travel extensively overland should visit in the dry season, which spans the months from November until about April. Cambodia's mud and laterite roads are difficult to impossible to pass in the wet season when travel is slow and desperately uncomfortable. This being said, it is probably when the country is at its most beautiful, a million shades of electric green set against stormy grey skies. The dry season offers its own challenges as wind-blown dust invades all bodily cavities and from late March to early April it starts to get unbearably hot. Seasonal festivities are fun to witness but hardly the stuff around which to timetable a holiday. During Khmer New Year it a lot harder to organize travel as most buses are full and hotels booked up. If you wish to travel during this period you will need to book your transport and accommodation well in advance. For visitors from neighbouring countries with larger Chinese populations, Cambodia offers a pleasant escape from Chinese New Year: it is business almost as usual.

Tour operators

UK and Ireland

Audley Travel Ltd, 6 Willows Gate, Stratton Audley, Oxfordshire OX27 9AU, T01869-276200, www.audleytravel.com.

Coromandel, 29a Main St, Lyddington, Oakham, Rutland LE15 9LR, T01572-821330, www.coromandelabt.com.

Exodus Travels, 9 Weir Rd, London, SW12 0LT, T0870-240 5550, www.exodus.co.uk.

Explore Worldwide, 1 Frederick St, Aldershot, Hampshire GU11 1LQ, T0870-333 4001, www.exploreworldwide.com. Arranges small group tours (average 16 people), with many different types of trip offered including cultural excursions, adventure holidays and natural history tours.

Guerba Expeditions, Wessex House, 40 Station Rd, Westbury, Wiltshire BA13 3JN, T01373-858956, www.guerba.co.uk.

Magic of the Orient, 14 Frederick Place, Clifton, Bristol BS8 1AS, T0117-311 6051, www.magic-of-the-orient.com.

Maxwells Travel, D'Olier Chambers, 1 Hawkins St, Dublin 2, Ireland, T01-677 9479, F679 3948. An agent for **Explore Worldwide**.

Regent Holidays, 13 John St, Bristol BS1 2HR, T0117-921 1711, www.regent-holidays.co.uk. One of the leading UK tour operators to Cambodia.

Silk Steps, Deep Meadow, Edington, Bridgwater, TA7 9JH, T01278-722460, www.silksteps.co.uk.

Steppes Travel, 51 Castle St, Cirencester GL7 1QD, T01285-880980, www.steppestravel.co.uk.

Symbiosis, Holly House, Whilton, Daventry, Northamptonshire NN11 5NN, T0845-123 2844, www.symbiosis-travel.com. A company that offers tailor-made tours and expeditions for individuals and groups small and large – particularly expertise in bicycle tours. Symbiosis respects traditional values and cultures and has a high reputation.

Tennyson Travel, 30-32 Fulham High St, London SW6 3LQ, T020-7736 4347, www.visitasia.co.uk.

Travel Indochina, 2nd flr, Chester House, George St, Oxford, OX1 2AY, T01865 268950, www.travelindochina.co.uk.

USA

Adventure Centre, 1311 63rd St, Suite 200, Emeryville, CA 94608, T510-6541879, T1-800-228-8747, www.adventurecenter.com. A company supporting 'Trees for Life' which aims to re-forest denuded areas. Offers 7 different trips in Southeast Asia for 15-30 days.

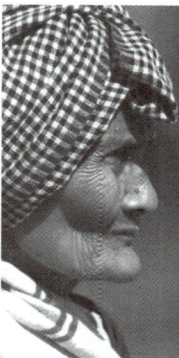
Essentials Planning your trip

14 **Global Spectrum**, 3907 Laro Ct, Fairfax, VA 22031, T1-800-4194446, www.asianpassages.com
Hidden Treasures Tours, 162 West Park Av, 2nd Floor, Long Beach, NY 11561, T888-8899906 (toll free), www.hiddentreasuretours.com.
Himalayan Travel Inc, 8 Berkshire Place, Danbury, CT 06810, T203-7432349, www.himalayantravelinc.com.
Journeys, 107 April Drive, Suite 3, Ann Arbor MI 46103, T734-6654407, www.journeys-intl.com.
Nine Dragons Travel & Tours, 2136 Fullerton Drive, Indianapolis, IN 46224-0105, T1-800-9099050, www.nine-dragons.com.

Australia
Adventure World, Level 20, 141 Walker St, North Sydney, NSW 2060, T02-8913 0755, www.adventureworld.com.au

Intrepid Travel Pty Ltd, 11 Spring St, Fitzroy, Victoria, T1300-360 667, www.intrepidtravel.com.au.
Travel Indochina, 403 George St, Sydney. NSW 2000, T02-9244 2133, T1300-367666, www.travelindochina.com.au.

South Africa
Shiralee Travel, 32 Main Rd, PO Box 1420, Hermanus, 7200, South Africa, T027-11452 6394, www.harveyworld.co.za.

Thailand
Asian Trails, 9th flr, SG Tower, 161/1 Soi Mahadlek Luang 3, Rajdamri Rd, Lumpini, Bangkok, T+66 2-6518111, www.asiantrails.com.
PaddleAsia, PO Box 1, Phuket 8300, www.paddleasia.com.

Finding out more

Tourist information

The national tourist authorities are light years behind Thailand's. They have not yet grasped the simple fact that tourists want accurate, up-to-date information. In fact it is probably best to view a visit to the tourist information office, at least in the more rural areas, as more of a social chat with the locals rather than a means of getting information. At the very best they might offer you their tour guide services for a nominal fee which is usually well-above the market rate. You will, however, be made incredibly welcome and invariably leave with at least a vague idea of what is around and, if you are lucky, you may also be given a map. Cambodia websites are improving year-by-year, and the national tourism authority's site (see below) is a good source of general, practical information on travel, visas, accommodation and so on.

• For a list of tour operators in Phnom Penh, see page 77.

One of the best sources of up-to-date information is through the visitors' guides produced by *Canby Publications*, www.canbypublications.com. Sihanoukville, Angkor and Phnom Penh are all covered in individual guides which can be picked up free of charge at most cafés and bars catering to tourists. The *Cambodian Pocket Guide*, www.cambodiapocketguide.com, also issues free guides for Siem Reap and Phnom Penh. A very good website on Siem Reap and beyond, with particulary pertinent advice on scams and border crossings, is www.talesofasia.com.

Useful websites

Travel

www.cambodian-online.com. Useful starting point with information ranging from visa requirements to hotel reservations. Site does tend to be a bit out of date.
www.tourismcambodia.com/. Cambodia's National Tourism Authority. Good source of general and practical information on travel, visas, accommodation and so on.
www.travel.state.gov. Useful info for travellers.
www.embassy.org/cambodia/.
A remarkably good website set up by the Royal Cambodian Embassy in Washington DC. Informative and reasonably up to date.
www.cambodia.org/. The Cambodian Info Centre. Wealth of information. News, clubs, organizations and politics, photos and facts. Also very good links academic essays, cultural essays, books etc.
www.khmer440.com. Although this site is a tad blokey, the forum is very good for bouncing any specific Cambodia questions to the predominantly expat crowd.
www.yellowpages.com.kh.
Comprehensive listing of phone numbers and addresses for businesses in Cambodia.
www.gocambodia.com. Useful range of practical information.

News

ww.phnompenhpost.com. The *Phnom Penh Post*, Cambodia's main English-language paper. Rather a slow download, but Cambodia's best English-language source of current news and events.
www.cambodiadaily.com. Selected features/stories from the *Cambodia Daily*.
www.cambodia.cc/. Good round-up of news on Cambodia from around the world.
www.bayonpearnik.com. Link for the magazine of the same name. Good up-to-date travel information, particularly good on motorbiking and more intrepid trips around Cambodia.

Art and architecture

www.khmernet.com/books/directory/link/art.html. Cambodian art, dance and culture. Could be of interest to specialists. Interesting site giving depth of knowledge.
www.orientalarchitecture.com. Good historical and archaeological information and maps of the temples in the Angkor area.
www.theangkorguide.com. Fantastic guide to Angkor. A translation of archaeologist Maurice Glaize's work. Good maps, history and photographs.

History and development sites

www.dccam.org. Site of the Documentation Centre of Cambodia which collects, collates and researches the genocide committed under the Khmer Rouge.

www.undp.org.kh. UNDP website gives a thorough, holistic overview of the current state of play in Cambodia's development. **www.licadho.org**. A Cambodian NGO creating awareness of the country's human rights issues including interesting research relating to women's and children's rights.

Language

The national language is Khmer (pronounced Khmei). Unlike other Southeast Asian languages it has no tones. The script is derived from the southern Indian alphabet. French is spoken by the older generation who survived the Khmer Rouge era. English is the language of the younger generations and those who can afford English lessons buy them. Phnom Penh is awash with schools and self-styled 'universities' offering English to the emerging middle class who, thus equipped, take the best jobs in business, in NGOs or in hotels and restaurants. Away from Phnom Penh, Siem Reap and Sihanoukville, to a degree, it can be difficult to communicate with the local population. ▸▸ *See also page 274.*

Disabled travellers

Cambodia may have the world's highest incidence of one-legged and no-legged people (because of landmine injuries) but this does not mean that facilities for the disabled are well developed. Indeed, the country makes no concessions to disabled travellers. Cambodia's own army of disabled simply get on with making their own living with determination and without self pity. In short, it is not an easy country for the disabled traveller. Pavements are often uneven, there are potholes galore, pedestrian crossings are ignored, ramps are unheard of and lifts are few and far between. On top of this, numerous other hazards abound, among the most dangerous of which must number the taxi and moto drivers whose philosophy on road safety remains eccentric. However, while there are scores of hurdles that disabled people will have to negotiate, the Cambodians themselves are likely to go out of their way to be helpful. ▸▸ *See Angkor, page 86, for specific information.*

Gay and lesbian travellers

Gay and lesbian travellers will have no problems in Cambodia. Men often hold other men's hands as do women, so this kind of affection is nothing short of commonplace. Any kind of passionate kissing or sexually-orientated affection in public is taboo – both for straight and gay people. The gay scene is just starting to develop in Cambodia but there is definitely a scene in the making – Linga Bar, Siem Reap and the Salt Lounge, Phnom Penh are both gay bars and are excellent choices for a night out.

Student travellers

Unlike other countries, the Cambodian government (at least post-Khmer Rouge) has not had an anti-backpacker philosophy. The guesthouse sector is well developed and there are sufficient numbers of budget travellers living on a handful of US dollars a day. But there are no specific student discounts in Cambodia but as most students follow the backpacker trail they are already enjoying the best prices available. It is a source of some hard feeling that foreigners pay up to five times the local rate for certain forms of transport (the boat to Siem Reap, for instance) but it is a useful reminder to penurious students that in the locals' minds they are fabulously rich.

ISIC

Anyone in full-time education is entitled to an International Student Identity Card (ISIC). These are issued by student travel offices and travel agencies across the world and offer special rates on all forms of transport and other concessions and services. They sometimes permit free admission to museums and sights, at other times a substantial discount on the entrance charge. **ISIC Association**, Box 9048, 1000 Copenhagen, Denmark, T45-33939303.

Travelling with children

Many people are daunted by the prospect of taking a child to Cambodia. Naturally, it is not something which is taken on lightly: travelling is slower and more expensive and there are additional health risks for the child or baby. But it can be a most rewarding experience, and with sufficient care and planning, it can also be safe. Children are excellent passports into a local culture. The Khmers love babies and children. You will also receive the best service and help from officials and members of the public when in difficulty.

Children in Cambodia are given 24-hour attention by parents, grandparents and siblings. They are rarely left to cry and are carried for most of the first eight months of their lives – crawling is considered animal-like. A non-Asian child is still something of a novelty and parents may find their child frequently taken off their hands, even mobbed in more remote areas. This can be a great relief (at mealtimes, for instance) or most alarming. Some children love the attention, others react against it; it is best simply to gauge your own child's reactions.

Sleeping

At the hottest time of year, air conditioning may be essential for a baby or young child's comfort. This rules out many of the cheaper hotels, but air-conditioned accommodation is available in all larger towns. When the child is bathing, be aware that the water could carry parasites, so avoid letting him or her drink it. Baby powder might help reduce some of the chaffing that comes with the dauntingly hot weather.

Food and drink

Be aware that expensive hotels may have squalid cooking conditions; the cheapest street stall is often more hygienic. Where possible, try to watch food being prepared. Stir-fried vegetables and rice or noodles are the best bet; meat and fish may be pre-cooked and then left out before being re-heated. Fruit can be bought cheaply: papaya and banana are excellent sources of nutrition, and can be self-peeled ensuring cleanliness. Many street stalls make fruit shakes, particularly safe if you ask for them to be ice-free. Powdered milk is available in provincial centres, although most brands have added sugar. Powdered food can also be bought in some towns – the quality may not be the same as equivalent foods bought in the west, but it is perfectly adequate for short periods. Bottled water and fizzy drinks are also sold widely.

Transport

Public transport may be a problem; long bus journeys are restrictive and uncomfortable. There is a limited domestic air network. Chartering a car is undoubtedly the most convenient way to travel overland. But rear seatbelts are scarce and child seats even rarer.

Disposable nappies

These can be bought in Phnom Penh, but are often expensive. If you are staying any length of time in one place, it may be worth taking Terry's (cloth) nappies. All you need is a bucket and some double-strength nappy cleanse (simply soak and rinse). Cotton nappies dry quickly in the heat and are generally more comfortable for the baby or child. They also reduce rubbish – Cambodia is not geared to the disposal of nappies.

Health

More preparation is probably necessary for babies and children than for an adult and perhaps a little more care should be taken when travelling to remote areas where health services are primitive. This is because children can be become more rapidly ill than adults (on the other hand they often recover more quickly). Diarrhoea and vomiting are the most common problems, so take the usual precautions, but more intensively. The treatment of diarrhoea is the same for adults, except that it should start earlier and be continued with more persistence. Children get dehydrated very quickly in hot countries and can become drowsy and uncooperative unless cajoled to drink water or juice plus salts. Upper respiratory infections, such as colds, catarrh and middle ear infections, are also common and if your child suffers from these normally take some antibiotics against the possibility. Outer ear infections after swimming are also common and antibiotic eardrops will help.

Emergencies

Babies and small children deteriorate very rapidly when ill. A travel insurance policy which has an air ambulance provision is strongly recommended. When planning a route, try to stay within 24 hours' travel of a hospital with good care and facilities. Many middle class Cambodians travel to Thailand for health care, and are suspicious of the ability of hospitals, even in the capital, of dealing with more than the most basic problems. Expats also leave the country for health care, usually for Bangkok.

Sunburn

Never allow your child to be exposed to the harsh tropical sun without protection. A child can burn in a matter of minutes. Loose cotton clothing, with long sleeves and legs, and a sunhat are best. High-factor sun-protection cream is essential.

Checklist

Baby wipes; child paracetamol; disinfectant; first aid kit; flannel; immersion element for boiling water; decongestant for colds; instant food for under-one year olds; mug/bottle/bowl/spoons; nappy cleanse, double-strength; ORS (Oral Rehydration Salts), such as Dioralyte, is the most effective way to alleviate diarrhoea (it is not a cure); portable baby chair (to hook onto tables; this is not essential but can be very useful); sarong or backpack for carrying child (and/or light weight collapsible buggy); sterilizing tablets (and container for sterilizing bottles, teats, utensils); cream for nappy rash and other skin complaints such as Sudocrem; sunblock, factor 15 or higher; sunhat; Terry's (cloth) nappies, liners, pins and plastic pants; thermometer; zip-lock bags for carrying snacks etc.

Women travellers

Women travelling alone are an unusual sight in Cambodia and can expect a good deal of curious attention. There are few reports of attacks and so it is a good idea to dress modestly and travel in the company of others in remote areas and after dark especially Phnom Penh.

While women travelling alone can generally face more potential problems than men or couples, these are far less pronounced in Cambodia than in most countries. Women's status is not equal to that of men, but the level of bias is comparatively small compared to other countries, such as Afghanistan for example. Women play a critical role in trade, household and reproductive decision-making; they are also prominent in Cambodian history. However, it is notable that the practice of Buddhism accords men a higher status and in national politics with women playing a very minor role. But the relative power, autonomy and status of women means that it is rare for women to be harassed. Nonetheless women should take care to dress modestly, especially in the smaller, more provincial towns. Here in particular, skimpy tops and micro-shorts still arouse in locals the sort of embarrassed shock their urban counterparts have had to get used to. The best piece of advice for female travellers is to spend a while watching how Khmer women behave and dress and try to follow suit wherever possible. If you·are a single woman and think you will get annoyed by relentlessly being asked if you are married it is recommended that you pop a ring on your wedding finger. Some more 'westernized' motos and tour guides will try to hit on their female passengers or clients so it is a good idea to meet with any guide or moto and suss them out before travelling with them. Older motos and guides tend to be more respectful that their younger counterparts.

Affection in public is not looked upon highly, especially in rural areas. What may be considered in the west as friendly affection, such as putting your arm around someone, could be misconstrued as romantic love in Cambodia, so try not to be too tactile with the men. If you don't have Kate Moss' physique, expect to be called fat – take it with grace as a backhanded compliment. Bring ample underwear and bathers as Cambodian synthetic underwear is uncomfortable (and very, very small) and some might find it hard trying to squeeze their breasts into the local Madonna-style, conical brassieres. Tampons and sanitary napkins can be purchased in major metropolitan centres but are thin on the ground in other areas, so a backup supply from home wouldn't hurt.

Working in the country

Work is not easily available in Cambodia. There is a vibrant expat community, mostly of aid workers (with NGOs or bilateral/multilateral agencies) as well as the usual diplomatic corps. The *Cambodia Daily* and *Phnom Penh Post* regularly advertise jobs. The locally-run website www.bongthom.com also has quite a large and regularly updated employment section. But unlike Thailand there is not great scope for people to, for example, stay here for a few months and teach English. More and more often western-run backpacker-orientated guesthouses are offering guests the free board in exchange for managing the fort for a week or so but this is about the only real short-term prospect available.

Before you travel

Visas and immigration

All foreign nationals, except for Malaysians, Thais and Filipinos, are required to obtain a visa either before arrival at a Cambodian embassy or on arrival. **Visas** for a 30-day stay are available on arrival at Phnom Penh's **Pochentong Airport,** Siem Reap's international airport, and at the border crossing point with Vietnam at Bah Vet and at the overland crossing points with Thailand at Pailin, O'Smach, Anlong Veng, Koh Kong and Poipet. Visas are not available at the Lao border, so organize in advance.

At the airport, fill in the form and hand over one photograph (4 x 6 cm). Tourist visas cost US$20, business visas US$25. Your passport must be valid for at least six months from date of entry into Cambodia. Children under 14 require a visa, but these are processed free of charge. Officials tend to demand the higher figure no matter which visa has been applied for, so bear this in mind when collecting change.

For all **other points of entry to Cambodia**, visas have to be obtained beforehand. The Cambodian Embassy in Bangkok issues visas in one day if you apply in the morning, as does the Consulate General in Ho Chi Minh City, Vietnam. In both Vietnam and Thailand, travel agencies are normally willing to obtain visas for a small fee. Cambodia has a few missions overseas from which visas can be obtained. Travellers using the Lao border should try to to arrange visa paperwork in advance in either Phnom Penh, Bangkok or in Laos' capital, Vientiane. If leaving Cambodia for Laos an exit permit will need to be obtained from Strung Treng's immigration police. This permit should be presented to the border guards, who in turn should provide the entry visa. However, as things are rarely this simple, expect to be charged anything up to US$40 for the privilege of crossing. There is a lot of confusion surrounding this permit as its availability changes all the time. Check details with local tourism authorities before contemplating this.

Travellers leaving Cambodia via Moc Bai must ensure their Vietnam visa specifies Moc Bai as point of entry otherwise they could be be turned back.

Extensions can be obtained at the Immigration Department, Confederation de la Russie, across the road from Phnom Penh International Airport, T023-9990380.Most travel agents arrange visa extensions for around US$40 for 30 days. Those overstaying their visas are fined US$5 per day, although the officials at the land crossings often try to squeeze out more.

Customs and duty free

Customs tend to be very relaxed both on arriving and leaving. A reasonable amount of tobacco products and spirits can be taken in without incurring customs duty – roughly 200 cigarettes or the equivalent quantity of tobacco, one bottle of liquor and perfume for personal use.Taking any Angkorian era images out of the country is strictly forbidden.

Vaccinations

Check with your doctor what vaccinations are necessary. Similarly check with your doctor for their recommendation on malaria prophylaxis. ▸▸ *For more detailed health information, see also page 21.*

Embassies abroad

Australia 5 Canterbury Cres, Deakin, Canberra, ACT 2600, T612-6273 1259, www.embassy ofcambodia.org.nz.
France 4 rue Adolphe Yvon, 75116 Paris, T331-4503 4720, ambcambodgeparis@mangoosta.fr.
Germany Benjamin-Vogelsdorf Strasse, 213187, Berlin, T4930-4863 7901, REC-Berlin@tonline.de.
Japan 8-6-9, Akasaka, Minato-Ku, Tokyo 1070052, T813-5412 8522, aap33850@hkg.odn.ne.jp.

Laos Thadeua Rd, KM2 Vientiane, BP34, T8562-1314950, F1314951.
Thailand 185 Rajdamri Rd, Lumpini Patumwan, Bangkok 10330, T662-2546630, recbkk@cscoms.com.
USA 4530, 16th St, NW Washington, DC20011, T202-7267742, www.embassy.org/cambodia.
Vietnam 71 Tran Hung Dao St, Hanoi, T844-9424788, arch@fpt.vn; 41 Phung Khac Khoan, Ho Chi Minh City, T848-8292751, cambocg@hcm.vmn.vn.

What to take

Travellers usually tend to take too much. In Phnom Penh it is possible to buy most toiletries and other personal items, although they are imported and therefore pricier than elsewhere in the region. Outside the capital the range of products, beyond items like soap, washing powder, batteries, shampoo and the like, is limited.

Suitcases are not appropriate if you are intending to travel overland by bus. A backpack, or even better a travelpack (where the straps can be zipped out of sight), is recommended. Travelpacks have the advantage of being hybrid backpacks/suitcases.

In terms of clothing, dress in Cambodia is relatively casual – even at formal functions. However, though formal attire may be the exception, dressing tidily is the norm. Travellers tend to take too many of the same articles of clothing: be aware, laundry services are quick and cheap.

Checklist

Bumbag; earplugs; first aid kit; insect repellent and/or electric mosquito mats and coils; international driving licence; photocopies of essential documents; spare passport photographs; sun-protection cream; sunglasses; Swiss Army knife; torch; umbrella; wet wipes; zip-lock bags. Those intending to stay in budget accommodation might also include a cotton sheet sleeping bag; money belt; padlock (for hotel room and pack); soap; toilet paper; towel; travel wash.

Insurance

Always take out travel insurance before you set off and read the small print carefully. Check that the policy covers the activities you intend or may end up doing. Also check exactly what your medical cover includes, ie ambulance, helicopter rescue or emergency flights back home. Also check the payment protocol. You may have to cough up first before the insurance company reimburses you. It is always best to dig out all the receipts for expensive personal effects like jewellery or cameras. Take photos of these items and note down all serial numbers. You are advised to shop around. **STA Travel** and other reputable student travel organizations offer good value policies. Young travellers from North America can try the **International Student Insurance Service** (ISIS), which is available through STA Travel, T1-800-7770112, www.sta-travel.com. Other recommended travel insurance companies in North

America include **Travel Guard**, T1-800-8261300, www.noelgroup.com; **Access America**, T1-800- 2848300; **Travel Insurance Services**, T1-800-9371387; and **Travel Assistance International**, T1-800-8212828. Older travellers should note that some companies will not cover people over 65 years old, or may charge higher premiums. The best policies for older travellers (UK) are offered by **Age Concern**, T01883-346964.

Money

Currency

The **riel** is the official currency. Notes in circulation are 50, 100, 200, 500, 1000, 2000, 5000, 10,000, 50,000 and 100,000 riel although higher value denominations are rarely seen. **American dollars** are widely accepted and easily exchanged across the country. In Phnom Penh and other towns most goods and services are priced in dollars and there is little need to buy riel. US notes with even the smallest tear are generally not accepted and some of the newer US notes aren't accepted in rural areas. Counterfeit dollars are reasonably common, so check for the watermark line and the texture of the paper notes are printed on. In remote rural areas prices are quoted in riel (except accommodation). In western border districts, particularly Poipet, Pailin and Koh Kong the **Thai baht** is widely used.

✦ In December 2005, US$1 was worth 4224 riel and 41.51 Thai baht.

Exchange

Money can be exchanged in banks and hotels. Rates are better in Phnom Penh but differ little between bank and street. US dollar traveller's cheques are easiest to exchange with commissionon encashment ranging from 1 to 3%. Outside Phnom Penh, Siem Reap and Sihanoukville it is hard to cash traveller's cheques. The banks often give a lower exchange rate than money changers in the markets etc. Cash advances on your credit card are available in Phnom Penh, Siem Reap, Sihanoukville and Battambang. Money can be wired through the branches of Western Union at most major Acleda branches and Moneygram through Canadia Bank branches.

Credit cards and ATMs

Credit card facilities are limited but some banks, hotels and restaurants do accept them, mostly in Phnom Penh, Sihanoukville and Siem Reap. **Canadia Bank**, a chain, has branches dotted all over the country and generally does credit cash advances. The most common bank is **Acleda**, which is present in almost every major town and although they don't do cash advances it does have a Western Union facility if you run out of cash. **UCB** also has a major presence across the country and will do cash advances on credit cards (without commission). If travelling outside the main tourist areas, do not count on plastic to keep you going. **ANZ Bank** has recently opened a number of ATMs throughout Phnom Penh, the first in Cambodia.

Cost of travelling

The budget traveller will find that a little goes a long way in Cambodia. Numerous guesthouses offer accommodation at around US$3-7 a night (often less if you're sharing). Food-wise, the seriously strapped can easily manage to survive healthily on US$4-5 per day, so an overall daily budget (not allowing for excursions) of US$7-9 should be enough for the really cost-conscious. For the less frugally minded, a daily allowance of US$30 should see you relatively well-housed and fed, while at the upper end of the scale, there are, in Phnom Penh and Siem Reap, plenty of restaurants and hotels for those looking for Cambodian-levels of luxury. A mid-range hotel (attached bathroom, hot water and air-conditioning) will normally cost around US$25 per night.

A good meal at a restaurant, perhaps US$5-10. The cost of travelling around Cambodia is dependent largely on your chosen method of transport. The variety of available domestic flights means that the bruised bottoms, dust-soaked clothes and stiff limbs that go hand-in-hand with some of the longer bus/boat rides can be avoided by those with thicker wallets and deeper pockets. As the roads improve and journey times diminish, the bus is now quite a viable option on certain routes.

Getting there

Air

International connections with Cambodia are still poor – but improving – and most travellers will need to route themselves through Bangkok as it is generally the cheapest regional hub to get to and offers the best connections with both Phnom Penh and Siem Reap. There are direct flights only from within the region. The most important entry point remains Phnom Penh but recently more international flights direct to Siem Reap have been launched (see below).

To/from Phnom Penh: there are connections with Thailand (Bangkok), Malaysia (Kuala Lumpur), Singapore, Hong Kong, China (Guangzhou and Shanghai), Vietnam (Ho Chi Minh City), Taiwan (Taipei) and Laos (Vientiane and Pakse). The following airlines currently operate international services to Phnom Penh's Pochentong Airport: **Bangkok Airways; Silk Air; Dragon Air; Thai; Malaysia Airlines; Vietnam Airlines; Siem Reap Airways; Lao Airlines; China Southern Airlines** and **Shanghai Airlines**.

To/from Siem Reap: there are connections with Bangkok, Kuala Lumpur, Taipei, Singapore, Ho Chi Minh City (Vietnam), Hanoi (Vietnam), Luang Prabang (Laos) and Vientiane (Laos). **Bangkok Airways, Vietnam Airlines, Silk Air** and **Lao Airlines** all operate flights to Siem Reap. Again the most popular international connection is with Bangkok.

Bangkok Airways, 99 Mu 14, Vibhavadirangsit Rd, Chom Phon, Chatuchak, Bangkok, Thailand T+66 2 2655555 and Bethmannstrasse 58, D-60311, Frankfurt/Main, Germany, T+49 69-13377565, www.bangkokair.com, siemriepairways.com. The airline offers useful air passes for the region.

Getting to Bangkok

Around 40 airlines and charter companies fly to Bangkok. **From Europe** the approximate flight time from London to Bangkok (non-stop) is 12 hours. There are direct flights from most major cities in Europe. From London Heathrow, airlines offering non-stop flights include **Qantas, British Airways, Thai Airways** and **Eva Air**. **Philippine Airlines** flies a two-stop service from Gatwick. There are non-stop flights from Athens with **Thai** and **Olympic**, Amsterdam with **KLM** and **China Airlines**, Copenhagen with **Thai** and **SAS**, Frankfurt with **Thai, Lufthansa** and **Garuda**, Paris with **Thai** and **Air France**, and Zurich with **Thai**.

From the USA and Canada the approximate flight time from Los Angeles to Bangkok is 21 hours. There are one-stop flights from Los Angeles with **Thai** and two-stops with **Delta**; one-stop flights from San Francisco with **Northwest** and **United** and two-stops with **Delta**; and one-stop flights from Vancouver with **Canadian**. There's also a direct flight from New York with **Thai**.

From Australasia there are flights from Sydney and Melbourne (approximately nine hours) daily with **Qantas, Malaysia Airlines** and **Thai**. There is also a choice of other flights with **British Airways, Alitalia, Lufthansa** and **Lauda Air** which are less frequent. There are flights from Perth with **Thai** and **Qantas**. From Auckland, **Air New Zealand, Thai** and **British Airways** fly to Bangkok.

Road

It is possible to enter Cambodia, overland, from Thailand, Vietnam and Laos. Travellers coming from Thailand usually cross at **Poipet** (they then face a long overland journey, on a particularly bad road, to Siem Reap) and obviously this is the choice of those wishing to stretch their travel budget as far as it will go. The Poipet crossing is usually not the most pleasant experience. There are now other overland entries from Thailand through Pailin (very rough roads), Anlong Veng (reasonably rough roads) and Koh Kong. As ever, the overland route from Vietnam via **Moc Bai** is the slow but cheap option for travellers coming from the east, and the border crossing at **Chau Doc** has enabled those coming from Vietnam to take the more scenic river route. There is a brand new scenic border open via Kep between Cambodia (Phnom Den) and Vietnam (Tinh Bien). The border crossing from Laos, close to the town at **Stung Treng**, is open bu no visas are issued at the border with Laos.

Entering from Vietnam

It is possible to travel the 245 km from Ho Chi Minh City to Phnom Penh on Highway 1, via the border crossing at **Moc Bai/Bavet** (on the Vietnamese/Cambodian sides of the border respectively). There is a daily through bus connection but it is desperately slow and overland travellers are better advised to travel by minibus organized by tour operators and change at the border to a share taxi. From Ho Chi Minh City to Moc Bai takes about three hours and from Moc Bai to Phnom Penh a further six hours or so with one ferry crossing. A share taxi from the border to Phnom Penh along National Route 1 should cost around US$10. There is a second overland entry point from Vietnam: the border crossing at **Chau Doc** has the advantage of offering a scenic river route. It is rumoured that the Vietnamese border crossing at Ha Tien, near Kep, will be open to the public shortly but travellers should check with the embassy before attempting this crossing. See below, under River, for further details.

❖ For road connections to Vietnam from Phnom Penh, see page 79.

Entering from Thailand

It is also possible to enter Cambodia overland from Thailand at two points: Aranya Prathet in northeast Thailand (to Poipet in Cambodia), and Trat in the far east of Thailand, on the Gulf of Thailand. Those entering from **Aranya Prathet** to **Poipet** can obtain a visa on arrival (US$20) and will need photographs. It is advisable, but not necessary, to organize a visa beforehand to avoid the corrupt officials overcharging at the border. From Bangkok to the Poipet border crossing takes four to five hours by air-conditioned coach. There are a number of scams with Bangkok based transport operators, most private bus companies (particularly around the Khao San Road area) are charging a ridiculous amount of money to get to the Cambodian border and taking about 10 hours longer than the trip should take. Public buses depart from Bangkok's Northern bus terminal (Morchit) every hour or less between 0400-1800. This way is recommended above any private operator as it is cheaper, more comfortable and a quicker option (four hours).

From Poipet taxis and pickups are available to Siem Reap for approximately 1000 baht (US$25) – this can be shared among all passengers (try and get a group together prior to bargaining with a taxi). The road to Siem Reap is particularly bad but should take between 2½-3½ hours. Despite the time involved this is a popular option for those wishing to explore Indochina and Southeast Asia overland. The border crossing closes at 1700.

The second crossing point from Thailand is via **Trat to Cham Yem** in Cambodia's Koh Kong Province. Visas are available on arrival. From Cham Yem there are boat connections to Sihanoukville (US$20, three hours) and from there to Phnom Penh (225 km, around three hours).

Entering from Laos

The recently opened border crossing from Laos is close to the town of **Stung Treng**. See under river below, for further details on this crossing point. This border crossing is yet to institutionalize any sort of standards and travellers will often have to negotiate with border officials over visa price etc. Often people will be stranded half way across the river and will be required to renegotiate their boat ride from there. You will need to obtain your visa in advance for this crossing.

Sea/river

There are sailings from **Ho Chi Minh City** (Saigon) to Phnom Penh. Saigon tour cafés run minibuses to Chau Doc and on to the border which is crossed on foot. Change to a speed boat which will take you to **Neak Luong** in Cambodia. Disembark here and take a taxi/pickup along Route 1 to Phnom Penh. From **Stung Treng** to the Lao border either charter a speed boat, which will take approximately 1½ hours, or board the slow ferry that leaves daily at around 0730 which will take approximately 3½ hours.

There are daily speedboat connections between **Hat Lek** in Thailand and **Koh Kong** and **Sre Ambel** in Cambodia. From Koh Kong there are connections direct to Sihanoukville. The sea route, in open speedboats, is not recommended to those who value their comfort and safety. The Sre Ambel connection is less reliable but it is quicker for visitors wishing to get to Phnom Penh. From Hat Lek or Trat there are buses to Pattaya, Bangkok and Bangkok's Don Muang airport. Check on timings before departing as Koh Kong is not a place where spending more than a day or two is good for peace of mind. Cruise ships visit the international seaport of Sihanoukville.

Touching down

Airport information

Phnom Penh

Collecting your visa on arrival, clearing immigration, reclaiming baggage and clearing customs at Phnom Penh's **Pochentong Airport** is a straightforward affair and the whole process is usually complete in around half an hour. For those wanting the luxury of extending their visa beyond the normal 30-day tourist visa, opt for a business visa. The airport has a limited range of facilities which include a café and money exchange. There is an enthusiastic but not too pushy crowd of taxi drivers who will grab your luggage unless you watch it closely. A taxi to town – just 8 km – costs US$5. Moto (motorbike taxi) into town, which is an easy option for those with light luggage, costs no more than US$2. There is an airport taxi desk inside the airport for those who prefer not to have to negotiate their ride into town.

Siem Reap

Siem Reap's airport is 7 km from the town. To get to the town hire a moto, US$1, or car, US$5-7. Guesthouse owners often meet flights and some offer free rides.

Taxes

Airport tax in Cambodia is US$25 for international flights and US$6 for internal flights.

Touching down

Business hours Government offices are open 0730-1700, banks 0800-1600 and most other businesses usually open 0700-2000.
Emergency services Police: 117, Fire: 118, Ambulance: 119.

Official time Seven hours ahead of GMT.
Voltage 220V. Round two-pin sockets.
Weights and measures Metric.

Local customs and laws

Cambodians are relaxed, easy-going people who are unlikely to take or give offence. Decent behaviour is never going to upset the Cambodians and it is difficult for normal people to offend them unwittingly. Only crass behaviour, such as patting people on the head or invading their homes uninvited, will upset them. One of the sheer joys of Cambodia and the reason for its enduring popularity among travellers is the simplicity of the way of life and the population's tolerance of others.

Clothing/conduct

Shoes should be removed before entering **temples** and a small donation is often appropriate. In private homes it is polite to take your shoes off on entering the house and a small present goes down well if you are invited for a meal.

Women should **dress appropriately**. Short skirts, midriff-baring and cleavage-exposing tops and tight outfits are deemed clothes that prostitutes wear. If you choose to dress like this then you may unwittingly attract undesirable attention and potentially offend some people.

Cambodians use their traditional **greeting** – the 'wai' – bowing with their hands held together. As a foreigner, shaking hands is perfectly acceptable.

When visiting a temple do dress respectfully (keep bare flesh to a minimum) and take off your hat and shoes. Put your legs to one side and try not to point the soles of your feet at anyone or the Buddha image. Females are not to touch monks or sit beside them on public transport.

Displays of anger or exasperation are considered unacceptable and therefore reflect very badly on the individual. Accordingly, even in adversity, Khmers (like the Thais) will keep smiling.

Displays of affection are also considered embarrassing and should be avoided in public areas. Try not to pat anyone on the head. To beckon someone, use your hand with the palm facing downwards. Pointing is rude.

Tipping

Tipping is rare but appreciated. Salaries in restaurants and hotels are low and many staff hope to make up the difference in tips. As with everywhere else, good service should be rewarded.

Prohibitions and getting out of trouble

As Amit Gilboa's book, *Off the Rails in Phnom Penh*, makes clear, **drugs** are not a problem in Cambodia, which is to say are readily available and cheap, or in other words, a big problem – depending on your point of view. Many places use marijuana in their cooking and the police seem to be quite ambivalent to dope smokers (unless they need to supplement their income with your bribe money, in which case – watch out). Other drugs are a definite 'no-no'. Drugs are illegal in Cambodia, so there is always a legal risk if you wish to indulge.

Without exaggeration, one of the biggest dangers for travellers in Cambodia today is dying of an overdose – a much higher risk than being shot, beaten, blown up by a landmine or other 'dangers' associated with this 'Off the Rails' lifestyle. Travellers are the highest risk group when it comes to drug overdoses (or at least the group most reported) and it was widely believed that during 2004-2005, at least one traveller a day was reported dead from a drug overdose. The backpacker areas around the lake in Phnom Penh and Sihanoukville are particularly prone to the problem, with travellers being pulled out of seedy guesthouses week in week out.

The frequency of overdoses is largely attributed to the fact that the people buying drugs aren't getting what they thought they were. Assume this as a given in Cambodia. Most people found dead (by overdose) thought they had bought ecstasy or cocaine and were given heroin. It is important to note that cocaine and ecstasy do not really exist in Cambodia, despite what you may be told.

Another particularly nasty side effect from the drugs explosion in Cambodia is the introduction of yaa baa. Although the drug has been around the region for a while it really has taken a stranglehold of Cambodia, especially in urban areas. This is a particularly insidious amphetamine that has sent numerous people mad – it has a corrosive effect on the mind, incites violence (which would make a rabid dog look calm) and can be lethal.

The legal component aside, the other risk in taking illicit drugs in Cambodia is the type of people associated with the scene – the dealers are known to be particularly nasty characters, lacking ethics and usually carrying guns. In a nutshell – don't buy illicit drugs in Cambodia, it is dangerous.

Religion

Most Cambodians are **Buddhist**. Cambodian Buddhism is an easy-going, tolerant religion which happily co-exists with more primitive worship of ancestors and spirits. Hill tribes tend to be **animist**, worshipping the spirits of trees, the land, the hearth and so on.

✷ For more information on Cambodia's religions, see page 269.

Responsible tourism

"Tourism is like fire. It can either cook your food or burn your house down". This sums up the ambivalent attitude that many people have regarding the effects of tourism. It is one of Cambodia's largest foreign exchange earners, and the world's largest single industry; yet many people in receiving countries would rather tourists go home. Tourism is seen to be the cause of polluted beaches, rising prices, loose morals, consumerism, and much else besides.

Most international tourists come from a handful of wealthy countries. This is why many see tourism as the new 'imperialism', imposing alien cultures and ideals on sensitive and 'unmodernized' peoples. But discussions of the effects of tourism cannot be reduced to a checklist of 'positive' and 'negative' effects. This is a complex issue. Different destinations will be affected in different ways; these effects are likely to vary over time; and different groups living in a particular destination will feel the effects of tourism in different ways and to varying degrees. At no time or place can tourism (or any other influence) be categorized as uniformly 'good' or 'bad'.

Some tourists are attracted to Cambodia because of its culture and supposed exoticism. When cultural erosion is identified, the tendency is to blame this on tourists and tourism who become the so-styled 'suntanned destroyers of culture'. The problem with views like this is that they assume that change is bad, and that indigenous cultures are unchanging. It makes local people victims of change rather than masters of their own destinies. It also assumes that tourism is an external

! How big is your footprint?

● Learn about the country you're visiting.

● Start enjoying your travels before you leave by tapping into as many sources of information as you can.

● Think about where your money goes – be fair and realistic about how cheaply you travel. Try and put money into local people's hands: drink local beer or fruit juice rather than imported brands and stay in locally-owned accommodation.

● Open your mind to new cultures and traditions. It can transform your holiday experience and you'll earn respect and be more readily welcomed by local people.

● Think about what happens to your rubbish – take biodegradable products and a water filter bottle.

Be sensitive to limited resources like water, fuel and electricity.

● Help preserve local wildlife and habitats by respecting rules and regulations, such as sticking to footpaths, not standing on coral and not buying products made from endangered plants or animals.

● Use your guidebook as a starting point, then talk to local people to discover your own adventure.

✖ Don't treat people as part of the landscape, they may not want their picture taken. Put yourself in their shoes, ask first and respect their wishes.

This is taken from the Tourism Concern website.

influence, when in fact it quickly becomes part of the local landscape. Cultural change is inevitable and on-going, and 'new' and 'traditional' are only judgements, not absolutes. Thus new cultural forms can quickly become key markers of tradition. Tourists searching for an 'authentic' experience are assuming that tradition is tangible, easily identifiable and unchanging. It is none of these.

Tourist art, both material (for instance, sculpture) and non-material (like dances), is another issue where views over the impacts of tourism sharply diverge. The mass of inferior 'airport' art on sale to tourists demonstrates, to some, the corrosive effects of tourism. It leads craftsmen and women to mass-produce second rate pieces for a market that appreciates neither their cultural or symbolic worth, nor their aesthetic value. Yet tourism can also give value to craft industries that would otherwise be undermined by cheap industrial goods.

The environmental deterioration that is linked to tourism is due to a destination area exceeding its 'carrying capacity' as a result of overcrowding. Hotel owners will always build those few more bungalows or that extra wing, to maximize their profits, reassured in the knowledge that the environmental costs will be shared among all hotel owners. So, despite most operators appreciating that over-development may 'kill the goose that lays the golden eggs', they do so anyway. Many areas of Cambodia have few other development opportunities and those with beautiful landscapes and/or exotic cultures find it difficult not to resist the temptation to market them and attract the tourist dollar. And why shouldn't they?

As a tourist there are actions and considerations one can take to promote responsible tourism.

Shop and eat locally. Tourism Concern estimates that 70-85% of tourism revenue is siphoned off to foreign-owned hotels, tourism operators, companies and businesses. Tourism is one of Cambodia's primary hopes in alleviating poverty, so please try to spend your money with local businesses, they desperately need it. And be generous. Even though tips aren't expected, if you think the service is exceptional you should tip, it helps incentivize good standards and generally waiters/waitresses etc don't receive very high wages. Although **haggling** is generally accepted in Cambodia, don't drag people down and cause them to lose face by fighting the price down, it's highly offensive and degrading. Often Cambodians will succumb to excessive heckling, just to put an end to it, even though they are selling things at cost price.

Avoid buying products that exploit native wildlife, especially souvenirs made from endangered species, such as ivory. See www.cites.org or www.traffic.org for further information.

Also avoid buying any objects that appear to be ancient artifacts; the looting of temples is a severe problem in Cambodia.

A survey conducted found that 80% of UK respondents would object if rich tourists came and took their **photograph** without permission. Always ask permission before taking people's photographs, particularly in minority groups where some believe photography can have a negative spiritual impact; it is basic courtesy.

Coral reefs are considered the most diverse of all marine systems and are believed to nurture nine million different species of marine life. Unfortunately 27% of the world's reefs have already been lost. If diving/snorkelling do not stand on coral reefs or touch them, it is highly damaging and definitely don't buy any coral off vendors around Cambodia's coastal areas. Ensure that the boat operators do not anchor onto coral reefs.

Sex tourism is always a major no-no. Many tourists try to justify the exploitation of women and children by saying they are less exploitative than local offenders. Regardless it's a highly oppressive practice, which takes advantage of the poor.

When visiting **minority villages**, try to ensure that the visit is endorsed/run by the local communities themselves. Ask local guides/guides about gifts to villages. School materials are generally more useful than lollies etc. Try to channel gifts through the village head or parents, so as not to disrupt traditional authority patterns (although sometimes this way it can be difficult to ensure they get to the end user).

Research the **cultural and social norms** of Cambodia before visiting, such as dress rules and taboos about public affection – it will help you to fit in. If you learn a few words of Khmer the locals really appreciate the extra effort. Be patient, Cambodians have a different concept of time. Try to avoid overt displays of wealth, jewellery, flaunting money etc. It creates a distance between you and the locals.

Pressure groups

Tourism Concern, a UK-based charity, works to resolve some of the issues sketched out above in a constructive manner. It is possible to subscribe to its magazine, *In Focus*, by writing to Tourism Concern, Stapleton House, 277-281 Holloway Road, London N7 8HN, www.tourismconcern.org.uk. The homepage of the **Nautilus Institute** (www.nautilus.org) focuses on issues connected with the environment and sustainability in the Asia-Pacific region.

Safety

Cambodia is not as dangerous as some would have us believe and it has been working on its tourism safety record in recent years. The country has really moved forward in protecting tourists and violent crimes towards visitors is, comparatively, low. Like any other country dangers and annoyances exist, but overall Cambodia is as safe as most other tourist destinations. Since large penalties have been introduced for those who hurt, kill or maim tourists, random acts of violence aren't as common these days. Regardless, it is important to exercise caution and listen to your instincts, they are usually never wrong. Khmer Rouge are no longer a problem, now it is simply unscrupulous men with guns.

❗ Mine safety

Very few foreign visitors have been injured, maimed or killed by landmines in Cambodia. Most that have were members of the UNTAC mission. However, mines do pose an ever-present danger (see the box on page 258) and as tourists venture further off the beaten track, so the risks increase proportionately.

The following is a short checklist of ways to avoid injury taken from a special supplement in the *Phnom Penh Post* published to coincide with Cambodia's first Mine Awareness Day in February 1995:

Ask local people whether mines are a problem in an area before venturing out by inquiring 'mian min teh?' Ask more than one local, just to make sure.

✅ Stick to known safe paths.
✅ Use a guide wherever possible.
❌ Do not remove the mine warning signs (some tourists, incredibly, have taken to removing signs as souvenirs).
❌ Do not touch mines.
✅ If you find yourself in a mine field retrace your steps **exactly**, stepping into each of your foot marks.

Safety on the nighttime streets of Phnom Penh is a problem. Unfortunately **robberies** and **hold-ups** are common. Many robbers are armed, so do not resist. As Phnom Penh does not really have a taxi service (too dangerous for them) travel after dark poses a problem. Stick to moto drivers you know. They will wait for hours outside a bar if you pay them well enough and it is better to go home with a man you know.

Women are particularly targeted by **bag snatchers** predominantly because fewer men carry handbags. A couple of simple risk prevention measures can decrease this risk dramatically. Firstly, don't carry your bag strap over your shoulder – it is a red flag to a bag snatcher. This is especially pertinent when riding on a moto as you have the double jeopardy of being pulled off a moving bike. When on a moto hold your bag in your hands between you and the driver. Secondly, if you are a female travelling with a man, get him to put your money in his pocket as he is harder to 'roll'. Thirdly, don't take out what you are not willing to lose – the risk of being robbed outside your hotel/guesthouse is much higher than theft from your room. Khmer New Year is known locally as the 'robbery season', so be on red alert. A common trick around New Year is for robbers to muck around with tourists (water and talcum powder in the eyes) and rob them blind. If you are robbed and draw it to attention of those around you, a mob will generally chase the thief and highly likely, beat them to death. This can be a far more terrifying experience than losing your bag/possessions. Vigilantism like this is endemic, as most Khmers are sick of the escalating crime and lack of police enforcement.

Try to hide your valuables in your room. This is not always easy when there's no furniture except a bed. With a bit of lateral thinking a place can be found (remember **robbers** think quickly not creatively). Pickpockets do arise from time-to-time so make sure your pockets are secured by a button or zip.

Sexual harassment, as we know it, is not uncommon. Many motos/tour guides will try their luck with women but generally it is more in a playboy fashion than anything serious. Still, it is advisable to know your guide/moto before you head out into any isolated areas, and set perimeters early in the day. Those who choose to entertain sex workers should take **safe sex** precautions. It is advisable not to take drink or food from prostitutes (or anyone you don't know for that matter) as **drugging**, and invariably theft, is common.

Motorbike accidents are another fatality area. In 2003, 824 people died in road accidents in Cambodia and the rate has been increasing by 30% a year. Increased

For those people planning to motorbike around the country it is important to know
that as a motorcyclist you do not exist to the average Khmer driver. The Khmers aren't
exactly renowned for their driving prowess and on the highways, particularly the
good, sealed ones, they speed along at a million km per hour with latent respect for
what is beside, behind and sometimes in front of them. If you do rent a motorbike
ensure it has a working horn (imperative) and buy some rear view mirrors so you can
keep an eye on the traffic. Do wear a helmet (even if using a motodop) – it may not be
cool but neither is a fractured skull.

Outside Phnom Penh safety is not as much of a problem but it is always sensible
to be alert to the dangers. Remember that to many Cambodians all foreigners are, by
definition, wealthy and most Cambodians are extremely poor.

Visit **www.travel.state.gov/travel_warnings.html,** the US State Department's
continually updated travel advisories on its Travel Warnings & Consular Information
Sheets page, or **www.fco.gov.uk/travel/,** the UK Foreign and Commonwealth Office's
travel warning section.

Mines

Visitors should be very cautious when walking in the countryside: landmines and
other unexploded ordnance is a ubiquitous hazard. Stick to well worn paths,
especially around Siem Reap and when visiting remote temples. There are said to be
more than seven million anti-personnel mines buried around the country and,
despite the best efforts of the Halo Trust and other de-mining organizations, many
still remain. See box opposite.

Getting around

Air

Cambodia has a modest domestic airline network serviced by two carriers: **Siem Reap
Airways** and **President Airlines**. There are three operational airports: **Phnom Penh,
Ratanakiri** (RBE) and **Siem Reap** (REP). Sihanoukville was in the
throws of developing its airport at the time of publication. The
majority of visitors use just Phnom Penh and Siem Reap.
Bookings should be made as soon as possible during the tourist
season (November to April) as services can become very booked up. Tickets can be
bought from travel agencies or direct from airline offices. The former is often a better bet
as it cuts out the waiting but is often a tad more expensive. Moreover, it is also possible
to secure tickets at the weekend this way, when the airline offices are closed.

Siem Reap Airways started flying between Phnom Penh and Siem Reap at the
end of October 2000 and operates French-built ATRs. **President Airlines** currently only
operates an intermittent service between Ratanakiri, Koh Kong and Siem Reap. This
airline usually operates with old Russian vessels which will test your disposition to
motion sickness. The short-lived national carrier **Royal Air Cambodge** went bankrupt
on 16 October 2001 and suspended all its operations.

❧ The baggage allowance for domestic flights is 10 kg.

Rail

Out of bounds to foreigners for many years Cambodia's railway system has cranked
into action once more. But lumbered with ancient locomotives and rolling stock and

with the permanent way in a pitiful state through lack of maintenance Cambodian state railways cannot be recommended. The railway is desperately slow, uncomfortable and

❣ The UK Foreign Office continues to advise against rail travel in Cambodia.

unreliable and it is a good idea to take a picnic and a good book and settle down for the long journey ahead. The train lumbers down the track so slowly that in many areas, such as Pursat and Battambang, locals have established their own 'public transport' system by building bamboo platforms and motor-powering people down the track. There are two lines out of Phnom Penh: one to Poipet on the Thai border which goes via Pursat, Battambang and Sisophon; the second, which runs south to Sihanoukville on the coast via Takeo, Kep and Kampot, is no longer operating.

Road

There is a basic road network of about 2000 km in total. But this doesn't mean that there are 2000 km of 'roads' in the North American or European sense of the word. Much of the network is in a poor state, and anyone travelling overland – at least those travelling long distances – should be prepared to put up not just with very long journeys (timewise) but also with very uncomortable ones. In the rainy season expect to be slowed down to a slither by mud and in the dry season get ready for dust to enter your most intimate crevices.

An extensive programme of road upgrading and maintenance has been taking place and has made things considerably better in the last few years. For example the Khmer-American Friendship Highway (Route 4) which runs from Phnom Penh to Sihanoukville (first built in the 1960s) is tarmacked from start to finish, the infamous National Highway 6 between Poipet and Phnom Penh via Siem Reap has also had extensive work, as has National Highway 1. The Japanese in particular have put considerable resources into road and bridge building. The roads from Phnom Penh are numbered 1-10 in a clockwise order starting from Highway 1 which runs to Saigon. The worst roads in the country are in the central region between Preah Vihear, Kompong Thom and T'Beng Meanchey. Some of the remote northeastern roads, particularly around Mondulkiri and Ratanakiri, can also be a bit rough.

The road from Sisophon to Siem Reap is in an appalling condition and can take from four to eight hours depending on the season. In the east the roads have improved in the last couple of years, due to the demands of logging: not the best of reasons. Even so they are still pretty nerve-wracking, particularly between Kratie and Stung Treng which takes approximately four to five hours. Stung Treng to Ban Lung should take three to four hours. Note that during the rainy season conditions can make travelling times substantially longer and sometimes roads are simply impassable.

Bicycle and motorbike

In Phnom Penh and other towns some visitors value the freedom that their own set of wheels bestows. For them a motorbike or bicycle rented from their guesthouse offers just that. It costs anywhere between US$5-8 per day to rent a motorbike and around US$1 per day for a bicycle. Others find a rented machine the biggest burden imaginable – they get endlessly lost and are loath to park it anywhere lest it be stolen. If riding either a motorbike or bicycle be aware that the accident rate is very high. This is partly because of the poor condition of many of the cars, trucks and other vehicles on the road; partly because of poor roads; and partly because of very poor driving.

Bus and shared taxi

There are buses and shared taxis to most parts of the country. Shared taxis (generally Toyota Camrys) or pickups are usually the quickest and most reliable public transport option. The taxi operators charge a premium for better seats and you can buy yourself more space. It is not uncommon for a taxi to fit 10 people in it, including two sitting on the driver's seat. Fares for riding in the back of the truck are half that for riding in the cab. The Sihanoukville run has an excellent and cheap air-conditioned bus service.

Car hire and taxi

Travel agents can organize vehicle hire. Expect to pay around US$30 or more per day, depending on make and model. Most hotels have cars for hire with a driver (US$30-50 per day). There is a limited proper taxi service in Phnom Penh.

Moto

The most popular and sensible option is the moto or motorbike taxi. This costs around the same as renting your own machine and with luck you will get a driver who speaks a bit of English and who knows where he's going. He snoozes on the bike whilst you sightsee so everyone is happy. If your moto driver doesn't follow instructions or is not helpful simply pay him off at the next stop and engage a new one. There are so many good and eager moto drivers in Phnom Penh that there is no need to get stranded with a dud. Once you have found a good one stick with him – the odd drink or packet of cigarettes it costs to reward him for waiting is a good investment. In order to pick out your driver from the throng of men outside the FCCC all claiming to have brought you there remember to take a careful look at his baseball cap memorizing colour, logos, words etc before going in. Outside Phnom Penh, Siem Reap and Battambang do not expect much English from your moto driver.

River

In such a wet environment as Cambodia it is not surprising that boats play an important part in getting around, particularly in the wet season when some roads are impassable. In theory all the Mekong towns and settlements around the Tonlé Sap are accessible by boat but road upgrades across the country have cut back services dramatically. Always check before setting out. Boat travel is a very quick and relatively comfortable way of travel and much cheaper than flying. For those on a budget it is the best way to go.

It is also possible to travel by boat between Siem Reap and Battambang. Note that in the dry season travel by boat on this route (and others) is often much slower (taking up to six hours for the Siem Reap/Battambang leg) as a result of having to be taken to and from the shore in smaller boats. Boats are used as a main form of transport in the northeast, generally Phnom Penh to Stung Treng via Kratie, though these can not be guaranteed in the dry season when the water level is low.

Maps

Regional maps **Bartholomew** Southeast Asia (1:5,800,000); **Nelles** Southeast Asia (1:4,000,000); **Hildebrand** Thailand, Burma, Malaysia and Singapore (1:2,800,000). **Country maps** **Gecko Maps** (1:750,000), highly recommended. **Periplus** Cambodia (1: 1,100,000); **Nelles** Vietnam, Laos and Cambodia (1:1,500,000); **Bartholomew** Vietnam, Laos and Cambodia (1:2,000,000). **City maps** The **Periplus Cambodia** map also has a good map of Phnom Penh (1:17,000) and a detailed map of Angkor (1:95,000). **Gecko Maps** (1:750,000) has a good map of Siem Reap, Sihanoukville and Phnom Penh. There is a 3D Map of Siem Reap and Phnom Penh, which is quite good and is distributed for free in restaurants, bars and guesthouses. **Other maps** **Tactical Pilotage Charts** (TPC, US Airforce) (1:500,000); **Operational Navigational Charts** (ONC, US Airforce) (1:500,000). Both of these are particularly

Hotel price codes explained

L US$200 + Luxury: this category applies to only a few places in Phnom Penh and Siem Reap. Some are superbly renovated and modernized colonial-era hotels with health centres, pools and tennis courts; others are newly-built affairs, with all the facilities and amenities you would expect at this price.

AL US$100-200 International: business services (fax, translation, seminar rooms etc), sports facilities (gym, swimming pool etc), Asian and western restaurants, bars, and discos.

A US$50-100 First class: business, sports and recreational facilities, with a range of restaurants and bars.

B US$25-50 Tourist class: most rooms will have a/c and an attached bathroom; swimming pool, restaurants and 24-hr coffee shop/room service. Cable films.

C US$15-25 Economy: no a/c, attached bathrooms. Restaurant and room service. No sports facilities.

D US$8-15 Budget: no a/c, attached hot-water bathroom. Bed linen and towels, and there may be a restaurant.

E US$4-8 Guesthouse: fan-cooled rooms, shared bathroom facilities. Bed linen but no towels. Rooms are small, facilities few.

F Less than US$4 Guesthouse: fan-cooled rooms, usually with shared bathroom facilities. Squat toilets. Variable standards of cleanliness.

good at showing relief features (useful for planning treks); less good on roads, towns and facilities.

On the web, try **www.lib.utexas.edu/maps/cambodia.html** which has up-to-date maps of Asia showing relief, political boundaries and major towns; **www.mapsofworld.com/cambodia/cambodia-river-map.html**, basic maps of Cambodia, highlighting rivers and other geographical markings; **www.visit-mekong.com/cambodia/maps/**, a clickable map of Cambodia, with pointer to individual provinces; or **www.expediamaps.com/** US biased but still pretty comprehensive. Key in a town and wait for it to magically appear.

In the UK, the best bookshop for maps is **Stanfords**, 12-14 Long Acre, Covent Garden, London, WC2E 9LP, T020-7836 1321, www.stanfords.co.uk.

Sleeping

With some exceptions hotel accommodation in Cambodia is still being developed to meet the demand of foreign tourists both in terms of standards and numbers. Some areas still lack decent accommodation but most will suffice. The exceptions are Phnom Penh, Sihanoukville and Siem Reap. Away from these towns, do not expect too much from hotels, particularly in levels of comfort and service. There are still some pleasant surprises, especially in places where you would least expect it, such as Anlong Veng or Sen Monorom. For those looking for budget accommodation the situation is rather more satisfactory: most towns, even in less frequently visited areas, have serviceable guesthouses. While facilities may be generally limited at the moment, Cambodia's tourism industry is fast developing and the trajectory is upwards. The government sees tourism as one of the country's few growth sectors – and one of the few ways of generating the economic vitality necessary to raise incomes from their current low levels.

Phnom Penh experienced a surge of hotel building in 1992 following the arrival of UNTAC peace-keeping forces and ever since then supply has exceeded demand. Over the last few years as investor confidence has slowly returned a number of very good business hotels have metamorphosed from hollow shells or have been built from scratch. Phnom Penh's top hotels **Le Royal, Intercontinental, Amanjaya, Sunway** and **Cambodiana** are very good and compare with their equivalents in neighbouring countries . Phnom Penh has a lot of low-cost guesthouse accommodation, not all of it good – check before signing in.

Siem Reap has a range of accommodation from middle to bottom with **Le Grand** posing at the top. It is well geared up to the needs of budget travellers. In the rest of the country, foreigners are a new phenomenon, so accommodation is geared only to the basic needs of Cambodians away from home. New guesthouses are appearing all the time, but the better ones are quickly snapped up by the staff of NGOs, so finding a decent place to stay can be difficult.

More expensive hotels have safety boxes in the rooms. In cheaper hotels it is not uncommon for things to be stolen from bedrooms. In Phnom Penh this poses a real dilemma for it is more dangerous to take valuables on to the nighttime streets. Most hotels and guesthouses will accept valuables for safekeeping but do keep a close eye on your cash.

Eating

Food

There are some good restaurants and things are getting better as tourism expands, but don't expect Cambodia to be a smaller version of Thailand, or its cuisine even to live up to the standards of Laos.

Cambodian food shows clear links with the cuisines of neighbouring countries: Thailand, Vietnam and, to a lesser extent, Laos. The influence of the French colonial period is also in evidence, most clearly in the availability of good French bread. Chinese food is also common place owing to strong business ties between Cambodia and China and overseas Chinese. Vietnamese baguette stands and pho soup (noodle soup) stalls are aplenty. True Khmer food is difficult to find and much that the Khmers would like to claim as indigenous food is actually of Thai, French or Vietnamese origin. Perhaps the simplest way to describe Cambodian food is that it is like Thai food – but less spicy and like Vietnamese minus the fish sauce. Curries, soups, rice and noodle-based dishes, salads, fried vegetables and sliced meats all feature in Khmer cooking, as they do in Thailand, Laos and Vietnam. Herbs and herb paste are usually used to flavour meals including lemon grass, ginger, galangal root, turmeric, lime zest, garlic, shallot and dried chilies. And, of course, another popular ingredient to add zest is prahok, a fermented fish paste (see box, page 37). A popular dish, ginger chicken, is absolutely superb if done well (ie not too boney).

Rice is obviously the staple of the Khmer's diet. The Cambodian verb 'to eat', sii bay, translates literally as 'eat rice' (the same is true in Thailand and Laos). Both steamed rice and sticky rice are eaten. Khao phonne, a noodle dish, is also popular.

Dried, salted fish is the most common accompaniment. In coastal areas, seafood is abundant – shrimps and crab (especially Kep crab) among the favourites. Most Cambodian dishes are cooked in a chhnang khteak (wok). Home-cooked meals usually consist of three courses (all served at once): a soup, grilled fish or meat and a vegetable dish – all usually accompanied by rice. The Tonlé Sap is one of the largest freshwater lakes in the world, carrying over 300 hundred fish species. So it is not surprising that fish is central to the Khmer diet, accounting for a whopping 75% of the country's protein.

Restaurant price codes explained

♉♉♉	Expensive US$6 or more	The prices refer to the cost of
♉♉	Mid-range US$2-6	one dish for one person.
♉	Cheap US$2 and under	

Other than fish, Cambodians eat poultry, beef, pork and game. An sam chruk is a Cambodian favourite: a fat roll of sticky rice filled with soya-bean cake and chopped pork. Local legend has it that an sam chruk was invented by the Buddha himself. Frogs are also considered a delicacy and one of Cambodia's signature dishes is barbecued, stuffed frog. Deep-fried spiders are also eaten as a snack.

A typical Cambodian meal consists of a bowl of fried or steamed rice, mixed with bits of fish and seasoned with chillies, mint or garlic. Most of the fish is freshwater from the Tonlé Sap. Bits of fish are often eaten with tuk trey, a spicy sauce with ground peanuts. More elaborate meals include barbecued shrimp, roasted sunflower seeds and such delicacies as pong tea kon (duck eggs, which are eaten just before they hatch) and chong roet (crunchy cicadas). Soup accompanies most meals and is eaten at the same time as the main dishes. Amok (usually steamed fish) is another popular dish. It is served in paste or soup form and consists of boneless fish mixed with coconut and flavoured with spices – delicious – but being highly time consuming to prepare is not widely available, try it whenever you see it on a menu.

There are a lot of good deserts around, such as sticky rice with coconut milk. There are also a wide range of tropical fruits around, which include banana, coconut, durian, jackfruit, longan, lychee, mangosteen, papaya, pineapple, rambutan, sugar palm and watermelon.

The French gastronomic influence is still in evidence – delicious fresh French bread can be bought in Phnom Penh. Western food, as well as Khmer, Thai, Chinese and Vietnamese, is available at all the hotels and quite a few restaurants. European style breakfasts are only available in the more expensive hotels, otherwise you can eat a local breakfast of sliced roast pork, rice and a bowl of clear soup. Seafood is readily obtainable. There are surprisingly few restaurants serving Cambodian food but plenty of stalls do (expect to pay about US$1 for a simple one-dish meal).

The expansion of backpacker travel has also meant a parallel expansion in backpacker cuisine and most guesthouses, if they have a restaurant, will serve the usual array of pizzas and pancakes and so on. Phnom Penh and Siem Reap are probably the best places to get started on Khmer food, as both have a number of particularly good local restaurants. Kep is the spot for freshly cooked crabs and Sihanoukville offers scrumptious (and exceptionally large) shrimps. The area surrounding Battambang is the country's primary rice bowl.

Drink

International soft drink brands are widely available in Cambodia. If there is a national drink in Cambodia, then it has to be tea which is drunk without sugar or milk. Coffee is also available black or 'crème' with sweetened condensed milk (not to everyone's taste). That ubiquitous and well-known brand of cola is available as well as most other international soft drinks. Soda water with lemon, soda kroch chhmar, is a popular drink. Bottled water is widely available; local mineral water too. Fruit smoothies – known locally as tikalok – are found at stalls with that give away food processor on the counter. If you want to avoid consuming your fruit with horrendous quantities of sugar then make sure you make your intentions clear. Most market stands will serve great fruit smoothies, but again, you might wish to request minimal

Fishy business

Every national cuisine has its signature dish and in Cambodia it is prahok, a strong, pungent, fermented fish paste that's been used to flavour Khmer dishes for centuries.

Cambodians swear by it and use it in everything from dips and soups, through to a simple accompaniment for rice. Reports suggest that 95% of Cambodians eat the delicacy, so it is no surprise that the practice of making prahok has passed down from generation to generation.

The Fisheries Department believe that in some areas 10% of fish caught are set aside for the manufacture of prahok. The paste is made by stomping on hundreds of small fish and fish heads in a large bucket. Once the fish is transformed into a thick brown paste it's left in the sun for a day to ferment. Salt is then added and the paste is put in jars and sold.

Locals suggest that prahok can be eaten after a month of maturation, but most consider the paste to be at its best after a few years of fermentation. This is a Cambodian delicacy, like sushi or parmesan cheese, and may taste a bit unusual at first but is somewhat of an acquired taste (if you can get past the smell).

sweet milk and stipulate whether you want egg or not. Fresh milk is hard to find outside of metropolitan areas. Interestingly enough, the literal translation for milk in Khmer is breast-cow-water.

Local and imported beers are available. Of the locally brewed beers the three most common are Angkor Beer, Anchor and ABC Stout – available on draught, in bottles and cans. VB or Victoria Bitter is also brewed locally but is much less common. Beer Lao, although imported, is usually the cheapest and also one of the best – popular with cost-conscious visitors.

Eating out

Phnom Penh and Siem Reap have the best restaurants. There is a wide selection of cuisines available in these hubs including French, Japanese, Italian and Indian. But for those who want to sample a range of dishes and get a feel for Khmer cuisine the best plan of action is to not to make for a restaurant but instead to head for the nearest market where dishes will be cooked on order in a wok – known locally as a chhnang khteak.

Entertainment

Cambodia has really established a widely diverse nightlife scene, although the majority of bars and clubs in the capital attract sex workers, there are still many places which do not. Phnom Penh has evolved into quite a cosmopolitan city and now offers something to suit everyone's taste.

During the Khmer Rouge period any semblance of a nightlife was well and truly snuffed out. Since then things have been improving steadily. But people don't come to Cambodia for the all-night raves or full-moon parties and, except in Phnom Penh, the nightlife is pretty rudimentary. On the music front things are even less well provided for, except in Phnom Penh, which is the only place where you will find a reasonable array of bars, clubs and discos. These tend to be fraternized by both locals and foreigners and things usually start relatively late – around 2300. It is normal for people to eat and then go to a club late in the evening. The price of a drink in a club is the highest in the country. Beyond Phnom Penh, don't expect a great deal. Most drinking occurs in restaurants and coffee/tea shops, not in bars or pubs. That said, tourist centres are beginning to catch onto the idea that foreigners like to hang out in bars.

Festivals and events

There are some 30 public holidays celebrated each year in Cambodia. Most are celebrated with public parades and special events to commemorate the particular holiday. The largest holidays also see many Khmers – although less than used to be the case – loosing off their guns, to the extent that red tracer fills the sky. The habit of firing weapons also extends to nights with a full moon and the onset of the rainy season. It is best to stay indoors at such times, as the concept of 'what goes up must come down' does not seem to be recognized in Cambodia. Several interesting festivals enliven the Cambodian calendar which festival-goers would be disappointed to miss. The major festivals mark important events in the farming year, determined by seasonal changes in the weather, and are listed below.

January

1 and 7 Jan New Year's Day (public holiday). **National Day** and **Victory over Pol Pot** (public holiday). Celebration of the fall of the Khmer Rouge in 1979. (It is also the anniversary of the beginning of the Vietnamese occupation of the country leading some people to lobby against it being declared a national holiday.)
Jan/Feb Chinese and Vietnamese New Year (movable). Celebrated by the Chinese and Vietnamese communities. **Anniversary of the last sermon of Buddha** (movable).

March

8 Mar Women's Day (public holiday). Processions, floats and banners in main towns.

April

13-15 Apr Cambodian New Year or Bonn Chaul Chhnam (public holiday). A 3-day celebration to mark the turn of the year. Predictions are made for the forthcoming year, the celebration is to show gratitude to the departing demi-god and to welcome the new one. Every household erects a small altar to welcome a new demi-god, filled with offerings of food and drink. Homes are spring cleaned. Householders visit temples and traditional games like boh angkunh and chhoal chhoung are played and festivities are performed.

17 Apr Independence Day (public holiday). Celebrates the fall of the Lon Nol government (17 April 1975) with floats and parades through Phnom Penh.
Chaul Chhnam (movable). 3-day celebration, which involves an inevitable drenching, to welcome in the new year. A similar festival to Pimai in Laos and Songkran in Thailand.

April/May

Visak Bauchea (movable – full moon, public holiday). The most important Buddhist festival; a triple anniversary commemorating Buddha's birth, enlightenment and his Paranirvana (state of final bliss).

May

1 May Labour Day (public holiday).
9 May Genocide Day (public holiday). To remember the atrocities of the Khmer Rouge in which nearly two million Cambodians lost their lives. The main ceremony is held at Choeng Ek, just south of Phnom Penh.
Royal Ploughing Ceremony (movable, public holiday). As in Thailand, this marks the beginning of the rainy season and traditionally is meant to alert farmers to the fact that the job of rice cultivation is set to begin (as if farmers need any advance warning!). Known as bonn chroat preah nongkoal in Khmer the ceremony is held on a field close to the Royal Palace in Phnom Penh. The land is ploughed by a man (King

of Meakh) while the seed is sowed by a woman (Queen Me Hour), reflecting the gender division of labour in agriculture and probably also symbolizing fertility. The sacred cows are led to silver trays holding rice, corn and other foods. Depending on their choice of food, this is taken as an omen for the coming year.

June

1 Jun International Children's Day (public holiday).
18 Jun Her Majesty Preah Akkaek Mohesey Norodom Monineath Sihanouk's birthday (public holiday).
19 Jun Anniversary of the Founding of the Revolutionary Armed Forces of Kampuchea. Founded in 1951, main parades and celebrations are in Phnom Penh.
28 Jun Anniversary of the founding of the People's Revolutionary Party of Cambodia. Founded in 1951, again, the main parades and celebrations are in Phnom Penh.

July

Chol Vassa The start of the rainy season retreat – a Buddhist 'lent' – for meditation.

September

24 Sep End of Buddhist 'lent' (movable). In certain areas it is celebrated with boat races. **Prachum Ben** (movable, public holiday). In remembrance of the dead, offerings are made to the ancestors. **Constitution Day** (public holiday).

October/November

Oct/Nov Water Festival, Bon Om Tuk (movable, public holiday) or **Festival of the Reversing Current**. To celebrate the movement of the waters out of the Tonlé Sap (see page 129), boat races are held in

Phnom Penh. The festival dates back to the 12th century when King Jayavarman VII and his navy defeated water-borne invaders. Most wats have ceremonial canoes which are rowed by the monks to summon the Naga King. Boat races extend over 3 days with more than 200 competitors but the highlight is the evening gala in Phnom Penh when a fleet of boats, studded with lights, row out under the full moon. Under the Cambodian monarchy, the king would command the waters to retreat. The festival was only revived in 1990. In addition to celebrating the reversing of the flow of the Tonlé Sap River, this festival marks the onset of the fishing season. (The Khmer diaspora in Vietnam celebrate the same festival at the same time further down the Mekong in Soc Trang.) The festival coincides with Ok Ambok (The Pounding of Rice) – which stems from a myth of a female giant who can control the weather and Sampeah Preah Khai, dedicated to a rabbit who took his own life in a fire to feed a dying man. Some celebrants look for the rabbit's figure drawn in the moon.
23 Oct Paris Peace Accord (public holiday). To mark the signing of the Paris Peace Accord.
30 Oct-1 Nov King Sihanouk's Birthday (public holiday). Public offices and museums close for about a week and a firework display is mounted by the river close to the Royal Palace in Phnom Penh.

November

9 Nov Independence Day (public holiday) Marks Cambodia's independence from French colonial rule in 1953.

December

10 Dec Human Rights' Day (public holiday).
Late Dec Half marathon. A half marathon is held at Angkor Wat, surely one of the most spectacular places to work up a sweat.

Shopping

Cambodia craftsmanship is excellent and whether you are in search of silverware, colourful kramas, hand-loomed sarongs or bronze buddhas you will find them all in abundance. A great favourite for its range and quality of antiques, jewellery and fabrics is the Russian Market (Psar Tuol Tom Pong) in Phnom Penh. Silverware, gold and gems are available in the Central Market (Psar Thmei). The contents of the shops and markets away from Phnom Penh are leaner and meaner although Siem Reap has a good selection. Until the purchasing power of the provinces picks up, or tourists start fanning out in greater numbers, you are advised to stock up on souvenirs in the two main centres.

Textiles The royal Cambodian court supported a vast retinue of weavers and wore sumptuous silk textiles, embellished with gold-patterned yarns in colours corresponding to the days of the week. They also wove beautiful scarves for the royal ballet troupe. Samphots (twice the size of a sarong, wrapped around the hips and pulled between the legs to form loose trousers) were traditionally woven in Cambodia. The same simple pictorial designs used on samphots were also woven into large banners for festivals. Banners for funerals have temple designs with a row of elephants underneath. Matmii – ikat – is also commonly found in Cambodia. It may have been an ancient import from Java, and is made by tie-dyeing the threads before weaving. Matmii is also found in central and southern Laos and in northeastern Thailand. It can be bought throughout the country but mainly in Siem Reap. Other local textile products to look out for are silk scarves bags and traditional wall-hangings – pedan – depicting great legends. Following years of civil war, traditional crafts, such as weaving, are being quickly re-established. Kramas – checked cotton scarves – can be found in local markets across the country and fine woven sarongs in cotton and silk are available in Phnom Penh and Siem Reap. Silk and other textiles products can be bought throughout the country but there are a couple of NGO-supported operations in T'Beng Meanchey and Stung Treng and some workshops rehabilitating people with disabilities in Phnom Penh. Otherwise the multitude of giftshops in touristy areas and the Old Market in Siem Reap and Russian Market in Phnom Penh are a really good bet.

Silver, gold and gems Cambodian craftsmen are well known for their high-quality silverwork, exemplified by betel nut boxes and jewellery. Dancers' anklets, decorated with tiny silver bells, are popular buys. Sylvia Fraser-Lu, author of *Silverware of South-East Asia*, believes the Cambodians represent some of the region's best silversmiths and excel in the areas of repoussé, niello, enamelling, gilding and mounting of precious stones. In the early 20th century, a fine arts college was opened in Phnom Penh to revive traditional Cambodian art forms, in particular the intricate craft of silver-smithing. This advent led to a renaissance in the crafting of silver. Innovative styles and materials were introduced: with a tendency to make animal-shaped boxes from thinly hammered sheets of silver decorated with delicately low-relief carvings. Most silver content in Cambodia is between 90-95% (usually 95%). There's a lot of 'silver' on sale, which simply isn't silver, just silver-plated copper – usually recognizable by the seller's propensity to bargain down to ridiculously low prices.

Gold is a completely different case altogether and isn't considered ornamental, or jewellery-like, moreover, an investment and status symbol. This helps to understand the Khmers' penchant for the gaudy, yellow, large, hulking rings and rope-thick necklaces. With little faith in the banking system, many Khmers, particularly in rural areas, accumulate gold items as a matter of security.

Most of the markets in Cambodia, even the tiniest of rural markets, sell gems. For the most part guarantees of authenticity are not readily available – the sapphires have been heated to create a sparkly blue colour, as have the rubies. When buying gems abide by the philosophy, if it's too good to be true it probably isn't. If you are looking to buy any gems, your best bet is to look into semi-precious stones such as either amethyst or zircon. In and around Ban Lung, many small-scale gem mines operate, where men are sent out to impossibly thin shafts to scavenge for stones. It is quite a remarkable and somewhat frightening sight to see. Ban Lung or the smaller villages around the town are the best place to buy gems.

Pottery and sculpture The history of **ceramics** in Cambodia stretches back to the ninth century, with large amounts of pottery produced in the 11th and 12th centuries. During the 13th century the production of ceramics ceased due to political instability. This was repeated again during the Khmer Rouge period, when the production of ceramics was banned. There has been a strong revival of pottery and ceramics in Cambodia in the last 30 years. Traditionally ceramics have been produced strictly for practical purposes but several international NGOs have been working alongside local artisans to help refine their skills and promote the trade as an art form. Cambodia now offers some brilliant ceramic works, particularly around the area of Kompong Chhnang.

The Khmers have had a centuries-old love affair with the art of carving and sculpture – testament to this is the country's greatest asset – Angkor. Today, it is possible to buy stone replica carvings and sculpture from almost any major town. Cambodians utilize a wide range of mediums for their carvings including wood, stone and marble. Marble carvings can be bought in Siem Reap and Phnom Penh but are best purchased at Pursat, Cambodia's marble-carving hub. There are some tremendous wood carvings around the country, ranging from the Bayon's faces through to life-sized dancing apsaras; **Chantiers Ecole** in Siem Reap is a particularly good place to pick up a well-crafted wood carving.

Handicrafts Other crafts include bamboo work, wooden panels with carvings of the Ramayana and temple rubbings.

Sport and activities

The dive industry in Cambodia is in its infant years, but the coastline boasts lots of pristine coral reefs and unexplored areas. There are several dive operators in Sihanoukville. Boating, fishing and snorkelling can also be done at Sihanoukville. In Mondulkiri and Ratanakiri you can go out trekking on an elephhant. There is a limited variety of eco-tours but it is expected in the next few years that Cambodia will be running lots of tours in some of the region's premier national parks.

Health

Hospitals are not recommended anywhere in Cambodia, even Phnom Penh's Calmette is horrible and good medical facilities are thin on the ground (even at some of the clinics that profess to be 'international'). If you fall ill or are injured the best bet is to get yourself quickly to either Bumrungrad Hospital, Soi 3 Sukhumvit, T+66 2-6671000, www.bumrungrad.com, or Bangkok Nursing Home in Bangkok. Both hospitals are of an exceptional standard, even in international terms.

See individual town directories for medical service information.

Before you go

Ideally, you should see your doctor or travel clinic at least six weeks before your departure for general advice on travel risks, malaria and vaccinations. Make sure you have travel insurance, get a dental check (especially if you are going to be away for more than a month), know your own blood group and if you suffer a long-term condition such as diabetes or epilepsy make sure someone knows that you have a Medic Alert bracelet/necklace with this information on it. It is particularly pertinent that you read the fine print on your medical insurance as it is absolutely essential to be evacuated out of Cambodia in the case of an emergency. Take advice on avian flu before leaving your country.

Malaria

The deadly **P.falciparum malaria**, in a form that is resistant to chloroquine, exists in most of the country except the capital Phnom Penh. You need special medical advice if you are travelling to the western provinces bordering Thailand because of mefloquine- resistant Plasmodium falciparum in the area. The choice of malaria prophylaxis will need to be something other than chloroquine for most people, since there is such a high level of resistance to it. See below.

Items to take with you

Anti-malarials Important to take for the key areas. Specialist advice is required as to which type to take. General principles are that all except Malarone should be continued for four weeks after leaving the malarial area. Malarone needs to be continued for only seven days afterwards (if a tablet is missed or vomited seek specialist advice). The start times for the anti-malarials vary in that if you have never taken Lariam (Mefloquine) before it is advised to start it at least two to three weeks before the entry to a malarial zone (this is to help identify serious side effects early). Chloroquine and Paludrine are often started a week before the trip to establish a pattern but Doxycycline and Malarone can be started only one to two days before entry to the malarial area. It is risky to buy medicinal tablets abroad because the doses may differ.

For longer trips involving jungle treks taking a clean needle pack, clean dental pack and water filtration devices are common-sense measures.

Ciproxin (Ciprofloaxcin) A useful antibiotic for some forms of traveller's diarrhoea (see below).

Immodium A great standby for those diarrhoeas that occur at awkward times. It helps stop the flow of diarrhoea and is of more benefit than harm. (It was believed that letting the bacteria or viruses flow out had to be more beneficial. However, with Immodium they still come out, just in a more solid form.)

MedicAlert These simple bracelets, or an equivalent, should be carried or worn by anyone with a significant medical condition.

Mosquito repellents Remember that DEET (Di-ethyltoluamide) is the gold standard. Apply the repellent every four to six hours but more often if you are sweating heavily. If a non-DEET product is used check who tested it. Validated products (tested at the London School of Hygiene and Tropical Medicine) include Mosiguard, Non-DEET Jungle formula and non-DEET Autan. If you want to use citronella remember that it must be applied very frequently (ie hourly) to be effective. If you are popular target for insect bites or develop lumps quite soon after being bitten, carry an Aspivenin kit. This syringe suction device is available from many chemists and draws out some of the allergic materials and provides quick relief.

Sun block The Australians have a great campaign which has reduced skin cancer. It is called Slip, Slap, Slop. Slip on a shirt, Slap on a hat, Slop on sun screen.

Pain killers Paracetomol or a suitable painkiller can have multiple uses for symptoms
but remember that more than eight paracetmol a day can lead to liver failure.

Pepto-Bismol Used a lot by Americans for diarrhoea. It certainly relieves symptoms but like Immodium it is not a cure for underlying disease. Be aware that it turns the stool black as well as making it more solid.

Websites

www.fco.gov.uk Foreign and Commonwealth Office (FCO) (UK) This is a key travel advice site, with useful information on the country, people, climate and lists the UK embassies/consulates. The site also promotes the concept of 'Know Before You Go' and encourages travel insurance and appropriate travel health advice. It has links to the Department of Health travel advice site, see below.

www.doh.gov.uk/traveladvice Department of Health Travel Advice (UK) This excellent site is also available as a free booklet, the T6, from post offices. It lists the vaccine advice requirements for each country.

www.medicalert.co.uk Medic Alert (UK) This is the website of the foundation that produces bracelets and necklaces for those with existing medical problems. Once you have ordered your bracelet/necklace you write your medical details inside, so that if you collapse, people can identify your illness or allergy.

www.bloodcare.org.uk Blood Care Foundation (UK) The Blood Care Foundation is a charity "dedicated to the provision of screened blood and resuscitation fluids in countries where these are not readily available." They will dispatch certified non-infected blood of the right type to your hospital/clinic.

www.phls.org.uk Public Health Laboratory Service (UK) This site has up-to-date malaria advice guidelines for travel around the world. It gives specific advice about the right drugs for each location. It also has useful information for those who are pregnant, suffering from epilepsy or planning to travel with children.

www.cdc.gov Centers for Disease Control and Prevention (USA) This site from the US Government gives excellent advice on travel health, has useful disease maps and details of disease outbreaks.

www.who.int World Health Organisation The WHO site has links to the WHO Blue Book (it was Yellow up to last year) on travel advice. This lists the diseases in different regions of the world. It describes vaccination schedules and makes clear which countries have Yellow Fever Vaccination certificate requirements and malarial risk.

www.tmb.ie Tropical Medicine Bureau (Ireland) This Irish based site has a good collection of general travel health information and disease risks.

www.fitfortravel.scot.nhs.uk Fit for Travel (UK) This site from Scotland provides a quick A-Z of vaccine and travel health advice requirements for each country.

www.btha.org British Travel Health Association (UK) This is the official website of an organization of travel health professionals.

www.Netdoctor.co.uk NetDoctor (UK) This general health advice site has a useful section on travel and has an 'ask the expert', interactive chat forum.

www.travelscreening.co.uk Travel Screening Services (UK) This is the health author's website. A private clinic dedicated to integrated travel health. The clinic gives vaccine, travel health advice, email and SMS text vaccine reminders and screens returned travellers for tropical diseases.

On the road

The key viral disease is **Dengue fever,** which is transmitted by a mosquito that bites during the day. The south of Cambodia suffered a serious epidemic of Dengue in 1998. Westerners very rarely get the worst haemorrhagic form of the disease. Bacterial diseases include tuberculosis (TB) and some causes of the more common traveller's diarrhoea.

Dengue fever
Symptoms This disease can be contracted throughout Cambodia. In travellers this can cause a severe flu-like illness which includes symptoms of fever, lethargy, enlarged lymph glands and muscle pains. It starts suddenly, lasts for two to three days, seems to get better for two to three days and then kicks in again for another two to three days. It is usually all over in an unpleasant week. The local children are prone to the much nastier haemorrhagic form of the disease, which causes them to bleed from internal organs, mucous membranes and often leads to their death. **Cures** The traveller's version of the disease is self limiting and forces rest and recuperation on the sufferer. **Prevention** The mosquitoes that carry the Dengue virus bite during the day unlike the malaria mosquitoes. Which sadly means that repellent application and covered limbs are a 24-hour issue. Check your accommodation for flower pots and shallow pools of water since these are where the dengue-carrying mosquitoes breed.

Diarrhoea and intestinal upset
This is almost inevitable. One study showed that up to 70% of all travellers may suffer during their trip. **Symptoms** Diarrhoea can refer either to loose stools or an increased frequency; both of these can be a nuisance. It should be short lasting but persistence beyond two weeks, with blood or pain, require specialist medical attention. **Cures** Ciproxin (Ciprofloaxcin) is a useful antibiotic for bacterial traveller's diarrhoea. It can be obtained by private prescription in the UK which is expensive, or bought over the counter in Cambodian pharmacies. You need to take one 500 mg tablet when the diarrhoea starts and if you do not feel better in 24 hours, the diarrhoea is likely to have a non-bacterial cause and may be viral (in which case there is little you can do apart from keep yourself rehydrated and wait for it to settle on its own). The key treatment with all diarrhoeas is rehydration. Try to keep hydrated by taking the right mixture of salt and water. This is available as Oral Rehydration Salts (ORS) in ready-made sachets or can be made up by adding a teaspoon of sugar and a half teaspoon of salt to a litre of clean water. Drink at least one large cup of this drink for each loose stool. You can also use flat carbonated drinks as an alternative. Immodium and Pepto- Bismol provide symptomatic relief. **Prevention** The standard advice is to be careful with water and ice for drinking. Ask yourself where the water came from. If you have any doubts then boil it or filter and treat it. There are many filter/treatment devices now available on the market. Food can also transmit disease. Be wary of salads (what were they washed in, who handled them), re-heated foods or food that has been left out in the sun having been cooked earlier in the day. There is a simple adage that says wash it, peel it, boil it or forget it. Also be wary of unpasteurized dairy products, these can transmit a range of diseases from brucellosis (fevers and constipation), to listeria (meningitis) and tuberculosis of the gut (obstruction, constipation, fevers and weight loss).

Hepatitis
Symptoms Hepatitis means inflammation of the liver. Viral causes of the disease can be acquired anywhere in Cambodia. The most obvious symptom is a yellowing of your skin or the whites of your eyes. However, prior to this you may notice itching and tiredness. **Cures** Early on, depending on the type of hepatitis, a vaccine or immunoglobulin may reduce the duration of the illness. **Prevention** Pre-travel hepatitis A vaccine is the best bet. Hepatitis B (for which there is a vaccine) is spread through blood and unprotected sexual intercourse, both of these can be avoided. Unfortunately there is no vaccine for hepatitis C or the increasing alphabetical list of other Hepatitis viruses.

Malaria and insect bite prevention
Symptoms Malaria can cause death within 24 hours and Cambodia can be considered a high-risk country. It can start as something just resembling an attack of

flu. You may feel tired, lethargic, headachy; or worse, develop fits, followed by coma
and then death. Have a low index of suspicion because it is very easy to write off vague symptoms, which may actually be malaria. Whilst abroad and on return get tested as soon as possible – it could save your life. **Cures** Treatment is with drugs and may be oral or into a vein depending on the seriousness of the infection. Remember ABCD: Awareness (of whether the disease is present in the area you are travelling in), Bite avoidance, Chemoprohylaxis, Diagnosis. **Prevention** This is best summarized by the B and C of the ABCD, bite avoidance and chemoprophylaxis. Wear clothes that cover arms and legs and use effective insect repellents in areas with known risks of insect-spread disease. Use a mosquito net dipped in permethrin as both a physical and chemical barrier at night in the same areas. Guard against the contraction of malaria with the correct anti-malarials (see above). Some would prefer to take test kits for malaria with them and have standby treatment available. However, the field tests of the blood kits have had poor results: when you have malaria you are usually too ill to be able to do the tests correctly enough to make the right diagnosis. Standby treatment (treatment that you carry and take yourself for malaria) should still ideally be supervised by a doctor since the drugs themselves can be toxic if taken incorrectly. The Royal Homeopathic Hospital in the UK does not advocate homeopathic options for malaria prevention or treatment.

Rabies

Symptoms Dog bite, animal scratch etc. Once visible signs of rabies set in it is too late to seek help. **Cures** If you get bitten or scratched by an animal ensure that you get your rabies booster shot immediately as people have been known to die in Camodia due to not getting their shots. Better to be safe than sorry.

Sun protection

Symptoms White people are notorious for becoming red in hot countries because they like to stay out longer than everyone else and do not use adequate sun protection. This can lead to sunburn, which is painful and followed by flaking of skin. Aloe vera gel is a good pain reliever for sunburn. Long-term sun damage leads to a loss of elasticity of skin and the development of pre-cancerous lesions. Many years later a mild or a very malignant form of cancer may develop. The milder basal cell carcinoma, if detected early, can be treated by cutting it out or freezing it. The much nastier malignant melanoma may have already spread to bone and brain at the time that it is first noticed. **Prevention** Sun screen. SPF stands for Sun Protection Factor. It is measured by determining how long a given person takes to 'burn' with and without the sunscreen product on. So, if it takes 10 times longer to burn with the sunscreen product applied, then that product has an SPF of 10. If it only takes twice as long then the SPF is 2. The higher the SPF the greater the protection. However, do not just use higher factors just to stay out in the sun longer. 'Flash frying' (desperate bursts of excessive exposure), as it is called, is known to increase the risks of skin cancer.

Sexual health

Sex is part of travel and many see it as adding spice to a good trip but spices can be uncomfortable. Think about the sexual.souvenirs any potential new partner may have picked up or live with. The range of visible and invisible diseases is awesome. Unprotected sex can spread HIV, Hepatitis B and C, Gonorrhea (green discharge), chlamydia (nothing to see but may cause painful urination and later female infertility), painful recurrent herpes, syphilis and warts, just to name a few. You can cut down the risk by using condoms, a femidom or avoiding sex altogether. Commercial sex workers in Cambodia have high levels of HIV. If you do stray, consider getting a sexual health check on your return home, since these diseases are not the sort of gift people thank you for.

Tuberculosis

This old disease is still a significant problem in Ho Chi Minh City in Vietnam and many other parts of the region. The bus driver coughing as he takes your fare could expose you to the mycobacterium. **Symptoms** Cough, tiredness, fever and lethargy. **Cures** At least six months treatment with a combination of drugs is required. **Prevention** Have a BCG vaccination before you go and see a doctor early if you have a persistent cough, cough blood, fever or unexplained weight loss.

Underwater health

Symptoms If you go diving make sure that you are fit do so. The **British Scuba Association** (BSAC), Telford's Quay, South Pier Road, Ellesmere Port, Cheshire CH65 4FL, United Kingdom, T01513-506200, F01513-506215, www.bsac.com, can put you in touch with doctors who do medical examinations. Protect your feet from cuts, beach dog parasites (larva migrans) and sea urchins. The latter are almost impossible to remove but can be dissolved with lime or vinegar. Keep an eye out for secondary infection. **Cures** Antibiotics for secondary infections. Serious diving injuries may need time in a decompression chamber. **Prevention** Check that the dive company know what they are doing, have appropriate certification from BSAC or **Professional Association of Diving Instructors** (PADI), Unit 7, St Philips Central, Albert Rd, St Philips, Bristol, BS2 0TD, T0117-3007234, www.padi.com, and that the equipment is well maintained.

Keeping in touch

Communications

Internet

The country is surprisingly well connected and most medium-sized to large towns have internet access. There are more than 180 internet and email facilities in Cambodia, mostly concentrated in Phnom Penh, Siem Reap, Battambang, Kampot, Kratie and Sihanoukville. Most small towns will have at least one internet shop, usually in the form of a mobile phone shop, but prices vary according to scarcity and depend on whether a long distance call to an Internet Service Provider is required. Needless to say, internet is a lot more expensive in smaller towns, up to a whopping US$5 an hour. In some places, such as Ban Lung, it is very expensive and so unreliable as to be not worth bothering. However, if you do have a yen to contact home or find out what's happening in the wider world then there are ample internet cafés in Phnom Penh, Siem Reap, Kampot, Battambang and Sihanoukville. These are listed in the relevant entries. In Phnom Penh internet rates are US$1-2 per hour and in Siem Reap should be US$1 per hour or under. **www.netcafeguide.com/** lists around 2000 cybercafés in 113 countries and also provides discussion forums for travellers and a language section. Www.yellowpages-cambodia.com/Technology-and-Communication/Email-and-Internet-Services.html lists all the metropolitan internet cafes and email facilities in Cambodia (it doesn't really detail the provincial facilities).

It is now possible to use **internet phones** to call internationally. Most cyber cafés have them, although they are usually tucked away. Expect to pay around 1000 riel (US$0.25) a minute to the UK.

Post

International service is unpredictable (post can take anywhere between a week and a month) but it is reasonably priced and fairly reliable (at least from Phnom Penh).

Only send mail from the GPO in any given town rather than sub POs or mail boxes. There is a poste restante at the central post office in Phnom Penh. Fedex and DHL also offer in country services.

Telephone and fax

Landline linkages are so poor that many people and businesses prefer to use mobile phones instead (mobile rates have also become very competitive). International calls can be made from most guesthouses, hotels and phone booths. Use public MPTC or Camintel card phone boxes dotted around Phnom Penh to make calls. The cards are usually sold at shops near the booth. International calls are expensive, starting at US$4 per minute in Phnom Penh, and more in the provinces. To make an overseas call from Cambodia, dial 00 + IDD country code + area code minus first 0 + subscriber number. The three-digit prefix included in a nine-digit landline telephone number is the area (province) code. If dialling within a province, dial only the six-digit number. Communications within Cambodia are unreliable and international connections even more so. Don't anticipate being able to make international calls outside Phnom Penh, Siem Reap, Sihanoukville and Battambang. A multitude of unofficial phone boxes have cropped up across the country (marked by 012 signage). These booths have been established by entrepreneurial mobile phone owners who let people call domestically or to other mobile numbers for a set fee. This fee can usually be negotiated. Sending a **fax** can cost as much as US$7 per page.

Mobile phones are one of the best options for communicating overseas as you can receive calls pretty much countrywide. If you already have a mobile, you can buy a Cambodian sim card and a pay-as-you-go card with prepaid phone credit (usually sold in US$5 denominations). Sim card prices depend on the number - the cheapest Camshin and Mobitel cards are around US$10 and the more expensive $US25 - you need to buy the latter if you wish to call/text internationally. Foreigners require serious documentation and ID card to buy a sim card, so it's best to ask a moto to do it on your behalf for a couple of dollars. Mobitel (012) is the best network for calling internationally as they have excellent coverage throughout the country. For mobile telephones the three-digit prefix included in a nine-digit mobile telephone number designates the mobile network. There are five mobile telephone networks: 011, 012, 015, 016 and 018. When dialling within a network it is only necessary to dial the six-digit number, but if dialling between networks then the three-digit prefix needs to be included too.

Internet calls are without a doubt the cheapest way to call overseas. Most internet cafes have call booths for international calls charging between 500-1000 riel per minute depending where you are calling from, and where you are calling to. Even the smallest of towns have caught on to net calls, though calls are usually more expensive outside of metropolitan areas.

Media

Newspapers and magazines

Cambodia has a vigorous English language press which fights bravely for editorial independence and freedom to criticize politicians. The principal English language newspapers are the fortnightly *Phnom Penh Post*, www.phnompenhpost.com, which many regard as the best and the *Cambodia Daily*, /www.cambodiadaily.com, published five times per week. The centre pages of the *Phnom Penh Post* have a good city map and the quality of the journalism is high with some fine investigative reporting. Set up by American Michael Hayes and his wife Katheen O'Keefe with a princely investment of US$50,000, the newspaper celebrated its 10th anniversary in mid 2002. The circulation of 3500 belies its impact in Cambodia; the government

Essentials Keeping in touch

finds the hard-hitting but usually accurate reporting hard to handle. In 2002 Deputy Minister of Information Khieu Kanharith said that the paper's pieces lack objectivity and are overly western in outlook. That's a pretty good sign that the newspaper is digging the dirt in a country where it is possible to shovel the stuff from dawn to dusk. The *Cambodia Daily* covers world as well as Cambodian news and is, like most things in Cambodia, an NGO, training its Cambodian journalists in impartial reporting.

The *Bayon Pearnik* gives general travel information – some quite useful – and offers occasionally interesting articles. You can normally find this magazine at travellers' bars, restaurants and guesthouses in the four main cities and towns. The *Cambodian Magazine* is a more upmarket monthly lifestyle and travel magazine, with particularly good feature articles. **Canby Publications** produces a free Siem Reap, Sihanoukville and Phnom Penh tourism guide, which contains good maps and reviews, and can be picked up from most restaurants and hotels,

The *Bangkok Post*, www.bangkokpost.com is widely available in Phnom Penh and two-day-old copies of the *Financial Times*, *Figaro* and *International Tribune* can be bought in the bigger hotels. For lighter reading there is the monthly free magazine.

Radio
The **BBC World Service**'s Dateline East Asia provides probably the best news and views on Asia (available on 100 FM). Also with a strong Asia focus are the broadcasts of the **ABC** (Australian Broadcasting Corporation).

Short Wave **British Broadcasting Corporation** (BBC, London) Southeast Asian service 3915, 6195, 9570, 9740, 11750, 11955, 15360; Singapore service 88.9MHz; East Asian service 5995, 6195, 7180, 9740, 11715, 11750, 11945, 11955, 15140, 15280, 15360, 17830, 21715. **Voice of America** (VoA, Washington) Southeast Asian service 1143, 1575, 7120, 9760, 9770, 15185, 15425; Indonesian service 6110, 11760, 15425. **Radio Beijing** Southeast Asian service (English) 11600, 11660. **Radio Japan** (Tokyo) Southeast Asian service (English) 11815, 17810, 21610.

Television
More expensive hotels in Phnom Penh and Siem Reap have satellite television and will receive CNN, BBC and other channels.

Phnom Penh

Footprint features

Introduction

It is not hard to imagine Phnom Penh in its heyday, with wide shady boulevards, beautiful French buildings and exquisite pagodas. They're still all here but are in a derelict, dust-blown, decaying state surrounded by growing volumes of cars, pickup trucks and motorcyclists. It all leaves you wondering how a city like this works. But it does, somehow.

Phnom Penh is a city of contrasts: East and West, poor and rich, serenity and confusion. Although the city has a reputation as a frontier town, due to drugs, gun ownership and prostitution, a more cosmopolitan character is being forged out of the chaos. Monks' saffron robes are once again lending a splash of colour to the capital's streets, following the reinstatement of Buddhism as the national religion in 1989, and stylish restaurants and bars now line the riverside. However, the amputees on street corners are a constant reminder of Cambodia's tragic story. Perhaps the one constant in all the turmoil of the past century has been the monarchy – shifting, whimsical, pliant and, indeed, temporarily absent as it may have been. The splendid royal palace, visible to all, was a daily reminder of this ultimate authority whom even the Khmer Rouge had to treat with caution. The royal palace area, with its glittering spires, wats, stupas, national museum and broad green spaces, is perfectly sited alongside the river and is as pivotal to the city as the city is to the country.

★ Don't miss...

1 Royal Palace and Silver Pagoda
The city's 19th-century highlights, pages 53 and 56.

2 Tuol Sleng Museum
Remember those who died in the genocide, page 60.

3 Choeung Ek The infamous 'killing fields' are 15 km south of the city, page 61.

4 Kirirom National Park The nearest national park to the capital, page 64.

5 Central market The building is an art deco delight, page 76.

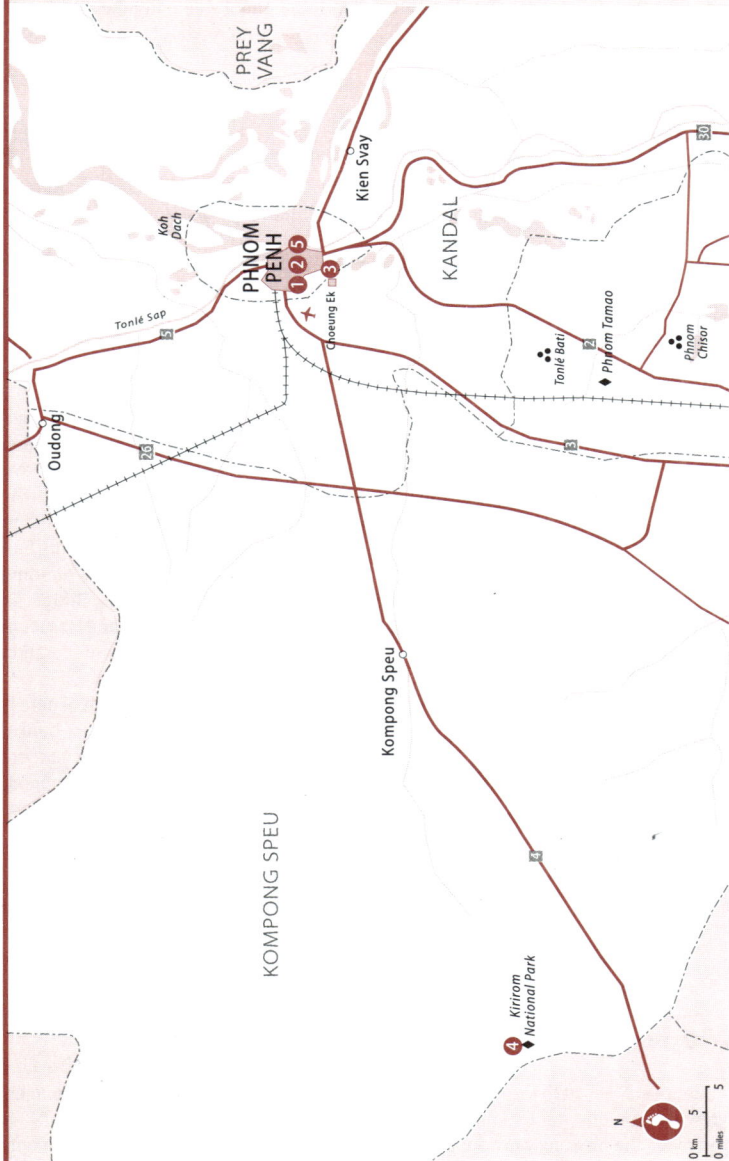

PREY VANG

Koh Dach

Tonlé Sap

PHNOM PENH
1 2 5
3

Choeung Ek

Kien Svay

KANDAL

Oudong

Tonlé Bati

Phnom Tamao

Phnom Chisor

Kompong Speu

KOMPONG SPEU

Kirirom National Park

N

0 km   5
0 miles   5

Ins and outs

Getting there

There are flights to Phnom Penh's Pochentong airport, 10 km west of the city on Road 4, from Bangkok, Ho Chi Minh City, Vientiane, Singapore, Hong Kong, Kuala Lumpur and Siem Reap. The river crossing with Laos is at Voen Kham, and alights at Stung Treng. It is also possible to get to Phnom Penh by boat and bus from Chau Doc in Vietnam and by road crossing at Moc Bai, Vietnam. Visitors travelling from Thailand can take the long overland route or go by sea to Sihanoukville and take a bus from there. A taxi from the airport to town costs US$7 and a moto should be about US$3.
▸▸ *See Transport, page 78, for further details.*

Getting around

Owing to the popular local custom of hijacking cars and the understandable reluctance of drivers to expose themselves to risk, taxis are rare on the streets of Phnom Penh, particularly after dark. Recently, a fleet of tuk tuks (*lomphata* in Khmer) has sprung up that provides a good, cheaper alternative to cars. Nevertheless, hotels can arrange car hire around town and surrounding areas. Motorbikes are ubiquitous. Most visitors use the local motodops (motorbike taxis) as a quick, cheap and efficient way of getting around. Some travellers rent motorbikes from their guesthouses. There are cyclos too which undoubtedly appeal to many tourists but for regular journeys they prove to be just too slow and expensive.

Orientation

Navigating Phnom Penh is pretty straightforward. The map shows a pretty rigid gridiron layout with a couple of diagonals and curves thrown in to lighten the picture. Every street is numbered but some major thoroughfares have names too. The key to unlocking Phnom Penh's geography is the simple fact that the horizontal steets are evenly numbered and odd numbers are used for the vertical ones. The rivers Tonlé Sap and Bassac run north-south and, with the exception of some houses and restaurants over the Japanese Friendship Bridge, all Phnom Penh lies to the west of the river. Monivong and Norodom boulevards are the main roads running north-south, and east-west are Confederation de Russie, Kampuchea Krom and Preah Sihanouk boulevards.

❣ Two areas popular with budget travellers for cheap accommodation and food are Street 182 around Capitol Guesthouse and Boeng Kak Lake.

The royal quarter lies to the east of the town not far from the river; north of here is what might be regarded as a colonial quarter with government ministries, banks, hotels, museums and other municipal functions, many housed in French era buildings. Chinatown, the commercial quarter, surrounds the central covered market, Psah Thmey. Sisowath Quay, the street which runs along the riverbank, is where many visitors head as it has the highest concentration of restaurants and bars.

❣ Mobile phones have prefixes which are listed in the text with the number, normally 012-, 018- and 016-.

Tourist information

There are two main tourist offices in Phnom Penh: **Ministry of Tourism**, 3 Monivong Boulevard, T023-427130, which organizes tours. Friendly and helpful.

Modern Phnom Penh

Phnom Penh lies at the confluence of the Sap, Mekong and Bassac rivers and quickly grew into an important commercial centre. The Cambodian capital relies heavily on the river. The Mekong provides the city's water supply and Phnom Penh is the only significant port on the Mekong above Can Tho in the delta. Years of war have taken a heavy toll on the city's infrastructure and economy, as well as its inhabitants. Refugees first began to flood in from the countryside in the early 1950s during the First Indochina War and the population grew from 100,000 to 600,000 by the late 1960s. In the early 1970s there was another surge as people streamed in from the countryside again, this time to escape US bombing and guerrilla warfare. On the eve of the Khmer Rouge takeover in 1975, the capital had a population of two million, but soon became a ghost town. On Pol Pot's orders it was forcibly emptied and the townspeople frog-marched into the countryside to work as labourers. Only 45,000 inhabitants were left in the city in 1975 and a large number were soldiers. In 1979, after four years of virtual abandonment, Phnom Penh had a population of a few thousand. People began to drift back following the Vietnamese invasion (1978/1979) and as hopes for peace rose in 1991, the floodgates opened yet again: today the population is approaching one million.

Phnom Penh has undergone an economic revival since the Paris Peace Accord of 1991. Following the 1998 coup, however, there was an exodus of businesses and investors for whom this bloody and futile atrocity was the final straw. The relative stability since the coup has seen a partial revival of confidence but few are willing to risk their capital in long term investments. Still, public health facilities are woefully inadequate – the city's services are overstretched and there are problems with everything from water and electricity supplies to sewage and refuse disposal. Electricity supply is so erratic that every hotel and many private houses have their own generator. The water supply will sometimes stop for a few hours. The Khmer Rouge saw to it that the plumbing network was completely destroyed before they left. The capital's streets are potholed and in bad need of repair. Even if the main thoroughfares are newly metalled many side streets remain ample justification for the capital's fleets of four-wheel drive vehicles. There are insufficient schools for the city's growing numbers of children: hence, for those that can afford them, private schools and language training centres have appeared.

Sights

Historic centre ⊟🛈🛆🛅🛇⚠🛈🛈 ▸ *pages 66-82*

Royal Palace

Of all the cultural sights in Phnom Penh, the Royal Palace, between Street 184 and Street 240, is the most impressive. The scale of the palace (and adjoining Silver Pagoda) dwarfs the others and given the rather gloomy recent history that pervades most of the city's sights, the Royal Palace holds nothing nasty in store.

Built mainly by the French in 1866, on the site of the old town, the Royal Palace, along with the Silver Pagoda in a pagoda-style compound, has since November 1991, been home to Prince Norodom Sihanouk and as of October 2004, King Norodom Sihamoni. The entrance is on Samdech Sothearos Boulevard via the Pavilion of Dancers (or Chan Chaya Pavilion). Opposite the entrance are the walls of the royal residence (closed to the public) and the stable of the white elephant (a highly auspicious and sacred animal treasured as a symbol of royal beneficence).

The **Throne Hall**, the main building facing the Victory Gate, was built in 1917 in Khmer style; it has a tiered roof and a 59-m tower, influenced by Angkor's Bayon Temple. The steps leading up to it are protected by multi-headed nagas. It is used for coronations and other official occasions such as the reception of foreign ambassadors when they present their official credentials: scenes from the *Ramayana*

Phnom Penh *Sights*

To Boat Piers & Route 5

French Embassy

British Embassy

International Mosque

Calmette Hospital

US Embassy

Monivong Blvd

Boeng Kak Lake

Tropical & Travellers Medical Clinic

Psar Thmei (Central Market)

Confederation de Russie Blvd

Kampuchea Krom Blvd

To Phnom Penh Water Park, Airport & Routes 3 & 4

Nehru Blvd

Charles de Gaulle Blvd

O Russei

Wat Koh

Croix Rouge

Mao Tse Tung Blvd

Mao Tse Tung Blvd

Olympic Stadium

Preah Sihanouk Blvd

Lucky Supermarket

Wat Moha Montrei

Montreth Blvd

To Choeung Ek

Dragon Air

Thai

Tuol Sleng Museum

Related map
A Sisowath Quay, page 67

Mao Tse Tung Blvd

Wat Tuol Tom Pong

Psar Tuol Tom Pong (Russian Market)

Rajana

Phnom Penh Sights

Sleeping 🛏
Billabong 1 *C3*
Boddhi Tree 2 *E3*
Café Freedom 4 *B3*
Cambodiana 30 *D5*
Capitol 5 *D3*
Diamond 6 *C3*
Flamingo 8 *C4*
Floating Island 9 *B2*
Golden Gate 10 *D4*
Goldiana 3 *E4*
Grandview Guesthouse 12 *B3*
Guesthouse Number 9 26 *A2*
Happy Guesthouse 14 *D3*
Hello Guesthouse 15 *D3*
Holiday Villa 16 *C3*
Imperial Garden Villa 11 *D5*
Intercontinental 18 *E1*
Juliana 19 *C2*
KIDS 7 *C4*
Lazy Fish Guesthouse 21 *B3*
Le Royal 22 *B3*
L'Imprévu 13 *F4*
Narin Guesthouse 24 *D3*
New York 25 *C3*
Number 10 Lakeside Guesthouse 27 *B3*
Palm Resort 17 *F4*
Phnom Penh 29 *A3*
Regent Park 31 *D5*
Royal Phnom Penh 23 *F5*
Scandic 32 *E4*
Simon 2 Guesthouse 34 *B3*
Spring Guesthouse 35 *D3*
Sunway 36 *B3*
Walkabout 37 *C4*

Eating 🍴
Asia Europe Bakery 1 *D3*
Baan Thai 2 *E4*
Boeung Bopha 5 *A4*
Comme a la Maison 3 *E4*
Elsewhere 6 *D4*
Family 7 *B3*
Garden Centre Café 4 *E4*
Jars of Clay 11 *F3*
Java 10 *D5*
Khmer Surin 12 *E4*
La Marmite 13 *B4*
Lazy Gecko 14 *B3*
Mount Everest 15 *D4*
Origami 16 *D5*
Pancho Villa 18 *B4*
Peking Canteen 17 *C3*
Pyong Yang 19 *E3*
Rendezvous 20 *B4*
Sam Doo 21 *C3*
Shiva Shakti 22 *D4*
Tamarind 23 *D4*
Tell 25 *B3*
Teukei 33 *D3*
The Shop 24 *D4*

Bars & clubs 🍸
Cathouse 26 *C4*
Heart of Darkness 27 *C4*
Manhattan 30 *A3*
Peace Café 32 *E4*
Sharkys 9 *C4*
Zepplin 34 *C3*

adorn the ceiling. Inside stand the sacred gong and French-style thrones only used by the sovereign. Above the thrones hangs Preah Maha Svetrachatr, a nine-tiered parasol, which symbolizes heaven. A huge carpet fills the hall. Woven into the carpet is the pattern found in the surrounding tiles and the steps leading up to the building. There are two chambers for the king and queen at the back of the hall, which are used only in the week before a coronation when the royal couple were barred from sleeping together. The other adjoining room is used to house the ashes of dead monarchs before they are placed in a royal stupa. Only the main throne room is open to the public. There are Buddha images in the left nave, before which the kings would pray each day. Returning to his former abode in November 1991, Sihanouk must have found it much as he had left it – although many of the state gifts from the display cases have sadly been smashed or stolen. The chairs closest to the entrance were reserved for high officials and the others were for visiting ambassadors. The yellow chairs were used by visiting heads of state.

Immediately to the south of the Throne Hall is a small unremarkable building which contains a collection of knick-knacks, curios, swords, small silver ornaments and costumes. There is a display of the different coloured costumes worn by staff at the royal palace each day of the week.

The **Royal Treasury** and the **Napoleon III Pavillion** – or summerhouse – built in 1866, are to the south of the Throne Hall. The latter was presented by Napoleon III to his Empress Eugenie as accommodation for the princess during the Suez Canal opening celebrations who later had it dismantled and dispatched it to Phnom Penh as a gift to the king. The building is constructed around a slender wrought iron frame. The elegant building is packed with bric-a-brac. Programmes of long forgotten but no doubt memorable royal command dance performances are strewn in glass cases. Upstairs there are some decidedly third rate portraits and some rather more interesting historical photographs of the royal family. The prefabricated folly was renovated and refurbished in 1990 and its ersatz marble walls remarbled – all with French money – but the graceful building is showing signs of age and much in need of more French money. 'Floor condition is under deterioration' reads one melancholy warning sign. Next to the villa are rooms built in 1959 by Sihanouk to accommodate his cabinet. Beyond is the north gate and the Silver Pagoda enclosure.

Silver Pagoda

① *Daily 0730-1100, 1430-1700, US$3, camera US$2, video US$5.*

It is a magpie-style collection, as the writer Norman Lewis said in 1957: "One imagined the Queen, or perhaps a succession of queens, making a periodic clear out of their cupboards and then tripping down to the Silver Pagoda with all the attractive useless things that had to be found a home somewhere".

The Silver Pagoda is often called the Pagoda of the Emerald Buddha or Wat Preah Keo Morokat after the statue housed here. The wooden temple was originally built by King Norodom in 1892 to enshrine royal ashes and then rebuilt by Sihanouk in 1962. The pagoda's steps are of Italian marble, and inside, its floor comprises more than 5000 silver blocks (mostly carpeted over to protect them from the bare feet of visitors) which together weigh nearly six tonnes. All around are cabinets filled with presents from foreign dignitaries. The pagoda is remarkably intact, having been granted special dispensation by the Khmer Rouge, although 60% of the Khmer treasures were stolen from here. In the centre of the pagoda is a magnificent 17th-century emerald Buddha statue made of Baccarat crystal. In front is a 90-kg golden Buddha studded with 9584 diamonds, dating from 1906. It was made from the jewellery of King Norodom and its vital statistics conform exactly to his – a tradition that can be traced

● *To the east of the Silver Pagoda is a statue of King Norodom on horseback (it is in fact a*
● *statue of Napoleon III with the head replaced with that of the Cambodian monarch).*

back to the god-kings of Angkor. The gold Buddha image is flanked by bronze and silver statues of the Buddha. Under a glass cover is a golden lotus – a Buddhist relic from India. At the back of the room there is a jade Buddha and a palanquin used for coronations which required 12 porters to carry it.

The 600-m-long wall enclosing the Silver Pagoda is galleried; its inward face is covered in frescoes, painted 1903-1904 by 40 local artists, which depict epic scenes from the *Ramayana* and numerous scenes of the Silver Pagoda and Royal Palace itself – the story starts by the east gate. The lower part of the fresco has deteriorated alarmingly under the combined assault of children's fingers and rising damp. To the east of the Silver Pagoda is a stupa containing the ashes of King Ang Duong (1845-1859). Beyond the stupa, on the south wall, are pavilions containing a footprint of the Buddha (to the east) and a pavilion for royal celebrations (to the west). Next to Phnom Mondap, an artificial hill with a building covering the Buddha's footprint, in the centre of the south wall is a stupa dedicated to Sihanouk's favourite daughter who died of leukaemia in 1953. On the west wall is a stupa of King Norodom Suramarit with a bell tower in the northwest corner. Beyond the bell tower on the north wall is the mondap (library), originally containing precious Buddhist texts. The whole courtyard is attractively filled with urns and vases containing flowering shrubs.

National Museum of Cambodia

ⓘ *Daily 0700-1130, 1400-1730. US$2. Camera US$2. Video US$3. Photographs only permitted in the garden.The shop sells reproductions of works from Angkor and a good selection of books, maps and cards. French- and English-speaking guides are available, mostly excellent.*

The National Museum of Cambodia is the desert-red building just north of the palace (entrance is on the corner of streets 13 and 178). It was built in 1920 following the design of French archaeologist and painter, George Groslier, in what, certainly from the outside, appears to be Khmer style. Closer acquaintance reveals a curious hybrid with French colonial influence much in evidence. It is built around a central courtyard and, for admirable reasons of ventilation and light, there are no doors or windows on the interior walls. Unfortunately the bats which live in the ample roof space exploit the open galleries covering the exhibits with several tons of guano each year. While sales of said guano may help bolster the museum's paltry income it doesn't do the sculptures any good at all. The museum was opened to exhibit works scattered throughout the country and in 1951 it was handed over to the Cambodians to run. The museum contains a collection of Khmer art – notably sculpture – throughout the ages (although some periods are not represented). Galleries are arranged chronologically in a clockwise direction. Most of the exhibits date from the Angkor period but there are several examples from the pre-Angkor era (that is from the kingdoms of Funan, Chenla and Cham). The collection of Buddhas from the sixth and seventh centuries includes a statue of Krishna Bovardhana found at Angkor Borei showing the freedom and grace of early Khmer sculpture. The chief attraction is probably the pre-Angkorian statue of Harihara, found at Prasat Andat near Kompong Thom. There is a fragment from a beautiful bronze statue of Vishnu found in the West Baray at Angkor, as well as frescoes and engraved doors. The library at the museum was one of the largest of its type in Southeast Asia but has now been dismantled and sold.

The riverside ⬛🌀🌀⬤🔺🔻⬤ ↦ *pages 66-82*

Sisowath Quay is Phnom Penh's Left Bank. A broad pavement runs along the side of the river and on the opposite side of the road a rather splendid assemblage of colonial buildings looks out over the broad expanse of waters of the quatre bras. The erstwhile administrative buildings and merchants' houses today form an unbroken chain –

Phnom de plume

Legend has it that the city is named after Penh, a rich Khmer lady, who lived on the banks of the Mekong River. Floodwaters are said to have washed a tree onto the riverbank and Penh found four statues of the Buddha hidden inside.

In 1372 she built a monastery to house the statues on a nearby hill – or 'phnom' in Cambodian. The people of Cambodia believed the statues were a sign from the gods that they wanted a new home.

When the Thais invaded in 1431 and after the collapse of the kingdom of Angkor, the capital duly moved to Oudong and then to a site near the important temple of Phnom Penh. The city lies at the confluence of the Sap, Mekong and Bassac rivers and it has grown into an important commerical centre. The French called the junction 'Les Quatre Bras'; in Khmer it is known as the Chameon Mon.

almost a mile long – of bars and restaurants, with the odd guesthouse thrown in. While foreign tourist commerce fills the street, the quayside itself is dominated by local Khmer families who stroll and sit in the cool of the evening, served by an army of hawkers.

Wat Ounalom

Phnom Penh's most important wat, Wat Ounalom, is north of the museum, at the junction of Street 154 and Samdech Sothearos Boulevard, facing the Tonlé Sap, ⓘ *0600-1800*. The first building on this site was a monastery, built in 1443 to house a hair of the Buddha. Before 1975, more than 500 monks lived at the wat but the Khmer Rouge murdered the Patriarch and did their best to demolish the capital's principal temple. Nonetheless it remains Cambodian Buddhism's headquarters. The complex has been restored since 1979 although its famous library was completely destroyed. The stupa behind the main sanctuary is the oldest part of the wat. The main sanctuary, which dates from 1952, now contains only the poorly assembled fragments of a Burmese marble Buddha. On the first level there is a fine bust of the Buddha, while frescoes on the second level represent scenes from the Buddha's life, painted in 1952. There are usually quite a few chatty monks about the place.

Wat Phnom and around 🔴🍴 ▸ *pages 66-82*

Wat Phnom stands on a small hill at the end of Boulevard Tou Samouth (in the north end of town, where it intersects Street 96) and is the temple from which the city takes its name. It was built by a wealthy Khmer lady called Penh (see above) in 1372. The sanctuary was rebuilt in 1434, 1890, 1894 and 1926. The main entrance is to the east, the steps are guarded by nagas and lions. The principal sanctuary is decorated inside with frescoes depicting scenes from Buddha's life and the *Ramayana*. At the front, on a pedestal, is a statue of the Buddha. There is a statue of Penh inside a small pavilion between the vihara and the stupa, with the latter containing the ashes of King Ponhea Yat (1405-1467). The surrounding park is tranquil and a nice escape from the madness of the city. Monkeys with attitude are in abundance but they tend to fight between themselves.

Wat Phnom is a favourite with the Phnom Penhois and is often teeming with worshippers praying for a dose of good fortune. Vietnamese devotees flock to the shrine of the spirit Preah Chau, north of the main sanctuary. Others buy birds to release in exchange for good luck (not that much luck for the bird though, which will probably be captured again). To the left of the image of Preah Chau is a statue of the

❧ Phnom de guerre

Of the original population of Phnom Penh thousands died during the Pol Pot era so the population of the city now seems rural in character. The population of the city tends to vary from season to season: in the dry season people pour into the capital when there is little work in the countryside but go back to their farms in the wet season when the rice has to be planted and so the population drops.

Phnom Penh has long faced a housing shortage – two-thirds of its houses were damaged by the Khmer Rouge between 1975 and 1979 and the rate of migration into the city exceeds the rate of building. Apart from the sheer cost of building new ones and renovating the crumbling colonial mansions, there has been a severe shortage of skilled workers in Cambodia: under Pol Pot 20,000 engineers were killed and nearly all the country's architects.

Exacerbating the problem is the issue of land ownership as so many people were removed from their homes. These days there are many more qualified workers but sky-rocketing property prices coupled with the confusing issue of land title has created a situation where a great land grab is occuring with people being tossed out of their homes or having their homes bulldozed to make way for more profitable developments.

Hindu god, Vishnu, 'the preserver', and the shrine is guarded by spirits wielding clubs. The summit affords nice views down Phnom Penh's tree-lined avenues, and there are plans to replant the hill with hundreds of trees to recall how it looked in former times. There is one resident, sad-looking elephant. On the slope behind the wat is an overgrown royal stupa ① *US$1.*

West of Wat Phnom in the **National Library** ① *0800-1100 and 1430-1700,* exemplifying the refinement of French colonial architecture. Original construction began in 1924, and the resplendent building was set in blossoming gardens. Not surprisingly and somewhat sacrilegiously, the Khmer Rouge ransacked the building, transforming it into, of all things, a stable. Books were either burnt or thrown out on to the streets. Fortunately many of the discarded books were grabbed by locals who kindly returned them to the library post 1979. There are some antiquated palm-leaf manuscripts, photo documentation from earlier years and some fascinating artworks.

French Embassy

The French Embassy, on the intersection of Monivong Boulevard and Street 76, was recently rebuilt as a low concrete whitewashed complex for the French to occupy once again. This was the building into which 800 expatriates and 600 Cambodians crowded when the Khmer Rouge first occupied the city in mid-April 1975. Within 48 hours of Pol Pot's troops' arrival

❧ *Jon Swain, who was caught up in the Khmer Rouge takeover, gives a graphic first-hand account of the sanctuary provided by the French Embassy, in his book,* River of Time.

in Phnom Penh, the French vice-consul was informed that the new regime did not recognize diplomatic privilege. Cambodian women married to foreigners were allowed to stay in the embassy (marriages were hastily arranged to safeguard the women), but all Cambodian men were ordered to leave. The foreigners were finally escorted out of Cambodia; everyone else was marched out of the compound.

Boeng Kak Lake

Boeng Kak Lake is the main area for budget accommodation. The lakeside setting with the all important westerly aspect – ie sunsets instead of the sunrises of Sisowath

Quay – appeals strongly to the nocturnal instincts of guests. The lake is quite beautiful, but close to the guesthouses it becomes more like a floating rubbish tip. The area is a bit far out, a walk to Central Market takes about 10 to 15 minutes, but will appeal to backpackers as it's well supplied with cheap food and guesthouses. Some bars and restaurants open 24 hours a day. On the water not much differentiates one guesthouse from another – all are of the same ilk. In the eyes of the law, the places on the lake are considered 'squatted' so their future is unsure.

Around Independence Monument 🔴🎷 ⟫ *pages 66-82*

South of the Royal Palace and Silver Pagoda, between Street 268 and Preah Sihanouk Boulevard, is Independence Monument. It was built in 1958 to commemorate independence but has now assumed the role of a cenotaph.

Wat Lang Ka, on the corner of Sihanouk and Norodom Boulevard (close to Independence Monument), was another beautiful pagoda that fell victim to Pol Pot's

❗ *The best colonial architecture is on streets 114 , 53, 178, Norodom Boulevard and Samdech Sothearos Boulevard.*

architectural holocaust. Like Wat Ounalom, it was restored in Khmer style on the direction of the Hanoi-backed government in the 1980s. It is a really soothing get-away from city madness and the monks here are particularly friendly. They hold a free meditation session every Monday and Thursday night at 6pm and anyone is welcome to join in.

South of the centre 🔴🎷 ⟫ *pages 66-82*

Tuol Sleng Museum

ⓘ *0800-1100, 1400-1700, closed Mon. Public holidays 0800-1800. US$2. There is a free film show at 1000 and 1500 each day. Recommended. The Documentation Centre of Cambodia website, www.welcome.to/dccam, is a Yale University project to investigate the crimes of the Khmer Rouge and document and record their atrocities. This information is available to those who may wish to pursue legal redress for genocide.*

Further southwest from Independence Monument, on Street 113 (close to Street 350), is the Tuol Sleng Museum (or Museum of Genocide). After 17 April 1975 the classrooms of Tuol Svay Prey High School became the Khmer Rouge main torture and interrogation centre, known as Security Prison 21 – or just S-21. More than 20,000 people were taken from S-21 to be executed at Choeung Ek extermination camp. Countless others died under torture and were thrown into mass graves in the school grounds. Only seven prisoners survived because they were sculptors or artists and could turn out countless busts of Pol Pot.

The school was converted into a 'museum of genocide' by the Vietnamese (with help from the East Germans who had experience in setting up the Auschwitz Museum). Classrooms were subdivided into small cells by means of crude brick walls (now liable to topple over). In some rooms there is a metal bedstead and on the wall a fuzzy black and white photograph showing how the room was found in 1979 with a body manacled to the bed. Walls on the stairways often have holes knocked in them and one can all too easily imagine the blood and filth that poured down the stairs making these outlets necessary. One block of classrooms is given over to photographs of the victims. All the Khmer Rouge victims were methodically numbered and photographed. The pictures on display include those of foreigners who fell into the hands of the Khmer Rouge but the vast majority are Cambodians – men, women, children and babies – all of whom were photographed. Some have obviously just been tortured or raped and stare with loathing and disgust into the camera, while others appear to be unaware of the fate that awaits them. The

block contains the simple but disturbing weapons of torture. It is a chilling reminder
that such sickening violence was done by such everyday objects.

South of Tuol Sleung Museum

Wat Tuol Tom Pong, next to a market of the same name (just off Mao Tse Tung
Boulevard – the entrance is on Street 135), is a modern pagoda – very bright, almost
kitsch. Surrounded by a high wall, it has entrances with mythical animals
associated with the Buddha.

Former US Embassy

The former US Embassy, now home to the Ministry of Fisheries, is at the intersection
of Norodom and Mao Tse Tung boulevards. As the Khmer Rouge closed on the city
from the north and the south in April 1975, US Ambassador John Gunther Dean
pleaded with Secretary of State Henry Kissinger for an urgent airlift of embassy staff.
But it was not until the very last minute (just after 1000 on 12 April 1975, with the
Khmer Rouge firing mortars from across the Bassac River onto the football pitch near
the compound that served as a landing zone) that the last US Marine helicopter left
the city. Flight 462, a convoy of military transport helicopters, evacuated the 82
remaining Americans, 159 Cambodians and 35 other foreigners to a US aircraft carrier
in the Gulf of Thailand. Their departure was overseen by 360 heavily armed marines.
Despite letters to all senior government figures from the ambassador, offering them
places on the helicopters, only one, Acting President Saukham Khoy, fled the country.
The American airlift was a deathblow to Cambodian morale. Within five days, the
Khmer Rouge had taken the city and within hours senior officials of the former Lon Nol
government were executed on the tennis courts of the embassy.

West of the centre 🛏🍴 ›› *pages 66-82*

There are two wats worthy of a visit lying to the west of the city centre. **Wat Koh**, on
Monivong Boulevard (between Streets 174 and 178), is popular for its lake. **Wat
Moha Montrei**, on Preah Sihanouk Boulevard (between Streets 173 and 163), was
used as a rice storage depot by the Pol Pot regime. A second brick mosque on
Chraing Chamres II, called **An-Nur an-Na'im Mosque**, is much smaller than the one
which previously occupied the site. The original building, built in 1901, was
destroyed by the Khmer Rouge.

Around Phnom Penh 🛏 ›› *pages 66-82*

Choeung Ek

ⓘ *US$2. Southwest on Monireth Blvd, about 15 km from town. By moto the return trip
should be between US$2-5. In a car it will be around US$10.*

Now in a peaceful setting surrounded by orchards and rice fields, Choeung Ek was the
execution ground for the torture victims of Tuol Sleng – the Khmer Rouge
extermination centre, S-21 (see page 60). It is referred to by
some as **'The killing fields'**. Today a huge glass tower stands on
the site, filled with the cracked skulls of men, women and
children exhumed from 129 mass graves in the area (which were
not discovered until 1980). To date 8985 corpses have been
exhumed from the site, although researchers believe the
number of victims buried is closer to double that figure. The site,
once an orchard, is peaceful with only the odd bird or quacking

❢ *Travel agents and hotels
will organize trips to
surrounding sights, but
it is often easier and
cheaper to hire your own
transport (see page 79)
or go by moto).*

duck to break the silence – and more numerous child beggars. Signs with rather an eloquent translation attempt to explain the inexplicable: "The method of massacre which the clique of Pol Pot criminals was carried upon the innocent people of Kampuchea cannot be described fully and clearly in words because the invention of this killing method was strangely cruel. So it is difficult for us to determine who they are for they have the human form but their hearts are demons' hearts…". The really sad part is that Choeung Ek is just one of 4973 gravesites uncovered by the Documentation Centre, dedicated to investigating Khmer Rouge atrocities.

Oudong

ⓘ *Take Route 5 north from Phnom Penh, turn left down a track before Oudong town (at Vihea Luong medical centre, by the big Angkor Beer and condom signs); it's approximately 1½ hours (40 km) by moto. Buses depart hourly from the Central Market with Pnhom Penh Public Transport Co. Alternatively, buses going to Kampong Chhnang pass through Oudong (get off at the Oudong billboard). The drive is a good one but to avoid too much climbing get your moto driver to drop you off at the foot of the steps. Oudong is busy with Phnom Penhois on Sun. There are drink stalls at the foot of the hill.*

Oudong, 35 km north of Phnom Penh, was the royal capital between 1618 and 1866 and only the foundations of the ancient palace remain. The skyward-soaring stupas can be seen from miles away emerging from the forest-clad hills. At the top of the larger of two ridges, just south of Oudong itself, are the ruins of **Phnom Chet Ath Roeus**. The vihara was built in 1911 by King Sisowath to house a large Buddha image, but was destroyed by the Khmer Rouge. Beyond the wat to the northwest is a string of viharas – now in ruins – and beyond them, several stupas, that house the ashes of King Ang Douong (1845-1859) and King Monivong (1927-1941). On the other side of the ridge stands a memorial to those murdered by the Khmer Rouge, whose remains were unearthed from mass graves on the site in the early 1980s. The stupas themselves are nothing special but the views over the vast surrounding plain are spectacular. The town itself is a nondescript, sleepy little place, a short ride north of the temples. Its chief function seems to be washing mud-caked cars and pick-ups coming in from the country so that their occupants can drive in to Phnom Penh with dignity. Oudong is also home to Prasat Nokor Vimean Sour, a kitsch, concrete model of Angkor Wat built in 1998.

Koh Dach (Koh Dait)

ⓘ *There are a few ways to get to the island which is 15 km north of the city, over the Japanese Bridge. You can take a moto to the ferry dock on Route 6 and catch a ferry from there (cheapest option) or you can take one of the small tourist boats on the riverfront, north of Street 178, which will do the trip for US$10-20 (for 1 or 2 hrs). Capitol Guesthouse also runs ½-day Mekong cruises for US$10 per person.*

Koh Dach (also known as Mekong Island) is a fairly touristy yet reasonably serene island jutting from the Mekong. The 12-km-long island is home to five villages who, for the most part, cultivate beans, corn, sesame seeds, peanuts and banana crops. However, the island is famed for its weaving and visitors are welcome to come and observe the crisscrossed weaving of looms. There are a few hut-style restaurants on the river edge, which make for a good lunch spot. In the dry season, the shore recedes, providing a good sandy cover for swimming.

Kien Svay

ⓘ *Kien Svay is about 12 km east of Phnom Penh, off Route 1. Follow Route 1 until you pass L'Imprevu Hotel and turn left 1 km later and follow the road through the archway. There is quite a good Khmer restaurant on the highway before the turn-off. Buses can be caught to Kien Svay from the Central Market (US$0.50).*

The small resort of Kien Svay (also known as Koki Beach) has become the definitive Cambodian picnic spot. Every weekend the folks from Phnom Penh descend on the site, to get a bit of rest and rejuvenation by the small Mekong tributary. The main attraction is the multitude of water houses for rent – small, sheltered bamboo stilt platforms protruding from the water. The huts are accessible via a small boat trip and usually the huts' owner will take you there and back. The plethora of fried insect and bug hawkers could fulfill anyone's monthly nutrition quota but for those not fond of six-legged creatures there are numerous food vendors and stalls selling chicken, rice and other Khmer dishes, so food isn't a problem. Longer boat rides around the area can be also organized. The boat trip to the hut and rental of the hut for an hour should cost around US$0.50-1 but this needs to be negotiated from the outset. The trip takes about 40 minutes and a moto from Phnom Penh should cost US$6-7. Possibly more interesting than the riverside itself are the surrounding villages. Most of the surrounding area comprises of silk weaving villages and provides an insight into quintessential Khmer life. This is probably one of the best places to pick up a krama.

Tonlé Bati

ⓘ *US$3 (includes a free drink). 33 km south of Phnom Penh on Route 2 and about 2½ km from the main road. If driving yourself, don't go straight over at the Takhmau roundabout or you'll end up at Sa'ong. If you are taking public transport it is best to catch the bus to Takeo, which departs regularly from the Central Market from 0700, several buses a day. There are a number that make the return trip in the afternoon (up until 1300). Make sure you indicate where you wish to hop off (31 km from Phnom Penh) or you could wind up at Takeo, 46 km away. A shared taxi enroute to Takeo is also an option.*

This is a popular local weekend picnic site, 33 km south of Phnom Penh. Beside the tranquillity of the Bati River and shady foliage there is the added attraction of the temple of Ta Phrom. The temple dates from Jayavarman VII's reign (1181-1201) and, unusually, it is consecrated to both Brahma and the Buddha, though some of the Buddhist iconography is easily recognizable as being modern. The reclining Buddha carved on the front lintel is modern as are the Buddha statues inside. Interestingly two are fixed into Yoni – the Sivaist 'female' pedestal. The temple is made largely of laterite with a central tower of limestone – notice how the carving of Vishnu is superimposed with Buddha images. The temple has been modelled in traditional form: four outer sanctuaries and the central sanctuary in cruciform layout. Each sanctuary contains a linga. There is a smaller temple, Yeay Peau, 100 m north of Ta Prohm. Both temples have a number of fine bas-reliefs. This temple is steeped in legend and is believed to be named after King Ta Prohm's mother. King Preah Ket Mealea fell in love with a young fisherman's daughter, Peau. Together they produced a son, Prohm. As the king had to return back to his royal duties he left a ring for his son, to enable the boy to prove his royal lineage. Upon being told that his father was the king, Prohm set off to track him down. After showing his genealogical proof (the ring), Prohm took up residence in his father's court for several years. So much time was spent away that when he returned to Tonlé Bati he didn't recognize his mother. Besotted with her beauty, Prohm demanded that Peau should be his wife. Refusing to believe Peau's pleas that she was his mother, she suggested a contest to settle the dispute. She proposed a 'winner takes all' competition – they were both to build temples and whoever finished first would have the final say in whether the marriage was to proceed. The pair of them undertook their construction at night, the women villagers allied with Peau and the men aided Prohm. Peau called the men's bluff, lighting the sky with a candle and the men, who were easily duped, believed it was daybreak and headed off to bed. The women continued their slog through the night and eventually Peau's temple was completed. Devestated, Prohm conceded defeat and respected Peau's wishes to be known as his mother and not bride-to-be. The modern Wat Tonlé Bati is nearby. About 10 km from Tonlé Bati is a house belonging to Khmer royalty. Locals climb the hill (Phnom Tamao) on Sundays to make donations to the monks, but it is noisy, crowded and not advised on weekends.

Phnom Tamao

ⓘ *44 km south of Phnom Penh on Route 2 and about 8 km (to the left) off the main road. If driving/riding zero the odometer at the start of the trip and turn left at the sign for the zoo (at 36 km), follow the dirt road until you hit the zoo. On public transport it is best to take the bus to Takeo, which departs regularly from the Central Market from 0700. There are a number that make the return trip in the afternoon (up until 1300). Make sure you indicate where you wish to hop off (36 km from Phnom Penh – you will need a moto or other form of transport to take you up the road to the zoo). A shared taxi en route to Takeo is also an option. Admission US$2.*

Phnom Tamao, 45 km southeast of Phnom Penh, is considered by many as the country's premier wildlife sanctuary. Asian zoos aren't usually renowned for their humane treatment of animals but this one is markedly better (though there is still a long way to go). The sanctuary stretches over 1200 ha, 80 ha of which have been designated as a sprawling zoo and wildlife rescue centre. The zoo was established to preserve and rescue rare and endangered local species from the grip of poachers and smugglers and it has rescued a vast array of animals including tigers, lions, deers, bears, peacocks, herons, crocodiles and turtles, which can all be seen at here. The Sun Bear enclosure is a definite highlight and is now one of the best of its type in Asia. The enclosure is home to a number of Sun Bears rescued from the smugglers (see box, opposite page).

Phnom Chisor

ⓘ *55 km south of Phnom Penh on Route 2, the turn-off is marked by Prasat Neang Khmau (the temple of the Black Virgin); Phnom Chisor is approximately 4 km from the main road. Take moto or hire car. For public transport take the Takeo bus (see above travel advice) and ask to hop off at Prasat Neang Khmau. Admission US$3.*

Some 52 km south of Phnom Penh, this phnom (hill) is topped by a large rock platform on which many buildings from different eras have been built and from which are tremendous views over the surrounding plains. The principal remaining sanctuary (originally called Suryagiri, literally meaning 'Sun Mountain') is dedicated to Brahma and dates from the 11th century. Navigating the steep 55 steps is a bit of a task.

Kirirom National Park

ⓘ *The best way to get to the park from Phnom Penh is by hired motorbike (US$5-8 per day) or car (US$30 per day). To take a moto (ie motorbike taxi) could cost you up to US$15 but should be less depending on your bargaining skills. From Phnom Penh head out on the Pochentong Airport road along Route 4. The entrance to the park is 78 km from the airport, passing first through the major town of Kompong Speu. As you near the park bundles of firewood can be seen for sale along the roadside. The other option is to take the bus to Sihanoukville and ask to be let off at Kirirom (or Preah Suramarit Kossomak Park Park in Khmer). From there you will have to arrange your own transport.*

The Preah Suramarit Kossomak Park, better known as Kirirom National Park, is 82 km southwest of Phnom Penh. It is a wooded upland area which has become deservedly famed for its huge and beautiful trees and its peaceful tranquillity. Capitalizing on its beauty, King Sihanouk established a settlement here in 1944 called Chuolong City. After the return of the French in 1945-1946, it became a hideout for the Khmer Issarak guerrillas fighting for independence. During the 1960s Chuolong City became an exclusive holiday retreat for the French and Khmer élite. The Khmer Rouge destroyed the villas in the 1970s, but some ruins still remain. Amazingly, it was not until 1992 that the Khmer Rouge were finally dislodged from the area.

Kirirom, which covers 35,000 ha of upland forest set in the Elephant Mountain Range, was designated a national park in 1993. In the higher elevations of the park the predominate tree is the pine tree (*pinus merkuzi*). A 1995 survey of the area mentions munjac deer, sambar deer, tigers and leopards. The higher altitude (675 m above sea level) offers a brilliant climate change, particularly in the hotter seasons.

A not so sunny trade – sun bears in Cambodia

Sun bears are the smallest of all bear species distinguishable by a splash of gold on their chests which represented the sun in ancient Eastern folklore. The mammals are believed to live in northern Burma, Bangladesh, Thailand, Laos, Vietnam, Cambodia and Malaysia and are one of the most endangered bear species in the world, with population estimates somewhere in the region of 1000 to 10,000.

The Cambodian Government has undertaken several radio and billboard campaigns to prevent the poaching of the bears, yielding good results locally, as bears pretty much disappeared from the menus of Phnom Penh.

However, the main problem lies outside of Cambodia, with a very strong demand for the bears and bear by-products emanating from China. The Chinese have revered the bears' medicinal qualities for centuries and Chinese pharmacopoeia regularly exploits the animals' gallbladders and penises to remedy infection, inflammation and pain. In China, bear paws are seen to bestow power and vitality and bear paw soup, considered a delicacy, fetches up to US$270 a bowl. In China the bears that aren't hacked to pieces are kept in cages so their bile can be extracted for traditional medicines.

Bear bile is, quite literally, worth more than its weight in gold. This was quantified a few years ago when smugglers in the United States were busted with around 5 kg of bear gall bile – the estimated market price at the time was US$2 million.

Many organizations are working alongside the government to stop the illegal trade of the bears but when the average Cambodian earns less than US$40 a month the lure of smuggling sun bears for US$350-500 each can often prove too strong. For more information visit www.freethebears.org.au and www.wildaid.org.

The park has been cleared of mines and is suitable for hiking, which you have to do in select areas as motorbikes aren't permitted throughout certain parts. The park has become very popular as a weekend getaway. Pick-up trucks piled high with young Khmers and motorbikes with whole families squeezed on the back form a convoy to the park on weekends. It is considerably more peaceful to visit on a weekday when the park regains some of the tranquillity for which it became popular in the first place. Just before entering the park, near the ranger's office, there is a sign pointing to a waterfall (to the right, approximately 10 km). These falls are arguably more magnificent than those heralded as the best in Kirirom – with water roaring down a 25-m drop into the natural pool below.

Inside the park, a metalled road leads to an intersection with some food stalls. The road to the right marked 'Liu Shaq Qi' leads up a small hill to one of the villas laid waste by the Khmer Rouge. The ruins are covered in Khmer and Vietnamese graffiti. There are good views from here of the surrounding countryside and a large lake. The lake can be reached on foot by returning to the intersection but as the lake has been killed by some form of pollution it is best viewed from a distance. For those who wish to take their chance, locals hire life jackets and inner tubes for 1000 riel. Further along on the same road are some popular picnic and bathing spots near river rapids. Thatch huts can be rented for a nap/picnic for US$1. There are plenty of walks and tracks to explore. **O Traw Sek Resort** is a series of rapids within the resort. Rapid perhaps isn't the best term as the waters are quite slow moving, particularly in the dry season. Nonetheless, it is a tranquil area with lush greenery, a still, green pool perfect for a dip and swarms of dragonflies flitting around. Wat Kirirom is a small but pleasant enough place.

⊜ Sleeping

Phnom Penh boasts a wide range of accommodation from good 4- to 5-star international standards to lowly guesthouse dormitories. Boeng Kak Lake has become somewhat of a mini Khaosan Rd, with most backpackers opting to stay there. Street 182 also offers a selection of cheaper alternatives. Similarly the top end hotels are quite widely scattered around town. For general ease of access to restaurants and bars Sisowath Quay is hard to beat but with Phnom Penh being as compact as it is location is not a major issue. Many taxis will try and take you to a 'preferred' destination – as they get commissions. To avoid this, you can organize an airport pick up with your hotel; 80% of the hotels here offer this service, and most of them for free.

Historic centre *p53, map p54*

A Regent Park, 58 Samdech Sothearos Blvd, T023-427131, regentpark@online.com.kh. Despite the unappealing façade it boasts 50 comfortable serviced apartments suitable for anyone contemplating a prolonged stay. Thai and European restaurant.
Price includes breakfast.
A-B Diamond, 172-184 Monivong Blvd, T023- 217221/2, diamondhotel@ online.com.kh. Hotel in a good central location. A little overshadowed by some of the newer and better hotels but the staff is exceptionally helpful and friendly. Rooms are clean with TV, bath and IDD telephone.
A-B Holiday Villa, 89 Monivong Blvd, T023-990888, www.holiday villa.com.my. Bit 1970s but well appointed, with bath, internet, TV, safe deposit box, IDD phone. Breakfast included. Restaurant serving Halal.
B Flamingo Hotel, No 30 St 172, T023-221640, reservation@flamingo.com.kh. Reasonably new hotel, bit garish from the outside but good facilities. Well fitted rooms with all the amenities, including a bath. Free internet, gym and restaurant.
B New York Hotel, 256 Monivong Blvd, T023- 214116, www.newyork hotel.com.kh. The rooms aren't going to set the world on

fire but the facilities are good for the price – massage centre, sauna, restaurant and in-room safe. Complementary fruit.
C Billabong, No 5 St 158, T023-223703, www.thebilla bonghotel.com. Reasonably new hotel, well appointed and decorated rooms. Breakfast included. Swimming pool, poolside bar and de luxe rooms with private balconies overlooking the pool. Internet. Recommended.
C-D KIDS Guesthouse, No 17A St 178, T012-410406, ryan@ ryanhem.com. Rather a good find this. Guesthouse of the Khmer Internet Development Service (KIDS) set in a small tropical garden, spotted with a couple of cabana-style internet kiosks. A couple of rooms are a decent size, quite clean and equipped with a huge fridge. Discount on internet use for guests. Welcoming. Good deals for guests staying 4 nights or more. Soon to open a coffee shop.
C-E Walkabout Hotel, corner of St 51 and St 174, T023- 211715, www.walkabout hotel.com. In the heart of Phnom Penh, a popular Australian-run bar, café and guesthouse. 23 rooms ranging from small with no windows and shared facilities to large rooms with own bathroom and a/c. Rooms and bathrooms are okay but lower-end rooms are a little gloomy and cell-like. 24-hr bar downstairs so often noisy and quite a bit of traffic, clientele mostly there for the females that hangs around till dawn looking for a suitor.

The riverside *p57, map p67*

L-A Cambodiana, No 313 Sisowath Quay, T023-426288, www.hotelcambodiana.com. Originally built for Prince (as he then was) Sihanouk's guests. The eyesore of a building has all the modern day communist touches, it's not surprising that in a former life, under the Lol Non regime, this was a military base. The place is reedemed by its vista, which overlooks the confluence of the Mekong, Tonlé Sap and Bassac rivers. 300 rooms every one of which is equipped with an internet connection. Exceptional facilities – 2

For an explanation of the sleeping and eating price codes used in this guide, see inside the front cover. Other relevant information is found in Essentials, see pages 34-37

Sisowath Quay

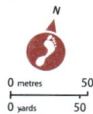

restaurants (French and Chinese), pool, tennis courts, health centre, boutique, business centre and a particularly good book shop – many French titles. Eclipsed as Phnom Penh's premier hotel by Le Royal it remains, nevertheless, a top class hotel.

AL Amanjaya, corner of St 1 and Sisowath Quay, T023-214747, amanjaya@ online.com.kh. Absolutely stunning rooms with full amenities, beautiful furniture and sitting area, creative finishing touches. Good location. K-West restaurant downstairs. Recommended.

AL-A Imperial Garden Villa and Hotel, 315 Sisowath Quay, T023-219991, www. imperialgarden-hotel.com. Another unsightly architectural development. The term garden, in this context, may simply refer to a garden of concrete, with the odd plant chucked in for good measure. The rooms (and suites) have a reasonably good view over the river, with wide screen TV, safe and all modern conveniences. Swimming pool, tennis, massage centre, restaurant.

A Bougainvillier Hotel, 277G Sisowath Quay, T023-220528, www.bougainvillierhotel.com. Lovely riverside boutique hotel, rooms decorated in a very edgy, modern Asian theme, with a/c, safe, cable TV, and mini bar. Good French restaurant.

A Foreign Correspondents Club of Cambodia (FCCC), No 363 Sisowath Quay, T023-210142, www.fcccambodia.com. Known locally as the FCC. 3 decent sized rooms are available in this well known Phnom Penh landmark. Not far to stagger home from the bar and handy for breakfast.

B Renakse, 40 Samdech Sotheros Blvd, T023- 215701, renakse-htl@ camnet.com.kh. Splendid yellow French colonial building in large grounds immediately opposite the Royal Palace. This hotel has the feel of a bygone era. Rooms are decorated in a tasteful, modern Asian style, with Thai-style cushion seats and adjoining mosaic-tiled bathroom. The management and staff are a bit iffy (particularly on room rates) but this aside, it is a simply stunning hotel. Recommended.

B River Star Hotel, corner of Sisowath Quay and St 118, T023-990501, river_star_hotel @yahoo.com. Decent hotel on the riverfront. The only thing extraordinary about the rooms is the view. All rooms have a/c, bathroom and seating area.

B XXL Auberge, No 277 Sisowath Quay, T023- 990691, xxlbouffe@ hotmail.com. Riverfront guesthouse with great balcony views (especially at sunset). Good but the restaurant is a tad pricey.

C Indochine, No 251 Sisowath Quay, T/F023- 427292. 14 rooms in this somewhat chaotically run hotel in a good location. Despite the price some rooms have cold shower only.

C-D Bright Lotus Guesthouse, sammy_ lotus @hotmail.com, No 22 St 178 (near the museum), T023-990 446. Fan and a/c rooms with private bathroom and balconies. Restaurant.

C-D Hotel California 2, No 317 Sisowath Quay, T023-982182. One block up from the Foreign Correspondents Club, overlooking the Tonlé Sap. TV, a/c, attached hot water bathroom with bath tub, in large, very white rooms, with Angkor-style bas-reliefs on the walls. Bored-looking staff. Front rooms are single only but with splendid views of the river.

C-D Indochine 2 Hotel, No 28-30 St 130, T023-211525. Great location and good, clean, comfortable rooms.

C-E Sunshine, No 253 Sisowath Quay, T023- 725684, F218256. 50 rooms in total a few of which get a glimpse of the river. Range of facilities, from a/c to fan in accordance with price.

Wat Phnom and around *p58, map p54*

L Le Royal, St 92 (off Monivong Blvd), T023-981888, www.raffles-hotel leroyal.com. A wonderful colonial era hotel built in 1929 which has been superbly renovated by the Raffles Group. The renovation was done tastefully, incorporating many of the original features and something of the old atmosphere. The hotel maintains an aura of history, mystery and even tranquillity despite the turbulent and bloody events it has witnessed. Jon Swain's *River of Time* is compulsory reading for any guest wishing to know something of the hotel during the

Khmer Rouge invasion of Phnom Penh. The hotel has excellent bars and restaurants, a delightful tree-lined pool and boasts a well stocked bookshop. 2 for 1 cocktails 1600 to 2000 daily at the **Elephant Bar** is a must. Reassuringly expensive and highly recommended.

AL-A Phnom Penh Hotel, 54 Monivong Blvd, T023-724851, www.phnompenh hotel.com. Exceptional value. This hotel comes most recommended from almost everyone in Cambodia's tourism industry. 407 well-appointed rooms with TV, a/c, IDD phone, internet, room safe. Health club, spa and an outdoor swimming pool. Within walking distance to the lake's cheap restaurants and bars. Highly recommended.

AL-A Sunway, No 1 St 92, T023-430333, asunway@on line.com.kh. Overlooking Wat Phnom this is a comfortable hotel in an excellent location. 140 elegant rooms including 12 spacious suites provide first class comfort, complemented by facilities and amenities to cater for the international business and leisure traveller.

E Last Home, No 172 St 21, T021-831702, sakith@forum. org.kh. A popular guesthouse, especially with journos. Just up from the old market (Psar Chas). For the most part, 25 average rooms with basic facilities, cheaper rooms have fan and shared toilet. The pricier rooms have a/c and shower. Dark, dilapidated hallways. Amicable staff, large selection of books, and good, cheap home-cooked food.

E-F Simon 2 Guesthouse, the road in front of the lake. This place has the largest, cleanest rooms.

F Café Freedom, lakeside, T012-807345, www.cafe freedom.org.uk. There are only seven rooms so more often than not this place is booked out. Nice, relaxing atmosphere, except for the fierce guard dogs.

F Floating Island, on the lake (formerly Shanti), T012-551227, floating island_pp@yahoo.com. Rooms emulate the feeling of being in a caravan, a small one. Some rooms have their own bathroom. Nice, breezy deck upstairs.

F **Grandview Guesthouse**, just off the lake, T023- 430766. This place is streets ahead of local competition. Clean, basic rooms. A few extra bucks gets you a/c. Nice rooftop restaurant affording good sunset views, with large breakfast menu, pizza, Indian and Khmer food (all under US$2, Travel services and internet.

F **Guesthouse Number 9**, No 9 St 93, Boeng Kak Lake, T012-766225. One of the original guesthouses here. Rock bottom prices, basic rooms, mosquito nets and fan are provided along with plenty of rats! Wooden complex of chalets perched on stilts in the lake.

F **Happy Guesthouse and Restaurant**, No 11 St 93, lakeside, T023-877232. If your idea of good accommodation is staying in a cupboard, then this is the place for you. 40 basic rooms, most with shared facilities but a few with private bathroom. Restaurant, free pool table and lovely veranda area.

F **Lazy Fish Guest House and Restaurant**, No 16 St 93, lakeside, T012-703368. Very basic guesthouse with shared bathroom facilities.

F **Number 9 Sister Guest house**, T012-424240, number9guesthouse@ hotmail.com. Cleaner than its counterpart. Hammocks, bar and restaurant.

F **No. 10 Lakeside Guest house**, No 10 St 93, Boeng Kak Lake, T012- 454373. Similar to Number 9. It is rather dingy and stuffy. Hammocks, pool table and lockers.

Around Independence Monument *p60, map p54*

B **Scandic Hotel** (also known as the **Scandanavian**) No 4 St 282, T023-214498, nisse@ online.com.kh. Well- appointed, clean rooms with a/c and TV. Very clean. Rooftop restaurant/bar. Pool and Finnish sauna. Motorcycle rental. Airport pick up. Recommended.

B-C **Golden Gate Hotel**, No 9 S 278 (just off St 51), T023-721161, goldengate htls@hotmail.com. Very popular and comparatively good value for the facilities offered. Clean rooms with TV, fridge, hot water and a/c. Within walking distance to restaurants and bars. Visa/MC.

South of central Phnom Penh
p60, map p54

A **Royal Phnom Penh**, Samdech Sothearos Blvd, T023-982673, royalphnom penh@bigpond.com.kh. On the Bassac River, a short drive south of the centre, this hotel is set in a large park. Tad run down but still sufficient. Swimming pool, spacious rooms.

B-C **Palm Resort**, on Route 1, 5 km out of Phnom Penh, T023-3086881. Beautiful bungalows surrounding by lush gardens and a very large swimming pool. A/c rooms with very clean bathrooms. Excellent French restaurant. Recommended.

C-D **Boddhi Tree**, No 50 St 113, T016-865445, www.boddhitree.com. A tranquil setting which belies its location just yards from the Tuol Sleng prison. Lovely old wooden building with guestrooms offering simple amenities, fan only, some rooms have private bathroom. Great gardens and fantastic food at very reasonable prices.

C-D **L'Imprevu**, on Highway Number 1, 6 km past the Monivong Bridge, T023- 360405, imprecas@everyday. com.kh. French run. Lovely bungalows with TV, fridge and hot water. Good pool and garden. Tennis court, petanque, snooker, table tennis and a gym.

West of the centre *p61, map p54*

A-L **Intercontinental**, 296 Mao Tse Tung Blvd, T023-430766, www.intercontinental.com. A 350 room hotel down at the southern end of town. Bit unsightly from the outside but comfortable with large, luxurious bathrooms and highly regarded by business guests. Cantonese restaurant, coffee shop and Clark Hatch fitness centre with aerobics room. Offers most of the facilities business visitors require as well as a large swimming pool.

A **Juliana**, No 16 St 152, T023-366070, www.juliana cambodia.com.kh. A very attractive resort-style hotel with 91 rooms, and decent sized pool in a secluded garden which provides plenty of shade; His and Hers, popular haircut and Thai massage centre and several excellent restaurants. Recommended.

D **Spring Guesthouse**, No 34 St 111 (next to the German Embassy), T023-222155, spring_guest house@yahoo.com. Newly established guesthouse in good location. Fan, cable, TV, a/c, hot shower.

D-F **Capitol**, No 14 St 182, T023-364104, capitol@ online.com.kh. As they say, 'A Phnom Penh institution'. What, in 1991, was a single guesthouse has expanded to 5 guesthouses all within a stone's throw. All are aimed at the budget traveller and offer travel services as well as a popular café and internet access. There are a number of other cheap guesthouses in close proximity, such as **Happy Guesthouse** (next door to Capitol Guesthouse) and **Hello Guesthouse** (No 242 Street 107) – all about the same ilk.

D-F **Narin Guesthouse**, No 20 St 111, off Sihanouk Blvd, T023-986131, touch narin@hotmail.com. In the western part of the city, not far from the Olympic stadium. Popular but has a bit of a seedy feel to it. Some with attached bathroom, some shared. Travel arrangements made (see page 79).

Kirirom National Park *p64*

D **Kirirom Restaurant and Guesthouse**, T018-815403, turn left before the intersection at the large Johnnie Walker sign about 10 km from the entrance to the park. 5 large twin rooms in a motel-style chalet, all rooms come equipped with ceiling fan, furnishings and attached cold water shower and toilet, tranquil with excellent views of the park, English spoken, electricity from 1500-2300. Adjacent restaurant serves Khmer and western food, US$15 per person.

❼ Eating

Most places are relatively inexpensive – US$3-6 per head. There are several cheaper cafés along Monivong Blvd, around the lake, Kampuchea Krom Blvd (St 128) and along the river as well as stalls by the main markets (see below). Generally the food is good and the restaurants surprisingly refined. One of the most remarkable assemblages of restaurants is to be found on Highway 6, several kilometres beyond the Japanese Friendship (Chruoy Changvar) Bridge. From late afternoon until early evening the road is packed with cars ferrying diners looking for a place to eat. Many establishments are embellished with strings of fairy lights, fountains and wedding cake architecture; others are more modest. Also around here is an area that the expats refer to as the 'hammock bar stretch'. A strip of restaurants and beer parlours with a multitude of hammocks which boast great sunset views. Excellent, cheap Khmer food and loads of cold beer are available – a must. To get there just look for the anchor beer signs on the side of the road.

Historic centre *p53, map p54*

¶ **Tamarind**, No 31 St 240, T012-830139. Stylish bar and restaurant specializing in French and Mediterranean, great kebabs and couscous. Bar and tapas. Atmospheric.

¶ **Peking Canteen**, No 393 St 136, T011-909548. Open until 2200. Hole in the wall Chinese restaurant famous for its cheap dumplings (which come either steamed or fried). Very busy at lunch time. Short walk from Psar Thmei.

¶ **Sam Doo**, 56 Kampuchea Krom Blvd, T023-218773. Open until 0200. Late night Chinese food and the best and cheapest dim sum in town.

¶ **The Shop**, No 39 St 240, T012-901964. Open 0900- 1800. Deli and bakery, sandwiches, juices, fruit teas, salads and light lunches.

The riverside *p57, map p67*

¶¶¶ **Bougainvillier Hotel**, 277G Sisowath Quay, T023-220528. Upmarket French and Khmer food.

¶¶¶ **Foreign Correspondents Club of Cambodia (FCCC)**, No 363 Sisowath Quay, T023-210142. A Phnom Penh institution that can't be missed. Superb colonial building, 2nd floor bar and restaurant overlooking the Tonlé Sap. Extensive menu with an international flavour, fantastic pizzas and creative salads. Bit pricey. Ironically, this is the last place in Phnom Penh most local journalists dine. WiFi internet and wonderful photography exhibitions.

K-West, corner of St 154 and Sisowath Quay, T023- 214747. Beautiful, spacious restaurant that offers respite from the outside world. Khmer and European food. Extensive cocktail list. Surprisingly, the prices aren't that expensive considering how upmarket it is.

Origami, No 88 Sothearos Blvd, T012-968095. Best Japanese in town, delectable and very fresh sushi and sashimi. Pricey – one local describes it as where "good things come in very small, expensive packages". Especially good for those craving sushi.

Riverhouse, corner of St 110 and Sisowath Quay, T023-220180. Happy hour 1700-1900, restaurant closes at 2200, bar shuts at 2400. Mediterranean/Thai restaurant in a lovely restored building overlooking the river. Brilliant food, particularly the steak, which is cooked to perfection. Upstairs is a comfortable lounge bar which also serves light meals. Recommended.

Bali, No 379 Sisowath Quay, T023-982211. Open 0700-2300. A wide range of very tempting Indonesian dishes on offer. Upstairs balcony setting facing the river.

Cantina, No 347 Sisowath Quay. Great Mexican restaurant and bar opened by long-time local identity, Hurley. Fantastic food made with the freshest of ingredients. The restaurant attracts an eclectic crowd and can be a source of great company. Terrific photography exhibition, featuring pictures from war-time photographers. Interestingly, the restaurant's sign is a sculpture crafted from old guns. Seating inside and on the street. Very popular. Recommended.

Khmer Borane, No 389 Sisowath Quay, T012- 290092. Open till 2300. Excellent Khmer restaurant just down from the FCC. Wide selection of very well prepared Khmer and Thai food, try the Amok.

La Croisette, No 241 Sisowath Quay, T023-882221. Authentically French and good value hors d'oeuvres and steak. Sit on the broad pavement dining contentedly with Edith Piaf singing softly in the background. Good selection of wines.

Pancho Villa, No 2 St 108 (just off Sisowath Quay). Good Mexican food, breakfast and excellent coffee. Bar that claims to be able to make any cocktail. T he Hawaiian-shirt clad owners are good for a chat.

Rendezvous, No 239 Sisowath Quay, T023-736622. Large comfortable chairs, great place for breakfast or a leisurely lunch and very popular for its 2 for 1 happy hour everyday from 1600-1800. Khmer owned.

Rising Sun, No 20 St 178 (just round the corner from the FCC). English restaurant with possibly the best breakfast in town. Ginormous roast and excellent iced coffee.

Riverside, corner 148 and Sisowath Quay, T023-766743. Enjoy omelettes and burgers while dining inside or out.

Veiyo (River Breeze), No 237 Sisowath Quay, T012-847419. Pizza, pasta and other western dishes. Also offers Thai and Khmer cuisine.

Chiang Mai Riverside, No 227 Sisowath Quay, T011-811456. Open until 2200. Riverfront location for this small but successful Thai restaurant. Simple picture menus (always a turn-off but common in Cambodia where little English is spoken). Endorsed by the Thai government.

Friends, No 215 St 13, T023- 426748. Non-profit restaurant run by street kids being trained in the hospitality industry. The food is delicious and cheap. Highly recommended.

Happy Herb Pizza, No 345 Sisowath Quay, T023-332349. Another Phnom Penh institution, open for over 10 years. Watch out for the 'happy' pizza full of hash – it has a nasty kick. Free pizza delivery.

Mikey's, No 213 Sisowath Quay, T023-991190. Khmer and western. Sensational breakfast.

Wat Phnom and around *p58, map p54*

Thankfully the restaurants at the lake are a notch above the accommodation standards. All of the restaurants here are exceptionally cheap, almost half the price of places in the city. All of the guesthouses on the lake have restaurants, most with identical western-Khmer- Thai menus and prices.

Tell, No 13 St 90, T023-430650. Restaurant closes at 2300 and bar shuts at 2400. Branch in Siem Reap. Swiss German specials including excellent raclette, fondue, wurst and schnitzel. Generous portions authentically prepared. Imported german beer. Owners maintain high standards in the kitchen and in the chalet-esque dining room.

La Marmite, No 80 St 108 (on the corner with Pasteur), T012-391746. Cheap French food. Extremely large portions. Closed Tue.

Boeung Bopha, Highway 6 (over the Japanese Friendship Bridge), T012- 928353. Open until 2300. Large Khmer restaurant with huge menu which includes a number of Khmer dishes and buffet.

The Family Restaurant, St 93, lakeside. A small, unassuming family-run, Vietnamese restaurant serving brilliant (and quite adventurous) food at ridiculously low prices. Great service, lovely owners. Highly recommended.

The Flying Elephant, No 3A St 93, just off the lake, T012-263332. Good cross-section of western foods and drinks. Good salads, burgers and cheap breakfast.

Lazy Gecko, St 93, lakeside. Popular, chilled out restaurant/café/bar offering a good selection of sandwiches, burgers and salads in large portions. Good home-cooked Sunday roast. Affable owner, Juan, is a good source of information. Selection of new and used books for sale. Good trivia night on Thu.

Around Independence Monument *p60, map p54*

Comme a La Maison, No 13 St 57, T023-360801. Great French delicatessen-type restaurant-cum-café. Good pizzas and the breakfast is exceptional.

Elsewhere, No 175 St 51, T023-211348. An oasis in the middle of the city offering delectable modern western cuisine. Seats are speckled across wonderful tropical gardens, all topped off by a well-lit pool. This place has everything right – the food, the setting, the music. 10 out of 10. Highly recommended.

Shiva Shakti, 70 Sihanouk Blvd, T012-813817. Open until 2230. Closed Mon. Facing the Independence Monument. Indian and Moghul specials, vegetarian and meat dishes. The option of pavement eating does not appeal by the side of this busy boulevard but the calm and aromatic atmosphere of the interior is enormously attractive. Quite expensive for Phnom Penh. A good range of excellent food. Selection of cigars.

Baan Thai, No 2 St 306, T023-362991. Open 1130-1400 and 1730-2200. Excellent Thai food and attentive service at this popular restaurant that has been running for 13 years. Main dishes US$4-5. Garden and old wooden Thai house with sit down cushions.

Mount Everest, 98 Sihanouk Blvd, T023-213821. Open 1000- 2300. Branch in Siem Reap. Acclaimed Nepalese and Indian specials. Operating for 5 years and attracts a loyal following.

Talkin to a Stranger, No 21 St 294, T012-798530. Open Wed-Sun. Fantastic bar and restaurant set in an old colonial building. Run a by friendly Australian couple, Derek and Wendy. High on atmosphere and with a brilliant photo- graphic display. Derek is a trained chef and you can tell: these people know how to do food and offer a wide selection of innovative meals. Excellent antipasto platter and delectable chocolate cake dessert. Creative cocktail list. Popular with the expat crowd who, at times, aren't the most engaging lot but the owners are good company. At the time of publication, the restaurant was being revamped to include a cocktail lounge. Highly Recommended.

Khmer Surin, No 9 St 57, T023-363050. Closes 2230. Set in an attractive building with some traditional Thai style seating on cushions, this restaurant is a little way south of Sihanouk Blvd. Quiet.

South of Central Phnom Penh *p60, map p54*

Boddhi Tree, No 50 St 113, T016-865445, www.boddhitree.com. Kitchen closes 2100. Bang opposite the Tuol Sleng Museum. A delightful garden setting and perfect for lunch, a snack or drink. Delicious salads (US$2-3) and sandwiches, barbecue chicken and cheddar is exquisite (US$3). Well run and managed and a great deal of care spent on preparation, presentation and service. Very, very good Khmer food. Very therapeutic garden setting. Highly recommended.

Pyong Yang Restaurant, 400 Monivong Blvd, T023- 993765. This North Korean restaurant is an all round experience not to be missed. The food is exceptional but you need to get there before 1900 to get a seat before their nightly show starts. All very bizarre – uniformed, clone-like waitresses double as singers in the nightly show, which later turns into open-mike style karaoke. Highly recommended.

West of the centre *p61, map p54*

Teukei, No 23 St 111, T012-707609. Good European food.

Cafés/bakeries

Asia Europe Bakery, No 95 Sihanouk Blvd, T012- 893177. Western style café/ bakery. Delicious pastries, cakes and excellent breakfast and lunch menu. Recommended.

Comme La Maison, No 13 St 57, T023-360801. French restaurant offering a selection of fresh French pastries.

Garden Centre Café, No 23 St 57, T023-363002. Popular place to go for lunch and breakfast (heart serves), perhaps not surprisingly, the garden is nice too.

Fresco, 365 Sisowath Quay, T023-217041. Delicatessen and purveyor of fine foods. Sandwiches, cakes and pastries.

Jars of Clay, No 39 St 155 (beside the Russian Market). Fresh cakes and pastries.

Java, No 56 Sihanouk Blvd. Contenders for best coffee in town. Nice use of space – open-air balcony and pleasant surroundings. Delightful food. Features art and photography exhibitions on a regular basis. Good place to come and eavesdrop on some NGO talk.

Kiwi Bakery, No 83 St 63, T023-215784. Bakery run by Cambodian returnees. Good pies and pastries.

Shop [The], No 39 St 240, T023-986964. Popular sandwich joint – fresh salads.

T&C Coffee World, numerous branches – 369 Preah Sihanouk Blvd; Sorya Shopping Centre; 335 Monivong Blvd. Vietnamese-run equivalent to **Starbucks**, but better. Surprisingly good food and very good coffee. Faultless service.

Foodstalls

According to a survey by the Ministry of Health, 75% of the street food tested contained high levels of bacteria. If locals with money avoid such places there is no good reason for visitors to patronize them. Those wishing to try should ensure their hepatitis antibody count is high. **Central Market**, just off Monivong Blvd (at the intersection of St 118 and Charles de Gaulle Blvd). Also good food stalls around the **Capitol Hotel** on St 182 St. Several Vietnamese stalls on St 242 and around most city markets. At the **Russian Market** on St 182, in the corner of the food hall area, is a stall with a sign saying 'best iced coffee in Phnom Penh'. They're right.

Bars and clubs

The vast majority of bars in Phnom Penh attract prostitutes.

California 2, 317 Sisowath Quay. Restaurant and bar, quite similar to the others on the riverfront. Staff not particularly helpful. US$0.75 pasties a major drawcard.

The Cathouse, corner of St 51 and St 18. Open till 2400. Around since the UNTAC days of the early 1990s and is one of the oldest running bars in the city. Not a bad place to have a beer and wonder what it would look like full of UN soldiers getting drunk, fighting and abusing women.

Elephant Bar, Le Royal Hotel. Stylish and elegant bar in Phnom Penh's top hotel, perfect for an evening gin. 2 for 1 happy hour everyday with unending supply of nachos, which makes for a cheap night out in sophisticated surroundings. Open until 2400. Potentially the best drinks in town. Cocktail hour is highly recommended.

Elsewhere, No 175 St 51. Highly atmospheric, up- market bar set in garden with illuminated pool and spot seating, lit by candle. Great cocktails and wine. Very popular with the expats, who have been known to strip off for a dip. Good for a drink before heading somewhere else or a late night spot for engaging conversation. Livens up on the last Sat of every month, when it has parties. Highly recommended.

Foreign Correspondents Club of Cambodia (FCCC), 363 Sisowath Quay. Satellite TV, pool, *Bangkok Post* and *The Nation* both available for reading here. Happy hour 1700-1900. Perfect location overlooking the river, excellent food.

Ginger Monkey, No 29 St 178. Stylish, well decorated bar with faux Angkorian reliefs. Chilled out atmosphere. Quite popular with the younger expat crowd. If you fancy yourself a pool challenge, ask Dave the owner for a game and see how you stack up. A good place to go if you don't want to be inundated with prostitutes. Also has good Asian fusion meals.

Heart of Darkness, No 26 St 51. Heaving with people. Reasonable prices, friendly staff and open late. Has been Phnom Penh's most popular hangout for a number of years. Absolutely full of prostitutes, but your best bet for a night of dancing. There have been many violent 'incidents' here, so it is advisable to be on your best behaviour in the bar as they do not tolerate any provocation. An increasingly popular option is **Howie's Bar** next door.

La Croisette has live music every Thu and Fri. See Eating.

Manhattan, in the rather dubious **Holiday International Hotel**, St 84, T023-427402. One of Phnom Penh's biggest discos. Security check and metal detectors at the door prevent you from bringing in small arms.

Memphis Pub, St 118 (off Sisowath Quay). Open till 0200. Small bar off the river. Very loyal following from the NGO crowd. Live rock and blues music from Tue to Sat.

Peace Café (Sontipheap), No 234 St 258. Chilled out bar with cheap drinks and friendly owner. Quiz night.

Pink Elephant Pub, 343 Sisowath Quay. Predominantly male bar with English football, pool and beer. Food.

The Rising Sun, No 20 St 178, T023-970719. Closes at 2400. Just around the corner from the FCCC. An English pub whose emphasis is just as much on food as beer.

Riverhouse Lounge, No 6 St 110 (Sisowath Quay). 1600-0200. Upmarket, cocktail bar and club. Good wine, cocktails and cigars. Nice views of the river and airy open balcony space. Live music (Sun) and DJs (Sat) with good music and crowd. Great restaurant attached – tad pricey. Atmospheric. Recommended.

Riverside Bar, 273a Sisowath Quay. Great riverfront bar. Tasty food. Recommended.

Salt Lounge, No 217 St 136, T012-289905, www.thesalt lounge.com. Relatively new, funky minimalist bar. Very atmospheric and stylish. Gay friendly.

Sharkys, No 126 St 130. 'Beware pickpockets and loose women' it warns. Large, plenty of pool tables and food served until late. Quite a 'blokey' hangout and advertized as the longest running rock and roll bar in Cambodia.

Talking to a Stranger, Villa 21 St 278. Great cocktails and relaxed atmosphere. In the throes of developing a cocktail lounge at the time of publication. Recommended.

Tom's Irish Bar, No 63 St 170, T023-363161. Comfortable, homely feeling. Very popular.

Zepplin Bar aka Rock Bar, No 128 St 136 (just off Monivong beside the Central Market). Open until 0200 or last customer. Hole in the wall bar owned by a Taiwanese man named Joon who is the human equivalent of a juke box and has over 1000 records for customers to choose from. Cheap beer and spirits. Truly unique concept and an excellent choice for rocking to your favourite songs.

● Entertainment

There are always events in Phnom Penh – the best bet is to pick up a copy of the *Cambodia Daily* and check out the back page which details up-and-coming events.

Casinos

Casinos are illegal within a 100-km radius of Phnom Penh. Those who think it surprising to find 2 in the heart of the city are clearly new to Cambodia.

Holiday International Hotel, St 84. This Singaporean-owned hotel opened the only casino in town in Nov 1994 – the first to begin operating since 1970. Roulette, blackjack and usual entertainments provided.

Naga is a floating casino moored near Cambodiana Hotel. Scarcely a week passes without a newspaper reporting the Naga's imminent closure owing to non-payment of rent or some other misdemeanour. It is open 24 hrs a day and continues to flourish. One useful tip: the **Cambodia Asia Bank**

on the ship never shuts, even on public holidays. Offers cash advances on Visa only.

Dance
National Museum of Cambodia, St 70 in the north of the city. Folk and national dances are performed by the National Dance group. Contact the National Museum directly or the Ministry of Information and Culture, 395 Monivong Blvd.
Pyongyang Restaurant has a North Korean show at 2000 but you need to be seated by 1900. See Eating.

Sovanna Phum Theatre, No 111 St 360 (on the corner of street 105), T023-987564, sovannaphum@camintel.com. Shadow puppets, traditional dance and circus. Every Fri and Sat, 1930, US$4.

Films
Check the *Cambodia Daily* for details.
MTV Video Studio, 1 block down from Lucky Super-market on Sihanouk Blvd. 20 private, a/c rooms which can be rented to watch movies. Hundreds of DVDs to choose from. US$4 for 2 hrs.

O Shopping

Art galleries
There is plenty of promising artistic talent coming out of Cambodia, with some tremendous works both in traditional and modernistic styles.
Apsara Art Gallery, No 170A St 450, T012-867390. Next to the Russian Market. Paintings, posters bronzes and a framing service. Studios of local work on St 178, Cambodian landscapes, Angkor and attractive ladies are the most common churned out themes but the quality is disappointing.
Asasax Gallery, No 192 St 178, T012-877795. Mixed media artist and sculptor using colourful modern materials to develop work based on traditional themes (apsaras and the sort).
Happy Cambodia Gallery, Cambodiana Hotel, www.happypainting.net. The gallery is owned by French-Canadian artist Stéphane Delaprée. His work is colourful in that naïve art kind of way. It is a shame that a foreigner is one of Cambodia's most famous artists. The Cambodian royal family, amongst many others, has bought his work. There is also another gallery below the FCC.
New Art Gallery, No 20 St 9, T012-824570. Contemporary paintings by local artists.
Reyum Institute of Arts and Culture, No 47 St 178 (across from the **National**, T023-217149, www.reyum.org. This is a great place to start for those interested in Cambodian modern art. Some absolutely world class artists have been mentored and exhibit here.

Books/maps
D's Books, No 79 St 240. Second-hand books and new (copied books). There is also a branch up from the **Rising Sun**.
The International Stationary and Book Centre, 37 Sihanouk Blvd. Better on stationery than international books. Lots of text books.
London Book Centre, No 51 St 240, T023-214258. 0800-1900 daily. Since the demise of Bert (who fled in the 1998 coup) and with 10,000 titles in stock this is easily the biggest collection of novels and second-hand books in Cambodia. Recommended.
Monument Books, 111 Norodom Blvd, T023-217617. Has the best selection of books on Cambodia and Southeast Asia and a fair range of other English and French language books and magazines. Shops in some of the top hotels, including **Le Royal** and **Cambodiana**, which both have excellent selections of Cambodia related titles.

Handicrafts
Many non-profit organizations have opened stores to help train or rehabilitate some of the country's underprivileged.
Disabled Handicrafts Promotion Association, No 317 St 63. Handicrafts and jewellery made by people with disabilities and widows.
The National Centre for Disabled People, 3 Norodom Blvd, T023-210140. Great store with handicrafts such as pillow cases, tapestries and bags made my people with disabilities. Recommended.

Le Rit's Nyemo, 131 Sisowath Quay. Non-profit shop with a wide range of silk products.

National Museum of Arts, corner of St 19 and St 184 (behind the National Museum), also sells reproductions of Khmer statues, prints and frescoes of Angkor.

Orange River, 361 Sisowath Quay (under FCC), T023-214594. Has a selection of beautifully designed decorative items and a very good stock of fabrics and silks which will leave many wishing for more luggage allowance. Pricier than most other stores.

Rajana, No 170 St 450, next to the Russian Market. Traditional crafts, silk paintings, silver and jewellery.

Photography

City Colour Photo, 123 Monivong Blvd, reasonably good photo processing. Stocks new and old cameras. Camera repairs.

Nikon Centre, 208 Preah Monivong. The most professional photographic shop.

Markets

Central Market (Psar Thmei), just off Monivong Blvd. Distinguished by its central art deco dome (built 1937), it is mostly full of stalls selling silver and gold jewellery, old coins and assorted fake antiques. Around the main building more mundane items are for sale, including, of course, kramas, the famous Cambodian checked scarf. The main gates into the Central Market are lined with stalls selling touristy items.

Old Market (Psar Chah), between St 13, St 106 and St 110. Sells stationery, clothes, jewellery, fabrics and kramas intended for locals rather than tourists, hence less fancy and cheaper.

O Russei Market, St 182, sells mainly fruit and vegetables. Terrible ladies fashion, worth a look if you can handle the smell of the food stalls.

Tuol Tom Pong, between St 155 and St 163 to east and west, and St 440 and St 450 to north and south, close to the pagoda of the same name. Known to many as the Russian Market. Sells antiques (genuine articles and fakes) and jewellery – nearby is an antique furniture market – as well as clothing, pirate CDs and computer software, videos, sarongs, fabrics and an immense variety of tobacco – an excellent place for buying souvenirs, especially silk. Most things at this market are about half the price of the Central Market. There are also several food stalls here.

Silverware and jewellery

Old silver boxes, belts, antique jewellery can be found along Monivong Blvd. Samdech Sothearos Blvd, just north of St 184, has a good cluster of silver shops, or **Tuol Tum Pong (Russian Market)**, which is recommended for gold and setting gems.

Cambodiana Hotel also has a good silver shop. There are plenty of jewellery stalls in the central covered market. Most modern silverware is no more than 80% silver.

Rachana, No 6B St 118, T023-211290, has nicely made silver animals and other crafts.

Music and film

Boom Boom Room, Boeng Kak Lake, T023-709096. A large selection of movies and music (over 2000 choices) US$2 each. iPod and MP3 recording.

Sorya Shopping Centre, St 63, besides the Central Market. The only 'mall' in the whole country. A modern, 7-floor, a/c shopping centre with goods ranging from shoes to plasma screen TV. Great view of the city from the look-out deck at the top.

Supermarkets

There are a number of petrol stations (**Star** and **Caltex**) which also serve as mini-marts – some are open 24 hrs.

Big A, Monivong Blvd. Good range.

Lucky Supermarket, 160 Sihanouk Blvd, and another branch in the **Parkway Centre**. Excellent French and Australian wine starting at US$5 per bottle (Cambodia has the cheapest wine in Southeast Asia). Lucky sells various English-language newspapers' weekly international editions.

Pencil Supercentre, St 214 and Norodom Blvd. Good range of products.

Sharky Mart. No 124 St 130 (below **Sharkys Bar**), T023- 990303. 24-hr convenience stocking everything from condoms and beer through to late night, junk food. Dubious hamburgers but a reasonably good selection of sandwiches. Free delivery during the day.

Veggy's, No 23 240 St, T023- 211534. An excellent green- grocer selling fresh vegetables and salads as well as a range of good imported food.

Badminton/squash
Cambodiana Hotel, US$10 per hr for court hire. **International Youth Club**, No 51 St 96.

Golf
Cambodia Golf and Country Club, Route 4, 35 km south of Phnom Penh, T023-363666. There is a driving range on the roof of the Parkway Centre.

Gym
All the top hotels have gyms and sports clubs which are usually open to non-members and non-guests for a fee.
Amrita Spa, Hotel Le Royal, T023-981888. Offers a gym, steam room, jacuzzi and pool.
Clark Hatch Fitness Centre, Hotel Inter-Continental, corner of Mao Tse Tong and Monireth blvds, T023-424888. Aerobics, gym, sauna, swimming pool, kick boxing.

Running
Cinder track at the **Olympic Stadium**.
Hash House Harriers meet 1500 Sun at the railway station.

Spectator sports
The 1960s Olympic Stadium is the centre of sport. Basketball (able-bodied and wheel-chaired), volleyball and training sessions of Tai-kwondo can be watched. University and schools football league play from Nov-Apr. A semi-professional league plays Jan-Jun. The standard is good. Crowds reach several thousand for the big games. Worth a look even if nothing is going on there.

Swimming
Some of the large hotels allow non-residents to use their pool: Inter-Continental, Juliana and so on.
International Youth Club, No 51 St 96, 50-m pool, US$10. **Phnom Penh Hotel**, Monivong Blvd. **Phnom Penh Water Park**, Confederation de Russie Blvd (airport road), Mon-Fri 1030-1830, weekends 0900-2000. Entrance US$7 or US$5 for children under 1 m. What a disappointment. Shoddy finish, complete absence of shade, poor rides and shocking mismanagement at an horrendous price. Take care of your children. Satisfactory for getting wet but little else.

Tennis
Hotel Cambodiana, US$5-15 per hr.
International Youth Club, No 51 96 St. US$10 per hr. **L'Imprévu**, see Sleeping. Tennis court US$5 per hr.

Therapies
Seeing Hands on Norodom Blvd is the place to go for a therapeutic massage. All masseurs are blind. There are several other branches around town.

Water skiing
Alligator, 2 km over the Japanese Friendship Bridge, T012-835850. Water skis and jet skis on the river, also a bar and weekend barbecue.

Tour operators

Most travel agencies or hotels can organize plane tickets, bus tickets and so forth. Some of the tour operators listed here also have offices in Siem Reap, see page 138.
Art Suriya Travel, No 40 Samdech Sotheros (St 3) at the **Renakse Hotel**, T023-351742, www.art suriyatravel.com. Offering more upmarket tours for smaller groups. Tailor made tours to unique destinations offered, particularly in the south.
Asian Trails, No 33 St 240, T023-216555, www.asian trails.com. Offers a broad selection of tours: Angkor, river cruises, remote tours, biking trips.
Capitol Tours, No 14AE0, Rd 182 (see **Capitol Guest-house**), T023-217627, www.bigpond.com.kh/users/capitol. Cheap tours around Phnom Penh's main sites. Also organizes tours around the country. Targeted at budget travellers.
Diethelm Travel, No 65 St 240, T023-219151, www.diethelm-travel.com. Well-known Southeast Asian tour operator, operating multi-country tours and Cambodia specific tours (coastal areas, temple tours, boat trips.)
Exotissimo Travel, 46 Norodom Blvd, T023-218948, www.exotissimo. com. Wide range of day trips and classic tours covering Angkor, Sihanoukville etc. Also offers tailor-made trips.
Hanuman Tourism-Voyages, No 128 Norodom Blvd, T023-218356, www.hanumantourism.com.

Offering a diverse selection of short and long tours across the country. Also boat trips.
Local Adventures Cambodia, No 14 St 258, T023-990460, www.cambodia.nl. Modestly prices tours to some more off the beaten track locations. Recommended for intrepid travelers, excellent Khmer guides.
PTM Tours, No 333B Monivong Blvd, T023-986363, www.ptm-travel.com. Reasonably priced package tours.

RTR Tours, No 54E Charles de Gaulle Blvd, T023-210468, www.rtrtours.com.kh. Organizes tours plus other travel services, including ticketing. Friendly and helpful.
Travel Indochina, No 43-44 St108, T023-991978, www.travelindochina.com. Well-established travel company offering group travel within Cambodia and multi-destination tours.

⊖ Transport

Air

Bangkok/Siem Reap Airways has connections with Siem Reap. See page 23 for details. Flights should be booked in advance.

Airline offices Most airline offices are open Mon-Fri 0800-1700, Sat 0800-1200.
Air France, Samdech Sothearos Blvd, T023-219220. **Bangkok/ Siem Reap Airways**, No 61A St 214, T023-46624. **Dragon Air**, Unit A3, 168 Monireth Blvd, T023-424300. **Lao Airlines**, 58C Sihanouk Blvd, T023-216563. **Malaysian Airlines**, Diamond Hotel, 172-174 Monivong Blvd, T023-426688. **President Airline**, 13-14, 296 Mao Tse Tung Blvd, T023-993088-89. **Silk Air**, Micasa Hotel, 313 Sisowath Quay, T023- 426808. **Thai**, 294 Mao Tse Tung Blvd, T023-214359. **Vietnam Airlines**, No 41 St 214, T023-363396/97.

Bicycle

Hire from guesthouses for around US$1 per day. The city is mostly flat, so not too exhausting. Bicycles can be bought cheaply (around US$40) from the shops that cluster on St 107 near Capitol Guesthouse.

Boat

Fast boats to Siem Reap depart from the tourist boat dock on Sisowath Quay at the end of 106 St. Ferries leave from wharves on the river north of the Japanese Friendship Bridge. Moto drivers get paid commission by the ferry companies so it should be possible to get a free ride to the boat. There are supposed to be connections to **Siem Reap** (Angkor), **Kratie**, **Stung Treng**, **Kompong Cham** and **Kompong Chhnang**.
In recent times the Mekong service (Kratie, Stung Treng, Kompong Cham and Kompong Chhnang) hasn't been running as they can't

get enough customers now the roads have been improved. Fast boat connections (5 hrs) with Siem Reap, US$25 1-way, Kompong Cham, US$2.50, Kratie, US$7.85, and Stung Treng US$15.70. Boats do sometimes breakdown and promised express boats often turn out to be old chuggers but they do cost less than flying. All boats leave early, 0700 or earlier. Most hotels will supply ferry tickets (happy to collect the commission).

International It is possible to get to **Vietnam** (crossing at Chau Doc) by bus and boat. **Capitol** and **Narin** guesthouses organize buses to the Neak Luong ferry crossing on the Mekong from where a fast boat transports passengers to the Vietnamese border. After the border crossing there is a boat to Chau Doc in the Mekong Delta. Departs 0800, arrive Chau Doc 1400, US$12.

Bus

See the bus timetables, page 80 and 81. Most buses leave southwest of Central Market (Psar Thmei) by the Shell petrol station.
Capitol Tours, No 14 St 182, T023-217627. **GST Buses**, T012-838910, depart from the southwest corner of the Central Market (on the corner of St 142).
Mekong Express Limousine Tour Bus, 87 Sisowath Quay, T023- 427518, www.mekongexpresstourboat.com.
Neak Krohorm, 127 St 108, T023-219496.
Phnom Penh Public Transport Company (formerly Ho Wah Genting Bus Company), T023- 210359, departs from Charles De Gaulle Blvd, near the Central Market.
To **Battambang**, 2 buses per day, first at 0700, US$5-6, from the Central Market; **Kompong**

Cham, 7 buses per day from 0700 until 1500, US$3; **Kompong Chhnang**, over 5 buses a day, 2-3 hrs, US$3. You can also get a minibus, US$1.60, pick-up, US$1.05, or shared taxi, US$2, to Kompong Chhnang (2 hrs). Most Siem Reap-bound buses will stop in **Kompong Thom** but you will usually be forced to pay the full-fare; to **Kratie**, 1 bus per day, US$4; **Sihanoukville**, 5 buses a day 0700, 0730, 0830, 1230, 1330, 4 hrs, US$3.50; **Takeo**, 6 buses a day, 3 hrs, departures from 0700-1400. **Kompong Speu**, 10 buses departing hourly from 0600; **Neak Leung**, 10 buses from 0600, 2 hrs. **Capitol Tours** runs a bus to **Kampot** departing 0800, US$2.50. GST Buses, runs 3 trips a day to **Pursat**, US$2.50. **Phnom Penh Public Transport Buses**, leave for **Pursat** 3 times daily, 0645, 0730, 1230, 10,000 riel. GST Buses, run to **Sisophon** at 0645, 0715, 0745, 18,000 riel. The Phnom Penh Public Transport Co buses leave for **Kratie** at 0715, US$4.50, 7 hrs. It also leaves

for **Sihanoukville** at 0700, 0730, 0830, 1230 and 1330. GST buses leave for Sihanoukville at 0715, 0815, 1230 and 1330. From **Phnom Penh Raksmei Bun Thaim Guesthouse**, T016-893949, a bus departs for **Koh Kong** at 0700, 7-8 hrs, ₱500.

Phnom Penh Public Transport Co. has buses to **Takeo** hourly between 0700-1600, 6000 riel, 2.5 hrs. **Neak Krohorm**, travels to **Siem Reap, Sisophon, Battambang** and **Poipet**.

International See also pages 24 and 25. If travelling to Vietnam by road, ensure that your visa is appropriately stamped (Moc Bai) or you will be turned back at the border. Don't forget visas for Vietnam are not available at the border. The bus from Phnom Penh to **Ho Chi Minh City** departs 0630 Tue, Thu and Sat (**Phnom Penh Public Transport Co**, Capitol Tour), 8 hrs, US$14 per 1-way ticket. **Narin Guesthouse** runs a bus service to the border and has a connecting bus waiting on the Vietnamese side, US$6, departs 0645.

Car
Chauffeur-driven cars are available at most hotels from US$25 per day upwards. Several travel agents will also hire cars. Prices increase if you're venturing out of town.

Cyclo
Plentiful but slow. Fares can be bargained down but are not that cheap – a short journey should be no more than 2,000-4,000 riel. A few cyclo drivers speak English or French. They are most likely to be found loitering around the big hotels and can also be hired for the day (around US$7).

Motorcycle
From guesthouses and some hotels (US$5-7 per day). Quite a few shops rent larger dirt-bikes from US$7-10 a day (depending on where you are going and for how long). You might want to book a big bike in advance, often if you turn up on the day there isn't a great selection.
Angkor Motorcycle Rentals, No 92 St 51, T012-916824. Highly reputable bike rental company.
Flying Bikes Shop, St 114, T012-841567. Does repairs if you damage your rented bike. When you rent a bike make sure the horn works. It provides you with a helmet and the odometer is hooked up (critical for navigating your way around the country). Repairs are usually at the expense of the customer, though third party insurance is available and recommended. A good investment is to buy some rear-view mirrors as it makes driving on the hellish highways a lot easier.
Lucky! Lucky!, 413 Monivong Blvd.

Moto
'Motodops' are 50-100cc motorbike taxis and the fastest way to get around Phnom Penh. Motodops are ubiquitous and most people will be inundated by offers from the hoardes that congregate outside any- where that tourists might be remotely inclined to visit. Standard cost per journey is around US$0.50 for a short hop but expect to pay double after dark. If you find a good English speaking moto driver, hang on to him and he can be yours for US$8-10 per day. A moto from the airport is US$2.

Shared taxi
These are either Toyota pick-ups or saloons. For the pick-ups the fare depends upon whether you wish to sit inside or in the open; vehicles depart when the driver has enough fares. Psar Chbam Pao, just over Monivong

❗ Cambodia bus timetable

Mekong Express Limousine Tour Bus, 87 Sisowath Quay, Phnom Penh,
T023- 427518, www.mekongexpresstourboat.com.

Buses from Phnom Penh to:	Departure	Price	Duration	Return
Siem Reap (14A Sivatha St)	0730, 1230	US$6	6 hrs	0730, 1230
Ho Chi Minh City (309 Pham Ngu Lao St, Q1)	0630, 0830	US$11	6 hrs	0600, 0900

Phnom Penh Public Transport Co Ltd, T023-210 359. Buses depart from the
Central Market.

Buses from Phnom Penh to:	Departure	Price	Duration	Return
Kompong Thom	0645, 0730,1215	US$3	3 hrs	No return
Kompong Cham (market)	0645, 0745, 0845, 1000, 1200, 1330, 1445	US$2	2.5 hrs	0700, 0915, 1030, 1115, 1345, 1430, 1515, 1630
Kratie (market, T016-862603)	0730	18,000 r	6 hrs	0830
Snoul	0730	15,000 r	4.5 hrs	0730
Stung Treng (market)	0700	40,000 r	8.5 hrs	0700
Takeo (market)	hourly between 0700 and 0400	6,000 r	2.5 hrs	hourly between 0600 and 1600
Sihanoukville (near Princess Hotel)	0715, 0830, 1230, 1330	US$3.5	4 hrs	0710, 0800, 1215, 1400
Oudong (market)	hourly between 0700 and 1600	3,500 r	1 hr	0700 and 1600
Pursat	0645, 0730, 1230	10,000 r	3 hrs	No exact times
Kompong Chhnang (Phsar Krom)	hourly between 0700 and 1600	6,000 r	2.5 hrs	hourly between 0700 and 1600
Battambang (near Thmor Thmey Bridge)	0645, 0730, 1230	US$3	5 hrs	0700, 0730, 1230
Sisophon	0700	20,000 r	7 hrs	0700
Siem Reap (Chong Kao Sou)	0645, 0730, 1215	14,000 r	6 hrs	0700, 0730, 1215
Ho Chi Minh City (309 Pham Ngu Lao, District 1, T+84-8-9203624)	0630, 0900	US$9	7 hrs	0600, 0900

Buses will only depart when they have enough passengers. Book a few days in
advance for public holidays

Bridge, on Route 1 for **Vietnam**. For **Sihanoukville**, **Battambang**, **Siem Riep** and **Thailand** take a shared taxi from the Central Market. Leave early (0500-0600). Prices will vary depending on the number of passengers in the car but expect to pay around US$2-3. To **Koh Kong**, 5-6 hrs, leaves from market, US$10 person (6 per car), US$60 own car, from 0600 onwards.

Taxi
There are only a few taxis in Phnom Penh as the risk of being held up at gunpoint is too high. It is possible to get a taxi into town from the airport (US$7) and one or two taxi companies can be reached by telephone. Taxi Vantha, T012-855000/ 023-982542, is available 24 hrs.

Golden Scaled Transport (GST), 13 St 142, Phnom Penh, T023-895 550.
(Departs from the Central Market)

Buses from Phnom Penn to:	Departure	Price	Duration	Return
Kompong Thom (Pich Chenda Restaurant)	0645, 0745, 1200	US$3/ 12,000 r	3 hrs	No return
Sihanoukville (near Paris Hotel, T012-820559)	0715, 0815, 1230, 1330	US$3.50	4 hrs	0715, 0815, 1230, 1330
Pursat (Railway Station)	0630, 0830, 1245	10,000 r	3 hrs	No return
Battambang (Por Khnung Pagoda, T012-414441)	0630, 0830, 1245	US$3	5 hrs	0630, 0830,1245
Sisophon (market, T012-445045)	0645, 0720, 0745	18,000 r	6 hrs	0715
Siem Reap (near Psar Chas, T012-777442)	0645, 0745, 1200	US$3.50	5 hrs	0700, 0730,1230

Capitol Tours, 14AEo St 132, Phnom Penh, T023-217 627, www.bigpond.com.kh/users/capitol,

Buses from Phnom Penh to:	Departure	Price	Duration	Return
Kompong Thom (Stong Restaurant)	0630, 0730, 0830, 1200	US$3.50	3 hrs	No return
Svay Reng	0645	US$4	3.5 hrs	No return
(Beng Meas restaurant)	0715	US$3	4 hrs	1230
Sihanoukville	Hourly-0700-1330	US$3	3.5 hrs	Hourly - 0700-1330
Pursat (Thmor Keo Guest House, T012-404650)				
Battambang (Beng Chhouk Market, T011-956105)	Hourly-0700-1330	US$3	5 hrs	Hourly-0700-1330
Sisophon (T012-525782)	0630, 0700, 0800	US$4.50	6.5 hrs	0630, 0730
Siem Reap (381 near Phsar Chas, T012-916165)	0630, 0730, 0830, 1200	US$3.50	6 hrs	0730, 1200

Train

The railway station is a fine old 1930s art deco French edifice, recently restored. Quite why is not readily apparent as the station's main function is to provide a place for the homeless to doss down. The station is located on Monivong Blvd between 106 and 108 streets. There are two lines but only one in operation: to the southern line to Kompong Som is no longer operating but the other north to Battambang is. One train per day leaves shortly after 0600, US$2. People have been known to wait until 1000 for the train to depart. Travel is very slow and unreliable and, though cheap, is not particularly advised. In fact, so slow is the train that locals can moto a piece of bamboo along the tracks more efficiently (and they do). The UK Foreign Office continues to advise against rail travel.

Banks

Most banks are now charging 1-2% commission on credit card advances.

ANZ Royal Bank, Russian Blvd, 20 Kramuon Sar (corner of St 67) has now opened ATMS across the city: also near the Independence Monument and at 265 Sisowath Quay.

Cambodia Asia Bank, No 252 Monivong Blvd, T023-722105. Western Union money wire. Branch also at the Naga Casino, which is open 24 hrs. Cash advances on credit cards.

Cambodia Commercial Bank (CCB), No 130 Monivong Blvd (close to the Central Market), T023 -426208. Cash advance on credit cards, TCs and currency exchange.

Canadia Bank, No 126 Charles de Gaulle Blvd, T023-214668, and 265-269 Ang Duong St, T023- 215286. Cash advances on credit cards.

Singapore Banking Corporation (SBC), No 68 St 214, T023-214466; No 203 Monivong Blvd, T023-882878; No 315 Sisowath Quay, T023-990688. Western Union money transfer and currency exchange.

Union Commercial Bank (UCB), No 61 St 130, T023-724931. Most banking services, no charge on credit card cash advances.

Embassies and consulates

Australia, No 11 St 254, T023- 213470, australia.embassy. cambodia@dfat.gov.au.

Belgium, No 8 St 352, T023- 987629, belco@online.com.kh.

Canada, No 11 St 254, T023- 213470, pnmpn@dfait- maeci.gc.ca.

France, 1 Monivong Blvd, T023- 430020, sctipcambodge@ online.com.kh.

Germany, No 76-78 St 214, T023-216381.

Japan, 194 Norodom Blvd, T023-217161-4, eojc@ online.com.kh.

Laos, 15-17 Mao Tse Tung Blvd, T023-983632.

Thailand, 196 Norodom Blvd, T023-726306-10, thaipnp@ mfa.go.th.

United Kingdom, No 29 St 75, T023-427124, britemb@ online.com.kh.

USA, No16 St 228, T023- 216436, usembassy@camnet. com.kh (A new embassy was under construction near Wat Phnom at the time of publication).

Vietnam, 436 Monivong Blvd, T023-362531, embvnpp@camnet.com.kh.

Emergency services

Ambulance, T119/724891. **Fire,** T118. **Police,** T117, 112 and T012-999999.

Internet

Cheap and ubiquitous. Rates can be as low as US$0.50 per hr.

Khmer Web, 150 Sihanouk Blvd, T023-219240 (has another store on St 182).

KIDS, No 17A St 178, T023- 218690, also a guesthouse (see page 66).

Mittapheap Cybercafe, on the corner of Monivong Blvd and St 174.

Medical services

It is highly advisable to try and get to Bangkok if you are seriously ill or have injured yourself.

Bumrungrad Hospital and **Bangkok Nursing Home** in Bangkok are state-of-the- art modern hospitals. Highly recommended.

Calmette Hospital, 3 Monivong Blvd, T023-426948, is generally considered the best, 24-hr emergency centre.

European Dental Clinic, 160 Norodom Blvd, T023-854408. French-run.

International SOS Medical and Dental Clinic, No 161 St 51, T023-216911.

Pharmacy de la Gare, 81 Monivong Blvd, T023-526855. There is also another good pharmacy opposite the **Rising Sun Restaurant**/bar.

Royal Optic, 220 Monivong Blvd.

Surya Medical Services, No 39 St 294, T016-8450000. Mon-Fri 0700-2000, Sat-Sun 0700-1800. 24 hrs emergency care available.

Tropical and Travellers Medical Clinic, No 88 St 108, T015-912100/012-898981. English doctor.

Post office and courier services

Main post office, St 13. Open 0700-2100. Possible to make international telephone calls from here.

DHL, 28 Monivong Blvd, T023-427726.

FedEx, 701D Monivong Blvd, T023-216712.

TNT, No 151F St 154, T023-211880.

UPS, No 27 St 134, T023-427511.

Visa extensions

Foreign Ministry, Sisowath Quay, at the intersection of St 240.

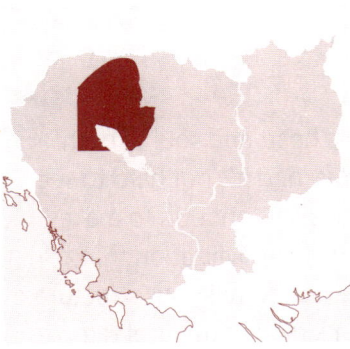

❗ Footprint features

Introduction

The magnificent Angkor Wat is the heart and soul of both ancient and modern-day Cambodia and it's not hard to see why. A glimpse of this majestic temple is enough to make most stop in their tracks and ponder the civilization that created what is believed to be the largest religious structure in the world. Beyond Angkor lies a legion of magical temples which further attest to the dexterity and dedication of bygone artisans, from the intricate Banteay Srei, with its detailed carvings to the beaming faces of the Bayon, whose large peaceful visages are synonymous with the Angkor complex. Visitors also flock to jungle-clad Ta Prohm, where foliage intertwines tentacle-like around the temple, providing an insight into how earlier explorers would have discovered it. A myriad of other temples within the Angkor complex ensure that visitors will be enthralled for days.

The town of Siem Reap has graduated from a minor service centre for Angkor to a thriving tourist hub, teeming with modern restaurants and upmarket hotels. Fortunately, the settlement still retains much of its original charm, with old colonial shopfronts, misty lamp-lit streets and a bustling market area. A short trip from Siem Reap is the Tonlé Sap, Southeast Asia's largest freshwater lake, scattered with many floating villages.

North of Siem Reap is Anlong Veng, the hauntingly beautiful former stronghold of the Khmer Rouge. Although short on tourist sights, the town will be of interest to history buffs and makes a good stopover en route to Preah Vihear.

★ Don't miss...

1 **Angkor Wat** Angkor Wat has been described as the largest religious monument in the world. Drink in the first glimpse of its five soaring towers – they cannot fail to stir the soul and quicken the pulse, see page 101.
2 **Angkor Thom** Enter the heart of the temple complex at Angkor – the colossal and magnificent royal city of Angkor Thom with the Bayon, Jayavarman VII's temple mountain, at its centre, see page 108.
3 **Ta Prohm** Discover this tree-engulfed temple, see page 116.
4 **Banteay Srei** Examine the fine artwork at this site, widely considered the most finely decorated temple in the Angkor complex, see page 123.
5 **Tonlé Sap** Meander through this vast lake's fascinating floating villages, see page 129.

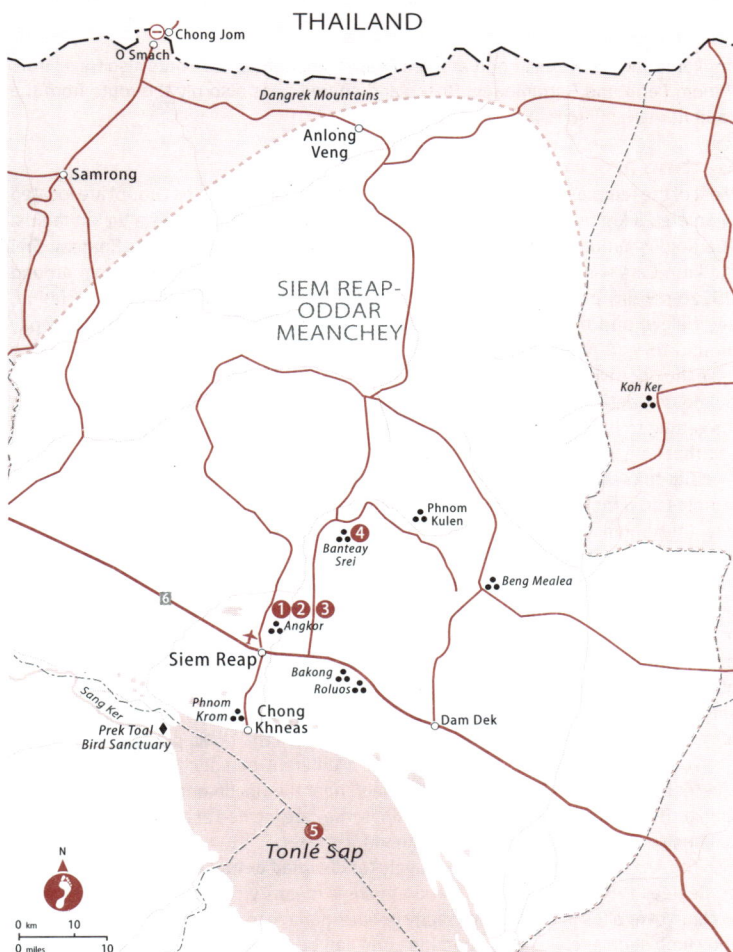

Angkor and around

The huge temple complex of Angkor, the ancient capital of the powerful Khmer Empire, is one of the archaeological treasures of Asia and the spiritual and cultural heart of Cambodia. Henri Mouhot, the Frenchman who rediscovered it, wrote that "it is grander than anything of Greece or Rome". Its mystical grandeur and architectural wonders are, to those that know them, unsurpassed by anything in Europe, Asia or Latin America.

The jungle around Angkor is scattered with many temple complexes which are also covered in this section. The former Khmer Rouge stronghold of Anlong Veng is found north of Siem Reap - the large town that serves the area. ▸▸ *For Sleeping, Eating and other listings see pages 130-140.*

Ins and outs

Getting there

Angkor is served by the airport at Siem Reap, 7 km from town. Boats also travel from Phnom Penh and Battambang. Buses and shared taxis also ply the route from the capital. ▸▸ *See Transport, page 139, for further details.*

Getting around

Most of the temples within the Angkor complex (except the Roluos Group) are located in an area 8 km north of Siem Reap, with the area extending across a 25 km radius. The Roluos Group are 13 km east of Siem Reap and further away is Banteay Srei (32 km). Cars with drivers and guides are available from larger hotels from around US$20 per day plus US$20 for a guide. The **Khmer Angkor Tour Guide Association**, see below, and most other travel agencies can also organize this. Expect to pay around US$7-8 per day for a moto unless the driver speaks good English in which case the price will be higher. This price will cover trips to the Roluos Group of temples but not to Banteay Srei. There is no need to add more than a dollar or two to the price for getting to Banteay Srei unless the driver is also a guide and can demonstrate to you that he is genuinely going to show you around.

Tuk-tuks and their ilk have appeared on the scene in recent years and a trip to the temples on a motorbike drawn cart is quite a popular option for two people, U$10 a day (maximum of two people). **Bicycle hire** costs US$2-3 per day from most guesthouses and represents a nice option for those who feel reasonably familiar with the area as the roads are pretty good. However, if you are on a limited schedule and only have a day or two at the temples you won't be able to cover an awful lot of the temples on a pedal bike as the searing temperatures and sprawling layout can limit even the most advanced cyclists a coverage. Angkor Wat and Banteay Srei have official parking sites, 1000 riel (US$0.25) and at the other temples you can quite safely park and lock your bikes in front of a drink stall. The government has just begun offering 300 **battery-powered bicycles** for tourists to rent, US$4 per day.

For those wishing to see Angkor from a different perspective it is possible to charter a **helicopter**. **Elephants** are stationed near the Bayon or at the South Gate of Angkor Thom during the day. In the evenings, they are located at the bottom of Phnom Bakheng, taking tourists up to the summit for sunset.

The Angkor site can be a real struggle for **disabled or frail persons**, the stairs are 90 degrees steep and semi-restoration of areas means visitors will sometimes need to climb over piles of bricks. Still, many people manage to do it. Hiring an aide to help you climb stairs etc. is a very good idea and can be hired for around $US5-10 a day.

⁞ Angkor tips

These days avoiding traffic within the Angkor complex is difficult but still moderately achievable.

As it stands there is a pretty standard one-day tour itinerary that includes: Angkor Wat (sunrise), Angkor Thom, Bayon etc (morning), break for lunch, Ta Prohm (afternoon), Preah Khan (afternoon) and Phnom Bakheng (sunset).

If you reverse the order, peak hour traffic at major temples is dramatically reduced. As many tour groups trip into Siem Reap for lunch this is an opportune time to catch a peaceful moment in the complex, just bring a packed lunch or eat at 1100 or 1400.

To avoid the masses at the draw-card attraction, Angkor Wat, try to walk around the temple, as opposed to through it. Sunset at Phnom Bakheng has turned into a circus fiasco, so aim for Angkor or the Bayon at this time as they are both relatively peaceful.

Sunrise is still relatively peaceful at Angkor, grab yourself the prime position behind the left-hand pond (you need to depart Siem Reap no later than 0530), though there are other stunning early morning options, such as Srah Srang or Bakong. Bakheng gives a beautiful vista of Angkor in the early-mid morning.

Best time to visit

Angkor's peak season coincides with the dry season, November to February. Not only is this the driest time of year it is also the coolest (which can still be unbearably hot). The monsoon lasts from June to October/November. At this time it can get very muddy.

Tourist information

Provincial Tourist Office, opposite *Grand Hotel d'Angkor*, T063-964347. Open 0700-1100 and 1400-1700 except Sun. They really aren't awfully helpful unless you are employing one of their guides. **Khmer Angkor Tour Guide Association** is in the same building and open every day. See below.

Guides can be invaluable when navigating the temples, with the majority being able to answer most questions about Angkor as well as providing additional information about Cambodian culture and history. Most hotels and travel agents will be able to point you in the direction of a good guide. The **Khmer Angkor Tour Guide Association** ① *T063-964347*, has pretty well-trained guides. Most of the guides here are very well-briefed and some speak English better than others. The going rate is US$20-25 per day. If you do wish to buy an additional guidebook Dawn Rooney's *Angkor: An Introduction to the Temples* and *Ancient Angkor* by Michael Freeman and Claude Jacques are recommended.

⁞ *A better option is to grab the free Siem Reap Angkor Visitor's Guide by Canby Publications available in most restaurants.*

Angkor Conservation is a specialist research institution, just off the main road to Angkor and about 1 km from the Grand Hotel (signed Conservation d'Angkor). Many statues, stelae and linga found at Angkor are stored here to prevent theft. It is accessible by special appointment only. Contact the Ministry of Culture in Phnom Penh for a written invitation which needs to describe the research objectives of the visitor.

Temple fees and opening hours

A one-day pass costs US$20, two- or three-day pass US$40, four- to seven-day pass US$60. Most people will be able to cover the majority of the temples within three days. If you buy your ticket after 1715 the day beforehand, you get a free sunset thrown in. For any ticket other than the one-day ticket you will need a passport photograph.

The destruction of Cambodia's heritage

The empire of Angkor produced some of the finest art and architecture that the world has seen. But Cambodia's heritage is in danger of being obliterated by art thieves intent on stealing anything that might have a market.

In January 1999 King Norodom Sihanouk remarked "It is very, very sad that Cambodian people were so masterful and skilful but now plunder their own history."

Khmer Rouge guerrillas moved into Angkor Wat in 1971, lit fires in the galleries, installed rocket launchers on Phnom Bakheng, looted temples and sliced the heads off sculptures. Like other guerrilla groups after them, they sold the extracted pieces on the black market in neighbouring Thailand to help finance their war efforts.

From the mid 1970s, ancient Khmer sculptures began to resurface in private art collections in the West, and on the floors of leading auction houses. But the real destruction only began with the onset of peace in 1993. Ironically, when the Khmer Rouge controlled much of the heartland of the former Angkorian kingdom the temples were safe from attack by all but Khmer Rouge guerrillas. With the pacification of the area it became a free-for-all.

In 1992 and 1993 there were reported thefts from many of the temples and from the conservation office in Siem Reap where about 7000 of the most valuable artefacts were stored. Between February and April 1993, there was a series of carefully organized break-ins into the conservation office; many priceless statues were stolen. In the most dramatic raid, in February 1993, thieves used machine guns to enter the conservation centre, shot one of the guards, fired a rocket-propelled grenade at the storeroom door and left with 11 of the most valuable statues. UN and local officials said they had been smuggled into Thailand. They also alleged that all four political factions were behind the thefts as well as soldiers "from a neighbouring country". And there was strong evidence that some of the thefts were orchestrated by conservation office staff themselves.

Despite the publicity that these thefts received, the destruction has continued on a truly monumental scale and, just like the destruction of Cambodia's forests, the army, it seems, has been closely involved in the pillage. Local villagers reported that at the end of 1998 at Banteay Chhmar more than 100 soldiers descended on the temple and used heavy equipment, including pneumatic drills, to remove nearly 50 sq ft of heavily carved relief work depicting the Hindu epics and decapitate scores of statues. So

The complex is open daily 0530-1830. You will need to pay additional fees if you wish to visit Beng Melea, Phnom Kulen or Koh Ker (payable at the individual sites.)

Safety

Landmines were planted on some outlying paths to prevent Khmer Rouge guerrillas from infiltrating the temples; they have pretty much all been cleared by now, but it is safer to stick to well-used paths. Wandering anywhere in the main temple complexes is perfectly safe. Be especially wary of snakes in the dry season. The very poisonous Hanuman snake (lurid green) is fairly common in the area.

Photography

A generalization, but somewhat true, is that black and white film tends to produce better-looking tourist pictures than those in colour. Plenty of hawkers have clicked thorough was their work that the main temple at the site is in imminent danger of collapse.

The main smuggling route for the pieces is across the border into Thailand, although some are shipped from the Cambodian ports of Kompong Som and Koh Kong to Bangkok and Singapore. In early 1999 a 10-wheeler truck was intercepted on the Thai border with 117 pieces stolen from Banteay Chhmar. Today Angkorian antiquities can be viewed and purchased in the air-conditioned antique shops of Bangkok's shopping complexes or Singapore's Tanglin Shopping Centre. There was even evidence that wealthy, but unethical, Western art buyers have been able to place orders for busts and sculptures of their choice through some of these shops. There are persistent rumours pointing to the existence of 'catalogues', containing detailed photographs of Angkorian statues and bas-reliefs. Shopkeepers will surreptitiously offer to 'organize' the acquisition of specific pieces.

Dealers in the antiquities-smuggling racket are reported to have links with organized crime. The underworld's labyrinthine networks – used in the trafficking of narcotics – facilitate the movement of statues around the world. 'Licences' for the illegal export of ancient works of art can be readily procured in Bangkok by dealers with good connections. Although Thailand does its best to prevent the smuggling of its own cultural treasures, it has refused to sign the UN's 1970 convention for preventing antiquities trafficking. This allows Bangkok dealers to trade Burmese and Cambodian pieces with impunity.

It is said that when Cambodia's Prime Minister, Hun Sen, booked into a Bangkok hotel all the Khmer artefacts of doubtful provenance were hastily removed from public display. Having survived a 1000 years of warfare and weather, many of Angkor's remaining statues are doomed to decapitation. The heads of many dancing apsaras – the most famous motif of Angkor's temples – have disappeared. As a rule of thumb, the more remote the site the easier it has been for art thieves to help themselves to Cambodia's heritage. Growing cultural consciousness – combined with uneasy consciences of some western collectors – may allow for some of this invaluable loot to be returned in the years to come. But for the present, Cambodia is losing tonnes of its cultural and artistic heritage to unscrupulous dealers and collectors.

Heritage Watch, www.heritagewatch.org, is an organization dedicated to stopping the illicit trade in Cambodian antiquities.

onto this and sell Fuji SS fine-grain black and white film (US$2-3 a roll). The best colour shots usually include some kind of contrast against the temples, a saffron-clad monk or a child. Don't forget to ask the permission of the people who you wish to include in your shots. In general, the best time to photograph the great majority of temples is before 0900 and after 1630.

Itineraries

The temples are scattered over an area in excess of 160 sq km. There are three so-called 'circuits'. The **Petit Circuit** (17 kms) takes in the main central temples including Angkor Wat, Bayon, Baphuon and the Terrace of the Elephants. The **Grand Circuit** (26 kms) takes a wider route, including smaller temples like Ta Prohm, East Mebon, Pre Rup and Neak Pean. The **Roluos Group Circuit** ventures further afield still, taking in the temples near Roluos: Lolei, Preah Ko and Bakong. The order of visiting is very much a matter of opinion and available time; here are some options:

Half day South Gate of Angkor Thom, Bayon, Angkor Wat.

One day Angkor Wat (sunrise or sunset), South Gate of Angkor Thom, Angkor Thom (Bayon, Terrace of the Elephants, Royal Palace) and Ta Prohm. This is a hefty schedule for one day; you'll need to arrive after 1615 and finish just after 1700 the following day.

Two days The same as above but with the inclusion of the rest of the Angkor Thom, Preah Srah Srang (sunrise) and at a push, Banteay Srei.

Three days – Day 1 Sunrise at Angkor Wat; morning South Gate of Angkor Thom, Angkor complex (aside from Bayon); Ta Prohm; late afternoon-sunset at Bayon. **Day 2** Srah Srang; morning Banteay Kdei and Banteay Srei; late afternoon Preah Khan; at Angkor Wat. **Day 3** Sunrise and morning Roluos; afternoon Ta Keo and sunset either Bakheng or Angkor Wat.

Those choosing to stay one or two days longer should try to work Banteay Samre, East Mebon, Neak Pean and Thomannon into their itinerary. A further two to three days warrants a trip to Prasat Kravan, Ta Som, Beng Melea and Kbal Spean.

Angkor's rulers

Jayavarman II (802-835)
Jayavarman III (835-860 or 877?)
Indravarman (877-889)
Yasovarman (889-900)
Harshavarman (900-923)
Ishnavarman II (923-928)
Jayavarman IV (928-941)
Harshavarman II (941-944)
Rajendravarman (944-968)
Jayavarman V (968-1001)
Udayadityavarman I (1001-1002)
Suryavarman (1002-1049)
Udayadityavarman II (1050-1066)
Harshavarman III (1066-1080)
Jayavarman VI (1080-1107)
Dharanindravarman I (1107-1112)
Suryavarman II (1113-1150)
Yasovarman II (c. 1150-1165)
Tribhuvanadityavarman (c.1165-1177)
Jayavarman VII (1181-1218)

History

Khmer Empire

Under Jayavarman VII (1181-1218) the Angkor complex stretched more than 25 km east to west and nearly 10 km north to south, approximately the same size as Manhattan. For five centuries (9th-13th) the court of Angkor held sway over a vast territory. At its height, according to a 12th-century Chinese account, Khmer influence spanned half of Southeast Asia, from Burma to the southernmost tip of Indochina and from the borders of Yunnan to the Malay Peninsula. Khmer monuments can be found in the south of Laos and East Thailand as well as in Cambodia. The only threat to this great empire was a riverborne invasion in 1177, when the Cham used a Chinese navigator to pilot their war canoes up the Mekong. Scenes are depicted in bas-reliefs of the Bayon temple.

The kings and construction – the temples and the creators

Jayavarman II (802-835) founded the Angkor Kingdom, then coined Hariharalaya the capital to the north of the Tonlé Sap, in the Roluos Region (Angkor), in 802. Later he moved the capital to Phnom Kulen, 40 km northeast of Angkor, where he built a Mountain Temple and Rong Shen shrine. After several years he moved the capital back to the Roluos Region.

Jayavarman III continued his father's legacy and built a number of shrines at Hariharalaya. Many historians believe that he was responsible for the initial construction of the impressive laterite pyramid, Bakong, considered the great precursor to Angkor Wat. Bakong, built to symbolize Mount Meru, was later embellished and developed by Indravarman. Indravarman (877-889) overthrew his predecessor violently and undertook a major renovation campaign in the capital Hariharalaya. The majority of what stands in the Roluos Group today is the work of Indravarman. Amongst his architectural feats are Preah Ko Temple, built in 880, and the remodelling of Bakong (with sandstone cladding). His greatest creation, initiated five days after his coronation, was the 'Sea of Indra', a massive baray (waterbasin), 3.8 km long by 800 m wide. Indravarman is credited with establishing many of the architectural 'norms' for the period that followed. A battle between Indravarman's sons destroyed the palace and the victor and new king Yasovarman I (889-900) moved the capital from Roluos and laid the foundations of Angkor itself. Prior to the move, he constructed Lolei Temple at Roluos on an island in the baray his father built. He dedicated the temple to his ancestors. His new capital at Angkor was called Yasodharapura, ('glory-bearing city'), and here he built 100 wooden ashramas (retreats), all of which have disintegrated today. Yasovarman selected Bakheng as the location for his temple-mountain and after flattening the mountain top, set about creating another Mount Meru. The temple he constructed was considered more complex than anything built beforehand – a five-storey pyramid with 108 shrines. A road was then built to link the former and present capitals of Roluos and Bakheng. Like the kings before him, Yasovarman was obliged to construct major waterworks and the construction of the reservoir – the East Baray (now completely dry) – was considered an incredible feat. The baray is eight times larger than his father's 'Sea of Indra' and historian, Claude Jacques, believes it would have taken no less than six million man days to construct. Some also suggest that Yasovarman constructed the temples of Phnom Bok and Phnom Krom.

After Yasovarman's death in 900 his son Harshavarman (900-923) assumed power for the next 23 years. During his brief reign, Harshavarman is believed to have built Baksei Chamkrong (northeast of Phnom Bakheng) and Prasat Kravan (the 'Cardamom Sanctuary'). His brother, Ishanarvarman II, resumed power upon his death but no great architectural feats were recorded in this time. In 928, Jayavarman IV moved the capital 120 km away to Koh Ker (see page 170). Here he built the grand state temple Prasat Thom, an impressive seven-storey sandstone pyramid. Over the next 20 years as king he undertook the construction of some smaller temples in the Koh Ker area and a baray. Many of the sculptures from his reign can be found in the National Museum in Phnom Penh.

Following the death of Jayavarman things took a turn for the worst. Chaos ensued under Harshavarman's II (941-944) weak leadership and over the next four years, no monuments were known to be erected. Jayavarman's IV nephew, Rajendravarman, took control of the situation and it's assumed he forcefully relocated the capital back to Angkor. Rather than moving back into the old capital Phnom Bakheng, he marked his own new territory, selecting an area south of the East Baray as his administrative centre. Here, in 1961, he constructed the state temple – Pre Rup and constructed the temple, East Mebon (953), in the middle of the baray. Srah Srang, Kutisvara and Bat Chum were also constructed, with the help of his chief architect, Kavindrarimathana. He also took to task the restoration of Baksei Chamkrong, a temple he held in the highest regard. It was towards the end of his reign that he started construction on Banteay Srei, considered one of the finest examples of Angkorian craftsmanship in the country. Rajendravarman's son became the new king Jayavarman V (968-1001) and he took the royal reigns. The administrative centre was renamed Jayendranagari and yet again, relocated. A new state temple, Ta Keo, was built west of the East Baray. The temple is believed to be somewhat cursed as it was struck by lightening during its construction and never completed. More than compensating for the unfinished Ta Keo was Jayavarman's V continued work on Banteay Srei. Under his supervision the splendid temple was completed and dedicated to his father.

Aside from successfully extending the Khmer Empire's territory King Suryavarman I (1002-1049), made a significant contribution to Khmer architectural heritage. He presided over the creation of a new administrative centre – the Royal Palace (in Angkor Thom) and the huge walls that surround it. Also built under his instruction was the colossal West Baray, still in use, measuring 8 km by 2 km, so large, it can be seen from outer space, and the sanctuary atop Preah Vihear. The next in line was Udayadityavarman II (1050-1066), the son of Suryavarman I. The Baphuon temple mountain and West Mebon (in the West Baray) were built during his relatively short appointment.

Jayavarman VI (1080-1107) never settled at Angkor living instead in the northern part of the kingdom. He constructed temples outside of the main Angkor region including Wat Phou (in southern Laos) and Phimai (in Thailand). After overthrowing his great-uncle Dharanindravarman, Suryavarman II (1113-1150), the greatest of Angkor's god-kings, came to power. His rule marked the highest point in Angkorian architecture and civilization. Not only was he victorious in conflict, having beat the Cham whom couldn't be defeated by China, he was responsible for extending the borders of the Khmer Empire into Myanmar, Malaya and Siam. This aside, he was also considered one of the era's most brilliant creators. Suryavarman II was responsible for the construction of Angkor Wat, the current day symbol of Cambodia. Beng Melea, Banteay Samre and Thommanon are also thought to be the works of this genius. He has been immortalized in his own creation – in a bas-relief in the South Gallery of Angkor Wat the glorious King Suryavarman II sits on top of an elephant. After a period of political turmoil, which included the sacking of Angkor, Jayavarman VII seized the throne in 1181 and set about rebuilding his fiefdom. Historian, Dawn Rooney, suggests that Jayavarman VII was the greatest builder, "constructing more monuments, roads, bridges and resthouses than all the other kings put together."

Jayavarman VII created a new administrative centre – the great city of Angkor Thom, a 3-km block, surrounded by a moat and laterite wall. The mid-point of Angkor Thom is marked by his brilliant Mahayana Buddhist state temple, the Bayon. It is said that the Bayon was completed in 21 years. Jayavarman took thousands of peasants from the rice fields to build it, which proved a fatal error, for rice yields decreased and the empire began its decline as resources were drained. The temple consists of sculptured faces of Avolokiteshvara (the Buddha of compassion and mercy) which are often said to also encompass the face of their great creator, Jayavarman VIII. He was also responsible for restoring the Royal Palace, renovating Srah Srang and constructing the Terrace of Elephants, the Terrace of the Leper King and the nearby baray (northeast of Angkor Thom), Jayatataka reservoir. At the centre of his reservoir he built Neak Pean.

Jayavarman VII adopted Mahayana Buddhism and so; Buddhist principles replaced the Hindu pantheon, and were invoked as the basis of royal authority. This spread of Buddhism is thought to have caused some of the earlier Hindu temples to be neglected. The king paid tribute to his Buddhist roots through his monastic temples: Ta Prohm and Preah Khan. Further afield in northwestern Cambodia he constructed Banteay Chhmar. He also built 102 hospitals throughout his kingdom, as well as a network of roads, along which he constructed resthouses. But because they were built of wood, none of these secular structures survive; only the foundations of four larger ones have been unearthed at Angkor.

Henri Mouhot's rediscovery of Angkor

Thai ascendency and their eventual occupation of Angkor in 1431 led to the city's abandonment and the subsequent invasion of the jungle. Four centuries later, in 1860, Henri Mouhot – a French naturalist – stumbled across the forgotten city, its temple towers enmeshed in the forest canopy. Locals told him they were the work of a race of giant gods. Only the stone temples remained; all the wooden secular buildings had decomposed in the intervening centuries. Mouhot's diaries, published

❝❞ The fig tree is the ruler of Angkor today... Over the temples which it has patiently prised apart, everywhere its dome of foliage triumphantly unfolds its sleek pale branches speckled like a serpent's skin...

in the 1860s, with his accounts of 'the lost city in the jungle', fired the imagination of archaeologists, adventurers and treasure hunters in Europe. In 1873 French archaeologist Louis Delaporte removed many of Angkor's finest statues for 'the cultural enrichment of France'.

French 'restoration'

In 1898, the École Française d'Extrême Orient started clearing the jungle, restoring the temples, mapping the complex and making an inventory of the site. Delaporte was later to write the two-volume *Les Monuments du Cambodge*, the most comprehensive Angkorian inventory of its time, and his earlier sketches, plans and reconstructions, published in *Voyage au Cambodge* in 1880 are without parallel. Henri Parmentier was chief of the school's archaeological service in Cambodia until 1930. Public interest was rekindled in the 1920s when French adventurer and novelist André Malraux was arrested in Phnom Penh, charged with stealing sculptures from one of the temples, Banteay Srei at Angkor. He published a thriller, *The Royal Way*, based on his experiences. Today around 400 sandstone, laterite and brick-built temples, walls, tombs and other structures remain scattered around the site.

Plundering of Angkor

Colonial souvenir hunters were not the first – or the last – to get their hands on Angkor's treasures. The great city's monuments were all subjected, at one time or another, to systematic plundering, mainly by the warring Cham (from South Vietnam) and Thais. Many temple pedestals were smashed to afford access to the treasure, hidden deep in pits under the central sanctuaries. Other looters knocked the tops off towers to reach the carefully concealed treasure chambers.

❣ UNESCO has trained up police in order to counteract the greatest scourge: the organized theft of carvings. Many believe prompt action is the only way to protect Angkor from a souvenir hunters' free-for-all.

Centuries of entanglement in the jungle also took their toll on the buildings – strangler figs caused much structural damage and roots and vines rent roofs and walls asunder. In 1912, French writer Pierre Loti noted: "The fig tree is the ruler of Angkor today... Over the temples which it has patiently prised apart, everywhere its dome of foliage triumphantly unfolds its sleek pale branches speckled like a serpent's skin." Even today, some roots and trees remain stubbornly tangled in the ancient masonry – affording visitors a Mouhot-style glimpse of the forgotten city. Between 1953 and 1970, the Angkor Conservancy – set up jointly by the French and Cambodian governments – maintained and restored the ruins. But when war broke out, the destructive forces of the Khmer Rouge – and other guerrilla factions – were unleashed on what the jungle had spared and the French archaeologists, such as Bernard Grosslier, had restored.

Restoration of Angkor

As if the conservation and protection of the complex was not already fraught with difficulties, a threat emerged in the mid 1980s, from the most unlikely of sources. The

Vietnamese-backed administration enlisted the services of Indian archaeologists to begin where the Angkor Conservancy had left off. They were given a six-year contract to clean and restore the galleries and towers of Angkor Wat itself. Prince Sihanouk is reported to have burst into tears when he heard that the Indians, using unskilled Cambodian workmen, had begun their concrete and chemical-assisted restoration effort. The cleaning agents stripped off the patina which for a millennium had protected the sandstone from erosion by the elements. Bas-reliefs depicting scenes from the *Ramayana* were scrubbed and scraped until some were barely discernible. Cement was used with abandon. Archaeologists around the world, who, since 1970, have only been dimly aware of the rape of Angkor, now consider the gimcrack restoration programme the last straw after two decades of pillage and destruction.

Whether the Indian team of archaeologists and conservators have really caused untold damage to the monuments of Angkor through insensitive restoration and the use of untested solvents is a source of some dispute. Generally, press reports in the west, as described above, have taken the latter line – that their work, rather than helping to restore and preserve the monuments, has helped to further ruin it. Cement has been used to fill in cracks, where western archaeologists would probably have left well alone. New stone has been cut and fitted where, again, other specialists might have been happy merely to have done sufficient restoration to prevent further degeneration. The Indian team also used chemical cleaning agents – an unorthodox and contentious approach to restoration. Although some of the methods used by the Indian team do seem rather crude and insensitive to the atmosphere of the place, the carping of some western archaeologists seems to have been motivated as much by professional envy as anything else. The Indians were called in by the government in Phnom Penh at a time when most western countries were boycotting the country, in protest at the Vietnamese occupation of the country. French archaeologists particularly, must have been pacing their offices in indignation and pique as a country with such 'primitive' skills took all the glory.

In 1989 UNESCO commissioned a Japanese art historian to draw up an Angkor plan of action. The top priority in its restoration, he said, was to underpin the foundations of Angkor Wat, Bayon, Baphuon, Preah Khan, Neak Khan and Pre Rup. Once the Paris Peace agreements had been signed in 1991, the Ecole Française, the New York based World Monuments Fund and the Japanese started work. UNESCO is co-ordinating the activities of the various teams and Angkor was declared a World Heritage site. Some temples are closed or partially closed for restoration work.

Whether the Japanese are any more sensitive than the Indians in their restoration work is an interesting subject for debate. For while the Indians may have been criticized for unsuitable techniques at least they were merely patching up. The Japanese approach is nothing less than renovation. Thus, while the traditional tools of the architect were brushes and hammers, visitors will be surprised to see huge cranes and lifts putting temples back as Japanese archaeologists think they once looked. Concrete and laterite blocks as well as newly carved sandstone are used to replace decayed stonework. Interestingly, in 2002 Indian archaeologists were again invited back to take part in the restoration process.

Documentation of Angkor

Sanskrit and Khmer inscriptions

About 900 inscriptions have been found in Indochina that give a jigsaw set of clues to Angkor civilization. Those written in Sanskrit are largely poetic praises dedicated to gods and kings; Khmer-language ones give a much more focused insight into life and customs under the great kings. Some give a remarkably detailed picture of everyday life: one documents a ruling that pigs had the right to forage in rice fields, another dictates that ginger and honey should be used in the preparation of ritual foods. Most of the inscriptions have now been deciphered. Contemporary palm-leaf and paper documents which would have added to this knowledge have long since rotted away in the humid climate.

Bas-reliefs

Bas-reliefs carved in perpetuity into Angkor's temple walls also give a fascinating pictorial impression of life in the great city. Its citizens are shown warring, hunting, playing and partying and the reliefs present a picture which is often reassuringly normal in its detail: men played chess, old women read palms and people ate and drank and gossiped while local musicians provided live entertainment. Young men went hunting and young women evidently spent hours at the Angkorian equivalent of the hairdressers and boutiques.

Chou Ta-kuan's account

The most complete eyewitness account of Angkor was written by Chou Ta-kuan, an envoy from the Chinese court, who visited Cambodia in 1296, around 75 years after the death of Jayavarman VII, the last great conqueror of the Angkor period. Chou Ta-kuan wrote detailed accounts of an outsider's observations and impressions during this time. He cast Angkor as a grand and highly sophisticated civilization, despite the fact that it was, by then, well past its heyday. His descriptions of daily life actually seem quite comparable with Khmer life today. Ordinary people generally built their houses out of wood and leaves and their homes, like today, were raised on stilts. He described a society highly suspicious of evil spirits, where parents would call their children 'ugly' names, like dog, in order to deflect the attention from the evil spirits (see page 226 for further accounts).

French interpretation

What the French archaeologists managed to do, with brilliance, was to apply scientific principles to deciphering the mysteries of Angkor. The French, and by extension the West, nonetheless managed to 'invent' Angkor for its own interests, moulding the Angkorian Empire and its art so that it fitted in with the accepted image of the Orient. (This notion that Europeans invented the Orient is most effectively argued in Edward Said's seminal book *Orientalism*, first published in 1978 and now widely available in paperback. It is a book that does not deal specifically with Angkor but much of the argument can be applied to the French appropriation of Angkor and the Khmers.) Much that has been written about the ruins at Angkor and the empire and people that built them says as much about what the French were trying to do in Indochina, as about the place and people themselves. What is perhaps ironic is that Cambodians then reappropriated the French vision and made it their own. Today, French invention and Cambodian 'tradition' are one. Cambodia, lacking the cultural integrity to resist the influence of the French, became French and in so doing they took on board the French image of themselves and made it their own.

Art and architecture

The Angkor period (ninth-13th centuries) encapsulated the greatest and best of Cambodia's art and architecture. Much of it shows strong Indian influence. The so-called 'Indianization' of Cambodia was more a product of trade than Hindu proselytism; there was no attempt made at formal conquest, and no great emigration of Indians to the region. In order to meet the Romans' demand for exotic oriental merchandise and commodities, Indian traders ventured into the South China Sea, well before the first century AD when it was discovered that monsoon winds could carry them to the Malay Peninsula and on to Indochina and Cambodia. Because of their reliance on seasonal winds, Indian navigators were obliged to while away many months in countries with which they traded and the influence of their sophisticated culture spread.

But although Khmer art and architecture was rooted in Indian prototypes, the expression and content was distinctively Cambodian. Most of the art from the Angkor period is Hindu although Mahayana Buddhism took hold in the late 12th century. Some Buddhist figures have been dated to as early as the sixth century – the standing Buddhas were carved in the same style as the Hindu deities, minus the sensuous voluptuousness.

Funan (First century AD-613) and Chenla (AD550-eighth century) eras

The ancient kingdoms of Funan (the Chinese name for the mercantile state encompassing the area southwest of the Mekong Delta, in what is now southern Vietnam and southern Cambodia) and Chenla (a mountain kingdom centred on northern Cambodia and southern Laos) were the first to be artistically and culturally influenced by India. In *The Art of Southeast Asia* Philip Rawson wrote that the art styles of Funan and Chenla were "the greatest phase of pre-Angkor Khmer art, and...

Khmer sanctuary tower 13th century after Stratton & Scott, 1981

1 Antefixes	4 Pediment	7 Pilaster	10 Cell
2 Arches	5 Lintel	8 Niche or door	11 Base
3 Tympanum	6 Capital	9 Superstructure	12 Platform

we can treat the evolution under these two kingdoms together as a stylistic unity. It was the foundation of classic Khmer art, just as archaic Greek sculpture was the foundation of later classical Greek art".

The Angkor region was strategically important to the Funan Empire as it helped control the trade routes around the region – specifically the Malay Peninsula and the Mekong Delta. The only traces of the kingdom of Funan – whose influence is thought to have spread as far afield as southern Burma and Indonesia – are limited to four Sanskrit inscriptions on stelae and a few sculptures. The earliest surviving Funanese statues were found at Angkor Borei and have been dated to the sixth century. Most represent the Hindu god, Vishnu (patron of King Rudravarman), and their faces are distinctly Angkorian. Scattered remains of these pre-Angkorian periods are all over southern Cambodia – especially between the Mekong and the Tonlé Sap. Most of the earliest buildings would have been made of wood rotted away – there being a paucity of stone in the delta region.

The kingdom of Chenla, based at Sambor and later at Sambor Prei Kuk (see page 168), expanded at the expense of Funan, which gradually became a vassal state. In the sixth century evidence of a new Chenla Kingdom started to appear in local inscriptions. Chenla inherited Funan's Indianized art and architectural traditions. Some buildings were built of brick and stone and typical architectural relics are brick towers with a square (or sometimes octagonal) plan: a shrine set atop a pedestal comprising of mounting tiers of decreasing size – a style which may have been structurally patterned on early Pallava temples in southeast India. The sculptural work was strongly rooted in Indian ideas but carved in a unique style – many of the statues from this era are in the museum at Phnom Penh (see page 57). Rawson wrote: "Among the few great stone icons which have survived are some of the world's outstanding masterpieces, while the smaller bronzes reflect the same sophisticated and profound style."

Srivijayan era

In the late eighth century the Chenla Kingdom collapsed and contact with India came to an end. Chenla is thought to have been eclipsed by the increasingly important Sumatran-based Srivijayan Empire. Jayavarman II, who had lived most of his life in the Sailendra court in Java but who was of royal lineage, returned to Cambodia in about AD 790. Jayavarman II's reign marked the transition period between pre-Angkorian and Angkorian styles – by the ninth century the larger images were recognizably Khmer in style. From Jayavarman II onwards, the kings of Cambodia were regarded as god-kings – or devaraja (see page 90).

Jayavarman II established a royal Siva-lingam (phallic) cult which was to prove the inspiration for successive generations of Khmer kings. "He summoned a Brahmin learned in the appropriate texts, and erected a lingam… with all the correct Indian ritual," Rawson said. "This lingam, in which the king's own soul was held to reside, became the source and centre of power for the Khmer Dynasty. At the same time – and by that act – he severed all ties of dependence upon Indonesia." To house the sacred lingam each king in turn built a new temple, some of the mightiest and finest of the monuments of the Khmer civilization.

Angkor temples

The temples at Angkor were modelled on those of the kingdom of Chenla, which in turn were modelled on Indian temples. They represent Mount Meru – the home of the gods of Indian cosmology. The central towers symbolize the peaks of Mount Meru, surrounded by a wall which represents the earth. The moats and basins represent the oceans. The devaraja, or god-king, was enshrined in the centre of the religious complex, which acted as the spiritual axis of the kingdom. The people believed their apotheosized king communicated directly with the gods.

The central tower sanctuaries housed the images of the Hindu gods to whom the temples were dedicated. Dead members of the royal and priestly families were accorded a status on a par with these gods. Libraries to store the sacred scriptures were also built within the ceremonial centre. The temples were mainly built to shelter the images of the gods. Unlike Christian churches, Muslim mosques and some Buddhist pagodas, they were not intended to accommodate worshippers. Only priests, the servants of the god, were allowed into the interiors. The

Angkor, Siem Reap & Roluos

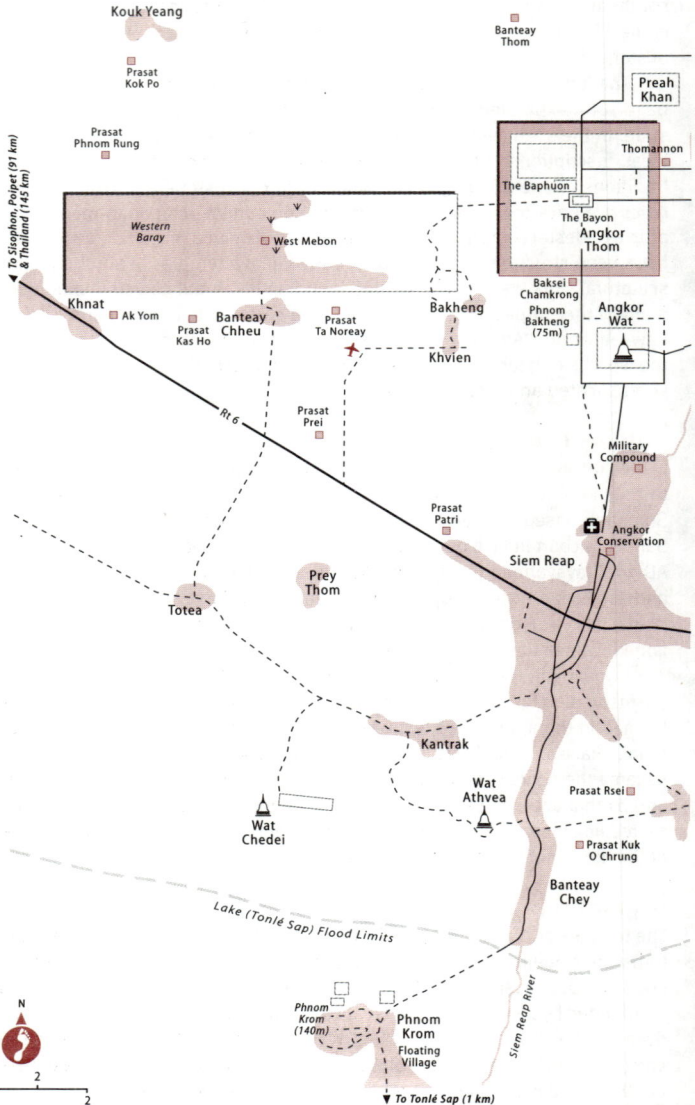

Kouk Yeang

Banteay Thom

Prasat Kok Po

Preah Khan

Prasat Phnom Rung

Thomannon

The Baphuon

Western Baray

The Bayon
Angkor Thom

West Mebon

Baksei Chamkrong
Phnom Bakheng (75m)

Angkor Wat

Khnat

Ak Yom

Banteay Chheu

Prasat Ta Noreay

Bakheng

Prasat Kas Ho

Khvien

Rt 6

Prasat Prei

Military Compound

Prasat Patri

Angkor Conservation

Siem Reap

Prey Thom

Totea

Kantrak

Wat Athvea

Prasat Rsei

Wat Chedei

Prasat Kuk O Chrung

Banteay Chey

Lake (Tonlé Sap) Flood Limits

N

Phnom Krom (140m)

Phnom Krom
Floating Village

Siem Reap River

0 km   2
0 miles   2

To Sisophon, Poipet (91 km) & Thailand (145 km)

To Tonlé Sap (1 km)

'congregation' would mill around outside in open courtyards or wooden pavilions. The first temples were of a very simple design but with time they became more grandiose and doors and galleries were added. Most of Angkor's buildings are made from a soft sandstone which is easy to work. It was transported to the site from Phnom Kulen, about 30 km to the northeast. Laterite was used for foundations, core material and enclosure walls as it was widely available and could be easily cut into blocks (see opposite). The Khmer sandstone architecture has echoes of earlier

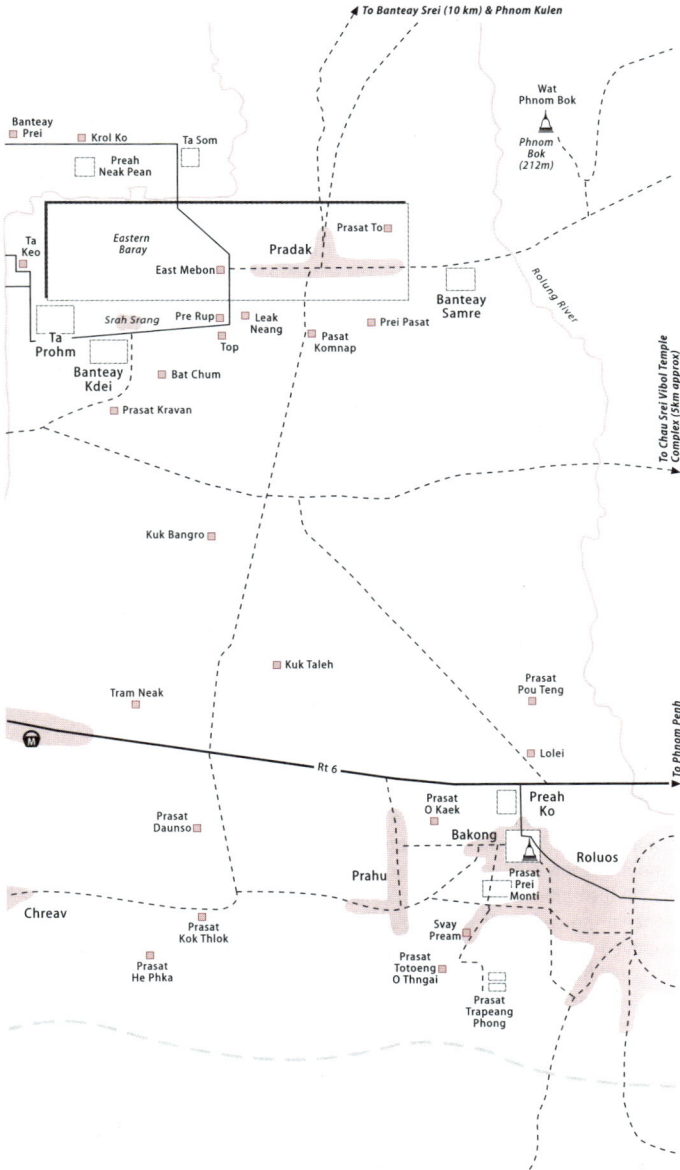

wooden structures: gallery roofs are sculpted with false tiles, while balustred windows imitate wooden ones. A common feature of Khmer temples was false doors and windows on the sides and backs of sanctuaries and other buildings. In most cases there was no need for well-lit rooms and corridors as hardly anyone ever went into them. That said, the galleries round the central towers in later temples, such as Angkor Wat, indicate that worshippers did use the temples for ceremonial circumambulation when they would contemplate the inspiring bas-reliefs from the *Ramayana* and *Mahabharata*.

In Europe and the Middle East the arch and vault were used in contemporary buildings but at Angkor architects used the false vault – also known as corbelling. It is strange that, despite the architectural innovation of the Khmer, the principle of the arch, used to such great effect in Christian and Muslim architecture, should have eluded them. Corbelling is a fairly primitive vaulting system so the interiors of sanctuaries could never be very large. The stones were often laid without staggering the vertical joints and mortar was not used. The builders relied on the weight of the structure, gravity and a good fit between the stones to hold their buildings together. This is why so many of the temples have collapsed.

Despite the court's conversion to Mahayana Buddhism in the 12th century (under Jayavarman VII) the architectural ground-plans of temples did not alter much – even though they were based on Hindu cosmology. The idea of the god-king was simply grafted onto the new state religion and statues of the Buddha rather than the gods of the Hindu pantheon were used to represent the god-king (see Bayon, page 109). One particular image of the Buddha predominated at Angkor in which he wears an Angkor-style crown, with a conical top which is encrusted with jewellery.

There are some scholars who maintain that Angkor has, perhaps, been over praised. The label of 'genius' that has been attached to the architects that conceived the edifices, the builders that worked on them, and the empire that financed their construction, demands that Angkor be put in the highest division of human artistic achievement. Anthony Barnett in the *New Left Review* in 1990, for example, wrote: "...to measure [Angkor's] greatness by the fact that it is nearly a mile square is to deny it a proper admiration through hyperbole. Thus the Church of Saint Sophia, to take one example, was for nearly a millennium the largest domed space in the world until St Peter's was constructed. Saint Sophia still stands in Istanbul. It was built 600 years before Angkor Wat, while Khmer architects never managed to discover the principles of the arch." (1990: 103)

Sculpture

The sculpture of the early temples at Angkor is rather stiff and plain, but forms the basis for the ornate bas-reliefs of the later Angkor Wat. Lintel-carving became a highly developed art form at an early stage in the evolution of Khmer architecture. (The lintel is a horizontal supporting stone at the top of a window or door opening.) The use of columns around doorways was another distinctive feature – they too had their antecedents in the earlier Chenla period. Frontons – the masonry covering originally used to conceal the corbelled end gables – were elaborate at Angkor. They were intricately carved and conveyed stories from the *Ramayana* and other great Hindu epics. The carved fronton is still used in temples throughout modern Thailand, Laos and Cambodia. Sanctuary doorways, through which priests would pass to enter the sacred heart of the temple, were an important site for icons. Ornately carved sandstone blocks were placed in front of and above the true lintel.

Angkor's most impressive carvings are its bas-reliefs which, like the fronton, were devoted to allegorical depictions and mostly illustrate stories from the Hindu classics, the *Mahabharata* and *Ramayana*. The latter is best exemplified at the Baphuon (11th century) – see page 113. Details of the everyday lives of the Angkor civilization can be pieced together thanks to these bas-reliefs. Those on the Bayon illustrate the weaponry and armour used in battle, market scenes, fishing and cockfighting – probably the Khmers' favourite excuse for gambling. In contrast to the highly sculpted outer walls of the temples, the interiors were typically bare; this has led to speculation that they may originally have been decorated with murals.

Laterite, which is a coarse soft stone, found widely across Southeast Asia, was excavated to form many of the moats and barays at Angkor. Early structures such as those at Preah Ko in the Roluos group were built in brick. The brickwork was often laid with dry joints and the only mortar used was a type of vegetable-based adhesive. Bricks were sometimes carved in situ and occasionally plastered. In the early temples sandstone was only used for architectural embellishments. But nearly all of the later temples were built entirely of sandstone. Most of the sandstone is thought to have been quarried from the northern hills around Kulen and brought by barge to Angkor.

The post-Angkor period was characterized by wooden buildings and fastidiously carved and decorated sculptures, but the humid climate has allowed little to survive. The contemporary art of 21st-century Cambodia is still redolent of the grandeur of the Angkor era and today, Khmer craftsmen retain their inherent skills and are renowned for their refined carvings. Art historians believe that the richness of Cambodia's heritage, and its incorporation into the modern artistic psyche, has enabled Khmer artists to produce work which is reckoned to be aesthetically superior to contemporary carving and sculpture in Thailand.

Angkor Wat 🕖 ▸ pages 130-140.

The awe-inspiring sight of Angkor Wat first thing in the morning is something you're not likely to forget. Angkor literally means 'city' or 'capital'. It is believed to be the biggest religious monument ever built and certainly one of the most spectacular. It was constructed between 1113 and 1150. British historian Arnold Toynbee said in his book *East to West* that: "Angkor is not orchestral; it is monumental." That sums it up.

Angkor Wat

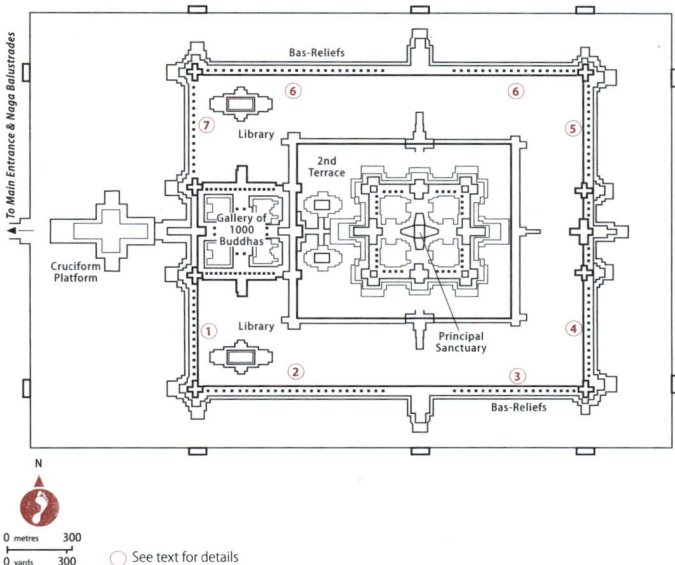

N

0 metres 300
0 yards 300

⟳ See text for details

Anti-clockwise round Angkor Wat's bas-reliefs

1. West gallery, southern half represents a scene from the Hindu *Mahabharata* epic. The Battle of Kurukshtra shows the clash between the Pandavas (with pointed headdresses, attacking from the right) and the Kauravas. The two armies come from the two ends of the panel and meet in the middle in a ferocious battle. Above the war scene is Bhima, head of the Kauravas, wounded and lying atop a pile of arrows, surrounded by grieving followers and loved ones. The centre of the sculpture reveals the chief of the Pandavas in his war chariot. (The larger the figure the more important the person.) The southwest corner has been badly damaged – some say by the Khmer Rouge – but shows scenes from Vishnu's life.

2. South gallery, western half depicts Suryavarman II (builder of Angkor Wat) leading a procession. He is riding a royal elephant and carrying an axe, giving orders to his army before leading them into battle against the Chams. Shade is provided to him by 15 umbrellas, while a gamut of servants cool him with fans. The rank of the army officers is indicated by the number of umbrellas. Other troops follow on elephants. While trailing behind them are musicians and priests bearing holy fire. The undisciplined, outlandishly dressed figures are the Thais helping the Khmers in battle against the Chams.

3. South gallery, eastern half was restored in 1946. It depicts the punishments and rewards one can expect in the afterlife. On the left-hand side, the upper and middle levels show the dead waiting for their moment of judgement with Yama (Judge of the Dead) and his assistants, Dharma and Sitragupta, as to whether they will go to either the 37 heavens or 32 hells. On the left, lead two roads one to the heavens (above), and the other to hell (below). The damned, depicted in the bottom row, are in for a rough ride: the chances of their being savaged by wild animals, seized by demons or having their tongues pulled out (or any combination thereof) are quite high. Yama was tough and some might suggest that the crime didn't exactly fit the punishment: those who damaged others property received broken bones; gluttons were sawn in half, and those who picked Shiva's flowers had their heads nailed. The blessed, depicted in the upper two rows, are borne along in palanquins surrounded by large numbers of bare-breasted apsaras dancing on lotuses.

4. Eastern gallery, southern half, is a 50-m-long panel that's probably Angkor's best known. The Churning of the Sea of Milk, portrays part of the Hindu legend, Bhagavata-

The temple complex covers 81 ha and is comparable in size to the Imperial Palace in Beijing. Its five towers are emblazoned on the Cambodian flag and the 12th-century masterpiece is considered by art historians to be the prime example of Classical Khmer art and architecture. It took more than 30 years to build and is contemporary with Notre Dame in Paris and Durham Cathedral in England. The temple is dedicated to the Hindu god Vishnu, personified in earthly form by its builder, the god-king Suryavarman II, and is aligned east to west.

Angkor Wat differs from other temples, primarily because it is facing westward, symbolically the direction of death, leading many to originally believe it was a tomb. However, as Vishnu is associated with the west, it is now generally accepted that it served both as a temple and a mausoleum for the king. Its moat is 190 m wide and is crossed from the west by a sandstone causeway. The sandstone was probably

Pourana. On the North are 92 deva (gods) and on the South 88 asura (demons) battling to win the coveted ambrosia (the nectar of the gods which gives immortality).

The serpent, Vasuki, is caught, quite literally, in the centre of their dispute. The asura hold onto the head of the serpent, whilst the devas hold onto the tail. The fighting causes the waters to churn, which in turn produces the elixir. In the centre, Vishnu commands the operation. Below are sea animals (cut in half by the churning close to the pivot) and above, apsaras encouraging the competitors in their fight for the mighty elixir. Eventually (approximately 1000 years later) the elixir is won by the asuras until Vishnu appears to claim the cup. Shortly before Cambodia collapsed into civil war in 1970, French archaeologists, who were repairing the roof and columns of the east gallery, dismantled the structure. Because they were unable to finish the job, the finest bas-reliefs have been left open to the elements.

5. Eastern gallery, northern half is unfinished and depicts the garuda-riding Krishna (Vishnu's incarnation) overcoming a wall of fire, with the help of a Garuda, to claim victory over Bana, the demon king. Having captured Bana and the ambrosia, Kailasa, Parvati and Ganesh,

plead with Krishna to spare Bana's life. The gate in the centre of the east gallery was used by Khmer royalty and dignitaries for mounting and dismounting elephants.

6. North gallery, eastern half shows Garuda-riding, Krishna claiming victory over the demons. Shiva is shown in meditation with Ganesh, Brahma and Krishna. Most of the other scenes are from the *Ramayana*, notably the visit of Hanuman (the monkey god) to Sita.

7. North gallery, western half pictures another battle scene: demons versus gods. 21 gods are pictured including Varuna, god of water, standing on a five-headed naga; Skanda, the god of war (several heads and a peacock with arms); Yama, the god of dead (chariot drawn by oxen): and Suva, the sun god (standing on a disc).

8. Western gallery, northern half has another scene from the *Ramayana* depicting another battle between the devas and asuras – this time in the form of Rama and Ravana. The demon king Ravana, who rides on a chariot pulled by monsters and commands an army of giants, has seduced and abducted Rama's beautiful wife Sita. The battle takes place in the centre of the relief.

quarried from a far-away mine and floated down the Siem Reap river on rafts. Like other Khmer temple mountains, Angkor Wat is an architectural allegory, depicting in stone the epic tales of Hindu mythology. The central sanctuary of the temple complex represents the sacred Mount Meru, the centre of the Hindu universe, on whose summit the gods reside. Angkor Wat's five towers symbolize Meru's five peaks; the enclosing wall represents the mountains at the edge of the world and the surrounding moat, the ocean beyond.

Angkor Wat was found in much better condition than most of the other temples in the complex because it seems to have been continuously inhabited by Buddhist monks after the Thais invaded in 1431. They were able to keep back the encroaching jungle. A giant stone Buddha was placed in the hall of the highest central tower, formerly sacred to the Hindu god, Vishnu. Three modern Buddhist monasteries flank the wat.

The temple complex is enclosed by a **square moat** – more than 5 km in length – and a high, galleried wall, which is covered in epic bas-reliefs and has four ceremonial tower gateways. The main gateway faces west and the temple is approached by a 475-m-long road, built along a **causeway**, which is lined with **naga balustrades**. There are small rectangular barays on either side of the roadway. To either side of the balustrades are two isolated buildings, thought to have been **libraries** – there are two more pairs of them within the temple precincts on the first and second terraces.

At the far end of the causeway stands a **cruciform platform**, guarded by stone lions, from which the devaraja may have held audiences; his backdrop being the three-tiered central sanctuary. Commonly referred to as the **Terrace of Honour**, it is entered through the colonnaded processional gateway of the outer gallery. The transitional enclosure beyond it is again cruciform in shape. Its four quadrants formed galleries, once stocked

In & around Angkor Thom

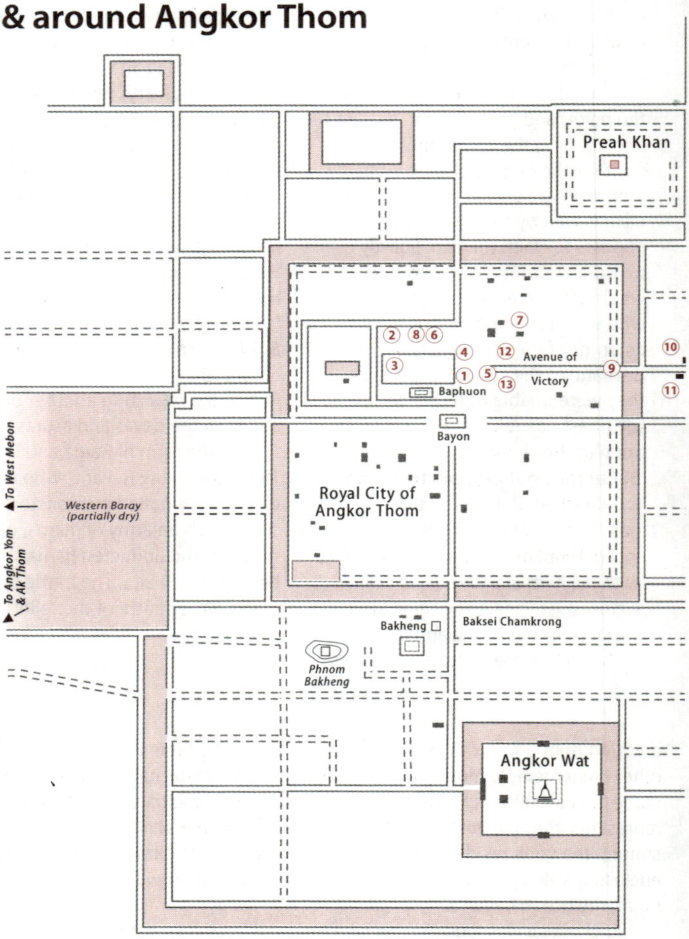

Terrace of the Elephants **1**
Royal Enclosure **2**
Phimeanakas **3**

Tep Tranam **6**
Preah Pithu Group **7**
Preah Palilay **8**

Chau Say Tevoda **11**
North Kleang **12**
South Kleang **13**

full of statues of the Buddha. Only a handful of the original 1000-odd images remain.
Each gallery also had a basin which would originally have contained water for priests' ritual ablution. The second terrace, which is also square, rises from behind the **Gallery of a Thousand Buddhas**. It has a tower at each corner.

The cluster of **central towers**, 12 m above the second terrace, is reached by 12 steep stairways, which represent the precipitous slopes of Mount Meru. Many historians believe that the upwards hike to this terrace was reserved for the high priests and king himself. Today, anyone is welcome but the difficult climb is best handled slowly by stepping sideways up the steep incline. The five lotus flower-shaped sandstone towers – the first appearance of these features in Khmer architecture – are believed to have once been covered in gold. The eight-storey towers are square, although they appear octagonal, and give the impression of a

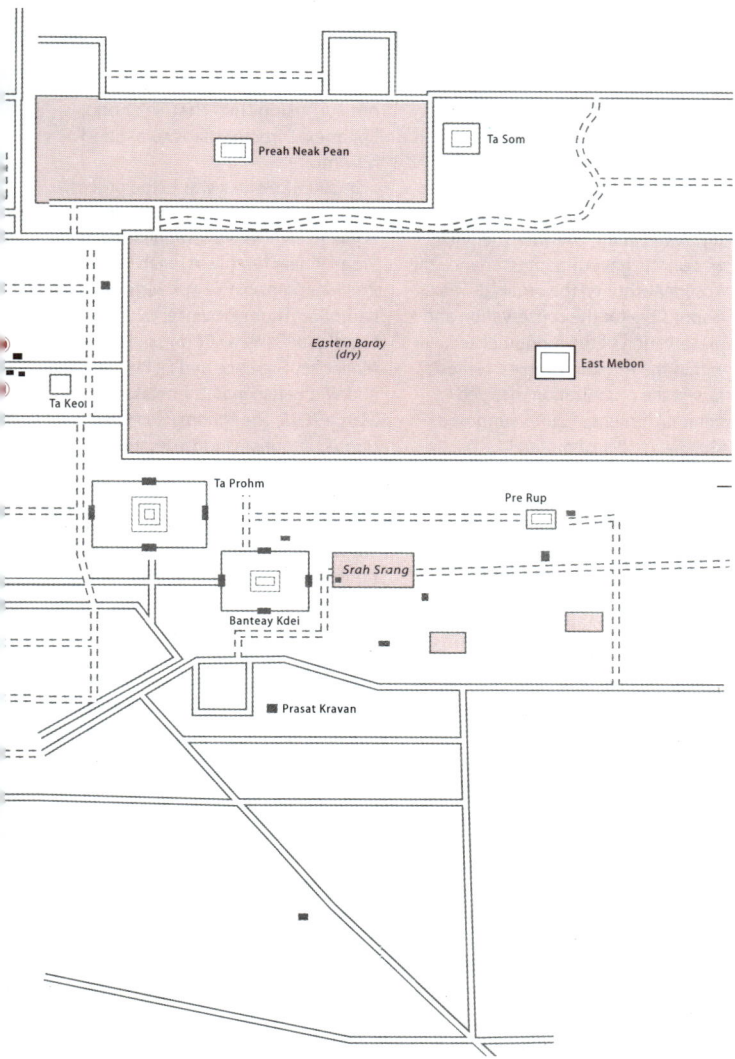

Preah Neak Pean

Ta Som

Eastern Baray
(dry)

East Mebon

Ta Keo

Ta Prohm

Pre Rup

Srah Srang

Banteay Kdei

Prasat Kravan

⦂ Who owns Angkor Wat?

The official line is that the Cambodian people own Angkor Wat. The Cambodian Constitution states that all of Cambodia's heritage sites are owned by the state and its people. However, the ticketing rights to Angkor are a completely different story. Cambodia's largest corporation, Sokimex, has held ticketing rights to Angkor since 1999. The company, which runs a huge chain of Cambodian petrol stations and hotels, struck a lucrative deal with the government in May 1999, whereby for US$1 million a year they received the exclusive right to ticketing at the Angkor complex.

All opposition to this transaction was completely overlooked. As stipulated in the contract, the onus was on the government to finance the Apsara Authority, the organization responsible for the conservation and preservation of the monuments within the Angkor complex. Needless to say, the organization received minimal funding, figures suggest as little as 5 to 8% of profits.

A new contract was renegotiated with Sokimex by the government and Apsara Authority in 2000 whereby approximately 78% of ticket revenue is given to the government. The Apsara Authority then applies for funding from the Ministry of Economy and Finance with approximately 10% of revenue allotted to their restoration projects. Whether the Apsara Authority gets its fair share is debatable but it claims to be happy with the current management system and is in a much better position to undertake restoration work than ever before.

In 2004, 450,000 tourists visited the Angkor complex, generating the minimum revenue of US$9 million (but is probably a higher figure). It is not surprising then that Sok Kong, Sokimex' Director plans to expand his empire.

In 2005, Sokimex was in the process of negotiating exclusive ticketing rights to another six temples including Preah Vihear temple in Preah Vihear Province Sambor Pre Kuk Temple in Kampong Thom Province, two temples at Banteay Chmmar, Banteay Meanchey Province and Ek Phnom and Wat Banan in Battambang. In March 2005, *The Phnom Penh Post* quoted a tourism industry source who described Sokimex as the business arm of the government. Quite befitting when one considers how easily the government is selling off rights to its heritage, qualm-free, to a local petroleum magnate.

sprouting bud. Above the ascending tiers of roofs – each jutting gable has an elaborately carved pediment – the tower tapers into a circular roof. A quincunx shape is formed by the towers with four on each corner and another marking the centre. The central tower is dominant, and is the Siva shrine and principal sanctuary, whose pinnacle rises more than 30 m above the third level and 55 m above ground level. This sanctuary would have contained an image of Siva in the likeness of King Suryavarman II, as it was his temple-mountain. But it is now a Buddhist shrine and contains statues of the Buddha. The steps leading up to the third level are worn and very steep. On the south side the steps have a hand rail (not recommended for vertigo sufferers).

Over 1000 sq m of bas-relief decorate the temple. Its greatest sculptural treasure is the 2-m-high **bas-relief**, around the walls of the outer gallery. It is the longest continuous bas-relief in the world. In some areas traces of the paint and gilt that once covered the carvings can still be seen. Most famous are the hundreds of figures of devatas and apsaras in niches along the walls. The apsaras – the celestial women – are modelled on the god-king's own bevy of bare-breasted beauties and the

The Churning of the Sea

The Hindu legend, the Churning of the Sea, relates how the gods and demons resolved matters in the turbulent days when the world was being created.

The elixir of immortality was one of 13 precious things lost in the churning of the cosmic sea. It took a 1000 years before the gods and demons, in a joint dredging operation aided by Sesha, the sea snake, and Vishnu, recovered them all.

The design of the temples of Angkor was based on this ancient legend. The moat represents the ocean and the gods use the top of Mount Meru – represented by the tower – as their churning stick. The cosmic serpent offered himself as a rope to enable the gods and demons to twirl the stick.

Paul Mus, a French archaeologist, suggests that the bridge with the naga balustrades which went over the moat from the world of men to the royal city was an image of the rainbow. Throughout Southeast Asia and India, the rainbow is alluded to as a multi-coloured serpent rearing its head in the sky.

Angkor Angkor Wat

sculptors' attention to detail provides an insight into the world of 12th-century haute couture. Their hair is often knotted on the crown and bejewelled – although all manner of wild and exotic coiffures are depicted. Jewelled collars and hip-girdles also are common and bracelets worn on the upper arms. Sadly many of the apsaras have been removed in recent years.

The bas-reliefs narrate stories from the *Ramayana* and *Mahabharata*, as well as legends of Vishnu, and are reminiscent of Pallava and Chola art in southeast India. Pious artisans and peasants were probably only allowed as far as Angkor Wat's outer gallery, where they could admire the bas-reliefs and pay homage to the god-king. In the open courtyards, statues of animals enliven the walls. Lions stand on guard beside the staircases. There were supposed to be 300 of them in the original building. Part of the bas-reliefs were hit by shrapnel in 1972, and some of its apsaras were used for target practice.

One of the great delights of Angkor, particularly at Angkor Wat, are the glorious trees. Huge tropical trees grow in Angkor's forests – a reminder of how much of Cambodia used to look. Driving out to Angkor from Siem Reap, the flat landscape is largely bare of trees but inside the protected area forests flourish. High in the treetops birds sing and call to each other all day. The trees and wildlife whose motto seems to be 'always watching: always waiting' are an integral part of Angkor. Keeping the prising tentacles and smothering creepers at bay requires constant vigilance and a sharp blade. A great deal of archaeology is still concealed in the embrace of the forest and exploring the less beaten paths will not uncommonly reveal some unknown and unmapped ruin.

The royal city of Angkor Thom

Construction of Jayavarman VII's spacious walled capital, Angkor Thom (which means 'great city'), began at the end of the 12th century: he rebuilt the capital after it had been captured and destroyed by the Cham.

Angkor Thom was colossal – the 100-m-wide moat surrounding the city, which was probably stocked with crocodiles as a protection against the enemy, extended more than 12 km.

Inside the moat was an 8-m-high stone wall, buttressed on the inner side by a high mound of earth along the top of which ran a terrace for troops to man the ramparts.

The area within the walls was more spacious than that of any walled city in medieval Europe – it could easily have encompassed the whole of ancient Rome. Yet it is believed that this enclosure, like the Forbidden City in Beijing, was only a royal, religious and administrative centre accommodating the court and dignitaries. The rest of the population lived outside the walls between the two artificial lakes – the east and west barays – and along the Siem Reap River.

Four great gateways in the city wall face north, south, east and west and lead to the city's geometric centre, the Bayon. The fifth, Victory Gate, leads from the royal palace (within the Royal Enclosure) to the East Baray. The height of the gates was determined by the headroom needed to accommodate an elephant and howdah complete with parasols. The flanks of each gateway are decorated by three-headed stone elephants and each gateway tower has four giant faces, which keep an eye on all four cardinal points.

Five causeways traverse the moat, each bordered by sculptured balustrades of nagas gripped, on one side, by 54 stern-looking giant gods and on the other by 54 fierce-faced demons. The balustrade depicts the Hindu legend of the churning of the sea (see box on the previous page).

Some stone buildings survived the sacking of the city by the Cham, such as the temples of Phimeanakas and Baphuon, and these were incorporated by Jayavarman in his new plan. He adopted the general layout of the royal centre conceived by Suryavarman II.

Inside Angkor Thom

The **South Gate** provides the most common access route to Angkor Thom, predominantly because it sits on the path between the two great Angkor complexes. The gate is a wonderful introduction to Angkor Thom with well-restored statues of asuras (demons) and gods lining the bridge. The figures on the left, exhibiting serene expression, are the gods, while those on the right, with grimaced, fierce-looking heads, are the asuras. The significance of the naga balustrade, across the moat, is believed to be symbolic of a link between the world of mortals, outside the complex, to the world of gods, inside the complex. The 23-m-high gates feature four faces in a similarly styled fashion to those of the Bayon.

The **Bayon** is one of Angkor's most famous sights and most people visiting Cambodia are familiar with the site of the beaming faces before even stepping foot in the temple. The Bayon was Jayavarman VII's own temple-mountain, built right in the middle of Angkor Thom; its large faces have now become synonymous with the Angkor complex. It is believed to have been built between the late 12th century to early 13th century, around 100 years after Angkor Wat. Unlike other Khmer monuments, the Bayon has no protective wall immediately enclosing it. The central tower, at the intersection of the diagonals city walls, indicates that the city walls and the temple were built at the same time.

The Bayon is a three-tiered, pyramid temple with a 45-m-high tower, topped by four gigantic carved heads. These faces are believed to be the images of Jayavarman VII as a Bodhisattra, and face the four compass points. They are crowned with lotus flowers, symbol of enlightenment, and are surrounded by 51 smaller towers each with heads facing north, south, east and west. There are over 2000 large faces carved throughout the structure.

Although the Bayon seems a complex, labyrinth structure, its overall layout is quite basic. The first two of the three levels feature galleries of bas-relief (which should be viewed clockwise), a circular central sanctuary dominates the third level.

When Pierre Loti, the French writer, first saw these towers in 1912 he was astounded: "I looked up at the tree-covered towers which dwarfed me, when all of a sudden my blood curdled as I saw an enormous smile looking down on me, and then another smile on another wall, then three, then five, then 10, appearing in every direction". The facial features are striking and the full lips, curling upwards at the corners, are known as 'the smile of Angkor'.

Even the archaeologists of the École Française d'Extrême Orient were not able to decide immediately whether the heads on the Bayon represented Brahma, Siva or the Buddha. There are many theories. One of the most plausible ones was conceived in 1934 by George Coedès, an archaeologist who spent many years studying the temples at Angkor. He postulated that the sculptures represented King Jayavarman VII in the form of Avaloketsvara, the Universal Buddha. If true, this would have meant that the Hindu concept of the god-king had been appended to Buddhist cosmology. Jayavarman VII, once a humble monk who twice renounced the throne and then became the mightiest of all the Khmer rulers, may be the smiling face, cast in stone, at the centre of his kingdom. The multiplication of faces, all looking out to the four cardinal points, may symbolize Jayavarman blessing the four quarters of the kingdom. After Jayavarman's death, the Brahmin priests turned the Bayon into a place of Hindu worship (confusing the archaeologists).

The Bayon has undergone a series of facelifts through its life, a point first observed by Henri Parmentier – a French archaeologist who worked for L'École Français d'Extrême Orient – in 1924 and later excavations revealed vestiges of a former building. It is thought that the first temple was planned as a two-tiered structure dedicated to Siva, which was then altered to its present form. As a result, it gives the impression of crowding – the towers rise right next to each other and the courtyards are narrow without much air or light. When Henri Mouhot rediscovered Angkor, local villagers had dubbed the Bayon 'the hide and seek sanctuary' because of its complex layout.

The Bayon

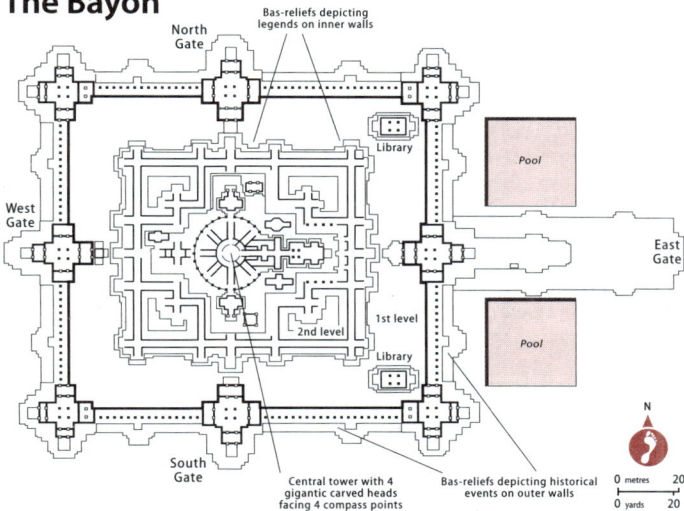

North Gate

Bas-reliefs depicting legends on inner walls

Library

Pool

West Gate

East Gate

2nd level

1st level

Library

Pool

South Gate

Central tower with 4 gigantic carved heads facing 4 compass points

Bas-reliefs depicting historical events on outer walls

N

0 metres 20

0 yards 20

Barays and the Jayavarman conundrum: the case for irrigation

By founding his capital at Roluos, just southeast of Angkor, in the middle of an arid plain annually plagued by drought and flash floods, Jayavarman II bequeathed to archaeologists and other scholars a geo-climatic conundrum. What possessed him to site the nerve centre of Khmer civilization at such an environmentally unfriendly spot and how did the great city sustain itself through the centuries?

Archaeologists have postulated that the Khmers engineered a complex irrigation system to grow enough rice to feed the city's population. In this view, Angkor was a classic hydraulic society.

In *The Art of Southeast Asia*, Philip Rawson wrote: "Angkor was a capital filled with temples and supporting many inhabitants. But its nucleus was a splendid irrigation project based on a number of huge artificial reservoirs fed by the local rivers and linked to each other by means of a rectangular grid system of canals." The barays, or man-made lakes, were used to feed an intricate network of irrigation channels. The first baray was Lolei, built by Indravarman at the city of Roluos. "The engineering involved at Angkor," Rawson said, "...was vaster and far more sophisticated than anything seen before in that part of the world." Lolei was more than 3½ km long and 800 m wide. The East Baray was twice the size of Lolei and the West Baray, built during Udayadityavarman II's reign, is thought to have held about 4 million cu m of water when full.

The barays were constructed by building dykes above the level of the land and waiting for the monsoon flood. Because the resultant reservoirs were higher than the surrounding land, there was no need to pump the water to flood the paddy fields: a gap was simply cut in the dyke. The water stored in the barays would have been replenished by each monsoon, making it possible to irrigate the ricelands. With their land being watered year round, the Khmers would be able to grow three crops of rice a year.

The barays were central to the health and vigour of Khmer civilization but because they were sitting targets for enemy saboteurs, they may also have played a part in its downfall. During successive Siamese invasions the fragile irrigation system would have been irreparably damaged and essential maintenance of the hydraulic works was neglected through a lack of manpower. The precarious, and artificial, balance of man and nature was disturbed and as the irrigation channels cracked and dried up so did the mighty Khmer Empire.

Why Angkor should have gone into decline from about the 13th century has exercised the minds of historians for years. Apart from the destruction of the fragile irrigation system, several other explanations as to Angkor's downfall have been suggested: climatic change, the shift of trade from land to sea-based empires and the corruption of a system which, like the Roman emperors, made the king a demi-god. Some think the builder King Jayavarman VII bankrupted the empire with his vast building schemes.

The **bas-reliefs** which decorate the walls of the Bayon all seem to tell a story but are much less imposing than those at Angkor Wat. The sculpture is carved deeper but is more naive and less sophisticated than the bas-reliefs at Angkor Wat.

The Bayon reliefs vary greatly in quality; this may have been because the sculptors' skills were being overstretched by Jayavarman's ambitious building programme. The

Barays and the Jayavarman conundrum: the case against irrigation

When the first westerners stumbled upon the Khmer ruins at Angkor – the lost city in the jungle – in the middle of the 19th century, they judged it to be the finest example of a civilization based upon the massive control of water for irrigation. The sheer size of the monuments, the vast barays storing millions of gallons of water, all seemed to lend force to the notion that here was the finest example of state-controlled irrigation. In Karl Marx's words, the Khmer Kingdom was a society based upon the Asiatic mode of production. The upshot of this was that, by necessity, there needed to be a centralized state and an all-powerful king – leading, in Professor Karl Wittfogel's famous phrase, to a system of 'Oriental Despotism'. Such a view seemed hard to refute – how could such enormous expanses of water in the baray be used for anything but irrigation?

However, in the past decade, archaeologists, irrigation engineers and geographers have challenged the view of the Khmer Kingdom as the hydraulic civilization par excellence. Their challenge rests on four main pillars of evidence. First, they point out that if irrigation was so central to life in Angkor, why is it not mentioned once in over 1000 inscriptions? Second, they question the usual interpretation of Angkorian agriculture contained in the Chinese emissary Chou Ta-kuan's account, *Notes on the customs of Cambodia*, written in 1312. This account talks of "three or four rice harvests a year" – which scholars have assumed means irrigated rice agriculture. However, the detractors put a different interpretation on Chou Ta-kuan's words, arguing that they in fact describe a system of flood retreat agriculture in which rice was sown as the waters of the Great Lake, the Tonlé Sap, receded at the end of the rainy season. Third, they note that aerial photographs show none of the feeder canals needed to carry water from the barays to the fields nor any of the other irrigation structures needed to control water.

Finally, the sceptics draw upon engineering evidence to support their case. They have calculated that the combined storage capacity of all the barays and reservoirs is sufficient to irrigate only 400 ha of riceland – hardly the stuff on which great civilizations are built.

The geographer Philip Stott maintains that flood retreat agriculture would have produced the surplus needed to feed the soldiers, priests and the court of the Khmer god-king, while postulating that the barays were only for urban use. He writes that they were "just like the temple mountains, essentially a part of the urban scene, providing urban symbolism, beauty, water for bathing and drinking, a means of transport, and perhaps a supply of fish as well. Yet, not one drop of their water is likely to have fed the rice fields of Angkor."

The East Baray is now dry but the West Baray is used for fish cultivation.

reliefs on the outer wall and on the inner gallery differ completely and seem to belong to two different worlds: the relief on the outside depicts historical events; those on the inside are drawn from the epic world of gods and legends, representing the creatures who were supposed to haunt the subterranean depths of Mount Meru. In fact the reliefs on the outer wall illustrating historical scenes and derring-do with marauding Cham were carved in the early 13th century during the reign of Jayavarman; those on the inside which illuminate the Hindu cosmology were carved after the king's death when his successors turned from Mahayana Buddhism back to Hinduism. In total, there are over 1.2 km of bas-reliefs, depicting over 11,000 characters.

Two recurring themes in the bas-reliefs are the powerful king and the Hindu epics. Jayavarman is depicted in the throes of battle with the Cham – who are recognizable thanks to their unusual and distinctive headdress, which looks like an inverted lotus flower. The naval battle pictured on the walls of Banteay Chhmar are almost identical. Funnily enough, there's a bas-relief in the north section of the west gallery depicting a huge fish eating a deer, a complimentary inscription says "the deer is its' food", an artistic directive, which the carver obviously forgot to remove. The other bas-reliefs give a good insight into Khmer life at the time – the warrior elephants, oxcarts, fishing with nets, cockfights and skewered fish drying on racks. Other vignettes show musicians, jugglers, hunters, chess-players, people nit-picking hair, palm readers and reassuringly down-to-earth scenes of Angkor citizens enjoying drinking sessions. In the naval battle scenes, the water around the war canoes is depicted by the presence of fish, crocodiles and floating corpses.

The **Royal Enclosure**, to the north of the Bayon, had already been laid out by Suryavarman I: the official palace was in the front with the domestic quarters behind, its gardens surrounded by a laterite wall and moat. Suryavarman I also beautified the royal city with ornamental pools. Jayavarman VII simply improved his designs.

In front of the Royal Enclosure, at the centre of Angkor Thom, Suryavarman I laid out the first Grand Plaza with the recently renovated **Terrace of the Elephants** (also called the Royal Terrace). The 300-m-long wall derives its name from the large, life-like carvings of elephants in a hunting scene, adorning its walls. The 2½-m wall also features elephants flanking the southern stairway. Believed to once be the foundations for the royal reception hall, lead tiles were found here in more recent years. This discovery corroborates Chinese diplomat Chou Ta-kuan's evidence that "the tiles of the king's main apartment are made of lead". Royalty once sat in gold-topped pavilions at the centre of the pavilion, and here there are rows of garudas (bird-men), their wings lifted as if in flight. They were intended to give the impression that the god-king's palace was floating in the heavens like the imagined flying celestial palaces of the gods. At the end of the terrace is an impressive sculpture of a five-headed horse. Arrive here before 1200 to catch the structure at its best. Also in front of the Royal Enclosure are the stately **North and South Kleangs**, which sit on the east side of the central square (opposite the Terrace of the Elephants). Although Kleang means storeroom, a royal oath of allegiance carved into one of the doorways indicates that they may have served as reception areas for foreign envoys. The North Kleang was was originally constructed in wood under Rajendravarman II, Jayavarman V reconstructed it with stone and Jayavarman VII later added 12 laterite victory towers, called the **Prasat Suor Prat**. The function of the towers is steeped in controversy. While some say they were intended as anchors for performing acrobats and clowns, Chou Ta-kuan stated that they were used to settle disputes between performing men (to see who could last the longest seated on a tower without illness or injury). Henri Mahout disagreed with both theories, suggesting that the towers were created to hold the crown jewels.

At the northeast corner of the 'central square' is the 12th-century **Terrace of the Leper King**, which may have been a cremation platform for the aristocracy of Angkor. Now rebuilt it is a little too fresh and contemporary for some tastes. The practice in some places of rebuilding as opposed to preservation has been questioned. The 7-m-high double terrace has bands of bas-reliefs, one on top of the other, with intricately sculptured scenes of royal pageantry and seated apsaras as well as nagas and garudas which frequented the slopes of Mount Meru. Above is a strange statue of an earlier date, which probably depicts the god of death, Yama, and once held a staff in its right hand. The statue's naked, lichen-covered body gives the terrace its name – the lichen gives the uncanny impression of leprosy. Jayavarman VII may have suffered from leprosy, but this statue is not a representation of him. Opposite the Terrace of the Elephants, on the south side of the Terrace of the Leper King, are the remains of an earlier wall, carved with bas-reliefs of demons. These reliefs were found by French archaeologists and had been intentionally concealed. This illustrates the lengths to which the Khmers went to recreate Mount Meru (the home of the gods) as faithfully as possible. According to Hindu mythology, Mount Meru extended into the bowels of the earth; the bas-relief section below ground level was carved with weird and wonderful creatures to symbolize the hidden depths of the underworld. The second layer of carving is the base of Mount Meru on earth. Flights of steps led through these to the lawns and pavilions of the royal gardens and Suryavarman's palace.

The **Phimeanakas** (meaning Celestial or Flying Palace in Sanskrit) inside the Royal Enclosure was started by Rajendravarman and used by all the later kings. The structure stands close to the walls of the Royal Palace, none of which much exists today. Suryavarman I rebuilt this pyramidal temple when he was renovating the Royal Enclosure. It rises from the centre of the former royal palace. Lions guard all four stairways to the central tower. It is now ruined but was originally covered in gold, as the Chinese envoy Chou Ta-kuan related in 1296: "The king sleeps in the summit of the palace's golden tower. All the people believe that the tower is also inhabited by the Lord of the Sun, who is a nine-headed serpent. Every night the serpent appears in the form of a woman with whom the king sleeps during the first watch. None of the royal wives are allowed in the tower. The king leaves at the second watch to go to his wives and concubines. If the naga spirit does not appear one night, it is a sign that the king's death is imminent. Should the king fail to visit the naga for a single night, the welfare of the kingdom will suffer dire consequences." The Phimeanakas represented a genuine architectural revolution: it was not square, but rectangular and on the upper terrace, surrounding the central tower, there was a gallery with corbelled vaults, used as a passageway. The Celestial Palace is now in a bad state of repair.

The **Srah Srei**, or the women's bath, to the north of the Celestial Palace is also within the walled enclosure. Chou Ta-kuan, whose Chinese delegation appears to have enjoyed watching Angkor's womenfolk bathe, noted that women, even of noble families, would shamelessly take off their clothes to bathe in public. "To enter the water, the women simply hide their sex with their left hand", he wrote. The Phimeanakas is linked by the **Avenue of Victory** to the Eastern Baray.

South of the Royal Enclosure and near the Terrace of the Elephants is the **Baphuon**, built by Udayadityavarman II. The temple was approached by a 200-m-long sandstone causeway, raised on pillars, which was probably constructed after the temple was built. The platform leads from the temple-mountain itself to the east gopura – an arched gateway leading to the temple courtyards (and offers quite good photographic opportunities below it). The Baphuon is not well preserved as it was erected on an artificial hill which weakened its foundations. Only the three terraces of its pyramidal, Mount Meru-style form remain and these afford little indication of its former glory: it was second only to the Bayon in size. Chou Ta-kuan, the Chinese envoy, reported that its great tower was made of bronze and that it was "truly marvellous to behold". With extensive restoration, the temple is starting to shape-up. Most of the bas-reliefs were carved in panels and refer to the Hindu epics. Some archaeologists believe the sculptors were trying to tell stories in the same way as the shadow plays. It is believed that the fourth level wall on the western side was originally created in the form of a large, reclining Buddha, though it is hard to make out today. There is a wonderful view from the summit. South of the Baphuon, returns you back to the Bayon.

Preah Palilay, just outside the north wall of the Royal Enclosure, was also built by Jayavarman VII. Just to the east of this temple is **Tep Tranam**, the base of a pagoda, with a pool in front of it. To the east of Tep Tranam and the other side of the Northern Avenue is the **Preah Pithu Group**, a cluster of five temples.

Motifs in Khmer sculpture

The **kala** is a jawless monster commanded by the gods to devour his own body – it made its first appearance in lintels at Roluos. The monster represented devouring time and was an early import from Java. **Singhas** or lions appeared in stylized forms and are often guardians to temples. The lions lack realism probably because the carvers had never seen one.

The **makara** was a mythical water monster with a scaley body, eagles' talons and an elephantine trunk. The **naga** or sacred snakes play an important part in Hindu mythology and the Khmers drew on them for architectural inspiration. Possibly more than any other single symbol or motif, the naga is characteristic of Southeast Asia. The naga is an aquatic serpent, the word being Sanskrit for snake, and is intimately associated with water (a key component of Khmer prosperity). In Hindu mythology the naga coils beneath and supports Vishnu on the cosmic ocean. The snake also swallows the waters of life, these only being set free to reinvigorate the world after Indra ruptures the serpent with a bolt of lightning. Another version has Vishnu's servants pulling at the serpent to squeeze the waters of life from it (the so-called churning of the sea. The naga permeates Southeast Asian life from royalty to villager. The bridge across the Bayon to Angkor Wat features nagas churning the oceans; men in Vietnam, Laos and Thailand used to tattoo their bodies with

Singha

Naga

South of Angkor Thom

Phnom Bakheng and Baksei Chamkrong

ⓘ *To get up to the ruins, either climb the steep and uneven hill where the vegetation has been cleared (slippery when wet), ride an elephant to the top of the hill (US$15) or walk up the gentle zig-zag path the elephants take.* Phnom Bakheng, Yasovarman's temple-mountain, stands at the top of a natural hill, 60 m high, affording good views of the plains of Angkor. There is also a roped off Buddha's footprint to see. It is just outside the south gate of Angkor Thom and was the centre of King Yasovarman's city, Yasodharapura – the 'City Endowed with Splendour'. A pyramid-temple dedicated to Siva, Bakheng was the home of the royal lingam and Yasovarman's mausoleum after his death. It is composed of five towers built on a sandstone platform. There are 108 nagas for protection; water, the gift of life in a region where wet rice is the staple crop, is measured in Thailand in terms of numbers of nagas; while objects from boats to water storage jars to temples to musical instruments are decorated with the naga motif throughout Southeast Asia.

The **garuda** appeared relatively late in Khmer architecture. This mythical creature – half man, half bird – was the vehicle of the Hindu god, Vishnu and the sworn enemy of the nagas. The **apsaras** are regarded as one of the greatest invention of the Khmers. The gorgeous temptresses – born, according to legend, 'during the churning of the Sea of Milk' – were Angkor's equivalent of pin-up girls and represented the ultimate ideal of feminine beauty. They lived in heaven where their sole raison d'être was to have eternal sex with Khmer heroes and holy men. The apsaras are carved with splendidly ornate jewellery and, clothed in the latest Angkor fashion, they strike seductive poses and seemingly compete with each other like models on a catwalk. Different facial features suggest the existence of several races at Angkor – it is possible that they might be modelled on women captured in war. Together with the five towers of Angkor Wat they have become the symbol of Khmer culture. The god-king himself possessed an apsara-like retinue of court dancers – impressive enough for Chinese envoy Chou Ta-kuan to write home about it in 1296.

Garuda

Apsaras

smaller towers scattered around the terraces. The main tower has been partially demolished and the others have completely disappeared. It was entered via a steep flight of steps which were guarded by squatting lions. The steps have deteriorated with the towers. Foliate scroll relief carving covers much of the main shrine – the first time this style was used. This strategically placed hill served as a camp for various combatants, including the Vietnamese, and suffered accordingly. Today the hill is disfigured by a radio mast.

Baksei Chamkrong was built by Harshavarman I at the beginning of the 10th century and dedicated to his father, Yasovarman I. It lies at the foot of Phnom Bakheng (between Bakheng and Angkor Thom), the centre of Yasovarman's city, and was one of the first temples to be built in brick on a stepped laterite base. An inscription tells of a golden image of Siva inside the temple.

East of Angkor Thom

Chau Say Tevoda and Thommanon

There are a close group of temples just outside the east gate of Angkor Thom. Chau Say Tevoda, built by Suryavarman II, is the first temple outside the east gate and is dwarfed by Ta Keo. The temple is dedicated to Siva but many of the carvings are of Vishnu. It is similar in plan to Thommanon, next door, whose surrounding walls have completely disappeared, leaving only the gateways on the east and west ends and a ruined central tower. Originally both temples would have had a hall linked to the central tower and enclosing walls with elaborate gateways. A library, to the southeast, is the only other building in the complex. There are repeated pediments above the doorways.

Ta Keo and Ta Nei

Ta Keo, begun during Jayavarman V's reign and left unfinished, stands east of the Royal Palace and just off the Avenue of Victory. The pyramid-temple rises over 50 m: its five tower shrines are supported on a five-tiered pyramid. This temple was one of the first to be entirely built of sandstone. Previous tower sanctuaries had entrances only on the east side, but Ta Keo has openings on all four sides. It was originally surrounded by a moat.

Deeper in the forest, 600 m north of Ta Keo, is Ta Nei. Built by Jayavarman VII the building has appropriated the Bayon's style but on a much smaller scale. Much of the building still remains in the collapsed state but ongoing work from the Apsara Authority means the building is being used for training purposes. It is an overgrown temple with lichen-covered bas-reliefs.

Ta Prohm

For all would-be Mouhots and closet Indiana Joneses, the temple of Ta Prohm, to the south of Ta Keo, is the perfect lost-in-the-jungle experience. Unlike most of the other monuments at Angkor, it has been only minimally cleared of its undergrowth, fig trees and creepers. It is widely regarded as one of Angkor's most enchanting temples and an absolute 'must-see'.

Ta Prohm was built to house the divine image of the Queen Mother and was consecrated in 1186 – five years after Jayavarman VII seized power.

The outer enclosures of Ta Prohm are somewhat obscured by dense foliage but reach well beyond the temple's heart (1 km by 650 m). The temple proper consists of a number of concentric galleries featuring corner towers and the standard gopuras. Other buildings and enclosures were built on a more ad hoc basis. The temple marked the end of an architectural style in which the temple's structure lay on a single plane with rising towers alluding to the notion of elevation rather than comprising multiple levels.

It underwent many transformations and an inscription gives detailed information on the complex. Within the complex walls lived 12,640 citizens. It contained 39 sanctuaries or prasats, 566 stone dwellings and 288 brick dwellings. Ta Prohm literally translates as the Royal Monastery and that is what it functioned as, home to 18 abbots and 2740 monks. By the 12th century temples were no longer exclusively places of worship – they also had to accommodate monks so roofed halls were increasingly built within the complexes. According to contemporary inscriptions, the temple required 79,365 people for its upkeep, relying on the income of 3140 villages to subsidize the 2740 officials and 615 dancers. The list of property it owned was on an equally impressive scale. It included 523 parasols, 35 diamonds and 40,620 pearls. Ta Prohm is one of the most beautiful temples in the area, as it has been relatively untouched since it was discovered and retains much of its mystery.

The French writer Elie Lauré wrote: "With its millions of knotted limbs, the forest embraces the ruins with a violent love". Roots entwine themselves around ancient stones like the tentacles of a giant octopus. Trunks and roots pour off temple roofs like lava flows. It was decided by the École Française d'Extrême Orient to leave the temple in its natural state. The trees burgeoning their way through the complex are predominantly the silk-cotton tree and the aptly named strangler fig. The plants are believed to have spawned in the temples cracks from seeds blown in or dropped by birds. Naturally, the roots of the trees have descended towards the soil, prying their way through the temples foundations in the process. As the vegetation has matured, growing stronger, it has forced its way further into the temples structure, damaging the man-built base and causing untold destruction. This has created a situation where the temples now rely on the trees for support. Herein lies the dilemma – if the trees die or are damaged, the now damaged and loose temple walls could easily crumble or collapse. Venerable trees weighing several tonnes growing on temple roofs also cause unimaginable stress, slowly shattering the stones. As historians Michael Freeman and Claude Jacques rightly believe the trees in Ta Prohm "are agents of destruction." There is currently a campaign to save Ta Prohm before it's too late.

In recent years a colossal tree, struck by lightening, fell on a gallery, causing quite serious damage. This has reignited the campaign to 'save Ta Prohm'. Already a project is underway to preserve Ta Prohm with some of the smaller trees being pruned and larger branches cut back.

Despite the damage this laissez faire is an enlightened policy as Ta Prohm is the only temple where one can gain any semblance of how Angkor would have looked, smelt and felt when it was rediscovered by those 19th-century Frenchmen.

Banteay Kdei, Srah Srang and Prasat Kravan

The massive complex of Banteay Kdei, otherwise known as 'the citadel of cells', is 3 km east of Angkor Thom and just to the southeast of Ta Prohm. Some archaeologists think it may be dedicated to Jayavarman VII's religious teacher. The temple has remained in much the same state it was discovered in – a crowded collection of ruined laterite towers and connecting galleries lying on a flat plan, surrounded by a galleried enclosure. It is presumed that the temple was a Buddhist monastery (because it is single level amongst other rationale) and in recent years hundreds of buried Buddha statues were excavated from the site. In recent times a community of monks would patronize the site, now less likely due to the strict restrictions imposed by temple management. The temple area is enclosed by a large laterite wall, 700 m by 500 m, and contains three main enclosures. Like Ta Prohm it contains a Hall of Dancers (east side), an open roof building with four separate quarters. The second enclosure runs around the perimeters of the inner enclosure. The third, inner enclosure contains a north and south library and central sanctuary. The central tower was never finished. And the square pillars in the middle of the courtyard still cannot be explained by scholars. There are few inscriptions here to indicate either its name or purpose, but it is almost certainly a Buddhist temple built in the 12th century, about the same time as Ta Prohm. It is quite similar to Ta Prohm in design but on a much smaller scale. Historians Freeman and Jacques believe that it was probably built over the site of another temple. The temple is being restored, slowly but surely. However, the 13th-century vandalism of Buddha images (common to most of Jayavarman's temples) will prove a little more difficult to restore. This temple offers a few good examples of Mahayanist Buddhist frontons and lintels that escaped the desecration.

The temple's similarity to Ta Prohm offers visitors the opportunity to experience and explore the temple without the hordes that its counterpart receives. However, most won't want to miss Ta Prohm in which case you should follow historians' Freeman and Jacques advice. They suggest that if you have time to spare (three hours) the temple should be explored on foot in conjunction with Srah Srang and Ta Prohm. From Srah Srang walk right through Banteay Kdei to its west entrance, turn north and follow the outer wall until you reach the east entrance of Ta Prohm and from there explore the overgrown temple.

The lake or baray next to Banteay Kdei is called Srah Srang – 'Royal Bath' – which was used for ritual bathing. The steps down to the water face the rising sun and are flanked with lions and nagas. This sandstone landing stage dates from the reign of Jayavarman VII but the lake itself is thought to date back two centuries earlier. A 10th-century inscription reads 'this water is stored for the use of all creatures except dyke breakers', ie elephants. This design is believed to be characteristic of that adopted in the Bayon. The Baray, which measures 700 m by 300 m, has been filled with turquoise-blue waters for over 1300 years. With a good view of Pre Rup across the lake, some archaeologists believe that this spot affords the best vista in the whole Angkor complex. The green landscape around the baray and beautiful views offer visitors a tranquil and cool resting place, perfect for a picnic lunch.

On the road between Angkor Wat and Banteay Kdei, on the small circuit, is Prasat Kravan. The temple, built in 921, means 'Cardamom Sanctuary' and is unusual in that it is built of brick. By that time brick had been replaced by laterite and sandstone. It consists of five brick towers arranged in a line. The bricklayers did a good job, especially considering they used a vegetable composite as their mortar. The temple's bas-reliefs are considered a bit of an anomaly as brick was hardly ever sculpted upon. In the early 10th century, temples were commissioned by individuals other than the king; Prasat Kravan is one of the earliest examples. It was probably built during the reign of Harshavarman I.

The Hindu temple, surrounded by a moat, is positioned in a north-south direction. Two of the five decorated brick towers contain bas-reliefs (the north and central towers). The central tower is probably the most impressive and contains a linga on a pedestal. The sanctuary's three walls all contain pictures of Vishnu; the left-hand wall depicts Vishnu disguised as Vamana the dwarf. The incarnation of Vamana was used to dupe the evil demon king, Bali, into letting the unassuming dwarf take a small space to meditate. Instead the mighty Vishnu rose up, taking three important steps – from a pedestal, across the ocean, to a lotus – in order to reclaim the world from the evil demon king. On the right-hand wall again is the mighty Vishnu riding his Garuda. Common to both the bas-reliefs is the four-armed Vishnu waving around a number of objects: disc, club, conch shell and ball – these are all symbolic of his personal attributes and power. On the opposing wall is Vishnu, this time with eight arms standing between six rows of people meditating above a giant reptile.

The Northern tower is devoted to Lakshimi, Vishnu's wife. Like her consort, she is also baring her personal attributes. The best light to view the relief is in the morning.

The Cardamom Sanctuary is named after a tree that grew on the grounds. Ironically, its ruin has been largely due to the roots of trees growing beneath it. The French have been involved in the temple's reconstruction by the French. The temple's twin, Prasat Neang Khamau (the Black Lady Sanctuary), can be found outside of Phnom Penh.

Pre Rup

Northeast of Srah Srang is Pre Rup, the State Temple of King Rajendravarman's capital. Built in 961, the temple-mountain representing Mount Meru is larger, higher and artistically superior than its predecessor, the East Mebon, which it closely

People originally thought Pre Rup was a funerary temple due to its misleading name (which means 'to turn the body') and a stone cistern nearby inscribed with the legend of a king who was accidentally poisoned by a cucumber. Its modern name, 'turning the body', derives from local legend and is named after a cremation ritual in which the outline of a body was traced in the cinders one way and then the other.

resembles. Keeping with tradition of state capitals, Pre Rup marked the centre of the
city, much of which doesn't exist today. The pyramid-structure, which is constructed
of laterite with brick prasats, sits at the apex of an artificial, purpose-built mountain, ·

The temple is enclosed by a laterite outer wall (127 m by 117 m) and inner wall
(87 m by 77 m) both which contain gopuras in the centre of each wall. The central
pyramid-level consists of a three-tiered, sandstone platform, with five central
towers sitting above. This was an important innovation at Pre Rup and East Mebon,
that the sanctuary at the top was no longer a single tower – but a group of five
towers, surrounded by smaller towers on the outer, lower levels. This more
complicated plan reached its final development at Angkor Wat 150 years later. The
group of five brick towers were originally elaborately decorated with plaster, but
most of it has now fallen off. However, the corners of each of the five towers contain
guardian figures – as per tradition, the eastern towers are female and the western
and central towers are male. The shrine has fine lintels and columns on its
doorways. But the intricate sandstone carvings on the doors of the upper levels are
reproductions. The upper levels of the pyramid offer a brilliant, panoramic view of
the countryside.

Eastern Baray, East Mebon and Banteay Samre

The Eastern Baray – or Baray Orientale – was built by Yasovarman I and fed by the
Siem Reap River. This large reservoir (7 km by 1.8 km), now dried up, was the labour of
love for Yasovarman I. Historian Dawn Rooney believes it took 6000 workers more
than three years to complete. The baray was Yasovarman I's first major work. To keep
the punters on side he needed to provide a reliable water supply to his new kingdom,
Yasodharataka. And that he did. At full capacity the baray could hold around 45-50
million cu m of water. He named the baray Yasodharataka and declared it protected
by the goddess Ganga (overseen by abbots from the ashramas south of the baray).
The four corners are marked by stelae.

Today, a boat isn't required to reach the middle of the Eastern Baray, where the
flamboyant five towers of the East Mebon are located. Intrepid traveller Helen
Churchill Candee remarked of the temple: "Could any conception be lovelier, a vast
expanse of sky-tinted water as wetting for a perfectly ordered temple."

The Hindu pyramid structure consists of three tiers. Guarding the corners of the
first and second levels are carefully sculpted elephants and sculptures (the best one
is in the southeast corner). The inner enclosure contains eight smaller towers and
skilfully carved lintels upon the gopuras featuring Lakshmi being watered down by
two elephants and Vishnu in his man-lion guise, Narasimha. The upper terrace
contains the five towers, the northwest tower features Ganesha riding his own trunk;
the southeast tower shows an elephant being eaten by a monster and the central
sanctuary's lintels depict Indra on his mount and Varuna the Guardian.

Finished in 952, Rajendravarman seems to have followed the Roluos trend and
dedicated East Mebon to his parents. The East Mebon and Pre Rup were the last
monuments in plaster and brick; they mark the end of a Khmer architectural epoch.
The overall temple construction utilizes all materials that were available at the time:
plaster, brick, laterite and sandstone. Although many believe East Mebon to be a
temple-mountain, that wasn't its original intention, it just appears that way now that
surrounding waters have disappeared. The Siem Reap River is said to have been
diverted while the temple was built.

Banteay Samre lies further to the east, around 500 m past the east end of the
East Baray. It is a Hindu temple dedicated to Vishnu, although reliefs decorating
some of the frontons (the triangular areas above arches) portray Buddhist scenes. It
is thought to have been built by Suryavarman II and has many characteristics of
Angkor Wat such as stone-vaulted galleries and a high central tower. The bas-reliefs
are in fine condition.

North of Angkor Thom

Preah Khan

Northeast of the walled city of Angkor Thom, about 3½ km from the Bayon, is the 12th-century complex of Preah Khan. One of the largest complexes within the Angkor area, it was Jayavarman VII's first capital before Angkor Thom was completed. Preah Khan means 'sacred sword' and is believed to have derived from a decisive battle against the Cham, which created a 'lake of blood', but was invariably won by Jayavarman VII.

Preah Khan is not uniform in style. It is highly likely that Jayavarman VII's initial very well-organized and detailed city plans went slightly pear-shaped during the working city's life. A number of alterations and buildings were added, in addition to a vast civilian habitation (huts and timber houses), which all came together to create a complex labyrinth of architectural chaos. It is similar in ground plan to Ta Prohm (see page 116) but attention was paid to the approaches: its east and west entrance avenues leading to ornamental causeways are lined with carved stone boundary posts. Evidence of 1000 teachers suggests that it was more than a mere Buddhist monastery but most likely a Buddhist university. Nonetheless an abundance of Brahmanic iconography is still present on site. Around the rectangular complex is a large laterite wall surrounded by large garudas wielding the naga (each over 5 m in height). The theme continues across the length of the whole 3-km external enclosure, with the motif dotted every 50 m. Within these walls lies the surrounding moat.

The city is conveniently located on the shores of its own baray, Jayataka, which measures 3½ km by 900 m. Some foundations and laterite steps lead from the reservoir, where two beautiful gajasimha lions guard the path. It is best to enter the temple from the baray's jetty in order to experience the magnificence of the divinities and devas of the Processional Way (causeway leading across the moat).

Preah Khan

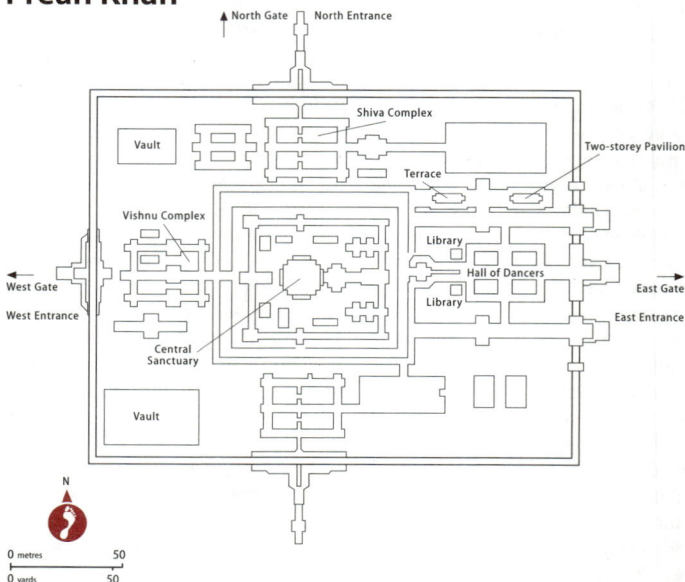

The construction's four walls meet in the centre creating two galleries and likewise, two enclosures. The outer enclosure contains the traditional four gopuras (adorned with stately bas-reliefs) and the Hall of Dancers. This hall contains an elaborate frieze of dancing apsaras and was used, in recent times, to host charity performances to help fund the area's restoration. Within the enclosure there are also a few ponds, libraries and supplementary buildings, most notably, a two-storey pavilion (north of the performance hall) which is believed to have housed the illustrious 'sacred sword'.

The second and inner-most walls run so closely together that it is possible to pass through the following enclosure without realizing you had entered it (this is probably due to an expansion undertaken very early on in the piece to offer additional protection to the shrines).

The inner enclosure is a bewildering array of constructions and shrines. Holes in the inner walls of the central sanctuary of Preah Khan suggest they may once have been decorated with brass plates – an obvious target for looters. One inscription implies that up to 1500 tonnes was used within the edifice. The temple was built to shelter the statue of Jayavarman VII's father, Dharanindravarman II, in the likeness of Bodhisattva Avatokitsvara, which has now probably been smashed. A stela was discovered at the site glorifying the builder, Jayavarman VII and detailing what it took to keep the place ticking over. The inventory mentions that for Preah Khan's upkeep, it required the services of 97,840 men and women, 444 chefs, 4606 footmen and 2298 servants. Preah Khan's inscriptions also refer to the existence of 515 other statues, 102 royal hospitals of the kingdom, 18 major annual festivals and 10 days public holiday a month.

The temple was starting to deteriorate due to some hard-core vegetation growth, but clearing and careful conservation have helped remedy this. During the dry season, the WMF, based in New York, undertakes archaeological site conservation activities here.

Preah Neak Pean, Ta Som and Krol Ko

To the east of Preah Khan and north of the Eastern Baray are two more Buddhist temples built by Jayavarman VII: Preah Neak Pean (the westernmost one) and the ruins of Ta Som. The exquisite temple of Neak Pean was also a fountain, built in the middle of a pool, and representing the paradisiacal Himalayan mountain-lake, Anaavatapta, from Hindu mythology. Two nagas form the edge of the island and their tails join at the back. In modern Khmer it is known as the Prea-sat neac pon – the 'tower of the intertwined dragons'. The colossal image of the horse is the compassionate Bodhisattva who is supposed to save sailors from drowning. The temple pools were an important part of the aesthetic experience of Preah Khan and Neak Pean – the ornate stone carving of both doubly visible by reflection. Such basins within a temple complex were used for religious ritual, while the larger moats and barays were used for practical purposes of bathing, transport and possibly for irrigation.

Located north of the East Baray is the pretty Ta Som. This mini temple has many of the same stylistic and design attributes of Ta Prohm and Banteay Kdei but on a much smaller scale. Unlike the larger constructions of Jayavarman VII, Ta Som's layout is extremely simple – three concentric enclosures and very few annex buildings. The main entrance is to the east, which would indicate some urbanization on the eastern side of the temple. The two inner enclosures are successively offset to the west. The outer (third) enclosure measures 240 m x 200 m and is pierced by two cruciform gopuras; the eastern one is preceded by a small terrace bound by naga balustrades. The current entry is through the western gopura as this faces the road between East Mebon and Preah Neak Pean and cuts across the moat.

Krol Ko sits north of Preah Neak Pean and about 2 km past Ta Som. The tower was built in the late 12th to early 13th century. Referred to as the Oxen Park, Krol Ko is a single, laterite tower which is about 30 m sq. The two frontons represent bodhisattva Lokesvara, whom it is believed the temple is dedicated to.

West of Angkor Thom

Western Baray, West Mebon and Ak Thom

ⓘ *Take Highway 6 west. About 3 km west of the airport turning a track leads north. It is 4 km from Highway 6 to Western Baray. Boats can be hired from the beach on the south of the Western Baray. The boat trip to West Mebon takes about 15 mins.*

The Western Baray was built by Udayaditavarman II possibly to increase the size of the irrigated farmlands. In the centre, on an island, is the West Mebon, where the famous bronze statue of Vishnu was discovered (now in the National Museum at Phnom Penh, see page 57). Today, the eastern end of the Western Baray is dry but the scale remains astonishing, more than 2 km across and 9 km long with an average depth of 7 m. It is believed that the reservoir could hold around 123 million cu l of water.

Just south of the Western Baray is Ak Thom, which marks the site of Jayavarman II's earlier city. It is the oldest surviving temple in the Angkor region and although little remains, it is worth a visit. The central towers are constructed mostly of brick, with some stone features. The bricks were cemented together with a mortar of vegetable sap, palm sugar and termite soil.

Outlying temples

It is possible to visit the other ancient Khmer sites dotted around the main temples at Angkor. Most of these temples can be reached by motos (motorbike taxi) or by car.

The Roluos Group

The Roluos Group, some 16 km southeast of Siem Reap, receives few visitors but is worth visiting if time permits. Jayavarman II built several capitals including one at Roluos, at that time called Hariharalaya. This was the site of his last city and remained the capital during the reigns of his three successors. The three remaining Hindu sanctuaries at Roluos are **Preah Ko**, **Bakong** and **Lolei**. They were finished in 879, 881 and 893 respectively by Indravarman I and his son Yashovarman I and are the best preserved of the early temples.

All three temples are built of brick with sandstone doorways and niches. The use of human figures as sculptural decoration in religious architecture developed around this time – and examples of these guardian spirits can be seen in the niches of Preah Ko and Lolei. Other sculptured figures which appear in the Roluos Group are the crouching lion, the reclining bull (Nandi – Siva's mount) and the naga. The gopura – an arched gateway leading to the temple courtyards – was also a contemporary innovation in Roluos. Libraries – used for the storage of sacred manuscripts – appeared for the first time, as did the concentric enclosures surrounding the central group of towers. Preah Ko and Lolei have characteristics in common: both were dedicated to the parents and grandparents of the kings who built them. Neither temple has a pyramid centre like Bakong as the pyramid temples were built exclusively for kings.

Preah Ko, meaning 'sacred ox', was named after the three statues of Nandi (the mount of the Hindu god, Siva) which stand in front of the temple. Orientated east-west, there is a cluster of six brick towers arranged in two rows on a low brick platform, the steps up to which are guarded by crouching lions while Nandi, looking back, blocks the way. The front row of towers was devoted to Indravarman's male ancestors and the second row to the female. The ancestors were represented in the image of a Hindu god. Only patches remain of the once magnificent stucco relief work, including a remnant of a kala – a motif also found on contemporary monuments in Java.

Indravarman's temple-mountain, **Bakong**, is a royal five-stepped pyramid temple with a sandstone central tower built on a series of successively receding terraces with

surrounding brick towers. It may have been inspired by Borobudur in Java.
Indravarman himself was buried in the temple. Bakong is the largest and most impressive temple in the Roluos Group by a long way. A bridge flanked by a naga balustrade leads over a dry moat to the temple. The central tower was built to replace the original one when the monument was restored in the 12th century and is probably larger than the original. Local children will point out to you that it is just possible to catch a glimpse of Angkor Wat from the top. The Bakong denotes the true beginning of classical Khmer architecture and contained the god-king Siva's lingam. The most important innovations of Indravarman's artists are the free-standing sandstone statues – such as the group of three figures, probably depicting the king with his two wives, who are represented as Siva with Uma, a Hindu goddess and consort of Siva, and Ganga, goddess of the Ganges river. The corners of the pyramid are mounted with statues of elephants and the steps guarded by crouching lions. Nandi watches the steps from below. The heads of all the figures are now missing but the simplicity of the sculpture is nonetheless distinctive; it is a good example of early Khmer craftsmanship. The statues are more static and stockier than the earlier statues of Chenla. There is now a Buddhist monastery in the grounds – originally it was dedicated to Siva.

Lolei was built by Yashovarman I in the middle of Indravarman's baray. The brick towers were dedicated to the king's ancestors, but over the centuries they have largely disintegrated; of the four towers two have partly collapsed. Much of the decoration has worn away but the inscriptions carved in the grey sandstone lintels and door jambs remain in good condition.

Phnom Krom and Phnom Bok

Today, Phnom Krom's main function is as a launching pad for nearby boat trips out to the Tonle Sap's floating villages. But a trip up the mountain is highly worthwhile as at the summit of the isolated, 140-m-high mountain stands a ruined temple. The temple is believed to have been built in the late 9th-10th century, presumably built by Yasovarman I but there are no inscriptions giving exact details. The square laterite enclosure measures 50 m by 50 m and features a gopura in the middle of each outer wall. The enclosure includes 10 halls, now mostly crumbled, that make an almost continuous inner square.

On a lower platform are three stone sanctuary towers, aligned north to south, dedicated to Shiva, Vishnu and Brahma. The temple affords amazing 360 degree panoramic views, which extend across to the Western Baray and Tonlé Sap's floating villages. Phnom Krom is 12 km southwest of Siem Reap.

Phnom Bok is the brother temple to Phnom Krom and features almost an identical layout to Phnom Krom. The carvings and decorative features here remain in far better condition due to their more protected location and relatively recent discovery. Located approximately 15 km northwest of Siem Riep, the temple sits at the pinnacle of the 235-m-high hill. It is the most elevated of the three temple peaks of Angkor; with Phnom Krom at 137 m and Phnom Bakheng at only 60 m (ironically the hill that is climbed the most by tourists is by far the smallest). All three temples were built by Yasovarman I; Phnom Bakheng was the first.

The ascent of Phnom Bok is a difficult climb but well rewarded, as the 20-30 minute hike up the southern slope reveals a limitless horizon, broken only to the north by the view of Phnom Kulen.

Banteay Srei ('Citadel of Women')

ⓘ *It is 25 km from Ta Prohm along a decent road and takes about 35-40 mins by motorbike. The way is well signed. There are lots of food and drink stalls.*

Banteay Srei, to the north of Angkor, is well worth the trip. This remarkable temple was built by the Brahmin tutor to King Rajendravarman, Yajnavaraha, grandson of Harshavarman (900-923), and founded in 967. The temple wasn't discovered by geographic officer Captain Marec until 1914, as its distance from Angkor and concealment by overgrown jungle meant it wasn't picked up in earlier expeditions. At the time of discovery, the site was so badly damaged that mounds of dirt had covered the main structure and foliage had bore its way through much of the site. It wasn't until 1924 that the site was cleared and by 1936 the site had been restored.

Banteay Srei translates as 'Citadel of Women', a title bestowed upon it in relatively recent years due to the intricate apsara carvings that adorn the interior. While many of Angkor's temples are impressive because of their sheer size, Banteay Srei stands out in the quality of craftsmanship. The temple is considered by many historians, to be the highest achievement of art from the Angkor period. Thierry Zeephir, a pre-eminent art historian, believes Banteay Srei constitutes one of the major contributions of Khmer art to the artistic heritage of the world. The explicit preservation of this temple reveals covered terraces, of which only the columns remain, which once lined both sides of the primary entrance. In keeping with tradition, a long causeway leads into the temple, across a moat, on the eastern side.

The main walls, entry pavilions and libraries have been constructed from laterite and the carvings from pink sandstone.The layout was inspired by Prasat Thom at Koh Ker. Three beautifully carved tower-shrines stand side by side on a low terrace in the middle of a quadrangle, with a pair of libraries on either side enclosed by a wall. Two of the shrines, the southern one and the central one, were dedicated to Siva and the northern one to Vishnu; both had libraries close by, with carvings depicting appropriate legends. The whole temple is dedicated to Brahma. Many believe this temple is closest to its Indian counterparts than any other in the vicinity. Beyond this inner group of buildings was a monastery surrounded by a moat.

In 1923 controversy surrounded the temple when it was targeted by famous French author André Lalraux for a major looting expedition. The author of *The Royal Way* (1930) shamefully attempted to pillage Banteay Srei of its treasures, having read that the temple not only contained a series of brilliant carvings in excellent condition but that was it was also unexcavated (which he took to mean abandoned). He travelled to Angkor and proceeded to cut out one tonne of the finest statues and bas-reliefs. Fortunately, he was arrested trying to leave the country with the treasures and was sentenced to three years in prison (a term that he did not serve). One of the best known statues from this site is a sculpture of Siva sitting down and holding his wife, Uma, on his knee: it is in the National Museum of Arts in Phnom Penh.

Having been built by a Brahmin priest, the temple was never intended for use by a king, which goes some way towards explaining its small size – you have to duck to get through the doorways to the sanctuary towers. Perhaps because of its modest scale Banteay Srei contains some of the finest examples of Khmer sculpture. Finely

Banteay Srei

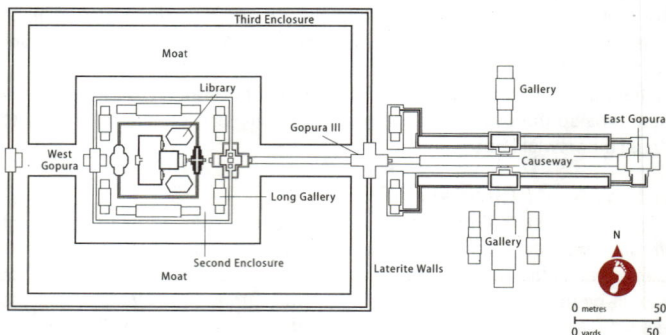

carved and rare pink sandstone replaces the plaster-coated carved brick decoration,
typical of earlier temples. All the buildings are covered in carvings: the jambs, the
lintels, the balustered windows. Banteay Srei's ornamentation is exceptional – its
roofs, pediments and lintels are magnificently carved with tongues of flame,
serpents' tails, gods, demons and floral garlands.

Phnom Kulen

*ⓘ It takes a good 2 hrs by moto to get there from Siem Reap; it is more than 1 hr
beyond Banteay Srei. At the height of the wet season the road will be virtually
impassable. Entering the park costs foreigners an extra US$20 (or US$12 from the
Angkor City Hotel beforehand) plus a fee for a motorbike or car (US$25-30) and it is not
covered by the Angkor ticket scheme.*

Phnom Kulen – or Mount Mohendrapura – 28 km northeast of Angkor and 48 km from
Siem Reap, is a sandstone plateau considered sacred by the Khmers. The site is the
mythical birthplace of the Cambodian Kingdom. At the hill's summit is the largest
reclining Buddha in the country – over 900 years old. Jayavarman II built his first brick
pyramid temple-mountain – to house the sacred golden Siva-lingam – here at the
beginning of the ninth century. Today the temple is only visible in fragments although,
over a millennium later, the phallic emblem is said to be still on display in the Phnom
Kulen complex. The temple is best known for its carved lintels and bas-reliefs. There
are also some remains of ninth-century Cham temples in the area. Today the hill is
clothed in forest and the nights here are cold and the days fresh and invigorating. As
with most of the other sites on Phnom Kulen it is necessary to have a guide to point
them out as they are small and well concealed in the forest. Khmer visitors to the area
seem only to be interested only in the reclining Buddha.

Phnom Kbal Spean

*ⓘ Kbal Spean is 50 km northeast of Siem Reap and should cost no more than US$10
by moto (last entry 1530). Upon arrival, follow the path for 1.5 km for about 40 mins up
the narrow path. The ideal time to visit is at the end of the wet season, when the fast
flowing water gushes around, but doesn't submerge most of the carvings.*

The intriguing spot of Kbal Spean is rich in both style and purpose. The name of the
river, and the mountain from which it springs, translates loosely to Headwater Bridge,
referring to a natural sandstone arch, marking the beginning of the 150 m of carvings,
upstream from the bridge. It is the downstream part, from the bridge to the waterfall,
that gives the river its Sanskrit name Sahasralinga, 'River of a Thousand Lingas'.

   Phnom Kbal Spean is regarded as highly auspicious so it is not surprising that the
remarkable 11th-century riverbed rock carvings display a gallery of gods and celestial
beings including Vishnu reclining on the serpent Anata, Shiva, Brahman, Lakshmi,
Rama and Hanuman. Some of the carvings are submerged by the river, while a few
have been hacked away by unscrupulous looters. The visibility of all carvings is really
dependent on the time of year.

   Downstream from the carvings are thousands of sculpted lingas (phallic images)
in the river bed and a large underwater representation of a yoni (womb). The lingas
stretch approximately 6 m downstream from the bridge, to 30 m upstream. Carved
from the coarse sandstone from the riverbed, some protrude as much as 10 cm from
the bed; others have been worn away by the flowing water. Finnish journalist Teppo
Turkki, who visited the site for the *Phnom Penh Post*, wrote at the beginning of 1995:
"The lingas, some of which date back to the ninth century, are about 25 cm square
and 10 cm deep and lined in a perfect grid pattern. The river runs over them, covering
them with about 5 cm of pristine water." He continued: "The holy objects are
designed to create a 'power path' for the Khmer kings." More likely the water which
would have fed Angkor was being sanctified before it entered the holy arena of the
temples. Beyond the series of carvings is a 15-m waterfall to a crystal clear pool.

Chau Srei Vibol

ⓘ *Turn east off the road from between Phnom Bok and Roluos, about 5 km south of Phnom Bok. Follow the road over several old bridges until you reach the compound of Wat Trach and the laterite wall at the bottom of the hill.*

The remote, 11th-century hilltop temple of Chau Srei Vibol is now in ruins but at least three major sandstone structures, a sanctuary and two libraries with decorative carvings, are readily identifiable. A couple of broken lions flank the steep eastern entrance gate.

Whilst viewing this small ruined temple in near silence it's worth reflecting on the building boom that occurred under the reign of Suryavarman I, a highpoint in the Khmer Empire. Suryavarman ruled a huge empire, covering much of southern Vietnam, Thailand, Laos and the Malay Peninsula and this was reflected in his large, grand, bustling city.

Beng Mealea

ⓘ *Beng Mealea is a full day trip from Siem Reap. There is an entrance fee of US$20.*
Beng Mealea, a huge 12th-century temple complex, 40 km east of the Bayon and about 7 km southeast of Phnom Kulen, is completely ruined even though it was built at about the same time as Angkor Wat. Its dimensions are similar (Beng Mealea is a bit smaller), but Beng Mealea has no central pyramid. It is widely believed that this temple acted as the 'blueprint' for Angkor. Most of the Buddhist temples built under Jayavarman VII – Preah Khan, Banteay Kdei, Ta Som and Ta Prohm – were modelled after this complex.

Further temples of interest include Banteay Chhmar, see page 152, Sambor Pre Kup, see page 168, Preah Khan, see page 170 and Koh Ker, see page 170, Preah Vihear, see page 171.

Anlong Veng and around 🚌🚐🚉🚌🚍 ›› *pages 130-140.*

From the outset Anlong Veng seems like your average Cambodian dusty, one street, frontier town with a towering mountain range in its midst. But the façade is deceiving. This small, unassuming town was once home to some of the country's most dangerous residents including the evil mastermind, Pol Pot, his right-hand man, Son Sen and Ta Mok, otherwise known as the "Butcher". Anlong Veng was the last Khmer Rouge stronghold and is now very safe, even though many of its citizens are families of the Khmer Rouge.

Sights

There aren't many 'tourist' sites per se but the town will appeal to those interested in Khmer Rouge history as it contains a number of sites decisive to the movement's downfall. These days the sleepy town gets a pretty bad rap by locals and expats alike but does have its merits: the people, for the most part, are tremendously friendly and it's surrounded by beautiful countryside and very hospitable rural villages. The town is a good launching pad for starting a trip to Preah Vihear Temple, see page 171, as the road between Anlong Veng to the temple is in relatively good shape (in the dry season).

The most popular destination around Anlong Veng is **Oh Chit**, Ta Mok's hauntingly beautiful lake, which was initially built as a moat for his house. A maniacal dam builder, Ta Mok (aka Brother Number Three) flooded much of the area while trying to develop the lake. Today the dead tree stumps, tranquil waters, grassy knolls and beautiful patches of lotus flower actually create a very beautiful but eerie atmosphere. On any given day packs of small kids swim in the lake while beneath the surface it is believed that the grisly remains of hundreds of people lie. Here tourists can visit **Ta Mok's Villa**, ⓘ *Admission $US1 which includes entrance to Pol Pot's* *residence*, the Khmer Rouge's last official headquarters after Pol Pot was overthrown. It was also the place where Pol Pot was tried by his own men, led by the one-legged Ta Mok. The villa is quite barren these days, looted by government officials, but still bares a few horrific reminders of the old days, including animal-like cages where prisoners were held captive. Inside the building there is a map marking Khmer Rouge territory and a few utopian paintings of Cambodia through the eyes of the regime. Across the lake is **Pol Pot's residence** (now reduced to a bathroom) accessed by a turn off on the right further from town on the same road heading north, where he was kept under house arrest under Ta Mok's direction. Some of the people working at the site are former Khmer Rouge, employed by Ta Mok. The villa and lake can be accessed by following the main road through town and turning right at the signpost.

8 km along Anlong Veng's main street is the bottom of **Dongrek mountain range**. The **Dongrek Enscarpment** is a site in itself, with spectacular, panoramic views from the cliffs over to Thailand. Pity about its history. Half way up the mountain is an old **Khmer Rouge checkpoint**. Here there are several life-size sculptures of Khmer Rouge troops (with AK47S, kramas and grenades). Considering that the Khmer Rouge were not purveyors of artistic culture these sculptures, are particularly detailed (and headless since the government decapitated them). As you move further along this road a small military house marks a path to **Pol Pot's cremation site**, where in 1998 he was burnt on a pyre of rubbish. The gravesite is now barricaded off with jungle swamping the area. Try and stay to the marked path as some of this area remains mined. Strangely enough some Khmers visit the site in the belief that winning lottery numbers will be bestowed upon them by greater forces. No doubt there will be a government official on site procuring some sort of entrance fee. Further along in the mountains, in a heavily mined area, are the former homes of Pol Pot, Son Sen and Ta Mok, all in close proximity to the border in case a quick get-away was required. It is probably no coincidence that the modern day houses of Nuon Chea and Khieu Samphan, who still had not been tried at the time of writing, also sit on the Thai border, near Pailin.

Siem Reap and around ⬛🏍️👤🏦⭕🔺⬛◐ ↠ *pages 130-140.*

The nearest town to Angkor, Siem Reap is seldom considered as anything other than a service centre and it is true that without the temples few people would ever find themselves here. But visitors exhausted by the temple trail might care to while away a morning or afternoon in Siem Reap itself. The town has smartened itself up quite substantially in the past couple of years and, with the blossoming of hotels, restaurants and bars, it is now a pleasant place in its own right. Hotel building has pretty much kept pace with tourist arrivals so the town is a hive of activity.

The town is laid out formally and because there is ample land on which to build, it is pleasantly airy. Buildings are often set in large overgrown grounds resembling mini wildernesses. The current level of unprecedented growth and development is set to continue, so this may not be the case five years from now. At the time of publication many people were being uprooted from their homes as greedy government officials, aware of the exponential increase in land value, were playing the game – the Great Land Grab (a big issue in modern day Cambodia).

The town proper has a romantic, French colonial feel, sprawling across a 10 km radius and carved apart by a pleasant lamp-lit river. The most popular tourist areas are around the Old Market (Psah Chas), the Wat Bo part of town and along the Airport Road.

The Old Market area is the most touristed part of the town with a gamut of restaurants, bars and boutiques catering for a wide range of tastes. Staying around here is recommended for independent travellers and those staying more than two or three days. A sprinkling of guesthouses are here but a much greater selection is offered just across the river in the Wat Bo area. The area has taken the on the name of

❖ The end of the line

In 1996 an internal conflict between high-ranking Khmer Rouge officials marked the disintegration of Pailin, the principal Khmer Rouge outpost. The conflict saw most of the movements' high-ranking officials relocate to Anlong Veng. Times were tough in the mountains without the riches (gems and timber) found in Pailin to bankroll the militia. Paranoia swelled.

Pol Pot ordered his cronies, Ta Mok, Son Sen and Nuon Chea to visit Pailin and settle the dispute. Their mission was a failure and Pol Pot, furious and suspicious that they were collaborating with the government, ordered the three of them to house arrest.

The Cambodian Government, aware of the major chasm, struck a deal with those left in Pailin, offering amnesty to those who defected. On November 6, 15,000 Khmer Rouge soldiers defected, including Ieng Sary, former Khmer Rouge Deputy Premier.

On June 9 1997, Pol Pot is believed to have sent his commander So Sarouen to request Son Sen's attendance at a meeting. But the meeting was never to be. Believing that Son Sen and his wife were conspiring against him through collusion with Hun Sen, he ordered their brutal execution. Son Sen, his wife Yun Yat, and nine of their children and grand-children were shot. Troops then crushed their skulls with a pickup.

Fearing the same fate, Ta Mok launched an anti-Pol Pot propaganda campaign generating the necessary

Siem Reap town's oldest pagoda, Wat Bo (built in the 18th century), which can be found at the end of Achamean Street.

The Airport Road area has been earmarked for mass tourism and wields countless cumbersome hotels and chains, geared towards package tourists, with packaged meals and packaged tours to go. You can still go into town from these hotels but it is a fair hike, especially at night. Still, this area holds appeal for those that want to fly in and out of Siem Reap and visit Angkor in the most simplistic, efficient fashion available.

A fair proportion of the buildings, particularly on the road south to Tonlé Sap, are built of wood and raised off the ground on stilts. The distance from Siem Reap to the water's edge fluctuates by many kilometres; the highest water levels occur towards the end of October at the end of the wet season. The name Siem Riep, as locals like to remind visitors, means Siam Defeated, marking a 16th-century victory against the Thais, one in a series of ping pong battles between the two neighbours.

Ins and outs

See under the Angkor section, page 86.

Sights

While Siem Reap is a pleasant enough place to hang out for a few hours, the main places of interest lie outside the town. Some 4 km south of Angkor Wat is the small **mine museum** ⓘ *0700-1800. Donations accepted. Follow the Angkor Wat road to the Krousar Thmey sign, after 700 m, turn left and follow the road to the museum*. Housed across several rundown shelters, the museum exhibits a vast collection of defused mines, bombs, ammunition and other ordinance. Former deminer, Mr Akira, commendably opened the mine museum in 1999 to create awareness about the insidious effect of mines and help fund his work with landmine victims. When on site, he goes to great lengths to explain the carnage caused by each type of mine (such as what part of the body they are aimed at) and often speaks openly of his experiences as a child conscript during the Khmer Rouge period and latter Vietnamese occupation.

military support to chase and capture Pol Pot in the surrounding jungle. In July 1997, Ta Mok put Pol Pot on trial at the local "People's Court", charging him with the murder of Son Sen and the attempted murder and detention of Ta Mok and Nuon Chea. Having ousted Pol Pot, Ta Mok became the new leader of the Khmer Rouge and ordered Pol Pot to be under house arrest. On April 15 1998 it was said that Pol Pot, aged 73, died of a heart attack and was cremated shortly after on a pyre of rubbish and tyres. Rumours surrounding his death are rife: some believe that he killed himself with malaria pills and tranquilizers after learning he was to be turned over to the US. Others suggest that Ta Mok had Pol Pot executed to protect himself. Locals around Along Veng suggest it is most likely that someone switched off his oxygen (presumably Ta Mok) or had been replacing his critical medication with placebos. When asked whether Pol Pot had been murdered, Mei Meakk, Pailin's cabinet chief and confidante said to the *Cambodia Daily*: "Pol Pot was cremated on a bed of tires. What do you think?"

Ta Mok's leadership was short-lived. He was captured by the government forces in 1998 but fled into the jungle. In 1999 he was recaptured and is now in jail in Phnom Penh. Anlong Veng proved to be, quite literally, the end of the line for Pol Pot and marked an important point in the demise of the Khmer Rouge.

On the Airport Road, near the airport, is the **War Museum** ⓘ *daily 0700-1700, US$3*. This government-run museum houses a collection of old tanks, guns and other war paraphernalia collected from the provinces. It's not at interesting as the mine museum but is worth a trip for those interested in war artillery and machinery.

Cambodian Cultural Village ⓘ *located 6 km from Siem Reap on the Airport Road, T063-963836, US$12*, is a park featuring smaller renditions of Cambodian architectural feats and models of the various ethnic housing, slightly on the kitsch side. Traditional dancing and wedding shows. Good if you have children.

Tonlé Sap

The Tonlé Sap, the Great Lake of Cambodia, is one of the natural wonders of Asia. Uniquely, the 100-km-long Tonlé Sap River, a tributary of the mighty Mekong, reverses its flow and runs uphill for six months of the year. Spring meltwaters in the Himalayas, coupled with seasonal rains, increase the flow of the Mekong to such an extent that some is deflected up the Tonlé Sap River. From June the lake begins to expand until, by the end of the rainy season, it has increased in area four-fold and in depth by up to 12 m. At its greatest extent, the lake occupies nearly a seventh of Cambodia's land area, around 1.5 million ha, making it the largest freshwater lake in Southeast Asia. From November, with the onset of the dry season, the Tonlé Sap River reverses its flow once more and begins to act like a regular tributary – flowing downhill into the Mekong. By February the lake has shrunk to a fraction of its wet season size and covers 'just' 300,000 ha.

This pattern of expansion and contraction has three major benefits. First, it helps to restrict flooding in the Mekong Delta in Vietnam. Second, it forms the basis for a substantial part of Cambodia's rice production. And third, it supports perhaps the world's largest and richest inland fisheries, yielding as much as 10 tonnes of fish per sq km. It is thought that four million people depend on the lake for their subsistence and three out of every 4 kg of fish caught in the country come from the Tonlé Sap.

Because of the dramatic changes in the size of the lake some of the fish, such as the 'walking catfish', have evolved to survive several hours out of water, flopping overland to find deeper pools. These *hok yue* – or elephant fish – are renowned as a delicacy well beyond Cambodia's borders. Large-scale commercial fishing is a major occupation during February to May and the fishing grounds are divided into plots and leased out. Recent lack of dredging means the lake is not as deep as it was and fish are tending to swim downstream into the Mekong and Tonlé Sap rivers. The annual flooding covers the surrounding countryside with a layer of moist, nutrient-rich mud which is ideal for rice growing. Farmers grow a deep water rice, long-stalked and fast growing – it grows with the rising lake to keep the grain above water and the stem can be up to 6 m long. The lake also houses people, and communities live in floating villages close to the shore.

Chong Khneas ⓘ *boats can be hired and trips to floating villages are offered; expect to pay about US$5-10 per hr; take a moto from Siem Reap (US$2); boats from Phnom Penh berth at Chong Khneas*, is 10 km south of Siem Reap. This floating settlement consists of some permanent buildings but is a largely floating settlement. The majority of the population live in houseboats and most services – including police, health, international aid agencies, retail and karaoke – are all provided on water. A trip around the village is testimony to the ingenuity of people living on this waterway with small kids paddling little tubs to each others houses.

Chong Khneas gets hundreds of visitors everyday. For a more authentic, less touristy village visitors should head out a bit further, 25 km east, to the village of **Kompong Phluk**. ⓘ *Costs to get to these villages are pretty high (up to US$50 per person) but are brought down if more passengers on the boat. See Terre Cambodge or Two Dragon's Guesthouse under Activities and tours to organize a tour.*

Also on the Tonlé Sap Lake is the **Prek Toal Biosphere** – a bird sanctuary which is home to 120 bird species, including cranes, stalks and pelicans. Boats can be organized from Chong Kneas to visit the Prek Toal Environment Office, ⓘ *US$30 return, 1 hr. From here you can arrange a guide and another boat for around US$20.* Terre Cambodia runs boat tours www.terrecambodge.com as does Osmose T012-832812, osmose@bigpond.com.kh, *upwards of US$80. There is basic accommodation at the Environment Office.*

● Sleeping

Anlong Veng *p126*
There is quite a lot of accommodation located on the main road in town.
D Monorom Villa, T012- 870840, on the main road towards the lake. The best accommodation in town by a very, very long way. Rooms are very clean and include a/c, fan, attached bathroom and free water and a pineapple! Don't be too surprised if the friendly owner asks you to join him and his family for dinner. Recommended.
E Mohaleap Guesthouse, on the main road before the roundabout. Pretty basic budget accommodation, with fan and toilet.
E Prean Chan Mean Rit Guesthouse, T011-205800, located past Monorom Villa, along the main road towards the lake. Very basic, spartan rooms well below the town's

average. Only the 'luxury rooms' have squat toilet and fan attached.
E-F Dorngrek Guesthouse, T011-679644. With rooms starting at US$2.50 it is not too bad in comparative terms. Rooms are a little pokey but are clean and have a fan. Rooms with attached western bathroom are also available.
E-F Sokhuntea Guesthouse, T011-205476. Wooden guesthouse with reasonable sized rooms and attached bathrooms. The psychedelic linoleum is a bit of an eye-sore and the service is a bit lack lustre but other than this the place is quite reasonable.

Siem Reap *p127, maps p132 and p134*
Hotel accommodation in Siem Reap has expanded dramatically in the past couple of

years reflecting the surge in demand triggered by the removal of the Khmer Rouge and the establishment of direct flights from Bangkok, Hanoi, Ho Chi Minh City, KL, Singapore and Vientiane.

At the time of writing there were 8000 rooms at over 200 establishments in the town and a few thousand more on their way.

Accommodation is spread across 3 main areas – east of the river in Wat Bo Village (cheaper accommodation), on the airport road (luxury hotels and others that cater to package tourists), and around the Old Market (the main bar and restaurant area). There are also quite a few hotels on the road to Angkor.

There are several well-run guesthouses and small hotels which for comfort and service match and sometimes surpass much pricier hotels. The words 'royal', 'palace' and 'Angkor' feature indiscriminately in their names. Note that although a few more streets in Siem Reap now have names, addresses are still fairly uncommon.

When arriving in Siem Reap, many motos/drivers will get a commission from the hotel/guesthouse they take you to. So don't necessarily believe that their recommendation is 'the best place in town' – similarly, if you request a particular hotel and are told that 'it is closed' or 'full' by your driver, don't take this as gospel.

When booking a high-end hotel in Siem Reap you can usually get a cheaper rate over the net with one of the many internet hotel agencies. If you are staying in a cheaper guesthouse, you might be able to get a cheaper price in person (note that arriving late at night decreases any bargaining power by about 200%.

Town centre

L Raffles Grand Hotel d'Angkor, 1 Charles de Gaulle Blvd, T063-963888, www.raffles.com. Magnificent from the outside, it seems churlish to carp about what is easily Siem Reap's best and oldest (1930) hotel but unlike its sister in Phnom Penh (Le Royal) this one fails to generate ambience, the rooms are sterile and the design of the huge new wings is uninspired (unforgivable in Angkor). However, it does have all the mod-cons, including sauna, tennis, health and beauty spa, lap pool, gym, 8 restaurants and bars, nightly traditional performances, landscaped

gardens, 24-hr valet service and in-house movie channels. Considering its astronomical rates guests have every right to feel disappointed.

L Sofitel Royal Angkor, Charles de Gaulle Blvd, T063-964600, www.sofitel. Com. A large 238-room hotel in a garden-like setting, a large attractive swimming pool and 5 restaurants and bars including Asian, International and French restaurants. Other perks include an open-air jacuzzi, health and beauty spa. Rates include buffet breakfast and dinner. Not as intimate as some of the other hotels in this price range.

L Victoria Angkor Hotel, Route 6, T063-760428, www.victoriahotels-asia.com. Perfection. A beautiful hotel with that 1930s, east meets west style that exemplifies the French tradition of Art de Vivre. The superb facilities make you feel like you are staying in another era – each room is beautifully decorated with local fabrics and fantastic furniture (some Japanese style others more Indian). Swimming pool, open-air salas, jacuzzi and spa. It's the small touches and attention to detail that stands this hotel apart from the rest. Highly recommended.

L-AL Angkor Village Resort, T023-963561, www.angkor village.com. Opened in 2004, the resort contains 40 rooms set in Balinese-style surroundings. The accommodation pays homage to traditional Asian architecture with lovely fittings, especially in the bathrooms. Traditional massage services, 2 restaurants, theatre shows and lovel pool. Elephant, boat and helicopter rides can be arranged. Recommended.

L-AL La Residence D Angkor Hotel, River Rd, T023-963390, www.pansea-angkor.com. Part of the Pansea luxury hotel group, this is a hotel to aspire to. With its beautifully laid out rooms all lavishly furnished with marble and hardwoods this reassuringly expensive hotel could persuade the most principled among us to sell their souls to the corporate beast. Each room has a huge, free-form bath tub – which is the perfect end to a day touring the temples. The pool is lined with handmade tiles in a variety of green hues and, like the rest of the hotel, is in true Angkor style. This and the Victoria hotel go head-to-head as offering the best room in town.

Siem Reap

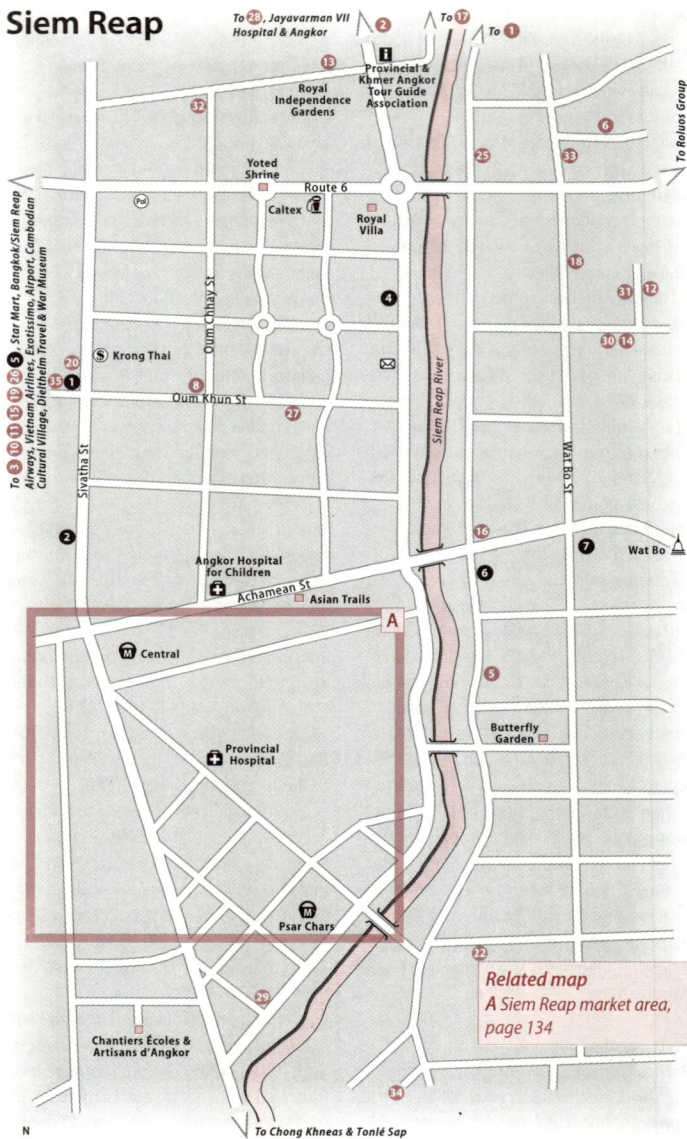

To **28**, Jayavarman VII Hospital & Angkor

To **17**

To **1**

Provincial & Khmer Angkor Tour Guide Association

Royal Independence Gardens

Yoted Shrine

Route 6

Caltex

Royal Villa

Krong Thai

Oum Khun St

Oum Chhay St

Siem Reap River

To Roluos Group

To **9 10 11 15 19 3 5** Star Mart, Bangkok/Siem Reap Airways, Vietnam Airlines, Exotissimo, Airport, Cambodian Cultural Village, Dieitheim Travel & War Museum

Sivatha St

Angkor Hospital for Children

Achamean St

Asian Trails

Wat Bo St

Wat Bo

A

Central

Provincial Hospital

Butterfly Garden

Psar Chars

Related map
A Siem Reap market area, page 134

Chantiers Écoles & Artisans d'Angkor

To Chong Khneas & Tonlé Sap

N

Not to scale

Sleeping
Angkoriana **2**
Angkor Village Resort **1**
Apsara Angkor **3**
Bopha **5**
Borann **6**
Casa Angkor **8**
Earthwalkers **10**

Empress Angkor **11**
European Guesthouse **12**
Golden Banana B&B **34**
Green Garden Home
 Guesthouse **35**
Home Sweet Home **14**
Jasmine Lodge **15**
La Residence D'Angkor **16**
La Villa Loti **17**
Mahogany Guesthouse **18**
Monoreach **19**
Neak Pean **20**

Passaggio **22**
Raffles Grand d'Angkor **13**
Rosa Guesthouse **35**
Rosy Guesthouse **25**
Secrets of Elephants
 Guesthouse **26**
Shinta Mani **27**
Sofitel Royal Angkor **28**
Sweet Dreams
 Guesthouse **31**
Ta Prohm **29**
Two Dragons Guesthouse **30**

Victoria Angkor **32**
Yaklom Angkor
 Lodge **33**

Eating
Abacus **1**
Barrio **2**
FCC **4**
Madame Butterfly **5**
Moloppor **6**
Viroth's **7**

L-AL Shinta Mani, Oum Khum and 14th St, T063- 761998, www.shintamani. com. This 18-room boutique, luxury hotel is wonderful in everyway: the design, the amenities, the food and the service. The hotel also offers a beautiful pool, library and has mountain bikes available. Provides vocational training to underprivileged youth. Listed in *Gourmet Magazine* as one of the 'Worlds Best Hotel Dining Rooms'. Recommended.

A-B Angkoriana Hotel, 297 Phum Boeng Daun Pa, Khum (the main road to the temples), T023-760274, www.angkorianahotel.com. Simply furnished rooms with a/c, mini-bar, cable TV etc. Renovated restaurant serving Khmer and French cuisine. Swimming pool.

A-B Casa Angkor, corner of Oum Chhay St and Oum Khun St, T023-963658, www.casaangkorhotel.com. This is a good looking, pleasant and well-managed 21-room hotel in a central location. 3 classes of room, all a decent size, well appointed and with cool wooden floors. Friendly reception and efficient staff. Restaurant, beer garden and reading room. Like all Siem Reap hotels this one offers the full range of tour services, airport run etc.

A-B Passaggio, near the Old Market, T023-964732, www.passaggio-hotel.com. 15 double and 2 family rooms, spacious, a/c, minibar and cable TV, internet, laundry service, bar and restaurant, outdoor terrace. Clean.

B Borann, T023-964740, borann@bigpond.com.kh. This is an attractive hotel in a delightful garden with a swimming pool. A short way down a quiet lane it is secluded and private. 5 small buildings each contain 4 comfortable rooms with terracotta floors and a lot of wood. Some rooms have a/c, some fan only: price varies accordingly. Restaurant.

B La Villa Loti (also known as Coconut House), 105 River Rd, T012-888403, resinf@ lavillaloti.com. Fantastic French-run guesthouse with 8 rooms in a big, wooden house. Good for lying back in a deckchair amongst its tropical gardens after a tiring day at the temples. Internet, massage, bicycles.

B Yaklom Angkor Lodge, Wat Bo St, T012-983510, www.yaklom.com. Perfectly nice but very simple, 10 small bungalows built slightly too close together. An attractive site and friendly, competent staff who speak good English but official rates are too high. Try to negotiate a discount. Breakfast and airport transfer included. Sawasdee Thai restaurant.

B-C Bopha, on the east side of the river, slightly up from **Passagio**, T023-964928, bopharesa@everyday.com.kh. Stunning hotel. Good rooms with all the amenities, decorated with local furniture and fabrics. Brilliant Thai-Khmer restaurant. Highly recommended.

C Home Sweet Home, T023-963245, sweethome@ camintel.com. Popular guesthouse and a favourite of the motos (who get a kickback). Regardless, it is still quite good accommodation. Good clean rooms, some with TV and a/c.

C-D Golden Banana Bed and Breakfast, Wat Damnak Area (past **Martini Bar**), T012- 885366, info@golden- banana.com. Good, clean rooms and decent restaurant.

C-D Two Dragons Guest- house, Wat Bo Village, T012-868551. Really nice, clean rooms with beautiful photographs decorating them. Good little Thai restaurant. Gordon, the owner of this place, is one of the well-briefed guys in Siem Reap and runs the www.talesofasia.com website. He can organize a whole range of unique and exciting tours in the area. Although it is slightly more expensive than surrounding hotels, you make up the value in all the extras, advice and other savings that comes from their expertise.

D Green Garden Home Guesthouse, down a small lane off Sivatha St, T012- 693393. Price varies according to facilities required. A/c or fan, hot water or cold water etc, cable TV. Garden not as great as their PR would suggest.

D Rosy Guesthouse, T063- 965059, east side of river before **Noria**. Good, clean rooms with bathroom. Very popular.

D-E European Guesthouse, T012-890917, jhoekstra@ angkorhospital.com. 12 fan rooms in a quiet lane off Wat Bo St occupied by 3 guesthouses.

D-E Sweet Dreams Guesthouse, off Wat Bo St, T012-783013, homesweet home@everyday.com.kh. Clean and well kept rooms in this small guesthouse in a quiet cul-de-sac. A favourite of the motos who obviously get a commission for bringing you here. Restaurant.

E Mahogany Guesthouse, Wat Bo St, T023-963417/ 012-768944, proeun@big pond.com.kh. Fan and now some a/c. An attractive and popular guesthouse, lovely wooden floor upstairs (try to avoid staying down- stairs), coffee making facilities and a friendly crowd of guests.

Around the Old Market (Psar Chars)

A Ta Prohm, T063-380117, www.angkorhotels.org/taprohm/EN/8.html. 95 large rooms in a well- kept and long-established property overlooking the river. Bathroom with bath tub. It is a touch overpriced but fair by Siem Reap standards. From the outside it can be difficult to tell whether the hotel is actually open but it is. Restaurant and tourist services.

A-B Molly Malone's, across from **Red Piano** in Old Market area, T023-963533. Fantastic rooms with 4-poster beds and good clean bathrooms. Irish pub downstairs. Lovely owners. Recommended.

A-B Neak Pean, 53 Sivatha St, T063-924429, neakpean @camintel.com. 100 rooms, many in large wooden bungalows behind the main building. Swimming pool and garden. Large restaurant.

C-D Red Piano, off Sivatha St (approximately 250 m from the restaurant), T012-854150, www.redpianocambodia.com. 15, clean a/c rooms with en suite bathroom.

D-E Ivy (across from the Old Market), T012-800860. Reasonable rooms above the restaurant and bar.

D-F Orchidae Guesthouse, T012-939964, 012939965@ mobitel.com.kh. A few houses down from the **Naga Guesthouse** and much better. Hammocks, restaurant and decent sized, clean rooms. With shower or shared facilities. Recommended.

D-F Rosa Guesthouse, down a small lane off Sivatha St (next to **Green Garden Home**), T012- 693393. Dilapadated building, average rooms.

Siem Reap market area

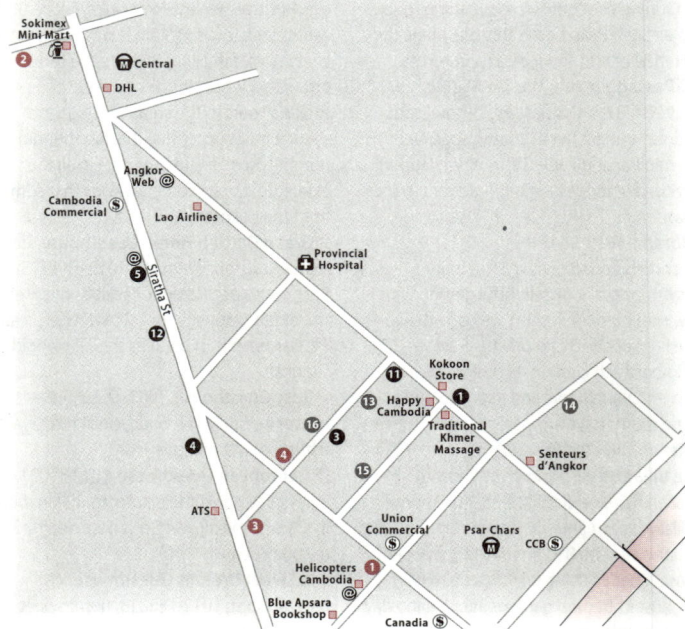

Sleeping	Red Piano 4	Carnets d'Asie 4	Bars & clubs
Ivy 1		Dead Fish Tower 5	Angkor What? 13
Molly Malone's 3	Eating	Soup Dragon 11	Laundry 14
Orchidae	Blue Pumpkin 1	Tell 12	Linga 15
Guesthouse 2	Buddha Lounge 3		Temple Bar 16

N
Not to scale

On the Airport Road

L-AL Apsara Angkor Hotel, Route 6, (between the airport and town), T063- 964999, www.apsara angkor.com. Pretty standard hotel for the money they are asking. Well-appointed rooms with all amenities but they are rather kitsch. Facilities include gym, internet, swimming pool. Visa/MC/AMEX.

L-AL Empress Angkor, Airport Rd, opposite cultural village, T063-963999, www.empressangkor.com. One of the newest luxury hotels in town. The wooden interior provides a much more pleasant interior than what one would presume from looking at the exterior. 207 cosy guestrooms with all the usual inclusions, plus cable TV and balcony. Hotel facilities include restaurant (international and local cuisine), bar, massage, gym, swimming pool, jacuzzi spa and sauna. Visa/AMEX/ MasterCard/JCB.

AL Monoreach Hotel, Airport Rd, T063-760182, www.monoreach.com.kh. Newly established international hotel, with 110 rooms and suites. Has a real Chinese-hotel feel to it. The room amenities include a/c, cable TV, IDD, minibar, hot water, bath tub. Onsite is a swimming pool, gym and restaurant. Rooms on average are about US$70 a night but there are a few more expensive ones that have pushed this hotel up into this category.

B Secrets of Elephants Guesthouse, Airport Rd, T016-901901, info@ angkortravel.com. Traditional wooden Khmer house, with just 8 rooms. French-run but English spoken. The garden is a mini jungle and concealed within are a small pavilion and bosky retreats. The house is beautifully furnished with antiques, silks, ornaments and hangings. There are secluded sitting areas. All rooms have their own private bathroom but not necessarily en suite. Breakfast included and other meals prepared to order. Some a/c rooms.

D-E Earthwalkers, just off the Airport Rd, T012-967901, mail@earthwalkers.no. Popular European-run budget guesthouse. Good gardens and pool table. Bit far out of town.

D-F Jasmine Lodge, Airport Rd, T012-784980, jasminelodge@ camnet.com.kh. Good budget accommodation, clean rooms (the outside ones are better). Lots of travel services. Often gets booked out in advance.

Apartments

Angkor Oasis Condo- miniums, Sala Kanseng Village, T063-693355, www.angkoroasis.com. Siem Reap's only medium- to, long-term apartments. Fully-furnished, pool, 24-hr security.

❼ Eating

Angkor Wat *p101*

Outside the entrance to Angkor Wat is a large selection of cafés and restaurants including the sister restaurant to the **Blue Pumpkin** serving good sand- wiches and breakfasts, ideal for takeaway. Near the pond there are a number of cheap food and drink stalls, bookshops and posse of hawkers selling film, souvenirs etc.

Anlong Veng *p126*

This small town shuts down relatively early so try to get in for dinner before 1900. Rumour has it between here and T'beng Meanchey lots of chickens used for cooking have died of starvation (which one could guess from looking at the mere carcasses). And without limiting choices too much, it is also advisable to avoid fish as some (but not all) have probably been caught at Ta Mok's lake, believed to contain human remains at some point in time (not particularly threatening these days but still largely unpleasant). At all restaurants most meals will come in under US$2.

† **Chom No Tror Cheak**, across from Ta Mok's Lake. Has the best variety of food in town. Mixed Thai and Khmer food. English menu.

† **Darareaksmei Restaurant**, on the main road near the roundabout, T011-559171. Whether you like this restaurant or not might depend on how you rate Khmer singing as it doubles as a local entertain- ment venue (provided by a synthesizer player and local talent). In this case, whoever invented karaoke has a lot to answer for. The music aside, this is one of the better restaurants in town with an English menu and Thai and Khmer food. Soup, quail, lok lok. Bit pricier than other places but that covers your entertainment for the night!

† **Lapia**, on the main road as you enter town. This little restaurant offers soup-style meals on individual cookers placed at each table. There is no English menu but with a few instructions

the children that run this restaurant can prepare something tasty. The noodles are fantastic.

☗ **Thou Thia**, at the same site as the guesthouse. The place doesn't have an English menu so some serious charades are in order. If you are a good enough actor they can make food on request. Chicken, fish, pork and beef dishes available.

Siem Reap *p127, maps p132 and p134*

Thanks to the growth in mainly foreign-owned restaurants there is now an excellent selection of eating places. As before, Thai, Indian and Asian are particularly well represented but a good number of French and other European restaurants also now compete for the traveller's dollar. Siem Reap is markedly more expensive than Phnom Penh (often double the price). The Old Market area has, over the last few years, become the main area to eat and drink, though the choice of hotels in this area is severely lacking.

Town centre

☗☗☗ **Abacus**, Oum Khun St, off Sivatha St, T012-644286. Considered one of the best restaurants in town offering French and Cambodian.
A little further out from the main Old Market area. Everything is fantastic here, the fish is superb, the steak is to die for. Recommended.

☗☗☗ **Barrio**, Sivatha St, away from the central area. Fantastic French and Khmer food. A favourite of the expats. Recommended.

☗☗☗ **FCC**, Pokamber Av, T063-760280. Sister to the Phnom Penh restaurant, this one is a bit more schmick. Good range of world-class food and drinks, nice surroundings, great armchairs, sophisticated.

☗☗☗ **Madame Butterfly**, Airport Rd. Fantastic French and Khmer food. A favourite of the expats.

☗☗ **Bopha**, on the east side of the river, slightly up from **Passagio**, T063-964928. Fantastic Thai-Khmer restaurant in lovely, tranquil garden setting. One of the absolute best in town. Highly recommended.

☗☗ **Viroth's Restaraunt**, No 246 Wat Bo St, T016- 951800. Upmarket place offering very good modern Khmer cuisine plus a few western staples. Looks more expensive than it actually is and is good value.

☗ **Moloppor**, east of the river, near **Bopha Hotel**. Good cheap Japanese and pizzas.

Around the Old Market (Psar Chars)

There are foodstalls along the northern side of the Old Market.

☗☗☗ **Carnets d'Asie**, 333 Sivatha St, T016-746701. Primarily a French restaurant also offering some Khmer and Thai dishes. Outdoor and indoor seating, amongst a garden, dotted with traditional Khmer parasols and a lovely water feature. Set menu and à la carte. Good Australian beef. Can't beat this one for atmosphere.

☗☗ **The Blue Pumpkin**, Old Market area, T063-963574. Western and Asian food and drinks. Sandwiches, ice cream, pitta, salads and pasta. Candidate for 'least likely eatery to find in Siem Reap' with its white minimalist decor reminiscent of the finest establishments in New York or London. Good breakfasts and cheap cocktails. Eat on the second level. Branches at both the International and domestic terminals at the airport and across from Angkor. Recommended if you need a retreat for half an hour.

☗☗ **Buddha Lounge**, 184 Mondol St. Bar and restaurant offering mostly western food.

☗☗ **Dead Fish Tower**, Sivatha Blvd, T063-963060. Thai and Khmer restaurant in a fantastically eclectic modern Thai setting. Multiple platforms, quirky decorations, sculptures, apsara dance shows, small putting range and a crocodile farm all add to the fantastic atmosphere of this popular restaurant.

☗☗ **Ivy** (across from the Old Market), T012-800860. Cosy, airy restaurant and bar offering British-style meals, plus a few Khmer dishes. Good breakfasts and roasts. Very popular.

☗☗ **Molly Malone's**, T063- 963533. Lovely Irish bar and restaurant offering classic dishes like Irish lamb stew, shepherd's pie, roasts and fish and chips.

☗☗ **The Red Piano**, northwest of the Old Market, T063-964750. An institution in Siem Reap, based in a 100-year-old colonial building. Coffee, sandwiches, salad and pastas. Cocktail bar, offering a range of tipples, including one dedicated to Angelina Jolie (who frequented the establishment while working on Tomb Raider).

¶¶ **Soup Dragon**, T063- 964933. Serves a variety of Khmer and Vietnamese dishes but its speciality is soups in earthenware pots cooked at the table. Breezy and clean, a light and colourful location sitting on a corner terrace surrounded by plants. Upstairs bar, happy hour 1600-1930.

¶¶ **Tell**, 374 Sivatha St, T063- 963289. Swiss, German, Austrian restaurant and bar. Branch of the long established Phnom Penh restaurant. Serves excellent fondue and raclette, imported beer and sausages. Reasonable prices and generous portions.

¶ **Orchidae Guesthouse**, fantastic Asian meals.

There are a number of cheap market-stall type restaurants around the Old Market and further up Sivatha St, near the Central Market, across from the Sokimex petrol station.

⊕ Bars and clubs

Siem Reap *p127, maps p132 and p134*

Angkor What?, on street known as 'bar street', Old Market Area, T012-631136. Open early evening to early morning. Bar run by friendly staff, popular with travellers and young expats.

Dead Fish bar and informal diner serving Thai food.

Easy Speaking, next to Angkor What?, T012- 865332. Good little bar with inside and outside seating.

Ivy is a popular bar and restaurant opposite Old Market. Open 0700 until late. Pool table, all day breakfast for US$4.

Linga, Laneway behind bar st, T012-246912. Gay- friendly bar offering a wide selection of cocktails. Great whiskey sours.

Laundry, near the Old Market, turn right off bar st, T016-962026. Open till late. Funky little bar.

Red Piano, Old Market Area, T012-854150. A comfortable bar/diner furnished with large wicker armchairs. The good international menu is fairly priced.

Temple Bar, on bar st. Popular drinking hole, dimly lit, good music. Not related to its seedier counterpart in Phnom Penh.

⊕ Entertainment

Siem Reap *p127, maps p132 and p134*
Dance performance

A number of hotels, notably **Le Grand**, **Sofitel** and **Angkor Village**, stage Khmer dancing performances in
the evening. Enquire at the hotels for details. **Cambodian Cultural Village**, on the airport road, 6 km from town. Shows performed for US$12.

Music concerts

A popular Sat evening attraction is the one man concert put on by Dr Beat Richner (**Beatocello**), founder of the Jayavarman VII hospital for children. Run entirely on voluntary donations the 3 hospitals in the foundation need US$9 million per year in order to treat Cambodian children free of charge. He performs at the hospital, on the road to Angkor, just north of the Sofitel hotel, at 1915 every Sat, lasts about 1 hr, free admission but donations gratefully accepted. A worthwhile experience.

Shadow puppetry

Shadow puppetry is one of the finest performing arts of the region and is an absolute must for visitors to the area. **Bayon Restaurant**, Wat Bo St. Has regular shadow puppet shows in the evening. **Krousar Thmey**, a local NGO, often tours its shadow puppet show to Siem Reap. The show is performed by underprivileged children (who have also made the puppets) at La Noria Restaurant. Wed at 1930 but check as they can be a tad irregular. Highly recommended. Donations accepted.

⊙ Shopping

Anlong Veng *p126*

Basic necessities can be obtained from the bustling market (a relatively new addition to a town that was forbidden to trade in anything too western or modern during the Khmer Rouge days.

Art

Happy Cambodia, Old Market Area. Sells the works of French Canadian Stéphane 'Stef' Delaprée. Colourful, cheerful images of everyday Khmer sights and scenes. Originals up to US$385, good quality prints US$25-40, cards and T-shirts.

Books

Street booksellers (usually people with disabilities) are in abundance, usually selling copied versions of the old favourites.
Blue Apsara, near the Old Market just down from **Helicopters Cambodia**, carries the best variety of used books in town.
Carnets d'Asie restaurant has a book shop/gift shop in front with a large selection of French titles.
Monument Books, near the Old Market, down from **Blue Pumpkin Restaurant**. The best selection of new books, maps and stationery in town.

Handicrafts

Chantiers Écoles, down a short lane off Sivatha St, T/F063-964097. School for orphaned children which trains them in carving, sewing and weaving. Products are on sale and raise 30% of the school's running costs. Outlets selling the school's products are dotted around town under the name **Les Artisans d'Angkor**. There is a silk production centre 15 km out of town, T063-380375, open daily 0730-1730.
Senteurs d'Angkor, opposite Old Market, T063- 964801. Sells a good selection of handicrafts, carvings, silverware, silks, handmade paper, cards, scented oils, incense, pepper and spices.

Markets

Outside Phnom Penh, Siem Reap is about the only place whose markets are worth browsing in for genuinely interesting souvenirs. Old Market (Psar Chars) is not a large market but stall holders and keepers of the surrounding shops have developed quite a good understanding of what tickles the appetite of foreigners. All manner of Buddhist statues and icons are on sale. Reproductions of Angkor figures are also available in various degrees of craftsmanship. There is a selection of silk and cotton fabrics, kramas and sarongs, nice

silverware, books, CDs and DVDs. Leather puppets and rice paper rubbings of Angkor bas-reliefs are unusual mementos.

Minimart

As elsewhere in Cambodia **Star Mart**, the supermarket attached to Caltex petrol stations, is very well stocked. Open 24 hrs.

▲ Activities and tours

Therapies

Khmer, Thai, reflexology and Japanese massage are readily available. Many masseuses will come to your hotel.
Frangipani, near Old Market, down side street opposite **Kokoon**, T063- 757120. Professional masseuse offering aromatherapy, reflexology and other treatments.
Seeing Hands, T063-836487. Massage by seeing impaired individuals. US$3 per hr. Highly recommended.
The Blue Pumpkin Restaurant has a large row of massage salons. **Secrets of Elephants Guesthouse** (see page 135) also offers Japanese massage.

Tour operators

Asian Trails, No 273, 1 Group, Kruos Village, T063-964595, www.asiantrails.com. Offers a broad selection of tours to Angkor and beyond. Also cruises and biking trips.
ATS, Sivatha St, T063-760041. All manner of local arrangements, boat tickets, minibus tickets, car hire. Visa service. Internet service. Very friendly and helpful.
Data Sight Travel, 430 Sivatha St, T063-963081, www.data sighttravel.com. Very, helpful travel agent, organizes tours, ticketing and a whole range of tourist services. Ask for Lim.
Diethelm Travel, No 4 Airport Rd, T063-963524, www.diet helm-travel.com.
Exotissimo Travel, No 300 Airport Rd, T063-964323, or head office (Phnom Penh), T023-218948, www.exotis simo.com. Tours of Angkor and sites beyond.
Hidden Cambodia Adventure Tours, Trang Village, House No 1, Slokram Commune, Siem Reap, T012-934412, www.hiddencambodia.com Specializing in dirt bike tours to some of Cambodia's

remote areas and off the track temple locations. Recommended for the adventurers. For example, to Koh Ker, 4 hrs. **Journeys Within**, on the outskirts of Siem Reap towards the temples, T063- 964748, www.journeys- within.com. Specializes in private, customized tours that allow visitors to enjoy the temples as well as go further afield to see the everyday lives of Cambodians.

PTM Tours, No 552, Group 6, Mondul 1, T063-964388, www.ptm-travel.com. Reasonably priced package tours to Angkor and around Phnom Penh. Also offers cheap hotel reservations.

RTR Tours, No 331, Group 7, Modul 1 (in the Old Market Area) T063-964646, www.rtr tours.com.kh. Organizes tours plus other travel services, including ticketing. Friendly and helpful.

Terre Cambodge, on **Frangipani** premises, Old Market area, T012-843401, www.terrecambodge.com. Offering tours with a twist, including cruises on an old sampan boat. Particularly good option for those wishing to tour the floating villages of the Tonle Sap. Not particularly cheap but worth it for the experience.

Two Dragon's Guesthouse can also organize some off-the-beaten-track tours. The owner Gordon Sharpless is a very knowledgeable and helpful fellow.

⊖ Transport

Anlong Veng p126

From Anlong to Siem Reap, T'beng Meanchey or Kompong Thom, one must endure enormously potholed roads and broken bridges. Shared taxis/ pickups leave in the morning for **Siem Reap**, US$3-4, 3-4 hrs. The road between Anlong Veng and Preah Vihear (90 km) is comparatively smooth for this region (in the dry season) and pickups leave from the market around 0700, U$2.

There is a **border crossing** 15 km north of Anlong Veng that is open to foreigners between Thailand and O'Smach in Cambodia. The crossing is open 0830-1600 (1700 at a push). Pick-ups leave from Anlong Veng market early in the morning, 3000 riel. Cambodian visas cost US$20 for a tourist visa and US$25 for a business visa. You need to bring 2 passport sized photographs. For

people travelling from Thailand the best bet is to take public transport to Surin (by bus or train) and then organize a tuk tuk from there to the border.

Siem Reap *p127, maps p132 and p134*
Air

The airport (REP), T063- 963148, is 7 km from Siem Reap, the town closest to the Angkor ruins, with flights from **Phnom Penh**, **Ho Chi Minh City**, **Hanoi Bangkok**, **Singapore**, **Kuala Lumpur**, **Pakse** and **Vientiane**. The airport has a taxi service, café, internet access, phone service and gift shop. A moto into town is US$1, taxi US$7. Guesthouse owners often offer free rides.

Airlines Airline availability and flight schedules are particularly prone to sudden change, so ensure you check/book well in advance. **Bangkok Airways/Siem Reap Airways**, Airport Rd, T063- 380191. 6 flights a day to **Bangkok**. Jetstar asia, www.jetstarasia.com, flies to **Singapore** 3 times a week. Malaysian budget airlines **Airasia**, www.airasia.com, is due to open new routes. **Helicopters Cambodia**, near Old Market, T012-814500. New Zealand company offering chartered flights around the temples (see Angkor chapter). **Lao Airlines**, close to provincial hospital, T/F063-963283. Mon- Fri 0800-1700, Sat 0800-1200. To **Vientiane**, 3 flights a week via **Pakse**. Malaysia Airlines, T063-964135. Flies 3 times a week to **Kuala Lumpur**. President Airlines, Sivatha St, T063-964338, flies to **Phnom Penh**. Vietnam Airlines, Airport Rd, T063-964488, www.vietnamairlines.com. Also general sales agent in town opposite provincial hospital, T03-964929. To **Ho Chi Minh City**. Silkair, T063-426 808. 5 flights a week to **Singapore**.

Boat

Boat to and from **Phnom Penh**, US$25, 5-6 hrs. The trip is fantastically atmospheric and a good way to kill two birds with one stone and see the mighty Tonlé Sap Lake. The boat is a less appealing option in the dry season when low water levels necessitate transfers to small, shallow draft vessels. In case of extremely low water levels a bus or pickup will need to be taken for part of the trip. The mudbank causeway between the lake and the outskirts of Siem Reap is hard to negotiate and may necessitate some walking (it is 12 km from

Bindonville harbour to Siem Reap). Boats depart from the Phnom Penh Port on Sisowath Quay (end of 106 St) 0700, departing Siem Reap 0700 from Chong Khneas on the Tonlé Sap Lake.

To **Battambang** the fast boat takes 4 hrs, US$12. Note that there are frequent mechanical breakdowns and occasional reports of boats being shot at by irate fishermen whose nets have been snagged.

Bus/pick-up/shared taxi

The a/c buses are one of the most convenient and comfortable ways to go to and from **Phnom Penh**, US$3.50-4, 6 hrs. Almost every guesthouse or hotel sells the tickets although it is easy enough to pick up from the bus stations/terminal. Companies include **Neak Krorhorm Travel, GST, Mekong Express** and **Capitol**. Most buses depart between 0630-0800 near the Old Market. The best bus service is the Mekong Express, US$6 if you buy in advance. It has the quickest service, 5 hrs and a/c with a little bit of info over the mike.

In peak periods, particularly Khmer New Year, it is important to purchase tickets a day or two prior to travel. A shared taxi to Phnom Penh will cost you US$10, minimum 4.

To **Battambang,** most guesthouses can organize a ticket for US$10, 7 hrs.

To **Anlong Veng**, roughly 3-4 hrs via NH67 on the way to Banteay Srei. Shared taxis/pickups leave from the market daily but not regularly, US$3-4. Siem Reap motodops will usually quote the price at US$30 a day for the trip but one should be discerning as you need a bike and driver who will be able to cope with the harsh roads. **Hidden Cambodia**, does tours with both dirt bike and 4WDs of the area (Anlong Veng, Preah Vihear, Preah Khan etc) for around US$100-130 per day.

Car and bicycle

Most hotels and guest- houses rent cars with drivers and US$2 per day for bicycles.

◑ Directory

Anlong Veng *p126*
Telephone
If you wish to make a phone call some of the local 'phone-boxes' (ie someone with a mobile) will let you make calls within Cambodia for 600 riel a min.

Siem Reap *p127, maps p132 and p134*
Banks
Cambodia Commercial Bank, 130 Sivatha St, 0900-1600. Open Sat and Sun. Currency and TC exchange. Advance on Visa, MasterCard, JCB, AMEX. **Canadia Bank**, Old Market Area, T063-964808. Moneygram, MasterCard advances, currency and TC exchange. Mon-Fri 0800-1500. **Krong Thai Bank**, 10-11 Sivatha Blvd. Mon-Fri 0800-1500, Sat 0800-1200. Currency exchange, TCs. **Mekong Bank**, 43 Sivatha St, T063-964417, Mon-Fri 0830-1600, Sat 0830-1200. US$ TCs cashed, 2% commission, cash advance on Visa and JCB cards only. Western Union services. **Union Commercial Bank**, north of Old Market, Mon-Fri 0800-1530, Sat 0800-1200. Cash advance on MasterCard and Visa. Cashes TCs.

Internet
Rates vary but should be around 3000-4000 riel per hr. Most internet places now offer internet calls. **The Internet Café**, Sivatha St, and **Angkor Web**, both north of Old Market. Both US$1 per hr.

Medical services
The medical facilities are okay here but by no means of an international standard. In most cases it is probably best to fly to Bangkok. **Naga International Clinic**, T063-964500, Airport Rd. International medical services. 24-hr emergency care. Children's hospitals: **Jayavarman VII Hospital**, on the road to Angkor Wat. **Angkor Hospital for Children**, Achamean St. Provincial hospital north of Old Market. Pharmacies: opposite the entrance of the provincial hospital.

Post office
Post offices and major hotels have IDD facilities but expensive. Main post office, Pokamber Av, west side of Siem Reap River, but it can take up to a month for mail to be delivered. 0700-1700. **DHL**, Sivatha St (opposite petrol station, will send urgent letters for US$50, guaranteed 4-day delivery.

Telephone
If you have a mobile you can buy a Mobitel sim card. US$10-25. 6 digit numbers let you call overseas, whereas 7 digit numbers don't. You will need someone with a Cambodia ID card to help you; motos will do this for a ll tip.

The Northwest

❗ Footprint features

Introduction

Southeast Asia's biggest fresh-water lake, the Tonlé Sap, is at the centre of the region making it one of the most agriculturally productive and prosperous parts of the country and has contributed to the great architectural and historical legacy of the area. The jewel in the crown of the northwest is, of course, Angkor, which is covered in a separate chapter, but there are many other spectacular archaeological remains including the stunning Banteay Chhmar. The riverside town of Battambang, with elegant French colonial buildings, exudes charm and is a great place to while away a day or two.

This vast region avoided the punishment inflicted on the east of the country by the Vietnamese and more particularly the Americans during the Second Indochina War but it was one of the most bitterly contested territories during the civil war. Thousands of civilians fled northwest from the advancing Khmer Rouge and sought refuge in the border areas of Thailand. Only, alas, in many cases to be forced back by the guns of the Thai army across minefields and into the arms of the waiting Khmer Rouge. Until recently places such as Battambang and Banteay Chhmar were Khmer Rouge strongholds; it is no surprise that Pol Pot should have breathed his last up here nor that Pailin is run by Khmer Rouge cadres as a semi-autonomous state under a flag of convenience.

★ Don't miss...

1 **Battambang** Take time to explore the provincial capital on the lovely Sangkei River, with its well-preserved French-era architecture and 16 monasteries, page 147.

2 **Wat Ek** Angkor may be impossible to match, but the 11th-century Wat Ek, about 10 km downstream from Battambang, is attractively decrepit, page 148.

3 **Bamboo train** For one of Cambodia's zanier journeys, hop on board Battambang's Bamboo train, page 149.

4 **Phnom Khieu Waterfall** Don't be put off by the cobras and landmines; the Phnom Khieu Waterfall, around 8 km outside Pailin, is an adventure not to be missed, page 150.

5 **Banteay Chhmar** These 12th-century ruins, 61 km north of Sisophon, are one of the least visited of the major Khmer sites. But though you'll feel like a true explorer, the site has been systematically looted, page 152.

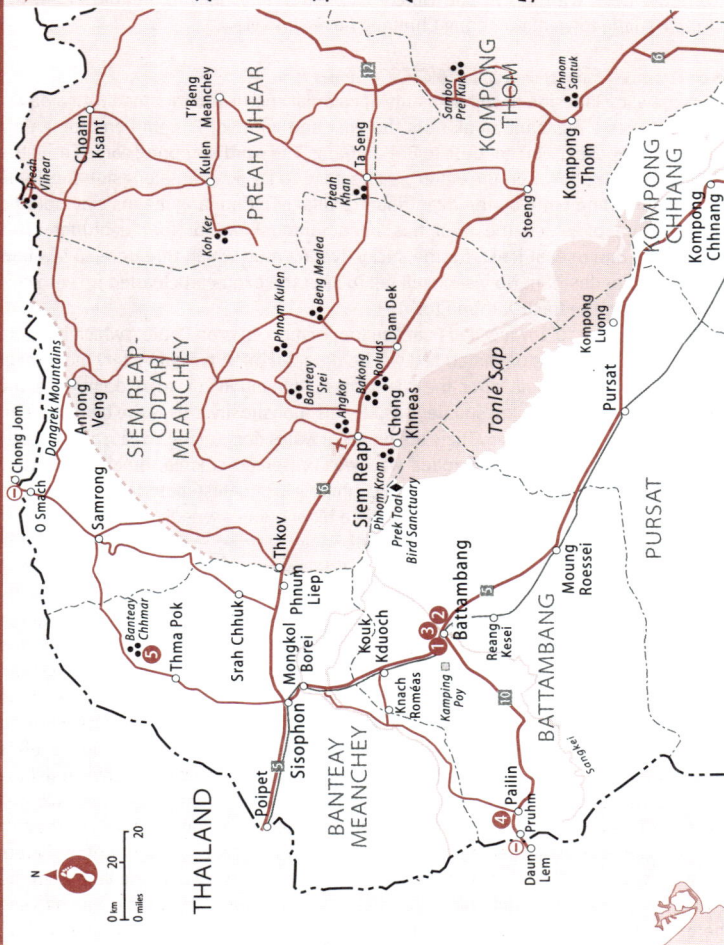

The Northwest

Battambang and around

Cuddled into various rivers, the laid-back towns of Kompong Chhnang and Battambang provide a lovely backdrop to sit back and soak up the atmosphere of Khmer life. Pursat is the gateway to the Tonle Sap and the Cardamom Mountains. Battambang oozes charm with its lovely colonial buildings and outlying sites.
▸▸ *For Sleeping, Eating and other listings, see pages 154-164.*

The Northwest Battambang & around

Towards Battambang

Heading north from Phnom Penh on Route 5 early in the morning the traveller quickly passes the ancient capital of Oudong, see page 62. The road is comfortable and fast and the scenery enchanting. In the wet season all hues of green predominate with flashes of red – soil, newly tiled roofs and kramas (Khmer scarves) – but the lakes and rivers are thick with brown silt. Ninety kilometres after leaving Phnom Penh, the attractive little town of Kompong Chhnang hoves into view.

Kompong Chhnang ⊜❼⊜❶ ▸▸ *pages 154-164.*

The sprawling lakeside town has plenty of colonial charm and for those with a day to spare, makes a pleasant break from the dust and grime of Phnom Penh, or even a pleasant stopover point en route to Battambang. The word Kompong comes from the Khmer meaning 'town on the water', a reference to its position alongside the Tonlé Sap and in some parts on the river (floating villages). Chhnang means clay pot, the manufacture of which the area has been famous for, for four centuries. This represents one use, at least, for the sticky riverine mud which threatens to swallow the unwary pedestrian. No visitor will fail to spot the oxen-carts loaded up with clay pots trundling the tracks around town.

The main part of town called **Psar Leu** (upper market) is on Route 5 which is where visitors arriving by bus or shared taxi will be dropped off. A typical Victory monument built after the Vietnamese 'liberation' of 1979 dominates the central square. Despite this monstrosity, this is the beautiful part of town. There are plenty of walks north of the square along shady tree-lined roads with well-preserved colonial buildings running alongside. Kompong Chhnang is underestimated by tourists – it is the perfect place to get a hit of quintessential Cambodian life. On one hand you have the heart and soul of Tonlé Sap life – the daily grind of the fishermen, buoyant homes drifting with the tide, merchants donning their archetypal conical hats and an endless stream of boats gliding through. On the other, you have the town – large, leafy boulevards, faded yellow buildings gathered in the French Quarter, the citizen's languid tempo and the even slower pace of meandering cows, and the town's parks which you must scour for a good stretch of grass. Kompong Chnnang is an amalgam of the country's diversity – Cambodia, Vietnam and France; the verve of the river and life on the land; rural and urban all rolled into one area. This place generates a feeling of simple, content, harmonious country life (although below the surface it has had a tumultuous history and still faces many problems – disputes between fishing villages, for example). It does evoke another place and another time: this town could well be one of Cambodia's friendliest spots, with locals literally flocking to simply say hello.

❧ The best way to tour the town and nearby villages is by bicycle or for those wishing to venture further outside, by moto.

The pier is at **Psar Kraom** (lower market) on the lakeside which is where visitors arriving by boat will land. It is at the end of a 2-km causeway over the lake from the main part of town. Although this is the shabbier side of the town there is much to see here. The lake is very beautiful and local inhabitants are keen to take visitors out on the water for around US$10 per day. The market activity on the lakeside – much of it taking place from boats – is interesting. You can buy fruit, meat, vegetables, cigarettes, clay pots and clothes. There is also a brightly painted wat on the corner of the causeway facing the lake.

Kompong Chhnang's claim to fame is its pottery and roadside **pottery** stalls line Route 5, particularly towards Battambang. A higher grade of pottery can be found at **Ban Chkol Village**, 6 km south of town. An NGO has actively been training the villagers in the art of pottery and the results are evident to see. To get there follow Route 5 until you see the turn off for the village.

Five hundred metres from the airport is **Tareak Cave** ⓘ *round trip by moto US$5*, a man-made construction also developed under the Khmer Rouge's auspices. Intended as a hideout, the cave was built by forced labour and required the indigent workers to carve a 2.5-m-high and 6-m-wide hole into a solid rock face. Like most developments under the brutal regime, many people lost their lives while working on this site. Neither of these sights hold great tourist appeal but might peak the curiosity of war buffs.

Kompong Chhnang

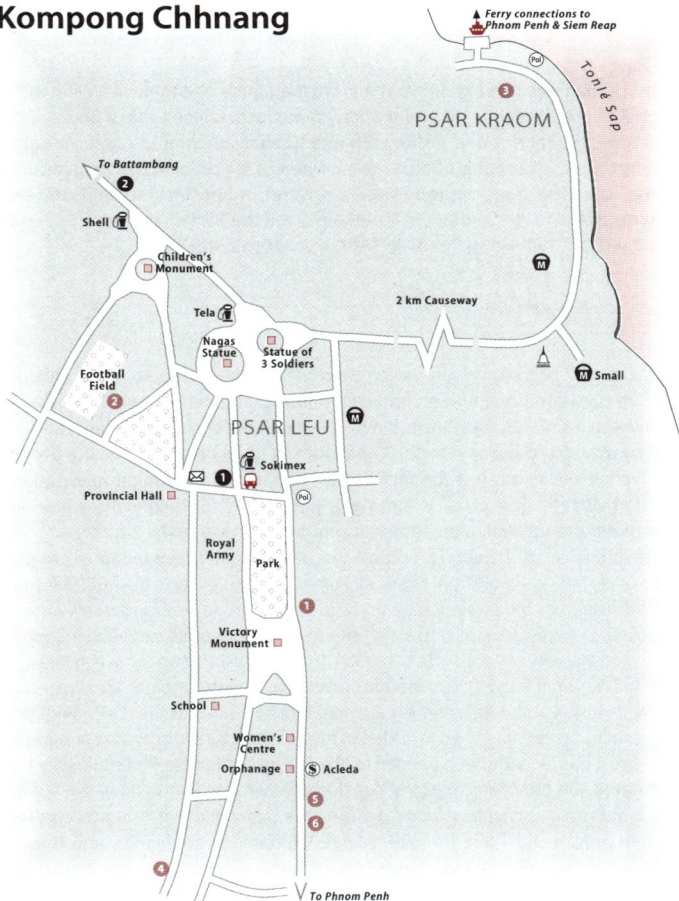

Sleeping
Bopha Angkor **5**
Krong Dei Meas **2**
Metapheap **1**
Phkay Proek
   Guesthouse **6**
Rithisen **3**
Sokha Guesthouse **4**

Eating
Mekong **2**
Soksen **1**

Across the river are the double peaks of **Mount Kong Ray**, the appellation deriving from the the legend of Kong Ray, a woman murdered when stuck in the middle of a dispute between her husband and mother-in-law. Many believe that the woman's spirit created the mountain, which today resembles a corpse, with feet to the north and hair to the south.

For the more intrepid travellers there are a few pre-Angkorian ruins across the river. The sites are scattered amongst small villages and bush land and are hard to find, so a good guide/moto is required for navigation. **Prasat Srei**, 'Girl Temple', is a seventh-eighth century Chenla-era structure. Like many of its kind, the temple has been severely looted. Swamped by bushes the structure features a single tower, with three artificial doors, stony stairs and crumbling lintels. **Prasat Broh**, 'Boy Temple', was constructed during the same period of brick and is in a pretty bad state of repair. There are several other Sambor-inspired temples in the area including **Prasat Srey Bee**, 'Twin Girl Temples', two identical temples sitting atop a beautiful mountain. The return boat trip, including waiting time, will cost around $US10. The temples span an area about 15 sq km, so you will need to either pick up a moto on the other side, at Kompong Layng port or organize for one to come across with you from Kompong Chhnang ($US5). The ever-obliging Mr Sophal from the **Holiday Guesthouse** can help make travel arrangements.

On the road south to Phnom Penh next to the orphanage there is a Womens' and Veterans' Centre. They run an outlet shop where local women make and sell crafts including woven fabrics and pottery. **Phnom Reabat** mountain temple 10 km from Kompong Chhnang probably affords the best view of the collection of temples around the area. The view from the top is nothing short of spectacular, with an outlook extending across to the Cardomom Mountains, and the Tonle Sap River. The signpost marking the site sums it up, reading: "Attractive 750 metres".

Pursat ⬤🏨🍴🛏🚌 ▸▸ *pages 154-164.*

Pursat is a town of major indifference to most travellers on the southern side of the Tonlé Sap between Phnom Penh and Battambang. The petite town is special in its own way with a sinuous river slowly lurching through the centre and little, leafy streets dotted by the odd cyclist or vehicle. Pursat doesn't quite have the bustling city feel of other riverine towns but has the facilities and population putting it miles ahead of most rural villages. The place is just right, particularly for those who would like a couple of days to unwind in an authentic, untouristed part of the country.

The province of Pursat is notable for its natural beauty and scenery, but unfortunately little is visible from the road. Pursat is the gateway to the fruitful Tonle Sap and the Cardomom Mountain Range and the settlement is surrounded by some truly spectacular countryside. Pursat town is renowned for its marble carvings (the province supplies the majority of Cambodia's marble). In the centre of town, between Road 1 and Road 2 (off National Road 5), is a **marble carving workshop**, where visitors can see the artisans at work. Cambodia's highest summit, Mount Aoral (1813 m – although no two maps seem to agree), has been included in the province by a slip of the cartographer's hand – and it has recently been opened to hikers. The Cardamom Mountains are thickly clad in forest and provide a source of considerable wealth. So too does the Tonlé Sap which is fished intensively. Around 79% of the population in this area are either fishermen or farmers. There is quite a large Vietnamese population and they have established a trade in fingerlings (immature fish) with Vietnam. It is estimated that one to two billion fingerlings are exported each year, causing grave concern to environmentalists. Many Vietnamese live in floating villages on the lake. The **floating village** of **Kompong Luong** can be reached via Krakor, which is 35 km east on Route 5. The area is rich is bird-life and the daily waterway life can be completely captivating.

Over 10,000 people live in this permanently floating town, with floating bars, restaurants, pool tables, school and medical clinics. The villagers here face the difficulty of relocating homes and businesses twice a year due to the seasonally shifting water levels. During the wet season, they move closer to the riverbanks to be protected from heavy storms. In the dry season they move towards the centre of the river where deeper water levels exist. The dwellings require between 1 and 4 m of water beneath them in order to float. Visitors can hire a boat for US$5 an hour and venture to the other floating villages of Raing Til, Kompong Thkol and Dey Roneat.

Pursat town has a small museum, on the west side of the bridge over Pursat River, containing ancient artefacts from the region.

Battambang ⊟🏧🏠🏪🅾️🔺🅱️ℹ️ » *pages 154-164.*

Cambodia's second largest city lies 40 km west of the Tonlé Sap at the centre of a fertile plain. Battambang, which translates to 'disappearing stick', is named after a magical stick that the king used to ensure his power. However, Battambang doesn't exude the power of a royal base, instead, it has the character of a provincial market town and, apart from a cluster of mobile phone stores and internet cafés near the market, it appears to be resolutely resisting any attempt to enter the 21st century. Battambang lies on the lovely Sangkei River and retains a lot of charming early 20th-century buildings as well

❢ Visitors travelling to or from Thailand who are in need of an overnight stop should choose Battambang over its neighbours without hesitation.

as 16 wats, some – so it is said – dating back to the Angkor period, which are scattered around the city and surrounding lush countryside. The town itself is quite beautiful, with a number of old colonial buildings sitting around the misty, river area. A large number of NGOs working in the northwest region have offices here so the town has quite good amenities and restaurants.

Ins and outs

Getting there and around Pick-ups and buses connect with Phnom Penh, Poipet and Pailin. Daily connections by boat with Siem Reap provide the most scenic and enjoyable way to get to Battambang but don't expect a serene drift where you can enjoy the bucolic charms of the Cambodian countryside. The speed boat tears across the Tonlé Sap for an hour or two then rips up the Sangkei River for a few hours more, but it cannot conceal the beauty of the river, its jumping shrimps and aquatic way of life. Dry season travellers will see in the distance the height of the houses above river level as evidence of the enormous growth of the lake in the wet season. Another scenic possibility is to take the train from Phnom Penh, via Pursat (the train departs at 0600, US$1.05). This journey normally takes up to 12 to 14 hours but it is a more comfortable option to the rollercoaster ride offered in the back of a pick-up. There are also rail connections with Sisophon. Motos can be used to get around town.
» See Transport, page 162, for details.

Sights

In 1975 the Khmer Rouge captured the town and made it a rebel stronghold. Much of the surrounding area was **mined** and even today many paddy fields are still abandoned as they have not been swept of their ordnance, contributing to a sharp decline in harvests. In the past, the area was considered a rice basket – but it is now better known for its fishing industry. More recently, and less bloodily, Battambang has been a fierce battleground for rival political factions – the royalist Funcinpec and Hun Sen's CPP (Cambodian People's Party).

Battambang retains almost all its original French **colonial architecture** including the splendid Governor's Residence. The original planners sited this grand building perfectly at the northern end of the main river crossing creating an imposing spectacle to impress the governor's visitors arriving from Phnom Penh. Most of the town's buildings are **shophouses**: business downstairs, residence upstairs. They were built to the same formula the British introduced into Malaya with a covered 5-ft walkway to provide shade and shelter for pedestrians. A number of occupants have 'privatized' the walkway by extending their side walls across the pavement down to the road. Most buildings on Street 2 remain as built, many with the original wooden doors and shutters.

The town has a small **museum** which contains a few items from local Khmer temples but the most pleasant way to while away the hours is to stroll along the riverfront or potter around the back streets reflecting on the irony that while the Khmer Rouge may have been savages to their compatriots, the colonial architectural heritage couldn't have been in safer hands.

Around Battambang

Around Battambang are the 11th-century temple of Wat Ek, the Bamboo train also known as the funny train, the lake of Kamping Poy, a mass grave of the Khmer Rouge and a 10th-century mountain-top temple and cave.

The Northwest Battambang & around

❣ *Around Battambang, by Ray Zepp (1991), is a good primer for those looking for intrepid travel. Ray, a local identity and English teacher, donates most of his profit from the guide to local charities.*

Wat Ek – or Ek Phnom – is 11 km downriver from Battambang. ⓘ *Take a moto on the road that follows the river; US$7 for full-day trip around these sites and others in the area.* It is a nice green drive past trees, shrubs, villages and covered bridges (the local architectural speciality, but of no great antiquity) to the 11th-century temple, built in 1027. It was built of huge sandstone blocks by Suryavarman and is now a pleasantly

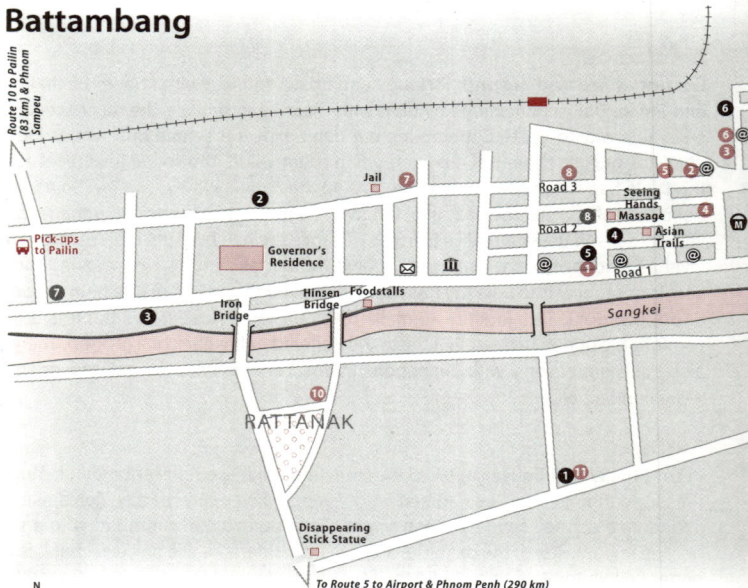

Battambang

Route 10 to Pailin
(83 km) & Phnom
Sampeu

Pick-ups
to Pailin

Jail

Governor's
Residence

Iron
Bridge

Hinsen
Bridge

Foodstalls

Road 3

Road 2

Seeing
Hands
Massage

Asian
Trails

Road 1

Sangkei

RATTANAK

Disappearing
Stick Statue

To Route 5 to Airport & Phnom Penh (290 km)

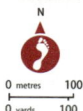

N

0 metres 100
0 yards 100

Sleeping ◉	Golden River **8**	Paris **5**	**Eating** ◉
Angkor **1**	International **4**	Park **10**	Cold Night **1**
Chhaya **2**	Leng Heng **11**	Royal **6**	Pkay Proek **2**
Golden Parrot **3**	Monorom **9**	Teo **7**	Riverside Balcony Bar **3**

abandoned ruin with one central tower leaning precariously. Many smaller structures and gateways have toppled or look as though they are about to topple. There are some carved lintels but nothing more. Local Buddhists are dutifully and busily staking out their own patch next door, as they are across the country, in an effort to pretend that they and their religion were authors of the site and its contents. The process is no different from what occurred in Europe as early Christian churches were established on existing pagan sites.

The Funny Train or **Bamboo Train** ① *US$5-6,* is a Heath Robinson affair and it probably comes closest to Britain's railway system in terms of sophistication, punctuality and comfort. A simple bamboo platform on wheels powered by a small petrol engine, the 'train' follows the railway track for approximately 40 km through the countryside stopping off at villages along the way (with two official 'train stations' at the 12 km and 6 km mark). The train, which consists of an engine from a water pump, wheels from a tank and bamboo platform, can miraculously carry up to three tonnes. The train, which was declared an official means of public transport for the area (1992), carries local villagers, young and old, women and men, who share the limited space with a smattering of farm animals and foreign tourists. Many of the moto drivers will suggest taking the 'train' from Ban Odomboing (one of the villages along the route) for a few kilometres and then take their moto the remainder of the journey passing through the beautiful countryside.

Kamping Poy ① *36 km west of Battambang; take a motorbike; many moto drivers will include it on a day trip of the area, US$6,* is the site of a lake and dam (spanning 8 km) which was built by the prisoners of the Khmer Rouge. Half of Battambang Province's population were involved in its construction and thousands are said to have perished during its construction. On weekdays this is a peaceful area where people go to swim and fish – and the horrors of its construction lie lost beneath the still waters. However, in a poignant twist, at the weekend it turns into a massive water playground and picnic area for the local population. The army, who help with its upkeep, dish out rubber rings to both adults and children.

Phnom Sampeu is 20 km southwest from town on Route 10 and 10 km from Kamping Poy, along a very poor road. The mountain is the site of some mass graves where victims of the Khmer Rouge were killed and dumped. There are two caves on site. The first one, Lang La'Coun (meaning **Punishment Cave**), was used as a torture ground during the Khmer Rouge days where people were beaten to death with sticks, stabbed or electrocuted. The second cave is much larger and houses a reclining Buddha (built in 1998). Many prisoners who were killed were thrown down the cave's 15-m-deep hole. A memorial holding some of the victims' remnants has been created. On the mountainside are two old government guns and some bunkers (which were supplied by the Russians). The guns are facing the former Khmer Rouge-controlled

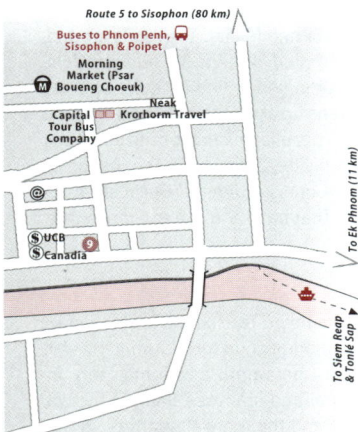

Route 5 to Sisophon (80 km)
Buses to Phnom Penh, Sisophon & Poipet
Morning Market (Psar Boeung Choeuk)
Neak Krorhorm Travel
Capital Tour Bus Company
To Ek Phnom (11 km)
UCB
Canadia
To Siem Reap & Tonlé Sap
To Siem Reap & Tonlé Sap

Smokin' Pot **5**
Sunrise
 Coffeehouse **6**
White Rose **4**

Bars & clubs 🎵
Bophatip Nightclub **7**
Paradise Nightclub **8**

Crocodile Mountain, named due to its bizarre crocodile-like shape. The site was a major outpost during the war and much cross-fire took place between the two mountains. At the top of the mountain is a tiny wat which was used as a prison during the Khmer Rouge era. Another wat was built in 2002 to promote a newer, more positive future. The new wat deviates from traditional style and has eight doors instead of the usual three or four. The eight doors symbolize the eight directions forward, all peaceful and positive. It is paradoxical that the mountain, with such a horrific history, is so serene and stunning today.

Phnom Banon, a mountain with a 10th-century temple at the top, is also worth a visit. The 80-m-high mountain, 25 km out of Battambang, is a 359-step hike to the top. The temple is believed to have been built by Suryavarman II and completed by Jayavarman VII and perhaps not surprisingly has an Angkorian feel with five prominent towers peeking above the roof line. Like most other temples of this era, many of the apsaras have been removed by looters. Alongside the temples, and not quite in keeping with the theme, is a huge anti-aircraft gun. On the other side of the mountain is **L'Ang But Meas Cave**, where locals believe Holy Waters are stored. The small, dark entrance leads into a large cave where a large jar is kept however, it is very dark so candles and a torch are required. Navigating your way to the cave is very difficult as a proper trail had not really been constructed. At the bottom of the mountain is a 150-year-old pagoda which is still in use today.

Pailin ⬤🍴⬤🚌⬤ » *pages 154-164.*

Pailin lies just 24 km from the Thai border on the edge of the Cardamom Mountain Range (Phnom Kravanh in Khmer). On the surface, Pailin belies its recent bloody history as it looks like any other town. The mountains surrounding the town and dust hanging in the air give this town an almost mystical feel (despite the serious lack of mysticism), especially from the higher ground of Wat Phnom Yaat. The roads around the town are in quite poor condition – dusty and potholed, so expect a bumpy ride if you came from either the border or Battambang. Gem shops line its quiet streets, which can almost feel like a ghost town by day. It livens up at night when the populace come out to eat and drink. The town itself contains a peculiar mixture of citizens: gem dealers are in abundance, prostitutes are on the high side, there is a fair sprinkling of former Khmer Rouge, as well as the odd genocidal mass murderer. Because of its proximity to the border most prices are quoted in Thai baht and the exchange rate from riel to US dollar is generally below the norm.

Sights

Beautiful **Wat Phnom Yaat** marks the entrance to the town. The temple is steeped in legend as it is renowned around the area and afar to bring good luck. During the war people would come here to pray to Madame Yaat (the patron and former nun in residence) for their lives to be spares. A brightly painted staircase flanked by two many-headed nagas leads up to a pagoda, temple and the monks' quarters. In the late afternoon, music rings out from the mountain top as a small band of local musicians meet for rehearsal. There are scenes from both Hindu mythology and Buddha's life depicted on the walls.

At the bottom of the hill is another important wat which dates back 570 years. The entrance gate is inscribed with Burmese characters (evidence of early Burmese colonists in this area). There is a rendition of the Churning of the Sea, in red stone along the perimeter wall.

There are some small **waterfalls** about 8 km from town. Most notable of these is the **Phnom Khieu (Blue Mountain) Waterfall** ① *The route is difficult as it follows dirt tracks and means entering an area which is sensitive militarily, so it is advisable to* *take a moto and, more importantly, a guide, US$10-15 per person*, which tumbles down several levels. The waterfall is 4 to 5 km into the jungle and up the mountain along a narrow winding path. Most of the obviously dangerous animals in the jungle have been hunted to oblivion but snakes, including cobras, are common. There are also landmines laid close to the path – hence the need for a guide. Whilst this may be enough to keep most people away, the birds, the clear, cooling pools at the foot of each fall, and the surrounding unspoilt forest makes this an adventure not to be missed. The drive into the mountains is spectacular. You can tour the countryside by yourself, but stick to the main roads. Thailand is a 24-km drive from town, but note that the border is not a legal crossing point for westerners. As at Poipet, there is a casino, called **Caesar International Casino**, on the border.

Sisophon and around ⬬🏍️🚌ℹ️ » *pages 154-164.*

Sisophon lies at the junction of Route 5 to Phnom Penh, Route 6 up to Siem Reap, the road north into the Dangrek Mountains and the pot-holed highway to Poipet and Thailand. Formerly part of Battambang Province, Sisophon is now the provincial capital of Banteay Meanchey Province. In the wet season Sisophon can be difficult to walk around as it gets very muddy. There are a handful of temples – two are very pleasant and are built next to lakes – some parks, a sleepy market, and thanks to the heavy NGO presence here, a choice of comfortable and well-equipped hotels. It makes a more convenient stopover en route between Siem Reap and Bangkok than Poipet.

Sights

Sisophon is small enough to explore on foot, although there are plenty of moto drivers willing to persuade you otherwise! There are two parks in town; both are on the main road that runs from Siem Reap to Poipet. The larger and scruffier one has a small **pavilion**, and comes alive at night with food vendors, lights, music and dancing. **Thien Po Park** alongside has well-tended lawns and shrubs, an elephant fountain and a plethora of benches and swings inside. However, the gate always seems to be locked and the park is deserted.

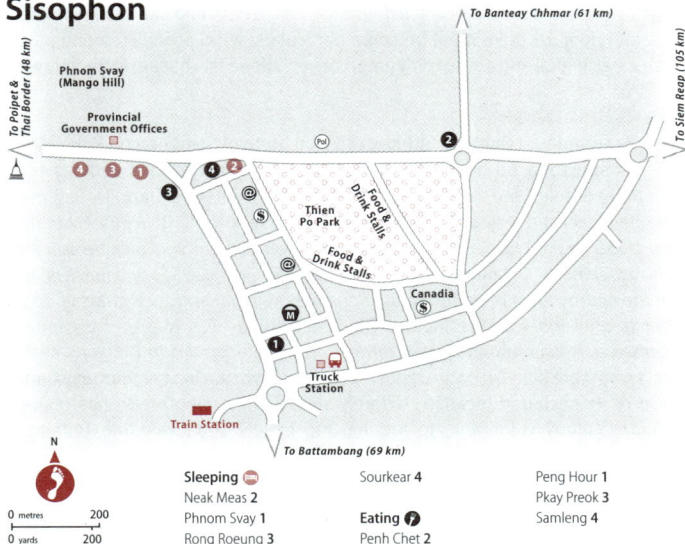

Sisophon

To Banteay Chhmar (61 km)
To Poipet & Thai Border (48 km)
To Siem Reap (105 km)
Phnom Svay (Mango Hill)
Provincial Government Offices
Pol
Thien Po Park
Food & Drink Stalls
Food & Drink Stalls
Canadia
Truck Station
Train Station
To Battambang (69 km)
N
0 metres 200
0 yards 200

Sleeping 🛏️
Neak Meas 2
Phnom Svay 1
Rong Roeung 3
Sourkear 4

Eating 🍴
Penh Chet 2

Peng Hour 1
Pkay Preok 3
Samleng 4

The tears of the Gods: rubies and sapphires

Major deposits of two of the world's most precious stones are found distributed right across mainland Southeast Asia: rubies and sapphires. They are mined in Thailand, Myanmar, Vietnam, Cambodia and Laos.

During the civil war in Cambodia, thousands of Thais were mining gems in Khmer Rouge-controlled territory (especially around Pailin) – with the protection of the vilified Khmer Rouge and the support of the Thai army. Bangkok has become one of the centres of the world's gem business and Thailand is the largest exporter of cut stones.

Rubies and sapphires are different colours of corundum, the crystalline form of aluminium oxide. Small quantities of various trace elements give the gems their colour; in the case of rubies, chromium and for blue sapphires, titanium. Sapphires are also found in a spectrum of other colours including green and yellow.

Rubies are among the rarest of gems, and command prices four times higher than equivalent diamonds.

The colour of sapphires can be changed through heat treatment (the most advanced form is called diffusion treatment) to 1500-1600°C (sapphires melt at 2050°C). For example, relatively valueless colourless geuda sapphires from Sri Lanka, turn a brilliant blue or yellow after heating. The technique is an ancient one: Pliny the Elder described the heating of agate by Romans nearly 2000 years ago while the Arabs had developed heat treatment into almost a science by the 13th century. Today, almost all sapphires and rubies are heat treated. The most valued colour for sapphires is cornflower blue. Dark, almost black, sapphires command a lower price. The value of a stone is based on the four 'C's: Colour, Clarity, Cut and Carat (1 carat = 200 mg).

Undoubtedly, the highlight of Sisophon is the horde of young drink and snack sellers at the truck station. These children have the biggest smiles and play the cheekiest games in their effort to sell their wilted baguettes and soft drinks. This place is quite an anomaly: there must be some particularly good schools around as most children are bilingual and are not only great conversationalists but are incredibly witty.

Around Sisophon

The temple complex at **Banteay Chhmar** is 61 km north of Sisophon on Route 69. The road is being resurfaced but there are still the usual obstructions such as broken bridges and potholes and there are some security concerns over banditry in this area. Check with locals and resident NGOs in town before setting off. ⓘ *A moto should cost around US$6 round trip. In the early morning you can catch a pick-up truck from Sisophon to Banteay Chhmar village for around US$2 inside, US$1 outside. It is best to stay in the nearby town of Samrong. Just outside the main entrance gates of Banteay Chhmar is an unnamed guesthouse.* Banteay Chhmar was one of the capitals of Jayavarman II. It was rebuilt by Jayavarman VII and dedicated to his sons and four generals who were killed in battle repelling a Cham invasion in 1177. Banteay Chhmar, because of its secluded location, is rarely visited. This remoteness has made the temple particularly vulnerable to looting and in July 1994 valuable 12th-century carvings were stolen from the site. Local officials say that Cambodian army units were involved in the looting using trucks to pull statues from their pedestals and then transport them the short 30-minute journey across the Thai border for sale. In 1998, the plunder of Banteay Chhmar reached a new peak with the boldest and best organized temple robbery of recent times. More than 500 sq ft of bas-relief was hacked off and discovered in a fleet of trucks en route for Thailand. The Cambodian army was, once again, implicated in the vandalism and theft.

Poipet ⊜𝟶⊝❶ ↠ *pages 154-164.*

Poipet is not a good introduction to Cambodia. To say the place is an unattractive town is a major understatement. The dusty streets are pockmarked by casinos, brothels, massage parlours, karaoke bars and all with an overriding sewer stench. To make matters worse, more than Cambodia's fair share of corrupt officials, hustlers, thieves, pimps, scamming touts, beggars, gamblers and prostitutes have chosen this mini hell as their haven. Scratch below the surface and the town's folk are as nice as anywhere else and Poipet isn't particularly dangerous for those passing through. Just keep your eye on the scammers (see box, page 154).

Most of the buildings have been hurriedly constructed in the wake of the war and unrest and others are still under construction. The streets are potholed dirt tracks and the sprawling market and many warehouses dominate the town. In the dry season Poipet is hot and dusty and in the rainy season the streets lie thick with mud: not just the kind which sticks to your shoes and makes walking difficult, or the slippery kind, which also makes walking difficult, but also the deep watery kind, which makes walking impossible.

Background
Poipet is tucked up in the northwest corner and sits on the border with Thailand. It was a long time Khmer Rouge stronghold and has now cultivated a reputation for being the very wild west of Cambodia. It is no doubt a frontier town and it is the main port of entry for Thai goods (such as smuggled Honda motorbikes and four-wheel drives). In early 1998 it became legal for foreign passport holders to cross into Cambodia at this point and what began as a nervous trickle of foreign tourists quickly escalated into a flood. The Poipet crossing can be quite depressing as it's the main people smuggling port of Cambodia and one can see the direst of scenes. The sight of pick-up trucks piled high with foreigners has become an almost hourly sight in this small market town. Until 1997 Poipet was the scene of heavy fighting and shelling between government troops and Khmer Rouge guerrillas. The last foreigners left in Phnom Penh were escorted out of the country through Poipet by the Khmer Rouge. In the following years refugee camps began to grow up around the border on the Thai side here. There are a number of scams operating in Poipet such as pick-ups stopping in the middle of nowhere and demanding more money or delaying the trip so that you arrive in Siem Reap very late and have to go to the guesthouse where they get a commission.

Sights
The **Friendship Bridge** (Klong Leuk in Khmer) which spans the murky O Chrov Creek joins Thailand with Cambodia. The bridge was funded by the UK and built by the Thais in 1996. The nearest Thai town is **Aranya Prathet**, about 7 km from the border. There is a busy covered market and a row of cafés next to the Thai immigration post.

The town is hoping to become the Las Vegas of Cambodia – they have even erected a sign declaring a street Las Vegas Boulevard. Not quite there yet, but casinos continue to crop up to satisfy the never-ending supply of Thais willing to cross the border to win or lose their fortunes (gambling is illegal in Thailand). One of the more bizarre sights in Poipet is **Casino Holiday Palace** located in no man's land between the two immigration posts. Built by a Thai company predominately for Thais it features blackjack, roulette, standard casino games, an array of fruit machines and a restaurant. The Thai government has placed signs on the Thai side warning of thieves

Scam central

Besides being known as a casino-filled frontier town, Poipet has become eponymous with the words 'tourist scam'. The ploys are usually pretty wily and at times can be very convincing. Don't be fooled (although sometimes it's unavoidable).

Overpriced bus tickets from Bangkok Private bus companies and travel agents in Bangkok (particularly around Khao San Road) routinely sell tickets to Poipet for nothing short of exorbitant prices. Not only are they seriously overcharging, but the trip, can take up to double the normal travel time, sometimes 12 hours. Another drawback with using these companies is that they have been known to take tourists to other border crossings, such as Pailin, which, believe it or not, is a much more difficult crossing and is a lot further away from Siem Reap. Avoid going with private bus companies from Bangkok. Public buses leave every half hour or so from Bangkok's Northern Bus Terminal (Morchit), ฿180-200. The trip takes approximately five hours and is a quarter of the price.

Bad exchange rate scam Upon arriving at Poipet many tourists are told US currency is no longer accepted and that a kindly money changer/gift shop/restaurant will exchange all your cash to riel/baht. The con artists are crafty and appear as if they are saving you trouble, suggesting the king has outlawed the US dollar or that the exchange rate in Siem Reap is weak. People have been known to lose up to 30% of their money through the dodgy exchange rate offered in Poipet. The US dollar is still widely used in Cambodia, so don't be duped. Traveller's cheques can be cashed in Phnom Penh and Siem Reap. Baht is widely used in Thai border areas and riel is good for smaller transactions.

Corrupt border officials More often than not border officials will overcharge on visas. It could be that they want to see proof of your medical insurance/vaccinations/SARS form, charging a fee when the relevant paperwork can't be provided. Or it could be blatant, outright corruption where they simply overcharge on the visa price or exit stamp (which should be free). Some people suggest obtaining your visa in Bangkok (but more often than not they will still find a hidden charge somewhere). Keep your cool. Try asking for a receipt. Others have suggested feigning a phone call to an embassy/tourist office has helped. The normal border fee should not be more than US$25/฿1000.

Touts. Most tourists will encounter a flock of hassling touts offering every

and swindlers at the casino. Whatever, it is an unsettling experience to witness the air-conditioned splendour and wealth inside, followed by the sight of local traders straining under loaded carts and amputees begging outside. There's another handful of casinos in the precinct including **Ceasar's**, **Star Vegas** and **Tropicana**.

The busy **market** is well worth a browse. The Friendship Bridge is bustling with human traffic loaded down with imported goods and is interesting to watch. There is not much else to do here, although Poipet makes a possible stopover point for those travelling overland from Bangkok to Phnom Penh.

Sleeping

Kompong Chhnang *p144, map p145*
E **Apsara Guesthouse**, T026-988744. Near the **Sokha Guesthouse**, the rooms are very clean with all the usual facilities.

E **Holiday Guesthouse**, on the road to Phnom Penh (beyond **Bopha Angkor Guesthouse**), T026-988802, haksophal02@hotmail.com. The newest service from carrying your bags through to helping you get your visa. Their assistance is completely unnecessary as all aspects can be handled by the individual and it is highly likely that they will charge you a fee or load your bags into their friend's truck, where you will be charged an excessive fee.

Taxi and pick-up scams Taxis and pick-ups routinely overcharge for the trip from Poipet to Siem Reap (it should be ₿1000 for the full car or ₿250 per person). It is best to find some fellow travellers going in the same direction as you have more bargaining power as a group. If you are paying full fare for the taxi, don't let them sneak anyone else in without your knowledge. Both taxi and pick-up drivers have been known to ask for payment (usually half) beforehand and then stop half-way, refusing to go any further until you pay them a new, inflated fare. To avoid this don't pay a cent until you have arrived at your destination, regardless of their protests. If you are travelling by pick-up you will need to change vehicles at Sisophon so only pay for the trip to Sisophon, around ₿30-60. You will need to negotiate the next leg once you hit Sisophon (Sisophon to Siem Reap ₿50-200, depending on where you are sitting in the vehicle). Try not to separate yourself from your bags, either by taxi or pick-up, as theft is common (particularly if your bags are in the back of a pick-up).

Guesthouse scam Most drivers will have pretty set ideas about where they want you to stay in Siem Reap – usually the place that pays them the highest commission. They have been known to stall the trip to Siem Reap so tourists arrive in Siem Reap late and disorientated and will stay at their selected place without debate. Many will try to tell you that the guesthouse you wish to stay at is 'full', or 'closed' or 'dangerous'. Outright lies. Taxis have been known to drop people at guesthouses and when those concerned have decided that they wish to move elsewhere, the guesthouse proprietors have seized their luggage. Select a guesthouse/hotel from the guide and inform your driver you have a booking at a certain guesthouse already – this they can't dispute.

Note that these scams aren't exclusive to Poipet – they are also known to occur around O'Smach, Pailin and Koh Kong. It would be very unlucky to encounter every single one of these scams in a single trip and for the most part the Bangkok to Siem Reap trip is a breeze.

place in town, clean rooms with TV and fan. 5 mins free internet per day and a free Khmer language lesson for guests. Charming owner, Sophal, worked on the UNTAC mission and the Genocide Documentation Centre and is good for a chat. Free transfers from bus station. Planning to build western/Cambodian restaurant. Good travel advice. Recommended.
E **Krong Dei Meas**. The basic rooms with attached bathrooms are spacious but rather gloomy and grubby, however, this guesthouse is set in the colonial area of town (close to the Central Park) and is an easy walk from the bus and taxi drop-off point.

E **Metapheap**, opposite the Victory Monument, T012-949287. Guesthouse above its restaurant. It has one of the only handful of restaurants in town, but they're not the friendliest lot.
E **Phkay Proek Guesthouse**, on the main road to Phnom Penh (up from **Acleda Bank**), T012-932919. Rooms with good amenities, clean. Nice gardens but vicious dogs. No English spoken.
E **Rithisen Hotel**, T026-988632. Convenient if arriving by boat as the hotel is opposite the pier, but about 2 km from the main town. An attractive 2-storey building. Lovely views of the lake from balconies, all rooms clean with

attached bathroom, fan. Very friendly staff, peaceful setting.

E Sokha Guesthouse, T026-988622. A 2-storey white house down a leafy lane in a peaceful location – a 5 to 10 min walk from the centre of town and 3 km from the lake. Reopened in 1997 and popular with NGO staff with large garden with swings and benches, basic rooms with fan only but clean (some have attached and some shared bathroom), family run, home cooking available. The only drawback is that there is no lighting around this area at night, so it can be a bit daunting walking around in the pitch black dark.

E-F Bopha Angkor, on main road to Phnom Penh, T012- 649268. Bit run down, basic rooms. No English spoken.

Pursat *p146*

D-E Phnom Pich Guest- house, on Road 1, near the bridge, T052-951515. The best hotel in town by miles. The staff are exceptionally friendly, the rooms are clean with TV, big bathroom and a/c or fan. Great restaurant attached. Nice views of the river.

D-E Tounsour Hotel, on Road 2, off Highway 5, behind the sculptural school, T052-951506. Clean, some well-sized and some small rooms all in a wooden structure with hot water, fan, a/c and TV. Despite the kitsch 1970s feel to this place the lobby has some very impressive wooden carved apsaras. Motorbike hire US$5 a day.

D-E Vimean Sourkea Guesthouse, on Road 1, on the riverfront. Rather large, unsightly building but the rooms are clean and have fan and a/c.

D-E Vimean Tip Guest- house, on Road 3, just off Highway 5, T012-836052. Good rooms with jazzed up rooms that include a large bath and granite basin. The staff are a bit of a bungling bunch but nice enough. A/c and fan rooms available.

E Sopheakmongkol Guesthouse, National Rd 5 (on the Phnom Penh side before you reach the bridge), T012-584548. Pokey rooms with TV, fan and lurid synthetic sheets and curtains to match. Little English spoken.

F Chock Meas Guesthouse, on Highway 5, before you cross the bridge, T092- 900669. Very average budget rooms with fan and attached bathroom, no English spoken.

F Penh Chet Guesthouse, National Road 5, 90 m from the bridge, T012-838859. Although the corridor smells like urine the place is generally quite clean. Rooms have attached bathroom, hot water, TV and fan. The fact that they quote US$1.50 for 3-hr room hire indicates that their target market is more of a transient ilk.

Battambang *p147, map p148*

There is quite a lot of accommodation in town with one or two guesthouses overlooking the river.

C International, Road 2, opposite the central market. 25 rooms in a bustling location which, due to its proximity to the market, will rarely leave you sleeping after 0500. Good for an early start but no English spoken and generally unhelpful. Proximity to the **Cold Night Restaurant** (see below) works in its favour and there's also a good restaurant attached.

C-D Teo Hotel, Road 3 (behind the post office),T012-857048, teohotelservices@ yahoo.com. A little way from the centre but it is clean, has a/c and hot water and restaurant. The management is so concerned with the safety of its guests and their olfactory comfort that guns and durians are forbidden. Accepts Visa and MasterCard.

D Angkor, Road 1, T012- 845761. Nice riverside location, quite busy, simple rooms, hot water but slightly overpriced.

D Chhaya Hotel, Road 3, T012- 733204. This large, older-style hotel, situated just off the market, is popular with travellers. The fan and a/c rooms are clean with attached bathrooms and western toilets. Lots of tourist services available.

D Leng Heng Hotel, on the east side of the river, T012- 882764/053-953088. Recently renovated but still smells of stale cigarettes. Rooms have a/c, cable TV and hot water and are slightly damp. The **Cold Night Restaurant** is located on the same premises.

D Monorom Hotel, T012- 878389. Ratty, ramshackle rooms. Most amenities available, such as TV, adjoining bathroom etc but no hot water.

● *For an explanation of the sleeping and eating price codes used in this guide, see inside the*
● *front cover. Other relevant information is found in Essentials, see pages 34-37*

D Park Hotel, Rattanak Village (on the East side of the river), T053-953773. Newest hotel in town, very clean, with good amenities and friendly staff. Rooms include TV, wardrobe, fan and hot water. A/c available.

D Paris, Road 3. Older building in a convenient and quiet location. Clean and well kept with a/c and fan, some hot water, like many others almost no English spoken but quite friendly.

D-E Golden Parrot, Rd 3. Basic cell-like rooms, some a/c, worth bargaining.

D-E Golden River Hotel, just off Road 3, T053-730165. The central location does not really compensate for the damp, dingy rooms on offer. Rooms are in a state of disrepair with paint peeling off the walls and general lack of upkeep. Fan, fridge and TV available.

D-E Royal, T016-912034, royal_asiahotelbb@hotmail.com. What sets this hotel apart from the others in this price range is the small rooftop terrace with restaurant where you can enjoy the sunset and panoramic views of the outlying countryside. The 42 rooms, all of which have attached bathrooms, are clean with a/c and fan. Usually at the ferry port and bus terminal a representative from the hotel will meet travellers. By far the best deal in town. Recommended.

Pailin *p150*

In Pailin there isn't a great selection of hotels to choose from, most of them rate somewhere between horrendous and average.

C-D Hang Meas (Golden Pheasant) Hotel, 100 m past the market on the left on the road to the Thai border, T012-787546. Pailin's grand hotel opened in early 1999 but the 50 a/c rooms are already shabby – though they all have hot-water bathrooms, TV and comfortable beds. There are great views from the roof and it has well tended grounds, massage, nightclub and dining hall. Staff seem to have better things to do than see to their guests' needs and are a little absent-minded. Although this is comparably expensive to other parts of Cambodia it is the best hotel in town, by a long way. Has an Interphone shop, though there are plenty around town.

D-E Kim Young Heng Guesthouse, near truck station on the road into town,

T016-727343. A film of dust covers the rooms and it is a bit noisy but is better than some of the other alternatives. TV, fan and attached bathroom.

E Cheng Lang Guesthouse, 2-storey wooden house, on the right before the turn-off to the market. No English sign apart from the word 'guesthouse'. A welcoming atmosphere and run by 2 friendly sisters with 8 doubles, some divided with wood panelling. Rooms are basically furnished and those with attached bathroom are a dollar or so pricier. Good views from both front and rear balconies. Bit pokey.

E Ponleu Pich Pailin, near the market, next to **Lao Lao Keng Guesthouse**. Very friendly owner. Clean rooms with fan and bathroom. Attached bathrooms.

Sisophon *p151, map p151*

There are plenty of guest-houses opposite the truck station and garage and on the way out of town towards Siem Reap. Facilities are basic and not always clean and the padded walls aren't a particularly good look.

D Neak Meas. The newest most resplendent hotel in town. Sparkling white but it will be only a matter of months before it collects the grime like the others. Large sized a/c rooms, bath and TV. Good Khmer restaurant. The only drawback is the number of karaoke booths but they are detached from the sleeping quarters so shouldn't be too disruptive. This hotel is probably the best pick in town.

D Phnom Svay Hotel, in a row of 3 hotels, next to the **Rong Roeung**, T012-971287. The grand palace of Sisophon: green deer and red lion statues flank the entranceway and the stairway and lobby are elegantly furnished with Khmer sculptures. Opened in 1996, it has reasonably spacious doubles equipped with a/c, TV, fridge and attached bathrooms with hot water. The place could do with a bit of an overhaul, otherwise it is pretty good value. Phnom Svay means Mango Hill, which is also the name of the large hill opposite the hotel.

E Rong Roeung (Glorious) Hotel, T054-958823, next to the **Sourkear**. Built during the UNTAC years it offers large doubles with TV. More expensive rooms have a/c and attached bathroom. Friendly English-speaking staff, nice seating area and balcony upstairs.

E Sourkear Hotel, T054- 958810. The first in the row of 3 hotels on the right of the road in from Poipet, opposite the Provincial Office. Surreal floor tiling and grand, high ceilings. Rooms are very shabby now, but with clean attached toilets and scoop showers. TV with some satellite channels. Very charming, friendly staff but with no English spoken.

Poipet *p153*

An overnight stop in Poipet is not advised and should not be necessary. Despite poor road conditions on the Cambodian side, it is possible to leave the Thai capital in the early morning and arrive in Siem Reap that night. Bangkok to Phnom Penh is more difficult to manage in a day but Battambang is a more agreeable overnight staging post than Poipet. The next town along, towards Phnom Penh, is Sisophon, still not the best stopover but marginally better than Poipet. If you do decide to stay overnight, there are plenty of guesthouses and a few hotels in town but beware, most places seem to operate as brothels for Thai customers.

There are a few flashier hotels attached to or associated with the casinos. Most of them are quite expensive and attract dodgy clientele but generally have quite good rooms if you can turn a blind eye or don't mind a bet or two, as in some places it is a prerequisite that you are gambling.

B Holiday Palace Casino, in the casino area. Although the room rate is ฿1000 guests are given ฿400 worth of non-redeemable vouchers which can be used for gambling. The rooms are of a better standard here and reasonably well-equipped.

B-C Grand Diamond City Hotel, in the casino area, T054-967344. Dodgy but cleanish modern rooms with all facilities. Patrons can be noisy.

E Poipet Pass Guesthouse, T011-940588. Reasonably good value as most rooms have fridge, attached bathroom and TV. A few extra dollars gets you hot water. The on-premises karaoke can be a bit grating.

E Poypad Phnom Pich Guesthouse, on the main road up from immigration. Red tiled throughout, clean but small rooms with basic facilities and attached bathroom. A lack of windows in some rooms make the place a little gloomy. Family run. For ฿350 you can get a room with a/c and TV.

F Bayon Guesthouse, is a basic guesthouse offering good, clean rooms, with fan, windows (a big plus compared to other places) and bathroom. One of the best restaurants in town, the **Hang Neak Restaurant**, is on the premises.

❼ Eating

Kompong Chnang *p144, map p145*
Considering the number of guesthouses in town, there aren't an awful lot of restaurants that cater for tourists. At the time of writing a new **Sarmarkey Restaurant** was under construction slightly up and across from the Victory Monument. It is possible to get spring rolls and other snacks down by the river.

❢ **Mekong Restaurant**, on the road from Battambang. Good Khmer food at reasonable prices.

❢ **Metapheap Restaurant**, on the corner opposite the Victory Monument. English menu, but little English is spoken. Chinese and Khmer dishes with an emphasis on soup, pricier than the restaurant by the truck stop but good service, US$2-4.

❢ **Sohka Guesthouse** will serve home-cooked food to guests (the cook is very hard to catch).

❢ **Soksen Restaurant**, on the corner beside the Sokimex Petrol Station. The name and menu are all in Khmer and the staff speaks no English, so it can be tricky. But they do very good, cheap Khmer food, ie noodles and vegetables. Best bet is to point at what another customer is having.

Pursat *p146*

The market on the west side has food stalls where it is possible to pick up a tasty meal or snack and there are various restaurants along the main road. Also a number of tikalok (fruit shakes) vendors.

❢ **Borei Thmei Restaurant**, on the corner of Road 4 and Route 5, T012-838332. Good little Khmer restaurant offering all the staples, fried fish etc. Most dishes come in under US$1.50.

❢ **Community Villa**, on Road 3, just off Highway 5, T012- 583860. A lovely little local NGO startup to train disadvantaged children and their families in the hospitality industry. A good selection of Khmer and

Thai-influenced dishes, including great papaya salad and tom yum soup. Very reasonable prices and the service, as you would expect, is nothing short of brilliant. Recommended,

Khmer BBQ Restaurant, at the start of the bridge on the Phnom Penh side. It has a bamboo platform that hangs over the riverside. This is a DIY operation where small burners are sat at each table and you cook your own food. More of a drinking atmosphere than fine food eatery.

Lamb Sewing, on Route 5 as you come in from Phnom Penh. Beer garden atmosphere with little thatched huts in a garden setting. Fantastic selection of Khmer food, though one must watch the beer girls hovering. The jovial, old one-legged owner is very accommodating. The only off putting thing about this place is that they have a slaughterhouse on sight and the sight of dead piggies hooked up could put you off your meal. If you eat in the cabanas this can quite easily be avoided. There are a couple of other similar places further along the road. Recommended.

Battambang *p147, map p148*

Battambang's selection of eateries has improved and widened considerably over the last few years. The best place to start is around the market where a number of stalls and small restaurants are open during the day and evening. Many have pans with ready cooked dishes. Just point to what you want. Rice, meat and vegetables costs US$0.50-0.80.

Cold Night Restaurant, next door to Leng Heng Hotel on the east side of the river, T012-994746. Locally known as Mr T's because of its likeable owner. It is a popular, quiet restaurant with an extensive menu of western, Thai and Khmer food. Expect to pay US$4 for a steak and less for local dishes. Beer garden, pool table and dart board.

Pkay Proek, St 3, west of Battambang Ct, T012- 571579. Large restaurant (with further extensions planned) offering a range of Cambodian, Chinese and Thai dishes. Considered the best Khmer food in town. Beer garden. Somewhat of a Khmer franchise, restaurants of the same name can be found in Phnom Penh, Pailin, Poipet and Banteay Meanchey.

Riverside Balcony Bar, located just down from the Governor's Residence where the road turns off for Pailin, this attractive wooden terraced bar, run by an entertaining Aussie, overlooks the river and is the best place to go if the ebb and flow of river life, particularly as dusk descends, is your idea of entertainment. Open from 1800, the comfortable bar is lit up by fairy lights. The menu is predominantly American and Mexican, and it has got the production of exceedingly good chips well and truly taped. Good value. Highly atmospheric. Recommended.

Royal Hotel Restaurant, good and well priced Khmer food served on the roof terrace.

Smokin' Pot, in the centre of town (between Road 1 and 2), T012-657125. Cambodian/Thai restaurant with very good food and lovely owner. Great fish amok. Also runs cooking classes.

White Rose is just up from the Angkor Hotel. It specializes in great fruit shakes (US$0.50- 0.60) but also has an extensive selection of dishes (predominantly Cambodian and Thai), 1 or 2 words of English spoken but for non-speakers of Khmer the best option is look and point.

Cafés
Sunrise Coffeehouse, slightly down from the Royal Hotel, T053-953426. A French-style bakery serving pastries, cakes, pies, bagels and cookies. Great breakfast and the best coffee and tea in town. Wraps, sandwiches and melts all between US$1-3. Good value. Open 0630-1700, closed Sun. Highly recommended.

Pailin *p150*

There are lots of cheap stalls and restaurants in the market area which are good for breakfast noodles and iced drinks. If you are in search of a quiet beer in the evening, head for the bottom of the hill on the road into town. Here there are numerous thatched drinking huts where you can perch on a stool. The Hang Meas Restaurant and Bamboo Restaurant are also popular drinking holes.

Bamboo Restaurant, on the main road towards the Thai border, T012-405818. Quite atmospheric with open salas and romantically lit gardens. Good selection of fish dishes, slightly on the pricey side. Over zealous beer girls.

Hang Meas Hotel, in the hotel's grounds. English menu, Khmer and Thai dishes. Good service and passable food – most expensive restaurant in town.

Reksmei Phnom Yat Restaurant. The owner of this place clearly couldn't decide whether to open a restaurant or a furniture shop specializing in teak products. The house speciality is the local smoked fish and the owners are planning to expand their rooftop empire.

Phkay Phreauk Restaurant, on Highway 10, towards the pagoda, T016-317027. This restaurant's brilliant food and extensive menu has easily made it the best restaurant in town. Very reasonable prices.

Sisophon *p151, map p151*

There really isn't a brilliant selection of restaurants in town. Surprisingly, eating at the street stalls is probably the best option, as the kids are extraordinarily bright and the food and service is usually nothing short of exceptional. At the time of publication the town was in a flutter over a new, impressive restaurant to be opened near the town hall. Watch this spot. The **Neak Meas** has a reasonably good Khmer restaurant. Just in front of the market is a Chinese coffee shop. At night the main park is packed with food vendors selling sweet desserts, sour wine, noodles, soup and rice. There is also a line of food and shake stalls lining the south and west side of Thien Po Park.

Peng Hour, between the truck station and the market. It's just behind the market and is hard to miss as it is lit up by flashing lights. Little Chinese restaurant- cum-coffee shop. English menu offering noodles, stir fries and other Sino-Khmer meals. Unexciting and expensive dishes.

Penh Chet, Khmer and Thai fare. The owner was in the throes of revamping his menu at the time of writing and indicated that there would be some kind of set menu option for customers. Little English spoken so lots of gestures required.

Pkay Preok Restaurant, just before the **Phnom Svay Guesthouse**, is popular with the NGO community. It is the preferred diner in

town serving unpretentious Khmer, Thai and western food at reasonable prices. English menu.

Reksmei Phnom Yat Restaurant. The owner of this place clearly couldn't decide whether to open a restaurant or a furniture shop specializing in teak products. The house speciality is the local smoked fish and the owners are planning to expand their rooftop empire.

Samleng, near the **Neak Meas Hotel**. Huge restaurant that spends more time closed than open. Khmer specialities, particularly banquets.

Poipet *p153*

There are plenty of noodle soup stalls around and inside the market. The restaurant at the **Bayon Guesthouse** is very popular and extremely good value.

Reksmei Phnom Yat Restaurant. The owner of this place clearly couldn't decide whether to open a restaurant or a furniture shop specializing in teak products. The house speciality is the local smoked fish and the owners are planning to expand their rooftop empire.**Srah Trocheck**, on the main road, is a favourite serving very good Khmer and Thai food.

● Bars and clubs

Battambang *p147, map p148*

There are a number of cheap market stalls offering Vietnamese rolls, shakes and various Khmer food on the riverfront in the museum area.

Bophatip Nightclub, beyond the **Riverside Balcony and Bar**, on the road to Pailin. Open 2000-2400. The most popular nightclub in town. Dancing and cheap beer.

Paradise Nightclub, in the centre of town adjacent to the **White Rose**. Open 2000-2400. Live music (usually in English). Beer girls in abundance.

Riverside Balcony Bar is the best option for a quiet sunset drink.

● Entertainment

Battambang *p147, map p148*

Sala Barang circus. This French- run circus is worth a visit. The circus is an initiative by a number of NGOs and organizations to provide opportunities for disabled children and those coming from underprivileged backgrounds. Starting at 2000, the circus includes trapeze artists, mono-cyclists, jugglers, clowns and scores of other entertaining acts. The circus is located 3 km out of town and runs infrequently (dependent on numbers) so it is best to check before-hand with **Asian Trails**, No 111 E1, St 2, T053-73008, asiantrails@online.com.kh.

O Shopping

Pursat *p146*
Aside from the local market which stocks most products Pursat is famous for its marble carvings. There is a Marble Carving Workshop in the centre of town.

Battambang *p147, map p148*
A range of shops selling local souvenirs can be found along Street 1 on the riverfront.

The **Central Market**, Phsar Nath, sells clothes, film and gems. Around its precinct there are several film shops.

Near Pailin is one of the central gem-mining areas in Cambodia so there are many gem dealers sprinkled around Battambang. There are some exceptionally good deals as well as some outright scams (heated stones, glass etc). Most of the gemmologists can be found around the Central Market area.

Danine mini-mart behind the **Chaya Hotel** stocks a wide range of foreign foodstuffs and other goods.

Pailin *p150*
The local market is stocked with a good variety of supplies due to the town's proximity to Thailand. Prices are usually quoted in baht. The signature trade business of Pailin is gems and there are a multitude of places where you can buy them around town, usually sapphires and rubies, though other precious and semi precious stones are in abundance. Watch out for artificially coloured gems – mostly through intensive heating (bright blues and reds are a tell-tale sign).

▲ Activities and tours

Battambang *p147, map p148*
Both **Intrepid** and **Asian Trails** run tours of the region.

Asian Trails, Rd 2, T053- 730088. Intrepid also has a head office in town.

However, there is no shortage of well-briefed moto-dops who speak good English. They usually hang around the **Royal Hotel** and **Chaya Hotel**. The standard tour includes a trip to some outlying villages, a trip to Phnom Sampeu and Wat Banon and a short ride on the Bamboo Train back to town again. Allocate a day for the tour and expect to pay US$6-8.

Mr Pou, T012 895442, is possibly one of the best guides in the country and arranges explorations around the circuit for US$7 a day.

Therapies
Seeing Hands Massage is located 10 m down from the corner of Street 3. Massage is US$4 for 1½ hrs.

⊖ Transport

Kompong Chhnang *p144, map p145*
Boat
The boat between Phnom Penh and Siem Reap will stop in Kompong Chhnang sometimes if you request. Catching it from Kompong Chhnang is quite tricky. Climb down the bank opposite the **Rithisen Hotel** to the police jetty. When you can see the boat (boat to Siem Reap is around 0830), hop onto a nearby craft, US$0.50-1, to take you into the middle of the lake. The fast boat should then stop, allowing you to board – but not always! The fee is usually the same as the whole journey (Phnom Penh-Siem Reap) ie US$25. Buy your ticket on board the boat; don't, despite their protests, pay your money to the marine policemen on the jetty.

Bus/pickup/taxi
Kompong Chhnang lies about 91 km from Phnom Penh and 201 km from Battambang along Route 5. The truck stop in Kompong Chhnang is opposite the Victory Monument. There is a bus station next to Sokimex Petrol Station and buses leave to **Phnom Penh**, invariably every hour (on the hour) from

0800-1600. Buses to **Battambang** can also be arranged here. Pick-up trucks from Phnom Penh onwards to **Pursat**, US$1.30, roughly 2½ hrs, and **Battambang**, US$2.60, 4-5 hrs,
pass the roundabout by the petrol station at around 0800.

Pursat *p146*

Shared taxi and pick-ups ply the route from Phnom Penh to Battambang and beyond (see page 162). The nearest boat stop is Krakor, 35 km east. It is possible to get to Phnom Penh and to Siem Reap from here. A train departs on alternate days for the north travelling as far as Battambang (at around 1300, US$0.40), and for the south down to Phnom Penh (at 1100, US$0.80). The train is notoriously unreliable and slow.

GST Buses to **Phnom Penh** depart from Pursat Railway Station at 0630, 0830, 1245 (10,000 riel), 3 hrs. **Phnom Penh Public Transport Buses**, T023- 210359, depart for Phnom Penh at 0645, 0730, 1230, 10,000 riel.

Battambang *p147, map p148*
Air
At time of printing there are no flights. **President Airlines** may offer flights in late 2005 but no longer have offices in town. The airport sits about 2 km from town centre, just off of Route 5.

Boat
River connections to **Siem Reap** daily from the pier just east of Route 5 river crossing. Departs at 0700, 3-4 hrs, US$15. In the dry season the boat can take up to 7 hrs and includes an hour long trip in the back of a pick-up, when the river becomes too low. From the boat to any hotel a moto should cost US$0.50.

Bus/pickup/taxi
Bus transport is pretty rough but still reasonably cheap.
Neak Krorhorm Travel, T023-219496, in Phnom Penh and **Phnom Penh Public Transport Company** run daily buses between Battambang and Phnom Penh (departure times vary but it is usually quite early in the morning).

Most guesthouses in Battambang sell

tickets onwards to **Siem Reap** or **Phnom Penh** (12 hrs) or tickets can be bought directly from the Capital Tour Bus Company or Neak Krorhorm Travel, near the morning market. Buses depart for **Siem Reap**, US$5 at 0700, and **Phnom Penh**, US$4 at 0700, 0730, 0800, 0900, 1200 daily from Psar Nath.
GST Buses, T012 895550, runs 3 trips day each way, US$3 at 0630, 0830, 1245 and departs from Phnom Penh, St 142, near the Central Market. The buses depart from Battambang near Por Khnung Pagoda, T012-414441, 5 hrs. **Phnom Penh Public Transport Buses**, T023-210359, depart from Battambang near Thmor Thmey Bridge. They depart 3 times a day to **Phnom Penh** at 0645, 0730, 1230, US$3.

Pick-ups and shared taxis depart from Boeung Choeuk Market, shared taxi US$7 per person to **Phnom Penh**, a 5-hr hard slog, **Sisophon**, US$4, and **Poipet**, US$6. Pick-ups to **Pailin** depart from Loeu Market at the western end of town, US$3. The roads are okay for about half the trip and horrible for the rest, so allow around 3 hrs for the trip from Battambang.

Train
To **Phnom Penh**, depart 0600, arrive 1800 approximately. The train leaves for Phnom Penh every second day, US$4. To **Sisophon** depart 0700 arrive 1100, US$2. The train to Sisophon is unreliable and does not run on a standard timetable.

Pailin *p150*
Motorbike
Cheng Lang Guesthouse rents motorbikes for ฿200 per day

Bus/pickup/taxi
There is only one way into Pailin on the Cambodian side and that is the 83 km along Route 10 from Battambang. Pick-ups leave all day (0600-1600) from the bus station next to the market to **Battambang**, US$3 inside. It is also possible to organize a motodop to take you for the night for around US$30-40.

There is an **international border crossing** 20 km from Pailin, identifiable by the tell-tale casino-out-in-the-middle-of-nowhere. Immigration visas are ฿1000, tourist visa and ฿1500, business visa. They could refuse dollars so ensure you have baht.

The crossing is known for scams similar to those found in Poipet (see box page 154). You will need to bring passport photographs with you as there is no photography processing facility here. From Pailin it is ฿50 per person in a shared taxi to the border which is around 20 km away. There are usually motos and taxis at the border crossing to take tourists at Pailin. From the Thai side it is a ฿20 motorbike ride to the songthaew station – which has songthaews to the nearest bus station at Chantaburi. It takes 1½ hrs to reach Chantaburi bus station and costs ฿35.

Sisophon *p151, map p151*
Bus

The trip between Sisophon and **Phnom Penh** takes 6 hrs. The buses depart from Sisophon Market bound for Phnom Penh, 18,000 riel at 0645, 0715, 0745. **Phnom Penh Public Transport Buses**, T023-210359, depart from Sisophon's central market, 0700, 20,000 riel.

To **Poipet**, 48 km, 2 hrs: pick-ups can be caught on the main road near the park and Provincial Offices. To **Battambang**, 69 km, 2 hrs, leaves from the truck station, US$2 inside. There are also vehicles travelling the 360 km to **Phnom Penh** (9-12 hrs). Route 5 to Battambang is poor. To **Siem Reap**, 105 km, 4-8 hrs, US$5 inside. Route 6 between Siem Reap and Sisophon was one of the worst highways in Cambodia but is being gradually repaired. The craters and potholes are being filled and the lunar landscape which once masqueraded as a road is fading into history. Even so, in the wet season the road becomes an ocean of thick mud and the journey can take almost a day to complete. Some of the bridges are also in a very poor state of repair. The wooden driveways of some bridges are missing. To cross the bridge the local bridge-keeper is engaged (for a small pecuniary interest) to return the planks to their original position. Many a small commune around the country is, one suspects, maintained by their bridge-keeping operations.

Train

There is a small railway station in Sisophon, and a daily service to Battambang, 3 hrs.

Poipet *p153*

The road from Poipet is absolutely horrendous.

To **Sisophon**, 48 km. Pick-ups ply the one and very potholed road out of Poipet. Pick them up from the bus station or anywhere along the main road. The drive is fairly unexciting, passing through rice fields but there are some interesting statues in the villages en route – in particular a curious rendition of Hanuman spearing a bull. To **Siem Reap**, 153 km, 4-7 hrs. Pick-ups converge on the Cambodian side of the border to collect passengers going to Siem Reap. However, one might get stuck waiting hours for other passengers to arrive to make the trip more worthwhile for the driver. If no direct ride to Siem Reap is available go to Sisophon and pick up a ride from there. To Battambang, 117 km, 3-4 hrs, US$5 inside. A shared taxi is quicker but more expensive.

Border with Thailand The border crossing is open daily 0730-1700. The last bus from Aranya Prathet to Bangkok departs at 1700. The immigration officials at the Poipet border can be difficult. Tourist visas are usually US$20 but expect to pay up to US$25 (฿1000). A business visa, by law, costs only US$30 (฿1200-1400). Prices will usually be charged in baht due to the weak dollar but rest assured that they will charge you whichever currency is best for them. In recent years all foreigners were required to take 2 pills supplied by the immigration officers, supposedly for cholera protection, for which a US$5 fee was demanded. The pills were clearly out of date and in fact they were doxycyclin – an antibiotic and ineffective against cholera. Exiting the country via Poipet can be just as exciting: border guards like to fine those overstaying their visas by charging double the official penalty set in Phnom Penh (US$5 per day). The increase depends on the mood of the official but bargaining has been known to work.

Transport from Thailand Bus: 4-5 hrs, a/c ฿160-200, non a/c ฿100 buses leave from the northern bus station in Bangkok. Take a motorbike, ฿25, or tuk tuk, ฿40-50, the 7 km from Aranya Prathet to the Cambodian border. **Train**, 6-8 hrs, ฿100 (US$1), from Bangkok to Arany Prathet.

❶ Directory

Kompong Chhnang *p144, map p145*

Banks The Acleda Bank, National Highway 5, on the way to Phnom Penh (2 blocks past the Victory Monument). Open Mon-Fri 0800-1600. Western Union money transfer but no credit card advances or traveller's cheque exchange. **Internet** Internet is very expensive in Kompong Chhnang as they have to connect via a long-distance landline. Sunway Computers, near Sokhimex Petrol Station, and Odec, on site at the Friendly Guesthouse, both have internet for US$5 an hr. **Telephone** Phone booths are scattered around the town, particularly concentrated around the Bus Station (Sokimex Petrol Station) and Psar Leu.

Battambang *p147, map p148*

Banks Most of the banks exchange traveller's cheques and change money but are closed frequently. Acleda Bank on the east side of the river has Western Union. Canadia Bank takes MasterCard and UCB accepts Visa and MasterCard. UCB is the best bet as it doesn't charge any commission for advances on Visa card. Money-changers/goldsellers are concentrated around the market with a few along Road 1.There are a number of banks in town but they are often shut so for simple exchange purposes the gold and gem shops are the best bet. **Internet** There are numerous internet cafés scattered around the market and along Road 1 (River road) and Road 3 (search around for the cheapest as the rates range from US$1-2). Some of the better ones are Kimsay Internet Café, opposite the Royal Hotel (US$0.75 an hr), and KCT, on Road 1 (along the Riverfront), quicker but more expensive at US$1.50 per hr. **Post office** Close to the museum on Road 1. **Telephone** The post office provides international connections as do a few of the better hotels. Telephone booths are scattered all over the town and internet cafés now offer net calls for a very cheap rate.

Pailin *p150*

Banks Canadia Bank has an outlet on Highway 10 towards the pagoda. Mon-Fri 0800-1600 and Sat until 1200. No credit card facilities only Western Union money transfer. **Internet** There are several phone booths located around the market. Buddhism for Development has an internet café on Highway 10, surprisingly cheap and quick.

Sisophon *p151, map p151*

Bank Canadia Bank, one street south of the park. **Internet** There are a couple of internet cafés on the road running parallel to Thien Bo Park. **Telephone** All the main hotels have interphone IDD facility. **Post office** The post office is next to the truck station.

Poipet *p153*

Banks There is an Acleda bank in town, which will do Western Union transfers only. **Telephone** Interphone shops with IDD facility are dotted around the town (around US$1 per min). Code for interphones here is 037.

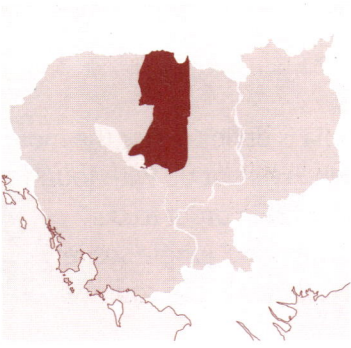

Central region

Footprint features

Introduction

The central north area of Cambodia is definitely for the more independent-minded traveller, who will put up with tough roads and sparse public transportation in order to be rewarded with amazing temples, beautiful jungle scenery and some of the friendliest small villages in the country.

The spectacular archaeological remains of Preah Vihear, Koh Ker, Sambor Prei Kuk and Preah Khan, all of which have been off-limits to visitors for several decades, are to be found in this region. They are not necessarily any more accessible these days but at least they are much safer to visit. The area is still littered with landmines but, by exercising caution, most people won't find this a problem. Visible evidence of both the Khmer Rouge fighting and the US bombings is ubiquitous.

★ Don't miss...

1 **Sambor Prei Kuk** Kompong Thom is a good place to base yourself to visit this Chenla-era, pre-Angkorian capital, a sprawling, peaceful romantic temple complex, see page 168.

2 **Preah Khan** A visit to this remote and isolated temple complex will satisfy the thirst of even the most independent, adventurous travellers. Terrible roads and isolation render it one of the least visited in the country, see page 170.

3 **Koh Ker** Be captivated by Jayavarman IV's former kingdom now shrouded in jungle, see page 170.

4 **Preah Vihear** Be left breathless by this mountaintop temple located atop the zig-zagging Dangrek Enscarpment, see page 171.

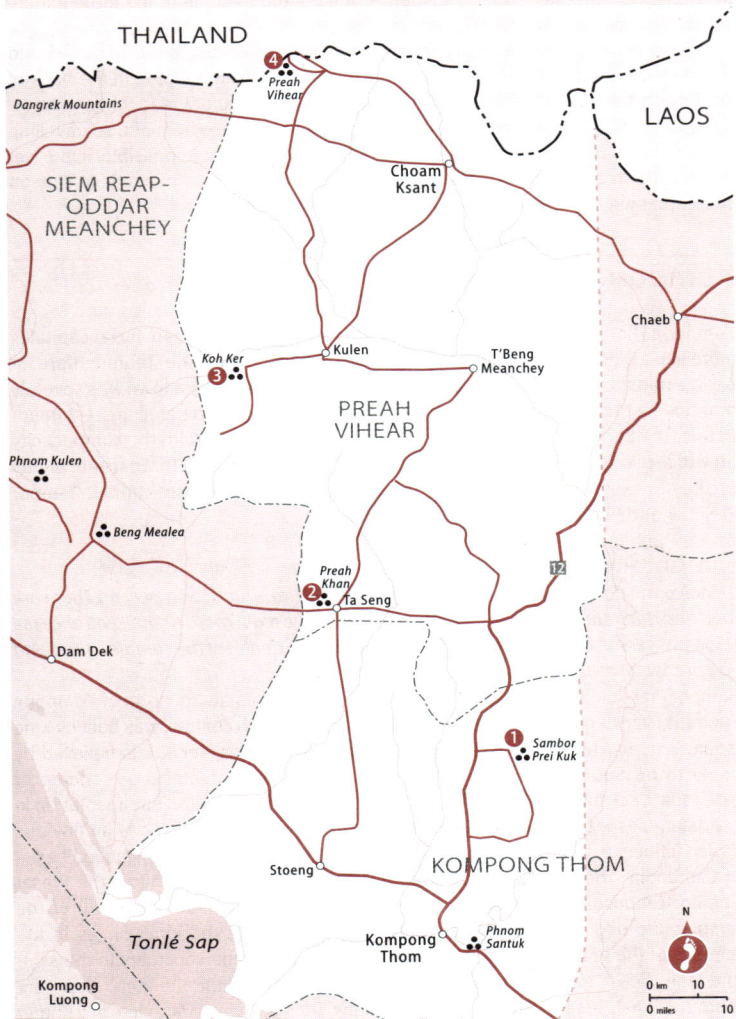

THAILAND

Dangrek Mountains

LAOS

4 *Preah Vihear*

Choam Ksant

SIEM REAP-ODDAR MEANCHEY

Chaeb

Koh Ker 3 ● Kulen

T'Beng Meanchey

PREAH VIHEAR

Phnom Kulen

● *Beng Mealea*

Preah Khan

2 ●Ta Seng

12

● Dam Dek

1 ● *Sambor Prei Kuk*

Stoeng

KOMPONG THOM

Tonlé Sap

Kompong Thom ○ *Phnom Santuk*

Kompong Luong ○

N

0 km   10
0 miles 10

Central region

The central provinces are among Cambodia's least visited regions yet contain a brilliant array of ancient temples and jungle scenery. Those who undertake the arduous journey to the remote sites of Preah Vihear, Koh Ker and Preah Khan will be duly rewarded. ⇥ *For Sleeping, Eating and other listings see pages 173-175.*

Ins and outs

Getting there and around

The Central provinces contain some of the country's worst roads making the area a little tricky to navigate. Public transport is limited and in some of the more remote areas, like around Preah Vihear, it is almost non-existent. In larger towns, like Kompong Thom, there are a range of options from shared taxi to buses but around Preah Khan or around Preah Vihear you might find yourself hopping in the back of someone's tractor. To access sites like Preah Khan, Koh Ker or Preah Vihear a larger dirt bike or 4WD is the best option. Most roads are constructed from dirt, so travelling to the temples or smaller towns becomes very difficult, or near impossible, in the wet season. The region is littered with mines, many of which aren't marked, so stay on clearly marked tracks. See Transport sections for further details.

Kompong Thom and around 🛏️🍴🚌📞 ⇥ *pages 173-175.*

Kompong Thom is Cambodia's second largest province and the provincial capital is more like a city than a town. It can be quite chaotic as it is a major thoroughfare for people transiting to Siem Reap and the regions further north. The town was severely bombed by the US in the 1970s and large craters spotted in the area are testament to this. The Sen River divides the town into two distinct areas with the compact city area to the south and a more sprawling, industrial area to the north. There are plenty of sites to explore around town including the magnificent former capital, Sambor Prei Kuk and Phnom Santuk.

Sambor Prei Kuk

ⓘ *Motos will do the return trip for US$6-9 a day and taxis for US$20 per car. There are food and drink stalls within the temple complex on the main road. A small entrance fee US$2 per person is charged at the Tourist Information Centre at the complex gates and you are required to pay extra to take the bike through.*

Sambor Prei Kuk is a group of over 100 temples which lies 28 km north of Kompong Thom. This ancient Chenla capital, dating from the seventh century, was built by King Ishanavarman I (616-635) and dedicated to Shiva. Sambor Prei Kuk is believed by many to be Southeast Asia's first temple city. The main temples are square or octagonal brick tower-shrines on high brick terraces with wonderful ornamentation in sandstone, especially the lintel stones. The finely sculptured brick has an obvious Indian influence, for example the use of lion sculptures, an animal which didn't exist in Cambodia. The temples are divided into three geographical groups: the Prasat Sambor Group, the Prasat Tao Group and the Prasat Yeay Peu Group. All of the temples are dedicated to Shiva. Some highlights include the inner lingas in the temples of the Prasat Sambor Group (try looking up from the sanctuary to the sky); and the lions guarding the temple of Prasat Tao (unfortunately they are reproductions). These temples are worth visiting: for many years they were in a Khmer

Rouge stronghold dominated by the commander Ta Mok and craters left by American bombing during the war are still visible. It is believed that there were originally between 180 to 200 monuments but many of these were completely shattered during the US bombardment. Paradoxically, even the park's conservation centre has been destroyed, so much so that one can consider it as one of Sambor Prei Kuk's ruins. Considering that these are some of the oldest temples in the country – 200 years before Angkor was built – they are well preserved and now that the area is safe, visitors can make their way around the temples and enjoy the forested solitude of the ruins. There are some amazing trees, some which look as old as the structures themselves. Botanists have been through the area and have put little identification signs on most foliage. There is a tranquil atmosphere and very few visitors, something which is difficult to say of Angkor. There is a really nice route via some beautiful small rural villages. Follow NH6 towards Siem Reap for 5 km until the road veers into a much worse road, NH64 (the road to T'Beng Meanchey). Follow this for another 10 km and turn right at the big colourful archway and follow the road through to the temples (another 19 km).This trip is highly scenic passing through rice paddies, small villages and little farming lots and should take about an hour to get here.

Phnom Santuk

ⓘ *Motos that congregate around the taxi stand and Arunreas Hotel will do the trip 20 km south of Kompong Thom for US$5-6 (roundtrip).*

The 980 steps to the pagoda at the top of Phnom Santuk Mountain is a great trip to do around noon in order to later catch the brilliant sunset and stunning panoramic views of the countryside. The holy mountain is the most significant in the region and around the brightly painted pagoda are some fascinating Buddha images carved out of large, stone boulders. Though many tourists might see the temple as a bit garish or kitsch, the site is hugely popular with the Khmers, who believe it to be somewhat auspicious. There are several vendors around the area, including a gamut of people touting traditional medicines and therapies.

Around T'Beng Meanchey ⊖⊘⊖⊜⊖» *pages 173-175.*

T'Beng Meanchey is a small, dusty, non-descript town that occupies a largely inflated land mass. The future of this sprawling town hinges on the development of the roads between the remote temple sites of Koh Ker, Preah Khan and Preah Vihear – in all likelihood this town will become a major gateway to these remote temples. At the time of writing only a dribble of tourists were making it to the town, which has a more 'remote' feel than those areas such as Ban Lung or Sen Monorom, which are usually ascribed remote status. Aside from being a 'gateway' to major temples in the region, T'Beng Meanchey also pierces the junction of some of the country's worst roads. However, the good news is that the roads are being overhauled courtesy of an Asian Development Bank loan so hopefully this will change in years to come. Oddly enough, wrestle mania has hit this town – big time. It is almost impossible to enter any restaurant without competing with the hordes of wrestling fans who swarm to see the matches broadcast via satellite TV.

Sights

The town itself doesn't have a whole lot of tourist attractions apart from the Joom Noon Silk Project and Wat Chey Preuk. The **Joom Noon Silk Project** is a local initiative started by Vietnam veteran, Bud Gibbons, to help rehabilitate people with disabilities through this silk weaving project. These days Bud has handed over the reins of the project to internationally acclaimed weaver, Carol Cassidy. This organization can be credited with producing some of the country's finest silk, its products available for sale across the country. The **Wat Chey Preuk** compound is almost opposite the hospital. It includes the few remaining structures of an ancient Pre-Angkorian temple built on the site, though it really isn't worth a trip out of your way to see.

Preah Khan

ⓘ *There is a small village about 5 km from the site where it is possible to pick up a drink or snack. Visiting Preah Khan is a long day trip for die-hard motorcyclists or temple enthusiasts. It is not easy as the sandy roads make for a very uncomfortable trip there. A very early start is required to make it there and back to T'Beng Meanchey in a day. It is advisable to take a hammock and torch (which can be hung in the temple) in case you get stuck out here the night. Only walk on well-trodden tracks as the area is still heftily mined. There are no official guides.*

Preah Khan ('sacred sword'), known as Bakan to most locals, ranks as one of the most remote temples in Cambodia. Surrounded by dense foliage that's presumably speckled with mines and near-impassable roads, a trip to Preah Khan is not for the light-hearted.

The development of Preah Khan is highly mysterious, though most believe that the complex was built in the ninth century and was home to both Suryavarman II and Jayavarman VII at some point (possibly during the Cham invasion). The temples were originally built for Hindu worship and later were transformed into a Buddhist complex. Scholars believe that the laterite and sandstone complex is the largest single enclosure ever constructed during the Angkor period, even superseding the mighty Angkor Thom. Preah Khan was originally linked to Angkor Wat via an ancient super-highway constructed of laterite and there are a number of fantastically carved stone bridges between the two points that still exist today.

The first temple most will see on approach is Prasat Preah Stung, with the Jayavarman VII trademark of large Bayon-like smiling faces peering out over the jungle. To the east is a massive 3-km-long baray and east of this is a petite ninth-century temple, Prasat Preah Damrei. This intricate pyramid is also known as Elephant Temple due to the two regal carved elephants gracing the temple. The main temple structure is now in ruins and is about 400 m from Prasat Preah Stung. Disappointingly, this temple has been so severely looted that no semblance exists whatsoever and much of the building, aside from the outer walls, has collapsed upon itself. Looting has long been a problem here: the recidivist French looter, Louis Delaporte, carted off thousands of kilograms of artefacts to the Guimet Museum in Paris and recently a couple of looters were killed when part of the building collapsed on them. The main structure is in a ruinous state and it's hard to distinguish many of its features as a result, though some bas-reliefs on the outer walls are quite good.

Here cows graze freely within the temple's walls and exploring the temples has a real Indiana Jones-caught-in-the-middle-of-nowhere feel. Tourists usually have the temples to themselves, aside from a few inquisitive village children.

Koh Ker

ⓘ *It may be possible to stay in a family home in nearby Seyong village, but don't count on it! At the time of writing there was nowhere to stay at the temples but Hidden Cambodia was in the process of building a guesthouse on site. It is possible to camp at the site, but you'll have to bring everything yourself. Kulen, 32 km away, is the closest village to Koh Ker. You can also access Koh Ker from Siem Reap via Beng Melea. A new toll road has been established which makes the 61 km from Beng Melea, and 146 km from Siem Reap, a breeze. If hiring a car or moto for this trip expect to pay upwards of US$50 and US$30 respectively. See also under Tour operators.*

Koh Ker (pronounced Koh Care) is the site of the old capital of Jayavarman IV (928-942). Many historians today still do not understand why Jayavarman IV moved the capital from Angkor to Koh Ker, after a feud with his family the capital was

Preah Vihear

Thailand Entrance ▲

Avenue to
Second Pavillion

N ▲

0 metres 100
0 yards 100

Grand Stairway (182 steps)

⊠

Food &
Drink Stalls ■

Baray

Second Gopuva ⊠

Lion Headed Pool

Avenue to First Court

⊠ Second
Enclosure

Naga Causeway

First
Enclosure
⊠ ⊠

⊠

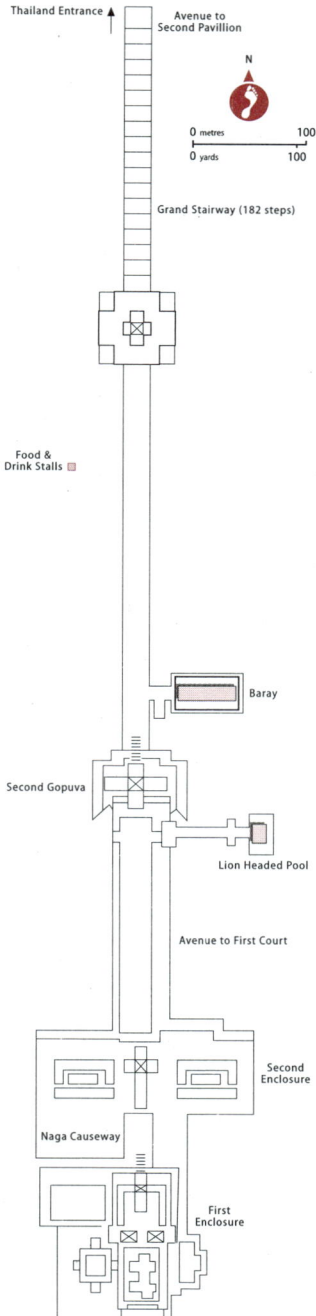

relocated. One inscription reads of Jayavarman IV and Koh Ker "founded by his own power, a city which was the seat of prosperities of the universe" – albeit a short-lived prosperous seat in the universe, as Koh Ker only remained the capital for 24 years. The main ruin here is **Prasat Thom**. Prasat Thom is an overgrown, seven-storey, stepped period in a pyramid style. The surrounding land was irrigated by baray, similar to, but smaller than, the ones at Angkor. The **Rahal Baray**, east of the pyramid, is 1200 m long by 560 m wide and made out of existing stone. The sculptors used sandstone for most of their carvings and were able to create great detailed scenes of movement that were not previously created in this era. Many of the great carvings, such as the fighting monkey men, are now kept in the National Museum of Phnom Penh. De-miners have been working a lot in this area and it is believed that over 80 ruined temples lie in the area.

Preah Vihear

ⓘ *This is a very remote place to get to and public transport can't be relied on. The site is accessible, although not easily, from both Anlong Veng and T'Beng Meanchey, see Transport and also Sleeping below.*

Well over 200 km northeast of Angkor, on the Thai border, is the breathtaking, mountain-top temple Preah Vihear (or Prasat Phra Viharn). This magical 'temple in the sky', as it is often referred to, is of utmost historical and political significance to the Khmers. One monk aptly described Angkor as the heart of Cambodia and Preah Vihear as its soul. Of all the country's temple mountains, this one is truly unbeatable – affording views that, on a clear day, reach all the way to Phnom Kulen (near Angkor) to the west and the intersection of the Lao, Thai and Cambodian borders to the east.

The sandstone temple was constructed at the height of the Khmer Empire and dates from the beginning of the ninth century with continual maintenance and development recorded through to the 11th century. In 1018, the

Cambodian nationalism

Nationalism is alive and well at Preah Vihear – the Cambodian flag waves furiously from the temple's peak, sellers ensure you know that they are Khmer and a huge sign at the temple's entrance reads "I have pride to be born as Khmer". This might give a few foreigners a laugh but its significance should not be underestimated.

Preah Vihear has long been a source of contention between Thailand and Cambodia. Thailand has made repeated attempts to annex the area in the past and has until recently provided the only reliable and safe access to the temple. However, in 1962, the argument was arbitrated by the International Court of Justice in the Hague. It ruled that the temple was the property of Cambodia.

Unfortunately this was not the last of the dispute. Thailand suddenly closed access to the site in the 1990s citing the illegal use of the border. And, in January 2003 there was further escalation of tensions after the misinterpretation of remarks allegedly made by a Thai actress insinuating that Thailand should regain control of the area. Once again the anti-Thai sentiment had been stoked and resulted in the evacuation of Thai citizens by their military and the closing of the border. The Thai embassy in Phnom Penh was badly damaged in rioting, fires and looting along with many Thai-owned businesses. The Cambodian government has since agreed to pay US$6 million in compensation for the damage to the embassy, as well as compensation to individual Thai businesses affected.

In May 2005 there were ongoing issues between the two countries with both sides deploying troops on the border surrounding Preah Vihear.

Khmer king Suryavarman I declared Preah Vihear marked the northernmost point of his empire.

The temple is unique as rather than being concentrically designed the complexes are linked by stone stairways and causeways leading in a straight row to the sacred summit.

Some restoration work was completed in the 1930s, but the temple suffered during the prolonged years of war in Cambodia. The central tower of the main shrine collapsed long ago; the size of the pieces lying on the ground inside the enclosure indicates it was very large. Preah Vihear means sacred monastery in Khmer and is believed to have been an operational monastery during this era.

The temple dominates the plain from its prominent position in the Dangrek Mountains at an altitude of more than 700 m. The mountain site itself was believed to be holy, seemingly designed by the gods to support the ascending series of stairs, walkways and structures which lie along a perfect north-south axis. In his book about Preah Vihear, historian Vittorio Roveda, indicated that the Dangrek Mountain was considered a holy place as: "the mountain was ascended because it offered spiritual rewards for pilgrims and provided the solitude necessary for religious meditation, not because it afforded spectacular views from its summit". This explanation has currency as the highest sanctuary faces in the opposite direction to the view.

The temple was recently floodlit and is stunning if you catch it on a night when the spots are on. In addition to the temple and the stunning views, there are a number of military guns and a crashed helicopter to inspect.

Kompong Thom *p168*

There a number of cheap budget guesthouses along the road on the north side of the bus/taxi station, including **Monorom Guesthouse** and **Santhipheap** (both under US$4 a night).

C Arunreas Hotel, on the corner, beside the market, on NH6, T062-961294. The accommodation is quite out of place in the town with lifts, Las Vegas-style lights and bell-hops. Rooms are clean with a/c, hot water and cable TV. Make sure you get a room towards the top of the hotel as the karaoke can be absolutely heinous, particularly if you are tired from a day of exploring the temples.

C Stung Sen Royal Hotel, T062-961228. The classiest hotel in town. Good sized rooms with a/c.

D-E Vimeansour Guesthouse, opposite the post office. Aside from the fact that there is a car park downstairs, this guesthouse is a bit lacking in atmosphere. The rooms are average with a fan, toilet and bed. No English spoken.

E Arunreas Guesthouse, T062-961238, right beside the market. Basic budget accommodation: fan rooms with attached cold-water bathroom. Popular restaurant downstairs. The proprietors have recently opened an upmarket sister hotel next door, the Arunreas Hotel.

E Mittapheap Hotel, on NH6 just before you cross the bridge into the town centre, T062-961213. This hotel is without a doubt the best value for money in town. Good, clean rooms with a/c, hot water and TV. Recommended.

T'Beng Meanchey *p169*

There is quite a lot of accommodation located on the main road in town.

D-F 27 May Guesthouse, on the main road beside the market, T011-214872. Concrete building with pokey rooms with TV and fan a/c.

D-F Diamond Guesthouse, opposite the market, T011- 676589. Tiny rooms adorned with Number One posters, suggesting that they aren't strictly catering to the tourism-related clientele.

D-F Prum Tep Guesthouse, on the main road about 2 km from the Vishnu traffic circle. Clean, hospital-like rooms with a/c, fan and bathroom. Recommended.

E-F Phnom Meas, opposite the taxi stand, T012-632017. Small, clean rooms with fan, attached bathroom and TV. The friendly staff have opted to paint the rooms a nauseating shade of green.

Preah Vihear *p171*

There are a few small simple and inexpensive guest- houses in the village at the foot of the mountain, but do not expect much. The general standard is a small basic fan room with mosquito net and shared squat toilet (US$3). However, due to the remoteness of the temple and the quality of the roads leading to it, those not wishing to spend 5 or 6 hrs coming and going in one day should plan to spend one night. It might be possible to stay at a village house but you will need to ask around. Rumour has it, that the Head of Police sometimes lets people stay at his house.

The option to sleep out in hammocks on Preah Vihear is still available, if that appeals. Those who do want to do this need to bring an extra layer of clothes as it get very cold at night.

● Eating

Kompong Thom *p168*

†† Stung Sen Royal Restaurant, attached to the hotel of the same name. The best pick for food in town. It is set-up for tour groups with white linen and silver spoon service. It feels a bit weird going in there to eat when you are the only diners (with 4 people waiting on you). Excellent Khmer food and some western dishes (omelettes etc). Good value

† Arunreas Restaurant. Despite smelling like a wet dog this place serves reasonably cheap, quick Chinese and Khmer food, large menu. Okay food and service. The waitresses are usually run off their feet dealing with local s.

● For an explanation of the sleeping and eating price codes used in this guide, see inside the
● front cover. Other relevant information is found in Essentials, see pages 34-37

Central region Listings

¶ **Lay Kim Seng Restaurant**, behind the market. Also doubles as a bus stop so turns out food very quickly. Large, cheap menu with Asian staples, noodles, rice, soups etc. There is often a hawker selling pretty good steamed pork rolls outside.

T'Beng Meanchey *p169*

There isn't a huge selection of restaurants in T'Beng Meanchey but the few there are offer Khmer food at very cheap prices (a meal and drinks under US$4). There is a row of Khmer restaurants all offering pretty much the same fare in town, on the road towards the Naga Traffic Circle.

¶ **Chan Reas Restaurant**, a block south of the **Acleda Bank**. Friendly restaurant with palatable Khmer food.

¶ **Dara Reah Restaurant**, on the corner, near the Vishnu roundabout. Despite the unfortunate name, this is probably the best place to eat in town, with an English menu and good selection of Khmer food. Its forte is dinner. Recommended.

¶ **Market Restaurant**, on the right-hand side of the market. This place is hugely popular with the locals who like to have a cuppa and tune into the wrestling. Worth a visit if only for the bizarre factor of watching what seems like the entire male population of town 'ooohh' and 'ahhh' over the wrestling. Its coffee is much better than its food.

¶ **Mlop Dong Restaurant**, opposite the taxi stand. Cute little restaurant offering good coffee, omelettes and noodles alongside other Cambodian fare. Good option for breakfast.

O Shopping

T'Beng Meanchay *p169*

The market in the centre of town is surprisingly the best point to get most essential items. The market services many of the smaller outlying villages so is surprisingly well stocked. Further along from the market is a Fuji Film shop which doesn't offer a great selection of film but is quite cheap. Buying black and white film in this area is impossible.

⊖ Transport

Kompong Thom *p168*

Kompong Thom is 146 km from Siem Reap and 162 km from Phnom Penh. To the north, T'Beng Meanchey is 151 km of mainly rough road with the turn-off to Preah Khan about 90 km from Kompong Thom. The taxi/bus station is just a block east of the main road in the centre of town. Shared taxis depart all morning for **Siem Reap**, US$4, **Phnom Penh**, 3 hrs, US$3, and the occasional one to **T'Beng Meanchey**, US$4-5. GST Bus Company runs 3 buses a day between **Phnom Penh** (from the Central Market) and Kompong Thom (from Pich Chenda Restaurant). The bus departs from both places at 0645, 0745, 1200, US$3/12,000 riel. **Phnom Penh Public Transport Buses** depart from the Central Market at 0645, 0730, 1215, US$3.

T'Beng Meanchey *p169*

Almost every way you approach T'Beng Meanchey is tough. T'Beng Meanchey is 151 km north of Kompong Thom and the road is not in great shape. The trip will take at least 4 hrs in the dry season and considerably more during the rains. A share-taxi to **Kompong Thom** is US$20-40. For a full taxi, hard bargaining is required. Pick-ups regularly make the trip and cost about US$4-5 to hop in the back.

Getting to **Preah Khan** is a lot more difficult and is really only for the most adventurous of souls. The temple is buried deep in mined jungles along very sandy roads which are difficult for inexperienced riders and smaller bikes to handle. From T'Beng Meanchey go to the traffic circle and turn down the south road towards Kompong Thom. Follow this road for 65 km and you hit a small village Phnom Dai. The turn-off (a small tiny, sandy path) to Preah Khan is on the right-hand side opposite a bunch of billboards and a new, larger road running parallel. It is a very slow 30-km trip to the temples through terrible roads and largely mined areas (allow 3-4 hrs each way).

For an explanation of the sleeping and eating price codes used in this guide, see inside the front cover. Other relevant information is found in Essentials, see pages 34-37

There are numerous motorbikes at the taxi stand that will make the trip to **Koh Ker**, 65 km, 3-4 hrs on motorbike, US$10-15 per day. Tackling these roads is best by motorbike, preferably a large dirt-bike with an experienced rider. To get there head to the Vishnu traffic circle and turn right (northwest towards Preah Vihear) and follow the road through to Kulen and continue through to Seyong village and nearby is Koh Ker. A moto costs US$10-20 per day.

Kulen and **Preah Vihea**r are about 100 km away. The new road in this direction is passable and should take around 3-5 hrs (shared taxi/pick-up US$10). **Stung Treng** is about 4 hrs east of T'Beng Meanchey and can be reached by shared taxi or pick-up, but not everyday.

Preah Vihear *p171*

Both routes to Preah Vihear on the Cambodian side, along with the mountain itself, are heavily mined and the subject of ongoing de-mining operations. As Preah Vihear was used by the Khmer Rouge as one of their last sanctuaries, it was chosen for its strategic location that was easily defended. By limiting the number of passable routes up the mountain, the Khmer Rouge could ensure their ability to keep unwanted visitors out. Approaching from Anlong Veng (120 km to the west), the road is in remarkably good shape by Cambodian standards, and takes around 2 hrs to reach the foot of the mountain. You may be able to travel on the back of a pick-up from Anlong Veng's market, US$6, but it is better if you have your own transport. Coming from T'Beng Meanchey, the road is not as good and takes over 3 hrs. Taxis depart from T'Beng Meanchey's taxi stand and cost $US30-40. Once you reach the foot of the mountain, there are two ways to the top depending on your preference for torment. When you arrive at the T-junction with a tree in the middle, head left, and you will soon see a small trail on your right marked by a UXO

warning sign. Following this slim trail, you will arrive at the ancient stone steps that lead to the top. The staircase definitely shows it age and the long hike to the top will take over 2 hrs. A few kilometres further down the road is the small village of Preah Vihear. Turning right will lead you up the treacherously steep and winding road to the top, a much quicker, yet far more nerve-racking way up. At the time of writing the road was still under construction. Taxis are available from the base of the mountain, but the negotiating will start at around US$25. From the Thai side a sealed road leads to the temple.

Directory

Kompong Thom *p168*
Banks Acleda Bank, NH6, before the bridge but it only does Western Union transfers (no credit card advances). There are a number of money changers in front of the market. **Internet** There are 2 internet shops on NH6 before the bridge, on the right-hand side of the road and a couple of other places around the market. Internet is quite expensive and ranges from US$2-4 per min. **Post office** There is quite a good post office, a block from the market, which can deliver international mail.

Telephone There are a number of local 'phone-boxes' (mobile phone providers) sprinkled around town, particularly in the market area. Overseas calls can be made at most internet shops for around 800 riel per min.

T'Beng Meanchay *p169*
Communications There isn't a whole lot of access here – the Post Office is nothing more than a two-way radio and mobiles phones don't have great coverage. **Buddhist for Development** has set up an internet café where you can make international calls for around 1000 riel per min; internet, US$2 per hr.

The Northeast

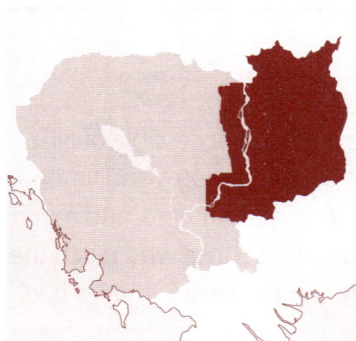

❗ **Footprint features**

Introduction

The northeast is the most remote and least accessible of all the regions in Cambodia. Difficult overland routes and limited air connections mean that few visitors make it here, and much depends on the season and the weather. Those who reach the northeast, however, can visit communities largely untouched by the western 20th century.

The region consists of the three provinces of Ratanakiri, Mondulkiri and Stung Treng. It is rugged upland that is forested, sparsely inhabited (the majority of Cambodia's small number of tigers live here) and desperately poor. It is home to several hilltribes notably Tampuan, Jarai and Kreung, whose clothes, livelihoods and villages are highly distinctive and, to those with a chance to get close, very different from the Khmer. Framing the western edge of the region, and cutting it off from the rest of the country, is the Mekong River. It bifurcates, meanders and braids its way through the country and represents in its width a yawning chasm and obstacle to transport and in its length a watery superhighway that connects three provincial capitals to Phnom Penh.

The history of the area has been dominated largely by local affairs – differences between neighbouring hill tribes being quickly settled. Northeast Cambodia was, alas, unwittingly sucked into the Second Indochina War. The Ho Chi Minh Trail snaked south, concealed in remote passes and dense jungle. Viet Cong cadres, holed up in pockets on the border beyond the reach of foot patrols, attracted the deadly attention of US bombers. Aerial bombing left the Viet Cong largely unscathed but inflicted untold destruction and damage on the local population.

★ Don't miss...

1 **Irrawaddy dolphins** Use the charming little town of Kratie as a base to see the dolphins that inhabit the Mekong nearby. Small trips from Kratie to the Mekong Island opposite provide an enchanting look at rural life, see page 181.

2 **Ethnic minority villages** Organize an elephant trek from a traditional Phnong village in Mondulkiri or visit some of Ratanakiri's many ethnic minorities, particularly the Tampeun and Kreung, see pages 184 and 186.

3 **Yaek Lom** Take a dip in the pristine waters of a volcanic lake, see page 188.

4 **Se San River** Make the enchanting journeys to **Ta Veng** and **Veng Xai**, on the Se San river, see page 188.

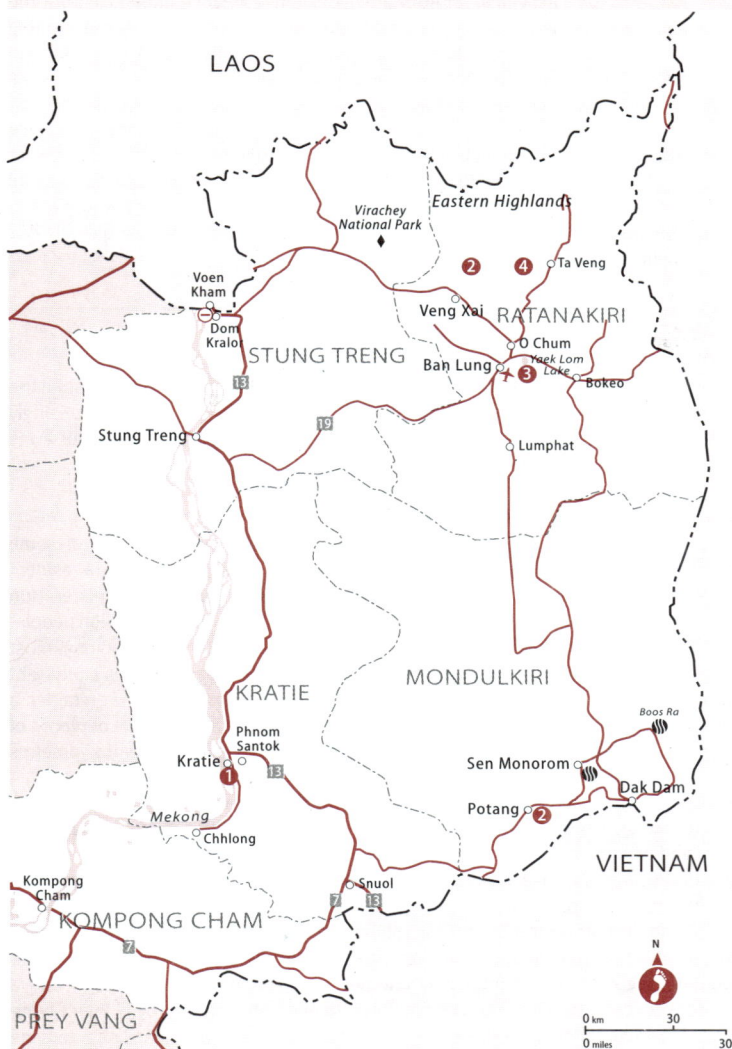

The Northeast

Background

The region has a very primitive economic base, primarily it is shifting cultivation: clearings in the forest are often hewn using hand tools. These are cultivated with rice,

❖ London based NGO, Global Witness, has conducted extensive research into the process of illegal logging and publishes details on www.oneworld.org/ globalwitness/.

corn, root crops and vegetables and, increasingly, a few cash crops such as cashews and coffee. In the 1960s the French attempted to establish rubber plantations but there was never sufficient labour for these to be profitable. Today, wealth accumulates in the hands of a few influential politicians and businessmen as a result of gem mining and logging. The remoteness of the area and the fact that vast tracts of land are controlled by the army make this ideal territory for illicit activities, far from the eyes of investigative journalists: but the swathes of cleared land cannot be concealed from the all-seeing eye of orbiting satellites. Nor can the huge volume of logging trucks rumbling down the roads to Vietnam be kept a secret for long, no matter how strenuously the two governments may try to deny such awkward facts.

The ethnic minorities are evicted from their ancestral lands as companies coerce them into signing documents, which they do not understand, in exchange for peanuts. Governor of Ratanakiri, Kep Chutkema, lamented: "They will strip away all the trees... everything will be gone." And he should know – it was he who granted logging rights to three companies to export timber to Vietnam. And predictably it is the minorities who get the blame for deforestation.

Mekong Provinces 🖥️🎯🗃️🚌🌀 » pages 190-198.

Kompong Cham, Kratie and Stung Treng make up the Mekong Provinces. Despite the Mekong River, its waterway and perpetual irrigation, these provinces are surprisingly unimportant and laid back. Not surprisingly they are accessible by boat but away from the river, transport is difficult.

Kompong Cham and around
Kompong Cham is the fourth largest town in Cambodia and is a town of some commercial prosperity owing to its thriving river port and also, it is said, as a result of preferential treatment received from local boy made good, the Prime Minister, Hun Sen. Town and province have a combined population of more than 1½ million people.

There is nothing in or around Kompong Cham to detain the visitor for long, most merely pass through, en route for Stung Treng and the northeast, but it is a pleasant enough town to rest awhile. In common with a lot of riverside towns it has retained a good deal of its **colonial shophouse architecture** and there are a couple of places of interest. **Wat Nokor** is a well preserved 11th-century monument several kilometres west of town off Route 7. At **Phnom Pros** and **Phnom Srei** ('Man and Woman Hill'), 5 km from town on highway Number 7, are the foundations of two early temples. The site reportedly derives its name from the legend of a competition between the town's men and women as to who could build the biggest hill (the women won). Here also are mass graves in which victims of the Khmer Rouge are buried. All three places can be visited in a couple of hours.

A short trip down the Tonle Tuok tributary is the **Maha Leap Pagoda**, a complex that survived the Khmer Rouge and has since been ascribed magical powers. The rare wooden pagoda features intricately adorned teak columns, a lovely pond and a modern concrete pagoda and reclining Buddha near the rear. Nearby is **Prey Chung Krap Weaving Village**, an epicentre for fine, detailed silk that has attracted the

attention of many silk traders. The **Koh Pen Bamboo Bridge**, 10 minutes' walk down
the river, is constructed every year during the low season and is worth a quick visit. Small villages and sandy beaches surround the area.

The small town of **Chhlong** ⓘ *get to Chhlong via boat from Kompong Cham, US$6-7; a whole boat, fitting 10 people, can be chartered for US$60; in the dry season access is probably best via road*, between Kompong Cham and Kratie is one of Cambodia's best kept secrets. The small town, nestled on the banks of the Mekong, 41 km from Kratie and 82 km from Kompong Cham, is one of the few places that survived the Khmer Rouge's ransacking and contains a multitude of French colonial buildings and traditional wooden Khmer houses. The locality features the foundations of 120 antique houses. Of particular note is the 19th-century wooden Khmer house supported by 100 columns. Formerly a base for workers to surrounding rubber plantations, it is easy to reminisce about a bygone era with dotted wats and monasteries, an old school and charming market set in a colonial-style building. There are a few smallish guesthouses on the riverfront, see Sleeping.

Kratie

Kratie (pronounced 'Kratcheay') is a port town on the Mekong roughly half way between Phnom Penh and Laos. It is a charming little town with a relaxed atmosphere and it too has some good examples of shophouse architecture. In the dry season the deep blue Mekong peels back to reveal sandy beaches like those you might find at the Thai seaside. Sunset is a real highlight in Kratie, as the burning red sun descends slowly below the shore line.

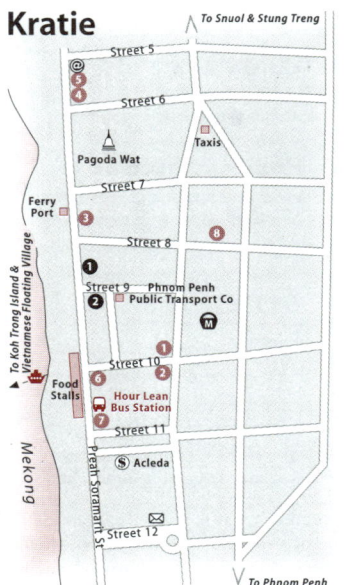
Kratie map

Koh Trong Beach, directly opposite Kratie town, is a lovely 8-km stretch of sandy dunes (in the dry season) where you can swim and relax. The island itself consists of small market farms with lovely scenes of simple, laid-back rural life. On the south side is a small Vietnamese floating village. A visit to this island is highly restorative and recommended for those who want to chill out. Kratie's main claim to some modicum of fame are the **Irrawaddy dolphins** ⓘ *go by moto, US$3 return, then hire a longboat, US$2-3 per person per hr, at the official viewpoint (signposted on the left of the road)*, that inhabit this portion of the Mekong (Kampi pool), 15 km north of the town on the road to Stung Treng. The best time to glimpse these rare and timid creatures is at sunrise or sunset when they are feeding. Verdant countryside surrounding the river provides romantic rural scenery with children on buffalos, cows munching haystacks, old men sorting out their fishing nets, lovers doubling on bicycles and people waving you through.

Kampi Rapids ⓘ *1000 riel* (also known as Kampi resort), 3 km north of Kampi Dolphin Pool, provides a refreshing and picturesque area to take a dip in the clear Mekong waters (during

Sleeping ⬤
Heng Heng **6**
Heng Heng II **7**
Heng Oudom **2**
Oudom Sambath **4**
Riverside
Guesthouse **5**
Santhepheap **3**
Star Guesthouse **1**
You Hong
Guesthouse **8**

Eating ⓐ
Mekong **2**
Red Sun Falling **1**

the dry season). A bridge leads down to a series of scenic thatched huts which provide shelter for the swimmers. Twenty one kilometres further north of the Kampi pool is **Sambor**, a pre-Angkorian settlement, but today unfortunately not a single trace of this ancient heritage exists. Replacing the ancient ruins are two temples. The first and most impressive is the 100-column pagoda, rumoured to be the largest new pagoda in the country. It is a replica of the 100-column, wooden original, which was built in 1529. During the war, Pol Pot based himself out of the complex, killing hundreds of people and destroying the pagoda. The new one was built in 1985; perhaps the builders were slightly overzealous as it features 116 columns. Three hundred metres behind the gigantic pagoda sits a much smaller, and arguably, more interesting temple. The wat still contains many of its original features including a number of wooden pylons which date back 537 years. Originally built in 1648 by the king, the temple has received a number of facelifts benefiting the beautiful Buddhist murals featured on the walls. The paintings, which depict the life and birth of Buddha, are believed to be about 40 years old. The highpoint of a trip to Sambor is more the journey through beautiful countryside rather than the actual temples themselves.

Stung Treng

Yet another eponymous provincial capital on the Mekong, Stung Treng is just 40 km from Laos and a stopping off place on the overland route to Ratanakiri. The town has a frontier feel to it – wild, remote, reckless and in the wet season it is all too easy to be trapped here for days owing to impassable roads. Pigs, cows and the odd ox-cart wander through the town's busy streets. There aren't a lot of activities for tourists around Stung Treng. Some tour guides will organize a boat run to the Laos border to see riverine life and some waterfalls but you will need a Laos visa in order to do this. **Lbak Khone**, the 26 km rocky area that the Mekong rapids flow through en route to the Laos border, is one of the country's most stunning areas. Many tour operators will offer land transport to this area (as only the very, very brave would try by boat). The **Stung Treng Women's Development Centre** on Street 1 is 1 km from Stung Treng Airport. It is a local NGO helping to train women in a variety of skills. Here they make some beautiful silk and welcome visitors. Some tour operators can also organize a trip to Siem Pang, where you can travel through to Virachey National Park, see page 189.

The borderlands

Mondulkiri and Ratanakiri are very different with green rolling hills, lush jungle areas and cascading falls. Many compare the areas to the green pastures of England or Tasmania. Here ethnic

Stung Treng

Boats to Laos

Tonlé Sekong

To Stung Treng Women's Development Centre (5km)

River Rd

Taxis

Kodak Shop

To Kratie & Ban Lung

N

0 metres 100
0 yards 100

Sleeping
Penh Chet Guesthouse 5
Preap Sor Guest House 3
Riverside 1
Sekong 4
Sok Sambath 2

Eating
Dara 3
New World 2
Prochum Tonle 4
Sophakmukal 1
Sun Tha 5

minorities comprise the majority of the population and a great fusion of diverse cultures and peoples populate the region. A great deal of natural attractions exist in the area, such as pristine lakes, national parks and beautiful rivers. During the dry season, the areas around Ban Lung and Sen Monorom appear windblown with stark terres rouge roads, snaking through desiccated landscapes.

Towards Mondulkiri

Snaking your way through the bumpy roads to Modulkiri is a good taster for what is to come - rolling hills, various minority groups, wooded areas and an altogether different feel to the rest of the country.

Snuol ●◑◒ » pages 190-198.

To put it bluntly, Snuol is a place where no-one really wants to stay for long. The town is a small red dust bowl which acts as a crossroads to destinations such as Ratanakiri and Mondulkiri. The town epitomizes the Wild West, with red dust gales blowing through its small wheeling and dealing central taxi area. Greener pastures rim the town's periphery with horse and carts and pleasant rural scenery. The town is set to expand over the next few years as it is geared to graduate from staging post to major border crossing. The town has a rather large market.

Sen Monorom (Mondulkiri Province)
●◑◒▲◓◔ » pages 190-198.

The other attraction of the northeast is Sen Monorom, provincial capital of Mondulkiri. Mondulkiri is one of Cambodia's largest provinces but it is the most sparsely inhabited, with approximately one person per 2 sq km. It is similar to Ratanakiri but by comparison with Sen Monorom, Ban Lung is considered cosmopolitan. Needless to say the provincial capital is particularly quaint and the surrounding environment is breathtakingly stunning.

Ins and outs

Getting there By river, you can get a boat to Chhlong (if the undependable boats are running) from Phnom Penh and from here it may be possible to catch a pick-up to Sen Monorom (220 km). The road is good for the first 180 km as it is used and looked after by a logging company. The final 40 km or so to Sen Monorom is unsurfaced and in very poor condition. This stretch of the road becomes virtually impassable in the rainy season. From Chhlong it may be necessary to overnight or change pick-up in Snuol, approximately 100 km away. It is also possible to travel by pick-up from Kratie and Sen Monorom, which is possibly the easiest option.

Getting around Most guesthouses and hotels can recommend a well-briefed, English speaking guide/moto driver for around US$10-15 and a few dollars more if lengthy trips are required.

Background

One of the most frequent epithets used to describe Mondulkiri is 'the Wild East'. At present the region is still underdeveloped but has the potential to become a major ecotourism Mecca. Sadly, not enough people make it here as the roads are pretty tricky – in the wet season hideously slippery and in the dry season, considerably dusty. However, they are a lot better now than a few years ago. A diamond in the rough, Mondulkiri's barren, red roads and harsh burnt out escarpment conceal in their midst virgin jungle, ethnic minority villages and some of the country's most unique flora and fauna. With an average elevation of 800 m, it is also a lot cooler than most other parts of Cambodia.

Dakramon Mountain is a large auspicious hill overshadowing Sen Monorom. It is a major place of worship for villagers as it was believed a wise old man called 'Ta Dakramon' who was a traditional healer, healed the masses up there.

Dam Nok Old Royal Palace, 3 km southwest of town and built in the 1960s, was pretty much destroyed during the Vietnam War. Once the holiday home for Sihanouk, only remnants of walls etc. exist today.

Ethnic minority villages and elephant trekking

The province of mountains and rainforests is dotted with hundreds of ethnic minority villages. Here, the term ethnic minority is a misnomer, with the majority of the population (80%) comprising 12 different ethnic groups. The largest ethnic group is the Phnong, 'the people of the mountain' which make up about 70% of the province's population and the indigenous people of Cambodia. Visiting a local minority village is a completely captivating experience and is highly recommended. Other minorities include Tampeun, Jarri, Krow, Steeng, Sumray and Rodai.

Most tour guides or guesthouses can arrange a visit to a village. It is best to stick with a local organization who is working alongside these groups.

The best village to visit is **Potang Village**, one of the closest and largest Phnong villages, with about 140 families spread across the area. The village consists of a collection of the very unique style of traditional Phnong thatched huts and raised wooden houses. The residents are very hospitable, inviting

Sen Monorom

To Phulung Village & Boos Ra Waterfall (38km)

To Boos Ra (38km)

Dakramon Mountain

Airstrip (Not in use)

Taxis

Wat Sen Monorom

To Dam Nok Old Royal Palace (3km) & Sen Monorom Waterfall

To Dak Dam Village (174km), Tray Tom Waterfall & Vietnam Border (353km)

To Potang Village, Kbal Prehear Waterfall, Putro Village, Rum Near Falls & Phnom Penh

N

0 metres 500
0 yards 500

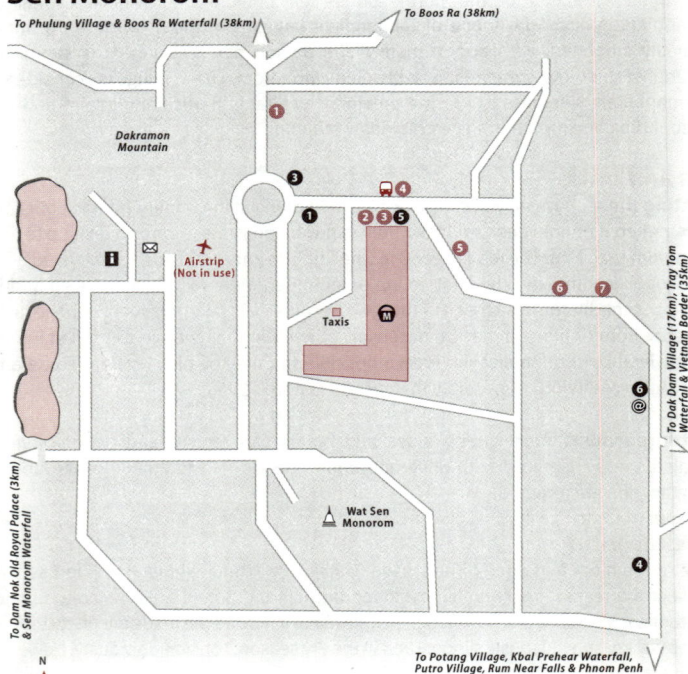

Sleeping
Bou Sra Guesthouse 2
Holiday Guesthouse 3
Long Vibal 1

Neak Meas 7
Pitch Kiri Guesthouse 5
Sovannkiri 4
Sum Dy Guesthouse 6

Eating
Arun Reah II 6
Chom Nor Thmei 1
Orameas 4

Sen Monorom 3
Spean Meanchey 5

❗ The Phnong

The Phnong revere their elephants holding an enormous amount of respect for these colossal creatures. Phnong legend states that the elephants were once Phnong people but after eating fish they transformed into their current mammoth form. They are considered the most sacred of all creatures. Because of this the Phnong do not let their village elephants breed as it is viewed as evil, akin to incest (ironic, considering the Phnong people will often marry their cousins). If a baby elephant is born in a village it is considered a very bad omen and large amounts of animals (ie four dogs, two buffalos, eight chickens etc) are sacrificed to appease the spirits.

To avoid this dilemma, musking bull elephants are tied to trees in the jungle, away from the village, until their sexual urges desist. This age-old custom presumably derives from the destruction caused by very aggressive, sexually-driven bull elephants.

The Phnong identify when their elephants are musking by a gland behind the restless creature's eye that starts oozing oil. In 2001, a musking elephant killed two local Phnong people and destroyed many villagers' houses. The elephant was shot and local Sen Monorom sources say that the elephant's owner died the next day. The whole incident was considered a seriously bad omen and the whole village moved, many burning their houses.

The downside of this animistic belief system is that the Phnong capture their elephants from the wild which is depleting the natural supply. In Mondulkiri the current wild elephant population is believed to be around 60 (the second biggest animal populace in the country).

Traditionally elephants were used for transport and to clear forests but this tradition has died out. Most Phnong villages now employ their elephants for tourist treks. A few years ago, impoverished locals sold their elephants to companies in Siem Reap where they are now used to transport tourists around Angkor Wat.

tourists into their surprisingly large abodes for a drink of rice wine or something to eat. It is still possible here to see some of the elders in their traditional attire including the not so politically correct elephant tusk earrings. The village is home to 15 elephants making it the most popular launching pad for elephant treks. Aside from elephant treks the main income base for this village is the collection of resin. A trip to this village could easily be combined with a trip to **Kbal Prehear Waterfall**, 18 km away.

Phulung Village, 8 km northwest of town, is home to about 80 families and four elephants used for trekking. The Potang and Phulung villages hold minority **cultural shows** for around US$30 per group. One can't be sure how culturally sensitive it is going to one of these 'shows', though it is a good way for the groups to benefit from tourism directly, while retaining their culture. The performance includes a large amount of dancing and singing in traditional attire while people play pipes, gongs, bells. The performance lasts for about two hours and a guide/moto can organize the day beforehand. Performances are usually held in the afternoon.

Dak Dam Village is 17 km east of town and home to a whopping 250 families of Phnong, Khmer and Vietnamese people. The village is renowned locally for its handicrafts, particularly bags and scarves. The **Tray Tom Waterfall** is 2 km from the village and cascades down up to 15 m in the wet season (see below).

Elephant treks can be organized by most guesthouses/hotels (**Long Vibol, Pich Kiri, Arun Reah II** etc) or motodops/guides. The treks start at one of the ethnic minority villages, typically Potang Village or Phulung Village. Treks can also be organized from Putru Village and Dak Dam Village. The pachyderms are not the most comfortable means of transport (expect a sore bottom for weeks to come) but offer a unique opportunity to explore surrounding jungle, habitat and ethnic minority villages. The slow moving creatures have the added benefit of transcending areas not usually accessible by motor vehicles. The elephant's 'passenger' basket fits up to two people and a day trek costs around US$25 (which is half the price of treks in Mondulkiri). Tourists also have the option of two- or three-day treks which usually involve camping by a lakeside or in jungle, romantically lit with fire flies. Routes vary depending on which village you start in.

Waterfalls

There are over 100 waterfalls in the area. **Sen Monorom Waterfall**, 5 km northwest of Sen Monorom, is the closest and most popular with tourists. The fall plunges 6 m into a lovely turquoise pool – perfect for a dip when the water levels are high enough. **Boos Ra Waterfall**, 35 km from town, is one of the region's best and the firm Khmer favourite. The fall became legendary when one of Cambodia's most famous singers, Sen Sisamoth, declared in tune that it was "the most beautiful waterfall in Cambodia". Unfortunately the singer was killed during the Pol Pot regime but the waterfall's legacy continues. From the summit, the water plunges 15 m to a second tier, where people can shower under the spray. The next tier features an even larger drop which plummets into an 8-m-deep bottle green pool which is perfect for bathing in. The fall is surrounded by dense foliage and chirping cicadas. There is a good new road to the waterfall. Boos Ra Village, 4 km from the waterfall, has a small handicraft shop and small rundown guesthouse for US$2.50 a night. Those taking the trip to the fall can either break the trip at the Phnong Phulong Village (8 km from Sen Monorom).

Kbal Prehear Waterfall is 27 km from Sen Monorom and 18 km from the ethnic minority settlement of Potang Village. It is usually possible to stay the night at a villager's abode in Potang Village for US$1-2. Kbal Prehear means 'Head of God' and is named due to its large breadth and 7-m drop. At its base is a large swimming pool.

Ol Leng Tang Waterfall, 40 km from Sen Monorom, near Memong Village, is possibly the province's most beautiful, with exceptionally clean water and a lovely spot to take a dip.

Dak Dam Waterfall, also known as **Tray Tom**, is located 30 km from Sen Monorom, near the Phnong Village of Dak Dam. The provincial tourist office has heavily promoted this fall as an alternative to Boos Ra, due to the formers inaccessibility during the wet season. The large fall has a 15-m drop and runs 2 m across but is difficult to find on your own. In nearby Dak Dam Village (2 km away) visitors can stop off for refreshments or purchase some locally produced handicrafts.

Rum Near Waterfall is not as impressive or large as its counterparts (it only has a 6-m drop) but has the added bonus of being close to town (13 km) and is on the way to the major Phnong settlement of Putru Village, 18 km from Sen Monorom. The fall has its own charm and is surrounded by large shady trees and jungle with a nice pool at the bottom.

Ratanakiri Province

Ratanakiri is like another planet compared to the rest of Cambodia - dusty, red roads curl through the landscape in summer, while in the rainy season the area becomes lush and green like Ireland or Tasmania. Adventure enthisiasts won't be disappointed, with waterfalls to discover, ethnic minorities to meet, elephants to ride, river trips to take and the beautiful Yaek Lom volcanic lake to take a dip in.

Ban Lung and around 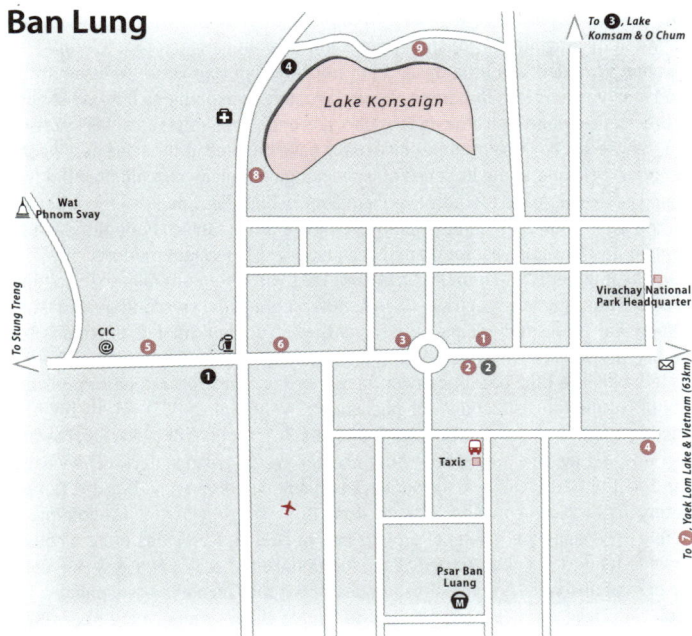 ▸▸ *pages 190-198.*

Ban Lung has been the dusty provincial capital of Ratanakiri Province ever since the previous capital Lumphat was flattened by US bombers trying to 'destroy' the footpaths and tracks that made up the Ho Chi Minh Trail. To the outside world, however, the town is of such insignificance that most refer to it as Ratanakiri. There are no paved roads in or around the town, merely dirt tracks which in the dry season suffocate the town with their dust and in the wet season turn into rivers of mud. The town is situated on a plateau dotted with lakes and hills, many of great beauty, and serves as a base from which visitors can explore the surrounding countryside. Basic guesthouse accommodation, food and drink can be obtained in town.

Ins and outs

Getting there Ban Lung is a back-jarring, bottom-bruising, brain-wobbling 13 hours from Phnom Penh. It is better to break your journey in Kratie and Stung Treng and take a pickup/taxi from there. It is also possible – when the river is high enough – to catch the boat from Phnom Penh to Stung Treng and travel overland to Ban Lung at quite a high price. Alternatively fly from Phnom Penh - although the planes are of worrying antiquity and doubtful provenance.

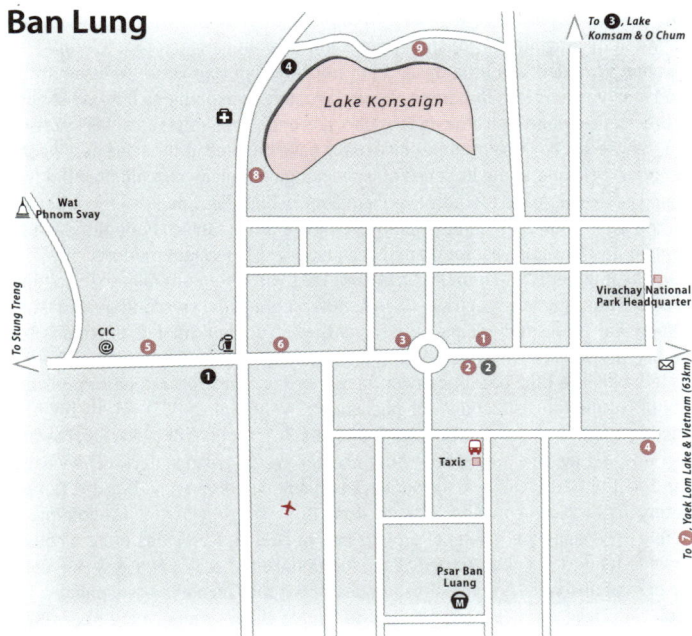

Ban Lung

Sleeping
Cheng Luk 2
Labansiek 3
Lakeside Chenglock 8
Mountain Guesthouse 6
Ratanak 1
Sovannikiri 5

Terres Rouges Lodge 9
Tribal 4
Yaklom Hill Lodge 7

Eating
American 1
Beoung Kamsan 3

Chum Nor Beoung
Konsaign 4

Bars & clubs
VP 2

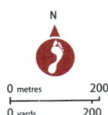

Getting around The chief mode of transport is the motorbike which comes with a driver, or not, as required (usually US$5 without driver and US$15 with - but bargain). Bus services are sporadic. Cars with driver can be hired for US$40-50 a day.

Sights around Ban Lung

The name Ratanakiri means 'jewel mountains' in Pali, presumably derived from the wealth of gems in the hills, but it could just as easily refer to the beauty of the landscape. **Yaek Lom** ① *US$1 and a parking charge of 500 riel, all of which goes into a fund to promote the conservation of the area; there is a visitors' centre which serves as an ethnic minority museum with a collection of instruments, baskets, tools and other curios.* It is a perfectly circular volcanic lake about 5 km east of town and easily reached by motorbike. The crystalline lake is rimmed by protected forest dominated by giant emergents (dipterocarps and shoreas) soaring high into the sky. Around the feet of these giant trees are a dense tangle of smaller woods and bamboos which filter the late afternoon sun into gorgeous hues of green and dappled patterns of light and shade. It takes about one hour to walk around the lake: in doing so plenty of secluded bathing spots will be found and given the lack of water in town it is not surprising that most locals and visitors bathe in the wonderfully clear and cool waters of the lake. There is a small 'museum' of ethnographia and a couple of minority stilt houses to be seen.

There are three **waterfalls** ① *all 2000 riel; to get to the falls follow Highway 19 out of town and branch off 2 km out on the main road in the first village out of Ban Lung: Chaa Ong Falls are 9 km northwest at the intersection; turn right at the village and head for about 5 km to head to Katien Waterfall (follow the signs); the same road heads to Kachaang Waterfall,* in close proximity to Ban Lung town.

Kachaang Waterfall is 6 km away. The 12-m high waterfall flows year round and is surrounded by magnificent, pristine jungle and fresh mist rising from the fall.

Katien Waterfall is a little oasis 7 km northwest of Ban Lung. Believed to have formed from volcanic lava hundreds of years ago, the 10-m plunging falls are sheltered from the outside world by a little rocky grotto. It is one of the better local falls to swim in as it is very secluded (most people will usually have the area to themselves), the water is completely clean and the bunches of vines hanging from its summit providing good swinging potential. Amongst the dotted ferns, rocky boulders and large meandering fig trees, the 40 m-wide pool peters off into a delicate brook, an offshoot of the Koutung Stream. Katien flows all year round and is a favourite of elephant trekkers.

The best waterfall is arguably **Chaa Ong Falls,** with the 30-m falls plunging into a large pool. Those game enough can have a shower behind the crescent-shaped ledge.

Veng Xai is a small village 35 km northwest of Ban Lung that straddles the charming Say San River. The trip to Veng Xai is quite pleasant – the green, curling road speckled with the odd basket-carrying family or lazy buffalo swining around offers plenty of wonderful distractions for passengers. Veng Xai itself is an itty-bitty town consisting of a few shops and outdoor foodstalls. A Tampeun Village is located about 20 km up the Say San (a one-hour boat ride up glassy green waters). The village of about 200 Tampeun, Lao and Khmer isn't particularly noteworthy, but the **Tampeun cemetery** (crunchiet cemetery), 200 m from the village, is rather fascinating. The cemetery possesses the graves of around 200 people and provides quite a colourful contrast to its western counterparts. Each memorial site houses two graves – usually those of man and wife. And the sites are decorated with an elaborately painted small pagoda with large wooden-carved male and female effigies marking the front corners. Whoever dies first will have their effigy placed on the right-hand side. Some of the more noteworthy effigies are the mushroom-headed man (who died from eating a poisonous mushroom); a western-like couple towards the back (distinguished by their large noses, and from the village to express gratitude to the tourists' support) and the military man, with CB radio, and his wife, with several big hearts.

Most people in this area belong to the Kreung minority. **Kreung villages** are often built around large and venerable trees such as flame trees and mango trees. One notable feature are brides' and grooms' houses which are built on stilts 5-10 m off the ground and reached via a rickety ladder. These are actually separate houses for the teenagers who entertain prospective spouses.

The woods, where slash and burn agriculture is increasingly common, are a twitcher's paradise: stand near a tall flame tree or fruit tree and listen to the cries, calls and songs of the birds. There are also trees of commercial value such as the sandalwood tree, the heart of which fetches thousands of dollars per kilo in Arab states. Out towards the south of the town you will come across rubber plantations where you can rest in the dappled light.

Both Veng Xai and Ta Veng (see below) have national park offices with rangers but it's best to organize any treks from the ranger office in the centre of town. It is possible to charter a boat from here upriver to Ta Veng for US$35.

The drive from Ban Lung to **Ta Veng** is roughly twice as long and certainly twice as pretty. Beyond the tiny hamlet of **O Chum** there is nothing: no water, no petrol, no puncture repair services – so go well prepared. The road undulates and winds and for much of its length it runs through dense forest providing welcome relief from sun or rain. Occasionally a family marching in file or workers returning from the fields will be seen and there are a few villages built by the roadside. Much the best option, however, is to be bold and steer your Honda down one of the many small tracks leading off to the side. After a while you will probably come into a village or pass an isolated house. Your reception will vary from warm to indifferent. Your presence may be regarded as an intrusion so it always a good idea to hover in a public area while gauging the response to your unannounced arrival. Expect no English to be spoken, those with a smattering of Khmer or Vietnamese will fare best. Some visitors will find the whole process uncomfortable and a little like visiting a zoo.

Virachey National Park is the country's largest national park and contains some of the nation's best forested areas. Organized tours of Virachey National Park are still being refined by local government officials. There are four national park headquarters, located at Veng Xai, Lumphat, Ta Veng and in Ban Lung Town. As the majority of guides/rangers at the smaller posts don't speak English it is recommended that you organize treks from the main ranger office in Ban Lung (see box). The park is host to a number of rare and not-so-rare animal species including wild cats, wild pigs, Asian elephants, the gau, and possibly the rare douc langur. Animal sightings are a lot more common during the wet season. The park also contains ancient rock formations, extinct volcanoes, the only high elevation forest in Cambodia and the Se Cong and Se San river catchments.

The trip to **Ou'Sean Lair Waterfall**, 35 km from Ban Lung, is a wonderful day excursion offering a fantastic cross-section of what is essentially Ratanakiri's main attractions (without the riverside element).

From Ban Lung, fields of wind-bent, spindly rubber trees provide a canopy over the road's rolling hills, a legacy left from the French in the 1960s. The kindly government has built a minority 'camp' near the rubber factory, to ensure they have a cheap labour force at hand to collect the rubber (with around 300 riel paid per litre of rubber, with 30 to 50 litres yielded daily in the wet and dry season respectively). The natural archway created by the surprisingly beautiful **rubber trees** provides a magical entrance into the oncoming territory. As the landscape transforms, so does the road, degenerating into a bumpy, sandy nightmare (which would be extremely difficult to navigate during the wet season). Here the scenery morphs from little fish farms and rugged jungle to bushy cashew nut farms and verdant mango plantations with hacked-up, depleted, slash and burn areas interspersed amongst the beautiful countryside (which some guides may try to tell you is a result of people 'recklessly throwing their cigarettes away'). Punctuating the mottled natural vista is an equally diverse range of ethnic minority settlements.

Tampeun and Kreung villages are dotted along the road and about half way (17 km from Ban Lung), in a lovely valley, is a tiny Cham village. The village has a small sugarcane drink stand and is an ultra-friendly spot to break the journey. From here the landscape becomes a bit more barren and burnt out, with old gem shafts dipped on the road. The township of **Bei Sruk Chomrom**, 32 km from Ban Lung and 3 km from the falls, is the epitome of hardship. The town could come straight from a country and western movie with its tough feel, wooden shopfronts and gales of dust blowing through. Here the townsfolk are seriously poor but still wear the necessary bling-bling you would expect from a mining town. They are largely a friendly mob who don't mind tourists poking around the mine shafts that have been burrowed absolutely anywhere and everywhere a hole can be dug. Amethyst is their holy grail and one must pity the poor miners who are sent down the extremely thin (60-70 cm) and deep (10-15 m) claustrophobic holes in searing temperatures – for the most part, bearing very little. The town has four cheap food stalls-cum-restaurants that actually provide very good food (although the hygiene of the buffets are a tad dubious). Food for the most part is pork, pork or...pork. Some 3 km from the mining town and the perfect end to the journey is the seven-tiered Ou'Sean Lair waterfalls. The falls were reportedly 'discovered' by a Tampeun villager five years ago, who debated as to whether he should tell the Department of Tourism of their existence. In return for turning over the falls, they were named after him. The falls are most spectacular in the wet season but are still pretty alluring during the dry season. Shaded by large Ta Prohm-like fig trees the pool at the bottom of the fall provides a nice swimming area (there is a little amount of rubbish but not too much). The ropey, sturdy roots of these gigantic trees provide good leverage into the 3-m-deep pool.

Bokeo is a gem mining town some 30 km east down Highway 19 on the road to Vietnam. This place was eclipsed by Pailin, close to the Thai border, but years of heavy duty mining there during the Khmer Rouge period means that Bokeo is now reputed to be a richer source of precious stones. Gem rushes are much like gold rushes and gem miners are equally careless about the effects of their actions on the environment. The rather unattractive town is booming as hopeful miners make their way here. The road is atrocious so few people make it. There is reported to be a guesthouse near the market.

Lumphat ⓘ *the most common way to arrive is with a motodop, US$15 (unless you are lucky enough to get a lift on one of the rare pick-ups heading this way); it is also possible to catch a boat down the river from Veng Xai but some tough negotiating may be required as the longboat drivers can be quite mercenary at times (the trip could cost up to US$30),* is approximately a two-hour drive south of Ban Lung (45 km). It is described as a 'ghost town' but occupies an attractive spot on the Se San River and boats can be hired for around US$15 to visit some of the nearby Lao villages. Prior to the war Sihanouk pumped loads of money into the town and some of the 1960s-era hospitals and school survived the massive bombing campaign. But for the most part, the place has been destroyed – buildings blown up and craters pockmarking the small town. Some tourists like to visit the now derelict and decrepit airport, once a major Khmer Rouge base.

🛏 Sleeping

Kompong Cham and around *p180*

B-C **La Relais de Marie Bopha**, Chhlong, T012- 501742. At the time of publication this beautiful large, colonial building was being restored into an upmarket, boutique hotel. D **Mekong**, T042-941536, F941465. On the river, a large hotel with 60 rooms, fan and a/c, fridge, TV and with bathrooms attached.

Easily the best hotel in town and popular with the NGO community. Excellent views from the rooms.

D **Pounleau Ramsey Hotel**, T042-941324, pounleaurasmey @yahoo.com. Good central location near the market area. Rooms with a/c, fan and attached bathroom. Not the most helpful staff.

E **Bopear**, Pasteur St, T012- 796803. Basic rooms that suit the adage: 'you get what you pay for'. Some rooms with attached bathroom.

E **Kim Srun Guesthouse**, on the river road, T042-941507. Scantily decorated, cell-like rooms but clean nonethe- less. Separate bathrooms with non-western toilet. Foyer eerily decorated with a gamut of wooden-carved moose-heads. Nice views from communal balcony. Small family hotel.

E **Spean Thmei**, on the river road, T016-998954. Cheap rooms with bathroom, TV and fan. Fawlty Towers like manager character who will go beyond the call of duty to assist. A bit dirty but the hospitality compensates.

Kratie p181, map p181

D **Santepheap Hotel**, on the river road, T072-971537. This is the nicest hotel in Kratie. The 20-room white building is located on the riverfront at the top of the steps leading from the pier. It has a quiet, intimate atmosphere and clean and airy rooms with attached bathrooms, fridge, fan or a/c. Dary, a female tour guide and one of a Cambodia's rare female motodops, bases herself out of this hotel. Good restaurant on site.

D-E **Heng Heng Hotel II**, 2 shops up from the original hotel, T012-929943, heng heng2hotel@yahoo.com. Nicely furnished, clean rooms, with fan, TV, hot water. Great balcony for taking in the wonderful red sunsets. The owner sometimes has internet facilities for guests.

D-E **Heng Oudom Hotel**, near the market, opposite the **Star Guesthouse**, T072- 971629. Relative newcomer to the Kratie hotel scene and you can tell. The rooms are impeccable, clean, TV, attached bathrooms and fan but the service isn't quite up to scratch.

D-E **Oudom Sambath Hotel**, on the river road (number 439), T072-971502. This newcomer will give the **Santapheap** a run for its money. The pink, wedding- cake-like exterior doesn't do this place justice. The rooms are huge, with a/c, TV, hot water etc. The more expensive rooms are fit for royalty with large ornate bath tub and very regal looking furniture.

E **Heng Heng Hotel**, T072- 971405. A small (11 rooms) hotel with rooms over- looking the Mekong. The rooms are on a bit cramped and furnished with 1970s wallpaper, but they are clean with fan or a/c and have attached bathrooms. There is a simple Khmer restaurant on the ground floor where a range of cheap food is served. Its sister hotel is much better.

E **Riverside Guesthouse**, on the riverfront next door to **Oudom Sabath**. Basic rooms with all the necessary facilities but a bit dingy. On the upside it is one of the cheaper places to stay on the waterfront.

E **Star Guesthouse**, T072- 971663. Situated beside the market, this has gained the reputation of being the friendliest guesthouse in town. Why exactly, one can't be sure. It is very popular with travellers, despite its rather small rooms.

E-F **You Hong Guesthouse**, between the taxi rank and the market, T012-957003. Clean rooms with attached bathroom and fan. One dollar extra gets you cable TV. Friendly, helpful owners and a fantastic restaurant. Recommended.

Stung Treng p182, map p182

C-D **Sok Sambath Hotel**, near the market, T016-746666. This hotel is quite literally suitable for royalty and is the choice of Cambodia's prince and princess when they are in town. The more expensive rooms are nicely furnished with a/c, TV and good bathrooms with hot water. Easily the best hotel in town.

D-E **Sekong**, on the river road, T074-973762, is one of the best places to stay but has become a little rundown. It has 15 rooms with a/c or fan and hot water. The riverfront hotel is quite picturesque and could easily be mistaken as a temple due to its unusual design. Try to avoid the cheaper rooms as they are a bit unkempt. The restaurant also provides good food and internet.

F **Preap Sor Guest House**, opposite the market. Average, basic rooms with fan and western toilet. Slight notch above others in the same price range.

● For an explanation of the sleeping and eating price codes used in this guide, see inside the
● front cover. Other relevant information is found in Essentials, see pages 34-37

The Northeast Listings

F Riverside, opposite taxi stand, T012-439454. The old adage 'you get what you pay for rings true here' rings true here. Dingy rooms with squat toilet and crud furniture. The owner, Mr T, is a tad overzealous but is actually quite well organized and informed and can 'fix' almost anything. The restaurant's food is about the same quality as its rooms.

F Penh Chet Guesthouse, opposite the town's 'park', T011-910111. Very basic rooms with squat toilet and fan. Reasonably clean.

Snuol *p183*

F Mettapheap Guesthouse, on the main road, T012- 317577. Surprisingly clean. Nice view of town roofs from balcony and surrounding countryside.

Sen Monorom *p183, map p184*

Electricity is irregular but usually 0600-1000, 1400-1700 and 1800-2200.

D Neak Meas, on the outskirts of town on road to Phnom Penh, T012-959110. A bit isolated and the dry, red plot it occupies makes it feel a bit desolate. The double-storey hotel still offers reasonably nice rooms with all amenities.

D Pitch Kiri Guesthouse, on a bend in the main road, behind the market. A bit past its use-by-date but popular. The rooms in the guesthouse are rundown and the bungalows are only marginally better. The restaurant food is double the price of anywhere else.

D Sum Dy Guesthouse, out of town on the road to Phnom Penh, T012-828533. Very cute bright orange bungalows. 10 out of 10 for distinctive character – nicely furnished, TV, mosquito net, free coffee and fan. Power supplied by generator so electricity is available around the clock.

D-E Bou Sra Guesthouse, in front of the market, on the road to Phnom Penh, T012- 527144. Clean rooms with attached bathroom. Some with TV – very useful considering the town's limited electricity supply. It rents bicycles, US$3 a day, motorbikes, US$7 a day, and cars with driver, US$70 a day.

D-E Long Vibal, 900 m past the roundabout in the centre of town, T012- 944647. Beautiful bungalows in a wonderful garden setting. Rooms with fan and attached bathroom. The owner is a very good source of local information. There is also a restaurant. A big plus is that they have a generator so you are not stuck bumbling around your room during the night. Recommended.

E-F Holiday Guesthouse, on the main road to Phnom Penh, T012-588060. Rooms are clean and comfortable but bordering on the smallish side – with bathroom and with shared facilities. TV, mosquito nets and candles supplied.

E-F Sovannkiri, on the main road to Phnom Penh, T092-821931. As this doubles as the bus terminal most people are put off. Nonetheless the rooms are extremely good value with attached bathroom. Big, airy rooms with mosquito nets, candles and free bottled water.

F Homestays. It is possible to stay in the home of one of the local ethnic minorities for around US$2 a night. You will need a moto or guide to arrange this prior to your stay as it is generally not customary or a tourism-driven practice. The huts or houses usually feature wooden beds (no mattress or linen) so you will need to bring fittings (and mosquito nets). A nice gesture would be to bring some food with you to share with the family at your homestay. See also Sights.

Ban Lung *p187, map p187*

The sheer volume of red dust that blows in through the doors and open windows makes washing and cleaning quite futile so guesthouse owners very sensibly gave up the fight against nature many years ago.

B-C Terres Rouges Lodge, T/F075-974051, www.ratanakiri -lodge.com. Run by Frenchman Pierre Yves and his friendly Khmer wife Chenda, this hotel is housed in a large traditional wooden Khmer lodge overlooking the lake and offers cool, spacious and beautiful rooms, with the added bonus of a great CD collection in the comfortable sitting area. The hotel's restaurant is first class. Pierre, like most other guesthouse and hotel owners in the area, runs a number of tour services, including elephant trekking and the use of a 4WD. Recommended.

B-C Tribal Hotel, 200 m from the centre of town, behind the post office, T075-974074, tribal_hotel@yahoo.com. Pleasant, comfortable hotel. The brightly decorated rooms have good amenities – fridge, hot shower, fan or a/c. Quite good restaurant attached (see Eating).

B-E Sovannkiri Hotel, on the outskirts of town, T075-974001. The hotel, which seems a bit ostentatious for Ban Lung, has a variety of rooms (and rates) – from basic rooms with TV, fan and attached bathroom through to the VIP suite with grandiose wooden furniture, a hot water bath (nice after a day's hiking) and fridge. The staff are rigidly formal but very helpful and friendly.

C-D Lakeside Chenglock Hotel, beside Lake Konsaign, T012-957422. An exponential improvement on its town counterpart. The rooms are very comfortable with the cheapest being roomy with fan and attached bathroom and, the more expensive fitted with lovely wooden furniture, attached bathroom with hot water and bath, a/c and a beautiful view over the lake. Internet is available for US$3 an hr if required. Recommended.

D Labansiek Hotel, clean and spacious rooms with fridge, TV and bathrooms. Undergoing major renovations at the time of writing so should be even better than before. It is friendly and well managed but lacks atmosphere.

D Yaklom Hill Lodge, near Yaklom Lake, 6 km east of Ban Lung, T012-644240, www.yaklom.com. This rustic ecolodge is a bit out of town but offers guests the opportunity to experience first-hand the wonderful surrounding environs. Bungalows are interspersed in the natural surroundings, with good-sized balconies to take in the starry-lit nights, and are decorated nicely with local handicrafts and fabrics. Fan, mosquito net, attached bathroom, shower and thermos (for those that wish to have a warm traditional scoop shower out of the earthenware pots provided). Power is supplied via generator and solar panels. The friendly owner, Sampon, is planning on turning the lodge into a bird sanctuary – with 22 different species identified on the premises at the time of publication.

D-E Cheng Luk Hotel, near the roundabout, in the centre of town, T075- 974121. Clean rooms with TV, fan and attached bathroom. Hot water and a/c rooms available. This hotel is relatively new and rooms are comfortable but after a day in the dust and mud, rooms can get dirty incredibly quickly and the

somewhat indolent staff appear reluctant to clean the rooms or even provide fresh towels (which are covered in dirt from day one). Otherwise nice hotel, but bring spare towels.

D- E The Ratanak Hotel, T012-958322, viraktravel@ yahoo.com. At this popular guesthouse you can get rooms with TV, attached bathroom, fan or a/c. It has a good restaurant and a roof on which you can sit and watch the shooting stars. Mr Leng, the proprietor, is a 'Mr Fix-It' and is happy to be at your beck and call – you want it, he gets it.

E Mountain Guesthouse, by the crossroads. This has basic rooms with fans and attached bathrooms with scoop loos. There is a simple wooden terrace where guests can mingle with the many guides who appear to have selected the guesthouse as the place to hang out after a day's work.

❼ Eating

Kompong Cham *p180*

❦❦ **Ho An Restaurant**, Monivong St, T042-941234. Large, Chinese restaurant with a good selection of dishes. Friendly service.

❦❦ **Mekong Crossing**, Pasteur St, 1 block from river, T012- 432427. Friendly restaurant and bar. Proprieter, Joe, is a great source of local information. Western dishes – hamburgers, sandwiches and steaks (US$2-4). A good selection of magazines and boardgames. Recommended.

Kratie *p181, map p181*

There are a number of food stalls set up along the river at night serving great fruit shakes. The market also sells simple dishes during the day.

❦❦-❦ **Red Sun Falling**, on the river road, is probably the best restaurant in town and offers a variety of excellent western dishes and a few Asian favourites. The full monty breakfast is fantastic. Good cocktails. The very friendly proprietor, Joe, also runs a very good bookshop on premises. Closed Sun. Recommended.

❦ **Mekong Restaurant**, just off Street 9 (near the river). A cheap selection of Khmer staples.

❦ **You Hong Guesthouse**, probably has the largest and most diverse menu in town – from muesli through to Amok. Good fresh juices. Friendly, helpful staff, who don't mind helping tourists with advice. Recommended.

The Santhepeap Hotel and Heng Heng Hotel restaurants both serve delicious Khmer food (and a sprinkling of western dishes) at very reasonable prices.

Stung Treng *p182, map p182*

There isn't a whole lot of choice when it comes to restaurants in Stung Treng. Most visitors choose to eat in their hotels. The market offers the usual array of food stalls serving simple but good one-dish meals.

Dara, opposite the taxi stand. An extensive menu of Khmer food plus a few western dishes (omelettes etc). Outdoor seating. Reasonably friendly.

New World Restaurant, adjacent to the market, T011-908584. Big clean restaurant serving Cambodian food. Bit pricey – Tom Yum US$2.50. The staff aren't friendly.

Prochum Tonle Restaurant, on site at the Sekong Hotel. Very good but short Khmer menu at reasonable prices.

Sophakmukal, near the market. Beer garden style- restaurant with very good, cheap Cambodian food, curry, amok, soup (all under US$1). Very friendly owner. Recommended.

Sun Tha, opposite the bus station. Very cheap soup shop popular with the locals. Soup for US$0.50. Next door is a fruit shake shop with a name in Khmer. It serves great fruit shakes and fruit salads for under US$0.25. If you don't like your fruit salad smothered with ice and condensed milk you may need to indicate this beforehand.

Snuol *p183*

There are 5 Cambodian restaurants on the main road opposite the taxi stand. They don't look like much but actually serve fantastic food.

Sen Monorom *p183, map p184*

Compared to the number of guesthouses there are relatively few restaurants.

Chom Nor Thmei, on the main road to Phnom Penh, in front of the market. The best restaurant in town by a longshot. Cheap Khmer food and a few western dishes (omelettes and French fries). Good, fresh orange juice and scrumptious guacamole (when in season). The lovely owners go well out of their way to satisfy customers. Recommended.

Orameas, further out on the road to Phnom Penh past the hospital. Khmer and western food. Good lok lok. Very cheap. The owner makes hydro-electric power.

Sen Monorom Restaurant, beside the roundabout in the centre of town. The oldest restaurant in town serving mostly Cambodian food. There is another Khmer restaurant beside this one, offering simple Cambodia dishes.

Spean Meanchey Restaurant, on road to Phnom Penh, away from the centre, T012-702183. Limited menu that offers 4 food options and 4 drink options. The menu states 'other command food bargaining price' – so other options are available for the right price.

A number of guesthouses have restaurants including **Pitch Kiri** (with prices double anywhere else), **Arun Reah II** (very atmospheric) and **Long Vibol** (recommended). There are also a number of good fruitshake shops around the market area.

Ban Lung *p187, map p187*

Terres Rouges Lodge Restaurant is considered the 'in' place to eat and is as fine dining as it gets in Ban Lung. Cambodian and French food. Pasta US$3, coq au vin US$8.50, beef steak US$5. Good wine list/bar and very ambient setting. Highly recommended.

Tribal Hotel Restaurant could give Terres Rouge's restaurant a good run for its money. In relative terms, the restaurant is of a similar standard and offers a very extensive menu, including some more obscure dishes for Bang Lung such as fish and chips (US$3) and kebabs (US$3). A number of local specialities are also offered.

Beoung Kamsan Restaurant, beside Lake Kamsan. The place offers a fantastic selection of Cambodian food including its own delicious speciality, chicken with cashew nuts (US$3) and the famous local delicacy, volcanic beef. It seems genuinely grateful to see foreign customers and the swift, attentive service reflects this.

The Mountain Guesthouse Restaurant has a selection of not particularly great western interpretations and Cambodian meals – from US$2-3.

American Restaurant, located on the crossroads opposite the petrol station and nicely shielded behind rose bushes. God knows where it got its name but the food works. The restaurant is simply marvellous and turns out a wide range of dishes, well prepared and highly satisfying. At 3000 riel (less than US$1) per dish it is also excellent value. The sweet and sour soup (with fish) and the fresh spring rolls are to die for.

¶ **Chum Nor Beoung Konsaign**, situated on the bend in the road around Lake Konsaign. This restaurant is not as atmospheric as its counterpart but offers a good selection of Khmer and Chinese food.

¶ **Ratanak Hotel Restaurant**. A quite popular restaurant that serves a spectacular barbecue which you cook at your table. Cambodian food between US$1-2.

¶ **Yaklom Hill Lodge** offers a good selection of tasty and cheap Lao, Khmer and Thai-inspired meals with a few dishes to please the more western-orientated palate. Curry US$2, burgers US$1.50.

⊕ Bars and clubs

Ban Lung *p187, map p187*
Since the local disco burnt down the town has been lacking any vivid nightlife. There is only one bona fide bar – the **VP Bar** – opposite the **Ratanak Hotel**. A small, intimate setting. Here, miles from any light 'pollution', you can see incredibly clear skies.

◘ Shopping

Kratie *p181, map p181*
The central market sells most things. There are a couple of pharmacies opposite the market. A good camera shop, Konica, is on the river road.

Sen Monorom *p183, map p184*
The central market in town has a variety of products (film, batteries etc) but not a great selection for those shopping. It is also possible to pick up ethnic minority handicrafts in some of the villages.

Ban Lung *p187, map p187*
Ban Lung **market** is large and set in a wasteland. Plastic bags blow in the wind and hungry dogs linger looking for scraps to eat. During the day there is very little of interest for purchase although a few shops sell

handicrafts but these have yet to develop and there are no local textiles, hence the eagerness with which kramas and T-shirts will be received. However from 0600-0700 the market is a hive of activity as nearby villagers come to sell their honey, nuts and other produce and catch up on the morning gossip whilst eating their breakfast. From 1700-1800 the food market opens at the back and, if you can face it, you can try their specialities.

▲ Activities and tours

Sen Monorom *p183, map p184*
A good tour guide is **Ok Sambol**, T012-944647, US$15 a day.

⊖ Transport

Kompong Cham *p180*
Boat
Due to improved roads the boat service to and from Kompong Cham is limited to non-existent. The boat service from Phnom Penh has been curtailed.

Moto/tuk-tuk/taxi
Local transport is by moto, tuk-tuk or taxi. A moto for a day is between US$6-8 and between 500-1000 riel for short trips. Local tuk-tuk driver and guide **Mr Vannat** has an excellent reputation and is fluent in French and English, T012995890. US$20 a day for a boat ride.

Shared taxi
The town is 120 km northeast of Phnom Penh via the well-surfaced Routes 5, 6 and 7. There are regular connections with **Phnom Penh** by **shared taxi**, US$1.85, 7000 riel. Several bus companies run services, US$2, 8000 riel, from Central Market, around 2 hrs, 8 buses a day. Pick-ups and shared taxis plough through to **Sen Monorom**, via Snuol, 2 hrs, US$3-4.

Kratie *p181, map p181*
Boat
The future of the express boat to and from Phnom Penh is uncertain but most believe the service won't resume.

195

Ecotourism in Virachey National Park

Virachey National Park has been recognized by international conservation experts as one of the top conservation priorities in Asia. The national park extends over three districts – Veng Xai, Taveng and Siem Pang in two provinces – Ratanakiri and Stung Treng. The park is bordered by Laos to the north and Vietnam to the east and is bound by two major rivers, the Sekong River in the west and the Se San River in the south.

The national park has relatively low population density. Most of those living in the park are ethnic minority peoples. Ethnic minorities comprise 4% of Cambodia's total population, and of this, 16% live in Ratanakiri.

A lot of tour operators are offering trips into Virachey National Park via the district ranger stations. These trips should be avoided as they are undermining local authorities in the effective management of the park. Those wishing to explore the area should contact the Biodiversity Protected Area and Management Project (BPAMP) who have been actively developing an ecotourism programme for Virachey National Park. The project focuses on small scale, low impact, culture, nature and adventure trekking-based tourism which benefits and involves local communities. They currently offer and are developing a number of different tours which combine jungle trekking with overnight camping, river journeys and village-based accommodation. These include a day trip from Ban Lung to the national park for a short forest walk, lunch and swim in the river; mountain biking to the national park boundary (a short two hour ride from Ban Lung), trekking and overnight stay beside a jungle waterfall in a known gibbon area, with a kayak return (three days, two nights); a river journey and trekking in Veng Xai district with village homestay (four days, three nights); extended wilderness trekking with patrolling rangers to a natural grassland deep in Taveng area (seven to eight days).

All visitors to the park require a permit which can be obtained from the national park headquarters either in Ban Lung (for Veng Xai and Taveng) or Stung Treng (for Siem Pang). For further information contact Ban Lung head office T075-974176, virachey@camintel.co

Bus

Getting to Kratie is easy now the roads have improved. Hour Lean Bus Company, T012-535387, on Kratie's riverfront runs daily buses to **Phnom Penh** for US$4.50 at 0715, 7 hrs. Phnom Penh Public Transport Co also runs the trip to Phnom Penh for the same price – the bus leaves at 0715 from the Central Market. The same bus company also charters buses to **Stung Treng** at around 1200. It is sometimes possible to hop on one of the buses coming from Phnom Penh to go to **Stung Treng** but seats can't be relied upon unless booked a few days in advance.

Motodop

Local transport by motodop US$1 per hr or US$6-7 per day.

Shared taxi

Shared taxis to **Stung Treng**, US$4 per person, 3 hrs. Shared taxis and pick-up to **Snuol** (2 hrs away) at 0700, US$2-3. Snuol is a good staging post for destinations such as **Sen Monorom** (a further 3 hrs away). Via Snuol, 5-6 hrs, US$4-5.

Stung Treng *p182, map p182*
Boat

The situation with boat travel to Phnom Penh/ Kratie is precarious. At the time of writing the roads were so good that the boat company could not recruit enough customers to maintain their service. In the wet season when the roads are a bit rougher they are more likely to resume their services (but they shouldn't be relied on). When they are running it is 4 hrs to **Kratie**, US$15 and 9-10 hrs to **Phnom Penh**, US$24.

The boat from Stung Treng to the **Lao border** costs US$7 per person or around US$35 to charter a boat and takes roughly 1 hr, 20 mins. Visas are not granted on the border and need to be organized from Phnom Penh. Boats depart quite regularly (depending on passengers), approximately every 2 hrs between 0700-1600. Once you have reached the border (open until 1700) you will need to cross the river to the other side. A departure tax of US$1-3 (and a small overtime fee on weekends and during lunch-time and after hours) will need to be paid at each side.

Most hotels (**Sekong, Riverside** etc) can organize tickets. Alternatively, you can go directly to the taxi/bus rank.

Bus

Buses to **Phnom Penh** leave from the bus stand (near the park but this office was declared 'temporary' at the time of writing) at 0700, 10 hrs, US$10. The same bus will stop at **Kratie**, US$5.

Shared taxis and pick-ups

Pick-ups and shared taxis connect regularly with **Phnom Penh** via **Kratie** and with recent road construction the roads should be okay to travel along (a little bumpy). Shared taxis to **Phnom Penh** leave at 0600 from the taxi rank near the river, 7 hrs, US$15. To **Ban Lung** at 0700 from the taxi rank and the trip takes 4-5 hrs, US$10. Please note with all shared taxi services that they will not run unless the driver has a full car (which can sometimes mean a squashy 8 people), so departure times and fares will vary depending on the amount of passengers in the car.

Snuol *p183*

Shared taxi to **Sen Monorom**, US$4, 3 hrs. The bus passes through from Phnom Penh to Snuol at about 1200. Taxis are constantly leaving for **Kratie** (usually around 1000-1200), US$2-3, 2 hrs. Bus to **Stung Treng** passes through at 1200, US$5, 5 hrs.

Sen Monorom *p183, map p184*

Local transport is US$10-15 a day with moto-guide.

It's 370 km from Phnom Penh to Sen Monorom. The trip takes between 6-8 hrs, depending on the speed of your car. Buses leave for **Phnom Penh** at 0730, 8 hrs, US$8 . The Phnom Penh bus goes via **Snuol** which is a staging post for buses and pick-ups to other destinations. Bus ticket to Snuol US$5. If you want to go to **Kratie** (change at Snuol), US$8, or **Stung Treng**, US$12. Pick-ups and shared taxis are probably the most comfortable travel option (particularly if you buy extra space). They depart from the morning market area between 0700-0800, US$6 or US$7 if you want inside – to go to Snuol.

Ban Lung *p187, map p187*
Air

The popular alternative to getting here overland is to fly although if you are a nervous flyer it might be better to arrive with a bruised backside. The ancient planes that operate on this leg are more Indiana Jones than Airbus Industrie. There is a return 4 days a week to **Phnom Penh**, 45 mins US$60-65. Two airlines operate, even though 'officially' there is only one - **President Airlines**. It is not uncommon to buy a ticket for one airline and be shafted onto the other (when you see the so-called airport this chaotic system all seems to make sense). US$4 departure tax must be paid.

Airline offices President Airlines, offices just off the market, T075-974059.

Pick-up/taxi

If you are a glutton for punishment or just want another after dinner story when you get home, it is possible to travel directly to **Phnom Penh** but be prepared to sit in a cramped pickup/taxi for around 13 hrs. Taxi to **Kratie**, US$12-13, leaving the taxi stand at approximately 0800, 7 hrs.

Taxis to **Stung Treng,** 0830, US$4-5, 8-10 hrs.

You can only get a moto to take you to **Lumphat** for around US$15 for the day trip. The road from Stung Treng is fairly well graded now and is constantly improving due to its use by logging companies. The trip to Ban Lung from Stung Treng takes about 4 hrs (if you get yourself in a nice new Camry), US$10. Unfortunately the same cannot be said of the road from Kratie to Stung Treng which barely deserves such an appellation, however, the road was being overhauled at the time of publication.

Tourists commonly ask about travelling between Ban Lung and **Sen Monorom**. At the time of publication this overland odyssey really wasn't an option, as the roads are almost impassable and difficult to navigate. Only experienced dirt-bike riders with very good local knowledge should attempt this trip.

Motorbike and moto
Several guesthouses have motorbikes for hire, or can arrange hire, for around US$5 per day without driver and triple that with a driver. The additional cost of the driver (plus a pack or two of Ara cigarettes) may be regarded as a worthwhile investment. There are very few 'excellent' guides around – with most merely pointing you in the right direction. For those with a reasonable sense of direction, it is actually quite hard to get completely lost. If this happens the local population is highly accommodating if a little uncommunicative. There are no garages/petrol stops outside the town of Ban Lung so it is advisable to set off with a full tank.

● Directory

Kompong Cham *p180*
Banks There are two banks in town – Acleda and Canadia Bank. Acleda will do Western Union transfers and Canadia will do advances on Visa and MasterCard. 0800-1600. **Internet** ABC computers, in the centre of town, was the only internet shop operating at the time of writing, US$1 per hr and overseas phone calls available. A new internet café was due to open on Pasteur St, opposite the Mekong Crossing.

Kratie *p181, map p181*
Banks There is an Acleda Bank half way down Street 11. It does not do advances on Visa or MasterCard but is a subsidiary for Western Union. **Internet** 10 m down from the wat on the river road. Quick, cheap internet. However, the NGO that runs it is likely to discontinue the project. **Three Star Internet** US$4 per hr. There is another internet café near Phnom Penh Transport bus office but at the time of writing it was US$4 per hr.

Stung Treng *p182, map p182*
Banks There are no banks in town. **Internet** Internet is available at the computer shop opposite the market and the Sekong Hotel, US$4 per hr. **Telephone** There are telephone shops all over town.

Sen Monorom *p183, map p184*
Banks There are no banks in town but dollar bills can be exchanged at gold stores in the market. There are no banks for Visa cash advances and no places to cash TC's in Sen Monorom, so bring enough cash to support your stay and activities. **Internet** At the time of writing the only place to have internet was **Arun Reah II Guesthouse** on the road to Phnom Penh at a whopping US$4 an hr.

Ban Lung *p187, map p187*
Banks The Mountain Guesthouse and the Ratanak Hotel both change TCs but allow at least 3 days for your cheques to clear. **Internet** CIC near *Sovannikiri Hotel*. **Medical services** The hospital is on the road north towards O Chum. Dr Vannara, T012-970359, speaks very good English. **Post office** In the centre of town.

Footprint features

Introduction

Cambodia's coast is fringed by mile after mile of fabulously soft white sand and is slowly become the place for a seaside holiday. With the new Sokha Beach Resort it won't be too long before Sihanoukville hosts a number of beach resorts comparable to other holiday destinations in Southeast Asia. Despite the lack of facilities, the beautiful coastal scenery between Sihanoukville and Kep should not be missed, particularly the stretch around Kampot.

The region includes the three provinces of Koh Kong, Kampot and Kampong Speu and is dominated and defined by the Cardamom and Elephant mountain ranges and by the coast. It is to the coast that modern Cambodia looks for its future wealth. Until now only fishing has been developed in any way but though tourism and trade lag lamentably behind they both have a bright future, particularly with the growth of Sihanoukville and the development of Route 4, which links it to Phnom Penh and is about to become a toll road. It is interesting how small a part the coast has played in Cambodia's history. This is partly because so much of the coast is hemmed in by hills and also because Cambodia is tucked away high up in the Gulf of Thailand away from all the international trade routes. Visitors of significance tended to arrive on the Mekong, which historically has carried more of Cambodia's trade than the coast. In recent decades attempts have been made to develop the coast but each time (until now) they have been thwarted by war and revolution.

★ Don't miss...

1 **Sihanoukville** Not many people come to Cambodia for a beach holiday experience, but Sihanoukville comes close, with clean water, good beaches and a picturesque location. Don't expect world class hotels and a host of amenities though, see page 202.

2 **Bokor Hill Station** 1000 m above the charming town of Kampot, this is a nifty getaway from the heat of the plains with its cool forest walks and waterfalls, see page 209.

3 **Kep** This small beach resort is mostly frequented by holidaying Cambodians. Come here not for the sea and sand but for the freshly caught crab – best eaten on the beach – and for the beautiful garden atmosphere, see page 210.

Ins and outs

Getting down to the south is easy as comfortable buses regularly make the trip down to Sihanoukville. From Sihanoukville, it is fairly easy to travel to Kampot and onwards to Kep. You can also travel to Koh Kong via road, both from Sihanoukville and Hat Lek, Thailand, or take a boat from Sihanoukville.

Sihanoukville 🚌🏍🏨🏊🍴🏕🚍🍷 ▸▸ *pages 213-222.*

Sihanoukville, or Kompong Som as it is called during the periods the king is in exile or 'out of office', was founded in 1964 by Prince Sihanouk to be the nation's sole deep-water port. It is also the country's prime seaside resort. In its short history it has crammed in as much excitement as most seaside towns see in a century – but not of the sort that resorts tend to encourage. Sihanoukville was used as a strategic transit point for weapons used in fighting the USA during the Vietnam War. In 1975, the US bombed the town when the Khmer Rouge seized the container ship *SS Mayaguez*.

Sihanoukville has turned a corner and with rapid development has firmly secured its place in Cambodia's 'tourism triangle', alongside Phnom Penh and Angkor Wat. Close by is the coastal Preah Sihanouk 'Ream' National Park.

Ins and outs

Getting there From Phnom Penh's Central Market there are regular departures in well-maintained, air-conditioned coaches with careful drivers which leave and arrive on time. Tickets are unbelievably cheap (US$3-4). Buses generally leave every 30 minutes from 0700-1330. Sihanoukville can also by reached from Thailand, crossing the border at Hat Lek and taking a boat from Koh Kong. Most taxi drivers are willing to take the trip to Sihanoukville, US$20-30, but it is much more comfortable to go by bus. Taxis depart from Kampot and Phnom Penh around 0700-0800, US$5-6. Pending the upgrading of Kang Keng Airport, about 20 km outside Sihanoukville, it may be possible in the future to fly there. ▸▸ *See Transport page 220, for further details.*

Getting around Most people take a moto from the coach drop to their hotel and then rent a motorbike for exploring. Within the beach area everything is close enough to reach on foot but from beach to beach or beach to town is definitely a ride. Check with locals before hiring a motorbike as there have been a number of scams including tourists having their bikes impounded and having to repay the bike shop. Don't ride with your bag strap across your shoulder as it screams out 'pull me off my bike'.

Sights

Sihanoukville occupies a lovely site on a small peninsula whose nobbly head juts out into the Gulf of Thailand. There are first rate beaches, clean water, trees and invigorating breezes. Cambodia's beaches are comparable to those in Thailand but are yet to yield the tourism masses, so make the most of it while you can as there are big plans for this area. Most people head for one of the three beaches close to the town which, starting from the north, are Victory, Independence and Ochheauteal. This is not so much because they cannot wait to immerse themselves in the balmy waters but because this is where the best hotels are. Sihanoukville's layout is unusual with the 'town' itself, inland acting as a satellite to the roughly equidistant three beaches. The urban area is pretty scattered and has the distinct feel of a place developing in an ad hoc basis. It has a few large Chinese hotels, a market, petrol stations and a couple of bars. Sihanoukville is primarily a resort for Cambodians although word is quickly spreading. It gets crowded at weekends as families from Phnom Penh descend in their newly acquired Toyotas, Mercedes and BMWs. The amount of litter they spread is astonishing – mile upon mile of families sit contentedly munching sandwiches while their detritus of cans, bottles, wrappers, newspapers, crab claws, chicken bones and plastic bags joins the strata of accumulated refuse at their feet.

Victory Beach is a thin, 2-km-long beach on the north of the peninsula, just down from the port, and offers reasonably secluded beaches. The original backpackers' beach, it's now somewhat deserted, usurped by the popularity of Ochheauteal Beach. Today, the large derelict buildings on the front fail to generate the seaside spirit of fun and frivolity and the grim hotels here quickly quench whatever joie de

Sihanoukville

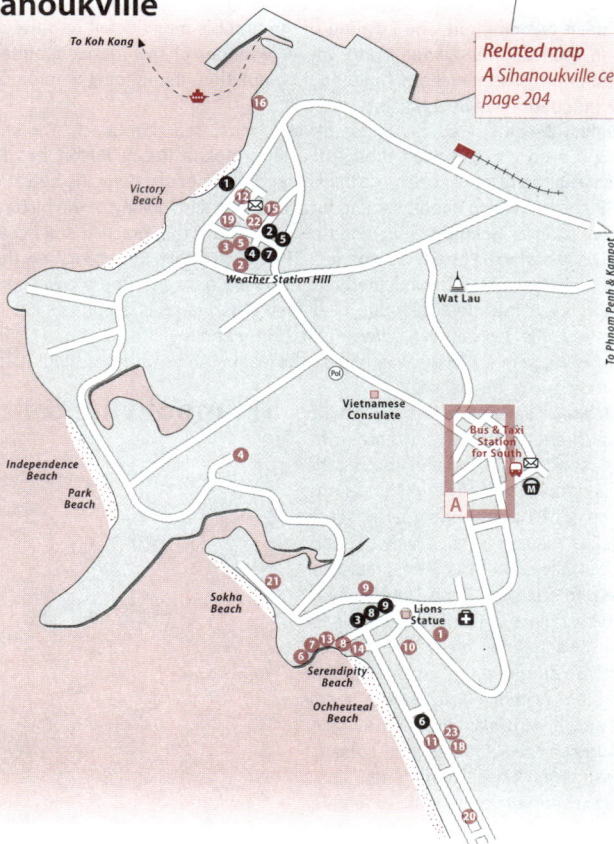

Related map
A Sihanoukville centre,
page 204

To Koh Kong

Victory Beach

Weather Station Hill

Wat Lau

To Phnom Penh & Kampot

Pol

Vietnamese Consulate

Bus & Taxi Station for South

A

Independence Beach

Park Beach

Sokha Beach

Lions Statue

Serendipity Beach

Ochheuteal Beach

The South Sihanoukville

N

0 metres 500
0 yards 500

Sleeping
Bar Ru **1**
Blue Frog **2**
Bungalow Village **3**
Chez Claude **4**
Chez Mari-yan **5**
Cloud 9 **6**
Coasters Guesthouse **7**
Eden Guesthouse **8**
Golden Castle **9**
Golden Sand **10**
Golden Sea **11**

Holiday Palace & Casino **12**
Malibu **13**
Mealy Chenda **15**
New Beach **16**
Orchidée **18**
Sakal Bungalows **19**
Seaside **20**
Sokha Beach Resort **21**
Sontapheap **23**
Sunset Garden Inn **22**
Unkle Bob's **14**

Eating
Chhner Molop Chrey **1**
Corner Bar **2**
Endless Summer
  Beach Club **3**
Indian Curry Pot **5**
Les Feuilles **6**
Mash Melting Pot **7**
Mick & Craig's **8**
Paillote **4**
Treasure Island Seafood **9**

vivre holidaymakers are able to muster. Beach hawkers are ubiquitous and outnumber tourists at a ratio of about three to one. The area does afford a good sunset view, however. A rocky point at the south end of Victory Beach divides the beach. Here is another small streak of sand referred to as **Hawaii Beach** or Lamherkey Beach. This quiet spot was a bustle of activity during the 1950s when French and Cambodian workers laid the groundwork for construction of the new Port of Kampong Som. North of the beach is the shipping port and a park. **Weather Station Hill** (or Backpackers Hill), above the beach, still proves to be a popular backpacker area, with several decent places to eat and stay in the vicinity.

Independence Beach does not currently have anywhere to stay other than the once bombed and charred **Independence Hotel** in which penurious Khmer appear to have been camping out. The location of the hotel is magnificent and the grounds, even in their mid-renovation state, are a reminder of the former grandeur. With restoration of this marvellous hotel near completion, its opening would do a lot to revive Independence Beach's fortunes.

Sokha Beach is arguably Sihanoukville's most beautiful beach. The shore laps around a 1-km arc and even though the large **Sokha Beach Resort** has taken up residence it is very rare to see more than a handful of people along the beach. It is said that Sihanouk used to import sand to local beaches and looking at the picture-perfect powdery sand of Sokha one wouldn't be surprised if this practice still occurs. Early risers will see why the beach is so perfect. The **Sokha Beach Resort** ensures the stretch remains obsessively well-manicured and every morning a troupe of sweepers rid the beach of even the most minutiae of debris. This beach is stunning and relatively hassle-free. It is best to swim between the centre and the end closest to Ochheauteal Beach, as the Sam At waterway appears to be leaking some rather dubious content into the farther end of the beach.

Ochheauteal Beach lies furthest to the south and is the all-round favourite. Like most of Sihanoukville's beaches, the sand is dazzling in its fine whiteness and copious deckchairs sporting large beach umbrellas shade the lovely beach. Sihanoukville is not a family resort but, for those with children, Ochheauteal would be the best place to come. Indeed it is for anyone wanting a break in relatively attractive surroundings with mottled green-blue waters, rock pools, shady trees and a wide sandy beach surface. The surfeit sellers touting fruit, colossal prawns, arm bands and sugar hair removal (whether you're male or female) and hordes of child vendors pursuing sales very aggressively (usually under duress) can all get a tad monotonous, if not exhausting. There is a fair whack of stray litter strewn along the shoreline and watch your stuff as theft is common.

The beach commonly referred to as **Serendipity Beach** is at the very north end of Ochheauteal. This little strand has gained flavour with travellers due in part to being the first beach in Sihanoukville to offer a wide range of

Sihanoukville centre

Sleeping 🛌
Chhoung Samoth **1**
Geckozy **2**
Neak Meas **3**
New Paris **4**
Oasis **5**
Small **6**
Spitfire
Guesthouse **7**

Eating 🍴
Bamboo Light **1**
Espresso
Kampuchea **2**
Holy Cow **4**
Starfish Café **5**

0 metres 100
0 yards 100

budget accommodation. This is definitely the most aesthetic piece of Ochheauteal with large ashen rocky outcrops, smaller rock pools, jungled hills and a much cleaner shoreline. At the time of publication, the many guesthouses and restaurants lining the shore of Serendipity and the extended Ochheauteal Beach area were at the centre of a land dispute with large developers hankering to clear the budget accommodation to make way for large Thai-style resorts. Tourists can get to Serendipity Beach by following Ekareach Street.

Around Sihanoukville

Preah Sihanouk 'Ream' National Park ⓘ *the park HQ is 18 km north of Sihanoukville, opposite the airport, T012-875096, daily 0700-1715. Visitors explore the park either by taking a boat trip (half or 1 day, US$30 for 4 people) or on foot with a guide (US$5 per person for a 3 to 5 hr nature trek). To arrange a guided tour visit the park office in Ream or arrange one through a guesthouse in Sihanoukville. Basic accommodation is available at the park headquarters for US$5 per person. To get there it is probably best to hire a motorbike or a moto driver from Sihanoukville. Head north on Route 4 out of Sihanoukville until you get to a major intersection at around 15 km. Turn right here and onto the road that was resurfaced by the Petroleum Authority of Thailand (PTT) in 1996. The road follows the coastline until you get to the PTT plant and the park can be accessed from here.* This beautiful park is a short 30-minute drive from Sihanoukville. The park was set up in 1993 and hugs the coastline of the Gulf of Thailand. It includes two islands and covers 21,000 ha of beach, mangrove swamp, offshore coral reef and the Prek Tuk Sap Estuary. Samba deer, endangered civet species, porcupines and pangolin are said to inhabit the park, as well as dolphins.

Kbal Chhay Waterfall ⓘ *at Khan Prey Nup Village, 8½ km from downtown Sihanoukville. Follow Highway 4 for 1 km until you have passed the 'Welcome to Sihanoukville' sign, turn left and follow this road for another 7½ km until you reach the falls.* This place is near the top of the motos and local tour operator 'must-see' list. The multiple falls are pleasant enough but don't live up to their reputation as one of the area's premier tourist attractions (funnily enough one tour operator refers to it as "something out of Hollywood"). The falls are at their best in the wet season with deeper swimming areas and clean flushes of water. In the drier months they're reduced to a stream, dotted with a few small pools in desperate need of a good clean. The waterfall was 'discovered' in 1960 but plans to establish it as Sihanoukville's primary reservoir were thwarted when the Khmer Rouge seized the area during the war. There are a number of food and drink vendors in the falls proximity but try to avoid a visit on weekends when scores of picnickers descend on the site.

Stung Hav ⓘ *take Hun Sen Beach Drive out past the Sokimex terminal*, is a small fishing village approximately 25 km north of Sihanoukville. The settlement isn't exactly a tourist site but a place where visitors can experience an authentic taste of Khmer life – watching fishing boats come and go, buyers checking out the catch of the day and other platitudes from waterfront life. Sometimes it reeks here due to the prahok factory – a less than palatable, pungent fermented fish paste.

For those not wanting to venture out of Sihanoukville, there is also a small fishing port, 2 km north of the ferry dock. Here, the motley collection of wharves comes alive at daybreak, when colourful fishing boats dock and the fish are sorted and bought by wheeling dealing merchants.

At the top of **Sihanoukville Mountain**, ⓘ *follow Route 4 about 2.5 km north of town and turn right at the brewery and follow the road up the hill*, is **Wat Leu**, a pretty but rather unexciting modern temple. Of more interest is the nearby **Chinese Cemetery**, which juts from the hill's side. The hill's 145m-high pinnacle affords brilliant panoramic views of Sihanoukville and the islands, particularly at sunset.

Sihanoukville's islands

More than 20 beautiful islands and pristine coral reefs lie off Sihanoukville's coastline. Most of the islands are uninhabited except Koh Russei (Bamboo Island), Koh Rong Salaam and a few others that contain small fishing villages. At the time of publication most of the islands were controlled by the Cambodian military with the odd chunk being leased out for tourism. Not all islands are accessible and admission to certain areas usually requires the go ahead from some military heavy (easy enough if you have a well-connected tour guide).

Regardless, diving and snorkelling around the islands is pretty good. The coast offers an abundance of marine life including star fish, sea anemones, lobsters and sponge and brain coral. Larger creatures like stingrays, angel fish, groupers, barracuda, moray eels and giant clams are ubiquitous. Baby whale sharks and reef sharks also roam the waters. More elusive are the black dolphins, pink dolphins, common dolphins and bottle-nosed dolphins but they are sighted from time to time. It is believed that further afield (closer to Koh Kong) are a family of dugongs (sea cows). No one has sighted these rare creatures except for one hotel owner who sadly saw a dugong head for sale in Sihanoukville's market.

The islands are divided into three separate groups: the Kampong Som Group, the Ream Group and the Royal Islands. The **Kampong Som Islands** are the closest to Sihanoukville and have quite good beaches. Here the visibility stretches up to 40 m. Koh Pos is the closest island to Sihanoukville, located just 800 m from Victory Beach. Most people prefer, Koh Koang Kang also known as Koh Thas, which is 45 minutes from shore. This island has two beautiful beaches (with one named after Elvis!) and the added attraction of shallow rocky reefs, teeming with wildlife, which are perfect for snorkelling. More rocky reefs and shallow water can be found at the **Rong Islands**. Koh Rong is about two hours west of Sihanoukville and has a stunning, 5-km-long sand beach (on the southwest side of the island). To the south of the Koh Rong is Koh Rong Salaam, a smaller island that is widely considered Cambodia's most beautiful. There are nine fantastic beaches spread across this island and on the east coast, a lovely heart-shaped bay. It takes about 2½ hours to get to Koh Rong from Sihanoukville. Koh Kok, a small island off Koh Rong Salaam, is one of the firm favourite dive sites, warranting it the nickname 'the garden' and takes 1¾ hours to get there.

During winter (November to February) the **Ream Islands** are the best group to visit as they are more sheltered than some of the other

The South Koh Kong & around

Koh Kong and around ▸ pages 213-222.

Dusty Koh Kong gets a bad rap. It's better known for its brothels, casinos and 'Wild West' atmosphere than as lying at the heart of a protected area with national park status (granted by Royal Decree in 1993). It is also often confused with its beautiful offshore namesake Koh Kong Island. Koh Kong town is also reputed to have the highest incidence of HIV infection of any place in Cambodia and is a haven for members of the Thai mafia trying to keep their heads down and launder large sums of money through the casino. Koh Kong is only really used by travellers as a transit stop on the way to and from Thailand. If you possibly can, move on before you have to spend a night here. Koh Kong is a great staging post to get to two of the most scenic places in the country – Koh Kong Island and the Cardamom Mountains.

islands but they are a lot further out. The Ream Islands encompass those islands just off the Ream coast: Prek Mo Peam and Prek Toek Sap, which don't offer the clearest waters. The islands of Koh Khteah, Koh Tres, Koh Chraloh and Koh Ta Kiev are best for snorkelling. Giant mussels can be seen on the north side of Koh Ta Kiev island. Some 50 km out are the outer Ream Islands which, without a doubt, offer the best diving in the area. The coral in these islands though has started to deteriorate and is now developing a fair bit of algae. Kondor Reef, 75 km west of Sihanoukville, is a favorite diving spot. A Chinese junk filled with gold and other precious treasures is believed to have sunk hundreds of years ago on the reef. Famous underwater treasure hunter, Michael Archer, has thoroughly searched the site but no one can confirm whether he struck gold.

Koh Tang, Koh Prins and Paulo Wai are seven hours away to the southwest. These islands are believed to have visibility that stretches for 40 m and are teeming with marine life. These islands are recommended as some of the best dive sites. It is believed that Koh Prins once had a modern shipwreck and sunken US helicopter but underwater scavengers looking for steel and US MIA guys have completely cleared the area. Large schools of yellow fin tuna are known to inhabit the island's

surrounding waters. Koh Tang is worth a visit but is quite far from the mainland so an overnight stay on board might be required. Many local dive experts believe Koh Tang represents the future of Cambodia's diving. The island became infamous in May 1975 when the US ship *SS Mayaguez* was seized by the Khmer Rouge just off here. The area surrounding Paulo Wai is not frequently explored, so most of the coral reefs are still in pristine condition.

Closer to Thailand lies Koh Sdach ('King's Island'), a stop off on the boat ride between Sihanoukville and Koh Kong. This undeveloped island is home to about 4000 people, mostly fishing families. The beaches are a bit rocky but there is some fabulous snorkelling. At the time of publication a guesthouse was being built on the island so it should be possible to stay.

The Cambodian diving industry is still in its fledgling years . The positive in this is that most of the islands and reefs are still in somewhat pristine condition and the opportunities to explore unchartered waters limitless. For those who wish to just kick back out on the islands, it is now possible. A young entrepreneur from Sihanoukville has just put up some bungalows on Bamboo Island for around US$5-10 a night (T012-388860). See Activities and tours, page 219, for a list of scuba operations.

Background

The sleepy town is quite scenic sitting between a large river and mountain range. There is no mistaking it as anything but a fishing port as women mend their nets and boats come and go. The town's infrastructure is quite low and much of what does exist hasn't been provided by the government but the casino. Power failure and an infrequent water supply are all too common.

Central Cardamoms Protected Forest

① *The area remains relatively inaccessible but over the next few years it is anticipated that ecotourism operators will flock to the area. For now, it is best to make short trips into the park as the area is sparsely populated and heavily mined (so stay on clearly marked paths). Take a motorbike (with an experienced rider) or a boat. The latter option is more convenient in Koh Kong. There are usually several men with boats*

❝❞ Needless to say, the 30-km boat trip down to the rapids reveals a dramatic backdrop of mountains, gorges, waterfalls and virgin wilderness...

willing to take the trip down the Mohaundait Rapids, cutting through the jungled hills and wilderness of the Cardomoms. Needless to say the 30-km trip down to the rapids reveals a dramatic backdrop of mountains, gorges, waterfalls and virgin wilderness and is spectacular. The cost of the trip is between US$25-30.

In 2002, the government announced the creation of the **Central Cardamoms Protected Forest**, a 402,000-ha area in Cambodia's Central Cardamom Mountains. With two other wildlife sanctuaries bordering the park, the total land under protection is 990,000 ha – the largest, most pristine wilderness in mainland Southeast Asia. The extended national park reaches widely across the country, running through the provinces of Koh Kong, Pursat, Kompong Speu and Battambang. Considering that Cambodia has been severely deforested and seen its wildlife hunted to near-extinction, this park represents a good opportunity for the country to regenerate both flora and fauna. The Cardamoms are home to most of Cambodia's large mammals and half of the country's birds, reptiles and amphibians. The mountains have retained large populations of the region's most rare and endangered animals, such as the Indochinese tigers, Asian elephants and sun bears. Globally threatened species like the pileated gibbon and the critically endangered Siamese crocodile, which has its only known wild breeding population, exist in the Cardamoms. Environmental surveyors have identified 30 large mammal species, 30 small mammal species, more than 500 bird species, 64 reptiles and 30 amphibians, that reside in the park. Conservationists are predicting they will discover other animals that have disappeared elsewhere in the region such as the Sumatran rhinoceros. With virgin jungles, waterfalls, rivers and rapids this area represents a huge untapped ecotourism potential. However, tourist services to the area are still quite limited.

Koh Kong Island

The island (often called Koh Kong Krau) is arguably one of Cambodia's best islands. There are six white powdery beaches each stretching kilometre after kilometre, while a canopy of coconut trees shade the glassy-smooth aqua waters. It's a truly stunning part of the country and has been earmarked by the government for further development, so go now, while it's still a little utopia. There are a few frisky dolphin pods that crop up from time to time – both from the black and the white species. Their intermittent appearances usually take place in the morning and in the late afternoon.

Kampot and around 🛏️🍴▲🚌🅾️❶ ↠ *pages 213-222.*

Kampot is a charming riverside town that was established in the early 1900s by the French. The town lies at the base of the Elephant Mountain Range, 5 km inland on the River Prek Thom and was for a long time the gateway to the beach resort at Kep. See page 210. On one side of the river are tree-lined streets, crumbling mustard yellow French shopfronts and a sleepy atmosphere whilst on the other side you will find locals working in the surrounding salt pans. The town has another era feel – with a dabbling of Chinese architecture and overall French colonial influence, which with a bit of restoration work, could easily be compared to UNESCO World Heritage sites such as Hoi An in Vietnam and Luang Prabang in Laos. Life is very laidback in Kampot and the town has become a regular expat retreat with Phnom Penh-ites ducking down here for a breath of fresh air and the cooler climate.

Despite its tranquil exterior Kampot has, like so many other Cambodian towns, a darker side to its history. In 1994, Khmer Rouge rebels kidnapped three foreign tourists on their way to Sihanoukville in a train just outside Kampot. When their ransom demands were not met, the tourists were killed. Later, in June 1996, sawmill workers north of Kampot were abducted and brutally executed by the Khmer Rouge.

Kampot has plenty to offer visitors with Bokor Mountain National Park close by, limestone mountains riddled with caves, temples and the former French health station of Kep.

Bokor Mountain National Park

① US$5. Park rangers can speak some English and have a small display board on the flora and fauna in the park at their office. Bokor is 42 km and 90 mins from Kampot. Head back 6 km towards Sihanoukville then take a right. The road up the mountain is steep and in a poor state of repair. 4WD or dirt bikes are recommended although in wet weather the road is slippery and the motorbike option is less advisable. A moto and driver for the day will cost around US$15 or a car for around US$30.

Bokor Mountain National Park's plateau, at 1,040 m, peers out from the southernmost end of the Elephant Mountains with a commanding view over the Gulf of Thailand and east to Vietnam. Bokor Hill (Phnom Bokor) is densely forested and in the remote and largely untouched woods scientists have discovered 30 species of plants unique to the area. Not for any reason are these called the Elephant Mountains and besides the Asian elephant there are tigers, leopards, wild cows, civets, pigs, gibbons and numerous bird species.

At the peak of the mountain is Bokor Hill Station where eerie, abandoned, moss-covered buildings sit in dense fog. The buildings were built by the French who,

The South Kampot & around

Kampot

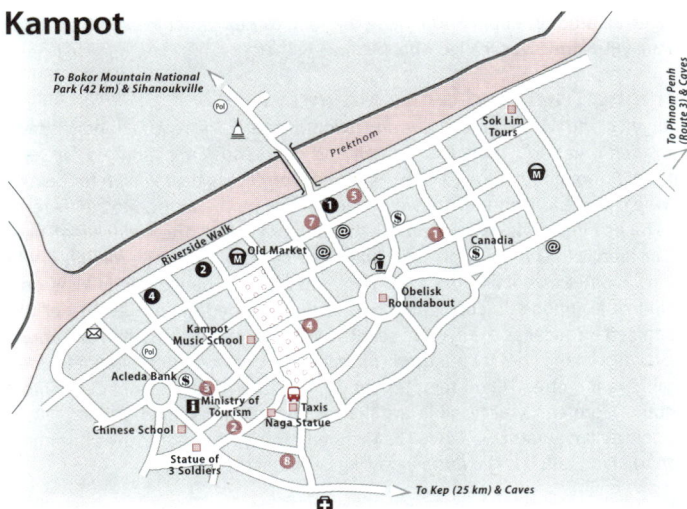

N

0 metres   200
0 yards   200

Sleeping
Blissful Guesthouse 3
Borey Bokor 1 1
Kampot Guesthouse 2
Little Garden Bar 5

Mealy Chenda
Guesthouse 4
Molieden 7
Ta Eng Guesthouse 8

Eating
Bamboo Light 2
Phnom Kamchay 1
Rusty Key Hole 4

attracted by Bokor's relative coolness, established a 'station climatique' on the mountain in the 1920s. In the grand old days there was a casino, a hotel, villas and a church with a graveyard for those for whom even the cool mountain air proved too oppressive. King Monivong established a residence which his son, Sihanouk, was later pleased to use. In 1970 Lon Nol shut it down and Bokor was quickly taken over by communist guerrillas; it later became a strategic military base for the Khmer Rouge. In more recent years there was a lot of guerrilla activity in the hills, but the area is now safe, with the exception of the ever-present danger of landmines.

The ruins are surprisingly well preserved but bear evidence of their tormented past. Many of the lower windows are bricked up, sandbags are packed into the lower floors and the walls are scarred by bullet holes. You could spend plenty of time poking around in the old settlement speculating where the king may once have lain his royal head, who lost what to whom in the casino and who wed whom in the church. Then there are lovely walks down into the forest. There is a double waterfall called **Popokvil Falls**, a 2-km walk from the station, which involves wading through a stream, though in the wet season this is nigh on impossible. In the last year or two Bokor has become very popular with Cambodian picnickers, especially on Sundays.

Kbal Romeas caves and temple

Some 10 km or so out of Kampot on both the roads to Phnom Penh and to Kep, limestone peaks harbour interesting **caves** with stalactites and pools. It is here that you can find one of Cambodia's hidden treasures – an 11th-century temple slowly being enveloped by stalactites and hidden away in a cave in **Phnom Chhnok**, next to the village of Kbal Romeas. The temple, which is protected by three friendly monks, was discovered by Adhemer Leclere in 1866. It was closed off due to thieving and now lies virtually forgotten by all bar the villagers who live here. The temple is on the road towards Kep but directions to get there are fairly complex and many of the motos and cars now do trips out there. If caves are more your cup of tea, take the Phnom Penh road out of town and turn right into the cement factory and head for the peaks; there are caves all around. About 8 km along the road to Kep under **Phnom Siap Ta'aun**, there are yet more caves, called Kbal Meal.

Kompong Trach and White Mountain

ⓘ *Bear left at the White Horse Statue and follow the road. The road is a combination of well graded and badly potholed. A torch and good shoes are required for serious exploring.* Although Kompong Trach, 35 km east of Kep, is best known for being the area where three foreign tourists were held captive by the Khmer Rouge in 1994, it makes for an interesting day trip out of either Kampot or Kep. The main reason people visit this area is to see the impressive limestone caves of the White Mountain which lie a few kilometres outside the town (look out also for the limestone kilns on the outskirts of Kompong Trach). Water erosion has created large outcrops of caves interspersed for as far as the eye can see. The White Mountain has been an important religious pilgrimage spot for hundreds of years and local rumour maintains there are several long forgotten Hindu temples within the caves which tunnel deep into the mountain. More easily accessible are the reclining Buddhas and shrines found in many of the cave entrances. As well as Kompong Trach's caves, the area has another reason to stand tall: it is the durian growing centre of the country.

Kep

Tucked in on the edge of the South China Sea, Kep was established in 1908 by the French as a health station for their government officials and families. Being the nearest beach to Phnom Penh, Kep was once very popular with Cambodian and French high society. The ruins of their holiday villas stand along the beachfront and in the surrounding hills. They were largely destroyed during the civil war under Lon Nol and by the Khmer Rouge. They were then further ransacked during the famine of the early 1980s when starving Cambodians raided the villas for valuables to exchange for food. The white villa on the hill is said to be Sihanouk's. In the past Sihanouk also had his own private island here – Ile des Ambassadeurs – where he entertained guests. Khmers will tell you that the name originates from the legend of Sa Kor Reach who cast a spell on the King of Angkor, stole the king's white horse, and rode to Kep where he was forced out of town by the king's soldiers leaving behind his saddle (Kep She which literally translates to horse seat in Khmer). The horsey statue on the way into town lends weight to this eponymous name.

At the time of publication, Kep still hadn't hit the radar of many international tourists. It is very popular on weekends with holidaying Cambodians who have managed to keep this idyllic town one of the country's best kept secrets. Beautiful gardens and lush green landscape juxtaposed against the blue waters makes it one of the most wonderfully relaxing places in the country. The town itself only has one major beach, a pebbly murky pool which doesn't really compare with Sihanoukville beaches, but they can be found at almost all of the 13 outlying islands, see below. However, it is considerably more beautiful than Sihanoukville and much more relaxing. It is famous for the freshly caught crab, which is best eaten on the beach (US$1.50 per kg), and the drink *tik tanaout jiu*, a palm wine. Along the waterfront lie a number of ruined holiday homes – testament to the town's wonderful past.

Kep is divided into two parts. The beach area features a **pier** with a large-buttocked mermaid statue, the best crab restaurants and the ruined colonial villas. It is here that you will find the sand. The **beachfront** is pleasant with plenty of shady trees and benches, but the beach itself can be quite dirty. From July to October Kep is subject to the southeast monsoon occasionally rendering the beach unswimmable because of the debris brought in. Vietnam is only 30 km from Kep and many of the islands that can be seen offshore belong to Vietnam. About 2 km further on, where the beach is stoney, is the administrative area and the **market**.

There are 13 islands off Kep's shore: Koh Trangol, Koh Korang, Koh Mtes, Koh Kok, Koh Svay, Koh Tbol, Koh Hal Trey, Koh Makprang, Koh Ses, Koh Sngout, Koh Pou, Koh Angkrang and Koh Toensay. The snorkelling and diving is not as good as around Sihanoukville's islands. From Kep it is possible to hire a boat to **Koh Toensay** ('Rabbit Island') ⓘ *expect to pay about US$10 to hire a boat for the day*. There are four half-moon beaches on this island which boast much finer, whiter sand than Kep beach. Further out is **Snake Island** which has beautiful white sandy beaches and coral. Local craft are generally too small to make the journey so it might be better to take a larger boat from Kampot. The Kampot to Kep road has some good caves about 8 km out of Kampot.

Takeo and around 🍽️🛏️🚌 ▸ *pages 213-222.*

There isn't a whole lot drawing tourists to Takeo. Most find themselves coming here to visit nearby sites such as Angkor Borei or Phnom Da. It's hard today to imagine Takeo being the powerhouse scholars presume it was. Third-century Chinese merchants referred to this area as the mighty Funan Kingdom and archaeological evidence discovered at Angkor Borei substantiates this theory that the area was probably an epicentre of some kind around AD 300-400.

Modern-day Takeo might lack the chutzpah of an ancient kingdom but is still delightful in its own way – bright red flame trees bloom about the town, these are charming parks and a very serene, lotus-filled lake. During the wet season Takeo becomes a wetlands almost overnight with over half the local land mass dedicated to rice cultivation. When heavy rains fall the hilltop of Phnom Da becomes a little island approachable by boat only. When the roads become impassable, a nifty canal system acts as a substitute.

The legend of Phnom Da

The mighty King of Champassack had a beautiful daughter, Princess Ak Or. As a young woman the princess fell hopelessly in love with a poor villager and the pair secretly married. The king was enraged when he found out and banished them from the kingdom, sailing them down the river on a small raft with only a few morsels to eat. They drifted for months and eventually washed up at Phnom Borei.

Poor, hungry and tired they immediately set about creating a new life, building a house and planting some crops. But they were desperately poor and nothing could quell Ak Or's pining for her old life. She prayed to the spirits every night for some luck and one night in her dream a man said: "I am an honest man. From now on I will watch over you and your fortunes will change. You will be rich and famous."

The next day, when her husband collected wood, she went to check, only to find he was collecting precious sandalwood. She was ecstatic and Ak Or's husband, desperate to keep her happy, went deeper into the forest, stumbling across a pile of colourful stones. He took them back to their house and Ak Or immediately knew he had found precious gems.

Eventually some traders came through and the couple sold their precious commodities and became very rich. Eventually Ak Or inherited the throne and as king and queen they constructed a huge castle out of bricks and stones and called it Da – the word for rock. Once their castle was completed they asked their subjects to build a small but beautiful stone temple on the mountain to pay tribute to the honest man who had kept his word. The temple they built was Phnom Da.

Sights

Angkor Borei is a lovely little settlement on the banks of the Prek Angkor, a tributary from the Bassac. The ancient Funan ruins here have attracted worldwide acclaim as research indicates the ancient walled city of Angkor Borei could date as far back as 2,000 years. There were probably hundreds of temples but today there is not much for tourists to see. The major draw card is the nearby **museum**ⓘ US$1, 0830-1630 (with a 2 hr lunch break in the middle of the day). Housed in a small colonial building, the museum has several reproductions of sculptures, statues, beads, rocks and inscriptions from the nearby ruins of Phnom Da. Many of these artifacts have been carbon-dated, some as far back as the 4th century. There is also small photography exhibition showing the extensive excavations undertaken by the University of Hawaii team to find out more about the Funan era.

Ten minutes away from the museum is **Phnom Da**ⓘ US$2, the oldest historical site in Cambodia. This site was a place of worship prior to the erection of the first temple here in the 6th century. There are two 45-m high hills and at the peak of one sits Prasat Phnom Da. On the way up the hill there are four caves utilized as shrines. Phnom Da is a square laterite tower with four doorways. Most of the precious artifacts have been relocated and false carvings and embellishments have been substituted (except for the east side).

Getting to Angkor Borei and Phnom Da is half the fun, taking a boat down the local canals and meandering down the river. The day excursion should cost US$20 by boat and is a scenic 40-minute trip through the rice fields, marshlands and criss-crossing the ancient canals.

Sihanoukville *p202, maps p203 and p204*

There is a lot of accommodation in Sihanoukville and not all of it good, but the situation is developing. Accommodation is changing hands so often that locals joke that opening a new business in Sihanoukville is like a sport. This aside, the future of Sihanoukville's guesthouses is somewhat insecure as locals suggest that many small operators will be cleared out (especially those on the beachfront) to make way for bigger developers.

Town centre

Travellers en route for Kampot or Thailand may choose to stay in town, otherwise one of the beach areas represents a more pleasant alternative.

B-C New Paris Hotel, corner of Sopheakmongkol and Ekareach St. Passable rooms with a/c, hot water, TV and fridge. Clean but nondescript and a serious overuse of wood panelling. Khmer and Thai restaurant with large menu of dishes charging between US$5-8.

D Oasis Hotel, Ekareach St. Large rooms with TV, a/c, fridge and hot water. Very large building with cavernous lobby behind the restaurant/ bar and mammoth staircase. Restaurant with large bar, western breakfast, pizza and generic Asian food. Ping pong, pool and big TV available.

D The Small Hotel, a block off Ekareach St, T012- 716385, thesmallhotel@ yahoo.com. As the name indicates this is a small hotel. Nonetheless it still manages to deliver much more than its name suggests and is very clean and friendly. Good-sized, bright rooms that are spotlessly clean offer fan, fridge, TV, new fixtures and big balconies. Swedish and Khmer restaurant. Recommended.

D Spitfire Guesthouse, off Ekareach St, behind GST Bus depot, T034-933774. Relatively new, clean guesthouse with good-sized rooms, bathroom, a/c, hot water. Discounts for long-term guests. Restaurant with small menu offering western food and snacks. The owners intend to expand the menu to include Mexican dishes.

Further on from the Spitfire Guesthouse are two similarly built and priced guesthouses sharing the same premises – the **Neak Meas** and the **Chhoung Samoth Hotel** (a cheaper version of the Neak Meas). Both have a/c, TV and western toilets.

E-F Bar Ru, east off the Golden Lion Traffic Circle, T012-388860. Well-kept, clean rooms with or without bathroom, geared towards backpackers. Ru, the young entrepreneur, also referred to as Ru Co, was expanding his mini empire to Bamboo Island, where he is building a small bungalow colony, see box page 219.

F Geckozy, 2 blocks back from Ekareach St, T012-495825, www.geckozy-guesthouse.com. Brightly painted guesthouse set in lovely gardens. Mid-sized rooms colourfully decorated in a beach theme with fan and balcony. Attached toilet. Great restaurant with modern Japanese and western cuisine. Travel services and motorbike rental.

Victory Beach Area

B New Beach Hotel, T034- 933822. Quite ostentatious, with an overly decorated lobby. Decent rooms with particularly good ocean views, well furnished, a/c, hot water and TV. Breakfast included. Bar and restaurant opens right onto the shore and the menu features typical western breakfasts, seafood dishes and a whole 'intestinal' section.

C-D Chez Mari-yan, Sankat 3, Khan Mittapheap, T034-916468. Currently the best bungalow- style place to stay in this end of town. It offers a block of hotel rooms and simple wooden and concrete bungalows perched on stilts at the top of a hill affording nice sea views. It is family-run (Swiss and Khmer). Occupants need to be nimble footed to scramble over the maze of pathways to get to their bungalow. Restaurant sports a short menu which features fish, squid and crab.

C-D Holiday Palace Hotel and Casino, near the Victory Monument, T034-933808, holiday_palace02@yahoo.com.140 rooms with a/c, TV, fridge and hot water. The casino can attract an undesirable element.

For an explanation of the sleeping and eating price codes used in this guide, see inside the front cover. Other relevant information is found in Essentials, see pages 34-37

D-E Blue Frog, at the top of Weather Station Hill, T012- 838004, www.bluefrog hotel.com. This big, blue monstrosity of a building has clean rooms with attached bathroom and fan. There's also a restaurant.

D-E Bungalow Village, halfway down Weather Station Hill, T034-933875, oliviercrusoe@yahoo.fr. Managed by a French chap – cheap clean rooms in a mild state of disrepair but the atmospheric restaurant affords lovely sea views and has quite nice food.

D-F Mealy Chenda, on the crest of Weather Station Hill on the triangle road, T034-670818. Very popular hotel offering accommodation to suit a wide range of budgets from dorm rooms through to a/c double rooms. Sparkly clean with fantastic views from the restaurant (the Korean BBQ is highly acclaimed here).

E-F Mash Melting Pot Guesthouse, Weather Station Hill, T012-913714. 4 rooms with fan, mosquito net and western toilet. Book exchange and small library.

E-F Sakal Bungalows, near the end of Weather Station Hill, T012-806155, 012806155@mobitel.com.kh. 10 simple but cheap bungalows in a garden setting. Restaurant, bar and cheap internet also available. Closest bungalows to Victory Beach. Popular and cheap.

F Sunset Garden Inn, near Mealey Chenda, T012- 562004. 3-storey guest- house tucked away on the hill with an unobstructed view of the ocean. Restaurant with not-so-impressive backpacker- orientated meals. Exceptionally clean, simple rooms with TV, western bathroom and fan. Very friendly family-run Khmer hotel. Recommended.

Sokha Beach

AL-A Sokha Beach Resort and Spa, Street 2 Thnou, Sangkat 4, T034-935999, www.sokhahotelsd.com. Sihanoukville's only luxury hotel. A de luxe, 180-room beachfront resort and spa, set amidst an expansive 15 ha of beachfront gardens fronting pristine white sandy beach. Guests have a choice between hotel suites or private bungalows dotted in the tropical gardens. The hotel has fantastic facilities including a large, land-scaped pool, tennis court, archery range, children's club and in-house Philipino band at

nights. Rooms are quite impressive, with beautiful Italian linen and lovely bath tubs. The hotel also has a somewhat incongruous stretched SUV, fitted out with minibar, karaoke and a 15-seat lounge (US$50). You can't imagine this car ever being able to get around the corners of any of Sihanoukville's pokey roads. The hotel has very low occupancy, so it is worthwhile checking if it can offer a discount as it's always running special deals.

B Chez Claude, between Sokha Beach and Independence Beach, on the hilltop, T012-824870. 9 bungalows occupy a beautiful hillside spot just behind Sokha Beach. The accommodation represents a cross-section of Indonesian-, Lao- and Khmer-style bungalows. Good for those with kids as it offers 2-room bungalows with western toilet, hot water and fan. The restaurant has fantastic views and is great (but pricey). Excellent selection of wines. Recommended.

C Malibu Hotel, T012-733 334. Offers both hotel rooms and bungalows set in the hills off the beautiful beach. The bungalows are the best pick (preferably the closest ones to the beach). Recommended.

Ochheuteal Beach Area

B Golden Castle Hotel, off the Golden Lion Traffic Circle on the road to Sokha beach, T034- 933919, goldencastlehotel@ yahoo.com. Large Chinese-run hotel with spacious rooms which include bath tub, telephone, fridge and big bay windows. 24-hr coffee shop and room service. Restaurant.

B-C Seaside Hotel, Mithona St, a block from the traffic circle, T034-933641, seasidehotel 2000n@yahoo.com. The building is designed to look like a wat. Some large, decent rooms with a/c, hot water, bath and fridge. Some rooms overlook the beach. Price varies according to floor. More of a hotel feel with restaurant (large Khmer menu, which is seafood intensive), gift shop and internet.

B-D Golden Sea Hotel, Ekareach St, just before the Golden Lion Traffic Circle, T034-966866, reservation@ golden-sea-hotel.com. Large, clean and nicely furnished rooms with a/c, TV, hot water and fridge. Fitness centre, sauna, Khmer restaurant, mini-mart and coffee shop also on site.

C **Golden Sand**, corner of Tola St, T034-933607, goldensand@everyday.com.kh. Large hotel with nice pool but somewhat soulless rooms, but at this price, it beats its competition, the **Sokha Hotel**. Nice views from some of the upper floors. Includes buffet breakfast. The restaurant serves Khmer, Chinese and Thai food.

C **Sontapheap**, next door to the **Orchidee Hotel** on Tola St. Clean rooms with new furnishings, fan and attached bathroom or, for a few extra dollars, a/c and hot water. Shared common balcony and restaurant with basic menu.

C-D **Orchidée Guesthouse**, Tola St, T034-933639, www.orchideeguesthouse. com This place does not belie its name and the courtyard full of beautiful orchids provides an auspicious welcome. It is well-run, properly maintained and clean offering well-aired rooms, a/c and hot water. Restaurant with Khmer and western seafood. Nice pool area, a 5-min walk to the beach. Great value. Highly recommended.

D **Ochheuteal Beachside Bungalows**, Mithona St, a few mins' walk to the beach, T034-953896. The name is slightly misleading as these bungalows aren't exactly on the beach but close enough to it. Good-sized rooms, brightly decorated (you may need sunglasses), with a/c, TV, hot water and fridge. Khmer and Chinese restaurant in garden setting. Pool tables available.

D-E **GST Guesthouse**, Mithona St, T016-210222. Popular guesthouse, in part because it is where the bus terminates and in part because they pay motos quite good commission for dropping you here. Regardless, the place is clean (fan, attached bathroom), cheap and reasonably close to the beach.

D-E **Markara Guesthouse**, Mithona St, near the golf course, T034-933448, markarashv@camintel.com. Big, clean rooms with relatively new furnishings in nice garden setting. Khmer restaurant with a few western dishes. Motorbike rental.

Serendipity Beach

At the north end of Ochheuteal Beach. These tenants have been given notice that they will be evicted for years so there is every possibility that these places won't be around too much longer. Most guest-houses along this strip organize boat trips, tickets and tours.

A-D **Coasters Guesthouse**, near the end of the cove, T034-933776, coasters@ camintel.com. The bungalows are pretty basic with western toilet and fan. The hotel rooms are good and have hot water and a/c. It boasts a restaurant right on the beach with a patio which affords lovely views.

B-C **Malibu Hotel**, between **Eden** and **Coasters guest-houses**, T012-733334. The nicest place on this beach strip. Rooms are clean and very well-furnished, with individual names rather than numbers. There is a small restaurant that serves western breakfast. Recommended.

C-D **Eden Guesthouse**, T034-933585, serendipityeden@yahoo.com. Popular guest-house and bar located on the beach. Basic rooms with fan or a/c. More expensive rooms have hot water, fridge and balcony overlooking the ocean. A penthouse 'suite' is also available.

D **Cloud 9**, on the hill above Serendipity Beach (at the very end of the beach). Basic wooden bungalows (the nicest 'huts' on the beach). Prices vary according to view, with western toilet and fan.

E **Unkle Bob's**, just off the beach, T012-752840, erling@camintel.com. Very basic western-managed accommodation. Cheap, small bungalows with fan. 24-hr bar.

Koh Kong and around *p206*

Many of the small guesthouses scattered around the town double as brothels.

C-D **Koh Kong International Resort Club**, T035-588173-82. This resort is surprisingly good value with lovely bungalows right near the beach. Some might be put off by the fact that it's a casino, which sometimes happens to attract dodgy people – don't be.

D-E **Bopha Koh Kong**, 2 blocks east of the boat pier, T035-936073. Good, clean rooms with all amenities – a/c, cable, fridge. More expensive rooms have bath tub and hot water. Pretty good value. Restaurant also.

D-E **Koh Pich Hotel**, T035-936113. One of the biggest and better establishments in town. Rooms are large and clean with a/c, TV, fridge and attached bathrooms. The large karaoke bar can be a bit of a nightmare. There are cheaper rooms with fan.

E-F Koh Kong Hotel, is the closest hotel to the ferry port and used to be very popular. The rooms are very basic with faux wooden panelling and squeezed in furniture.

E-F Otto's, a block south of the boat pier, T012-924249, 012924249@mobitel.com. kh. Basic fan rooms in a nice wooden house. Shared bath, fan, mosquito net, cartoon fish sheets, posters of random babies and fish, old wooden structure, feels like a bungalow, bit dirty, good size though. The German owner also runs the best restaurant in town serving western, Khmer and Thai food. Otto is a good source of tourist information. Books for sale/swap. Internet. Recommended.

F Cheap Charlie's, surprise surprise, the cheapest guest- house in town! Restaurant with western, Cambodian and Thai cuisine.

Kampot and around *p208, map p209*

C Little Garden Bar, T033- 256901, www.littlegardenbar. com. Basic, clean rooms, fan and bathroom. Restaurant offering panoramic views of Mt Bokor.

C-D Borey Bokor Hotel 1, T012-820826. In an ostentatious style with all rooms offering a/c, TV, fridge and comfy beds.

D-E Molieden, a block away from the main bridge, T033-932798, chuy_seth@ yahoo.com. A surprisingly good find, its hideous façade gives way to a very pleasant interior. Large, tastefully decorated modern art deco rooms with TV and fan. The rooftop restaurant also serves some of the best western food in town (see Eating). Very good value.

E Kampot Guesthouse, T012-956040. Converted from a private house, this guesthouse has a welcoming atmosphere with quiet, plain but comfortable fan or a/c rooms and attached bathrooms. It is tucked away on a small road 200 m from the taxi station.

E-F Blissful Guesthouse, next to Acleda Bank. Converted colonial building with lovely surrounding gardens. Rooms are simple with mosquito net, fan and attached bathroom. High on atmosphere and very popular with locals and expats alike, Affable Khmer manager, Elvis, and owner, Angela, make this a very pleasant place to stay. Recommended.

E-F Mealy Chenda Guesthouse, T012-831559. It may lack atmosphere but the management is friendly and the plain concrete building has dark and simple clean en suite rooms with fans. There is a restaurant with cable TV on the ground floor and a terraced roof where you can lie and relax in the sun.

E-F Ta Eng Guesthouse, T015-330058. 7 rooms furnished in 1970s style, with mosquito nets, ceiling fan, freaky green doors, and communal toilet and shower. Some English and French spoken, very friendly, a short walk from the bus station. There are also plans to make a rooftop terrace.

Bokor Mountain National Park *p209*

The park rangers run a simple guesthouse at the hill station – youth hostel style. There are bunk beds (US$5) and doubles (US$20), with clean, shared toilets and showers. There is no restaurant so you bring your own food: there is a large kitchen available for guests. Pack warm clothes and waterproofs.

Kep *p210*

The accommodation standards in Kep are higher than the rest of the country and are still considerably cheap.

B Champey Inn, on the Ocean road before you reach Kep beach, T012-501742, champeyinn@mobitel.com.kh. A notch above the others – elegant bungalows with 4-poster beds, open-air showers and large terraces all set in wonderful, manicured gardens, pool. Popular with the elite expat crowd. Internet for guests. Travel services. Good French restaurant. Recommended.

D Le Bout Du Monde, to get to the hotel turn left onto the small road going up hill just before the APSECA orphanage, in the first part of town, T012- 989106, viraneang@hotmail.com. Basic accommodation under a thatched roof, rattan-style walls, simple wooden beds, mosquito nets provided and attached shower and toilet (no fans). There are hammocks out on the front to relax and read while enjoying panoramic views. Comfortable restaurant area with a selection of western and seafood specialities. No electricity after 2300.

D Verandah Resort and Bungalows, next door to N4, further up Kep Mountain, T012-888619. Superb accommodation.

Large wooden bungalows set in a large, enchanting garden of ripe fruits, vines and tropical flowers which weave around the stairways criss-crossing the hillside. Each bungalow includes a good-sized balcony, fan, mosquito net and nicely decorated mosaic bathroom. The more expensive of these include very romantic open-air beds. A few extra upmarket bungalows are about to be built (a/c and hot water). The restaurant offers the perfect vista of the ocean and surrounding countryside. Epicureans will love the variety of international cuisines including poutine of Quebec, smoked ham linguini, fish fillet with olive sauce (all under US$3). Highly recommended.

E N4, at the foot of Kep Mountain, T011-908354. Still finishing their final touches at the time of publication, but this newcomer should turn out some reasonable accommodation. Small concrete bungalows set in a pruned-within-an-inch-of-its-life gardens. Clean double rooms with comfy beds, kitsch decorative style. The more expensive rooms have a/c.

E Seaside Guesthouse, the first right-hand turn as you enter Kep, before the APSECA turn-off, T012-684241. Owned by the Governor of Kep this waterfront concrete hotel lacks the ambience of some of those placed on the hill but is still clean, with fan, attached bathroom.

E The Vana Guesthouse, T011-926330. On the hill before **Le Bout Du Monde** this guesthouse comprises 4 attractive thatch-roofed bungalows with attached bathrooms and western toilet. They are clean but simple with double beds, mosquito nets and little more. The open, thatched restaurant and eating terrace has a friendly sedate atmosphere and the food is also good. Staff are friendly and more than willing to organize boat trips to the offshore islands.

Takeo and around *p211*

C-D Boeung Takeo Guesthouse, near the park, T032-931306. Reasonably good rooms with fan and western toilet and a nice view of the lake.

E Phnom Sorhng Guest- house, near the boat dock. Wide variety of rooms. Ask for one with en suite bathroom and TV.

❼ Eating

Sihanoukville *p202, maps p203 and p204*
Town centre
❢❢ Bamboo Light, Ekareach St, T012-602661. Sri Lankan restaurant offering a range of Sri Lankan/Indian dishes. Nice atmosphere. Good service. Recommended.

❢❢ Geckozy, in a small street down from the petrol stations. A lovely German- Japanese restaurant set in a large garden. A nifty selection of both German and Japanese fare at very reasonable prices. Recommended.

❢❢ Holy Cow, Ekareach St, on the way out of town. Ambient restaurant offering a selection of healthy, western meals – pasta, salads, baked potatoes. The English owner is a long-term resident and very good source of local information. To his credit he has created a lovely atmosphere and provides impeccable working conditions for his staff. Accommodation also available. Highly recommended.

❢❢ Starfish Café, behind Samudera Supermarket, T034- 952011. Small café-cum-bakery in a very peaceful garden setting. Here you can eat great food while knowing that you are supporting a good cause. The organization was originally established to help rehabilitate people with disabilities and has extended their services to cover a whole range of poverty-reducing schemes. A very positive place that oozes goodness in its food, environment and service – good western breakfasts, cakes, sandwiches, salads and coffees. A non-profit massage business has also opened on premises. Recommended.

❢❢-❢ Espresso Kampuchea. Best coffee in town and the owner is good for a chat. Limited breakfast menu.

Victory Beach Area
❢❢❢ Chez Mari-yan has a good seafood restaurant with probably the nicest setting in Sihanoukville, US$4-5 per dish.

❢❢❢-❢❢ Mash Melting Pot, a little backpacker café with predominantly Indian food run by an eccentric Dutch woman. Book shop and guesthouse rooms.

❢❢❢-❢❢ Paillote, at the top of Weather Station Hill. This is the finest dining establishment in town and one of the best in the country. They have everything right: the service can't be surpassed and it is high on atmosphere – cocooned from the noisy street and lit by soft glowing candles. The chef from Madagascar greets the customers (often to explain that he uses ganja as a flavour and not as a happy herb style ingredient) and the food is superb. The modern Asian-European fusion menu changes regularly. Highly recommended.

Chhner Molop Chrey Restauraunt, across the road from the casino, T034-933708. Big Khmer restaurant with a wide-open platform overlooking the beach. One of the most beautiful locations in town (perfect for a sunset drink). Specializing in some very delicious Cambodian, Thai and Vietnamese seafood dishes ($US2-5). Its menu also emphasizes a 'meat for drinking' section and a wide range of raw fish cuisines (non-Japanese).

The Corner Bar, T012-479395. Its pizzas have a reputation as the best in town. It also offers salads and baguettes for around the same price. Home delivery available. There is another restaurant upstairs called **La Barang**, T012-561845. A French restaurant with a big emphasis on seafood and daily specials.

Indian Curry Pot, on top of the hill. Very large Indian menu - lassis, dhal, tandoori etc, western breakfasts. Good fresh juices. A few basic rooms are for rent upstairs (US$3).

The Snake House, Soviet St (between North and South Victory beach) attached to the hotel of the same name, T012-673805. The biologist owner of this Russian restaurant has created a unique and captivating place to dine especially if snakes are your thing. A huge King Cobra and a multitude of enclosed vipers and pythons can provide hours of endless fascination. The fantastic staff can provide a miscellany of anecdotes about the reptiles. A particularly good place to bring children (but monitoring would be required). There is a wide range of traditional Russian dishes offered, some a tad too stodgy for the weather but otherwise very good. Recommended.

Treasure Island Seafood. Widely considered one of the best seafood restaurants in the town.

Yin-Yang, close to the Snake House between North and South Victory Beach. Predominantly German fare served in a nice beer garden atmosphere.

Ochheuteal Beach

Les Feuilles, near the Holiday Hotel, T034- 933910. An oldie but a goodie. Excellent but slightly overpriced little restaurant serving small dishes of (admittedly heavenly) prawns in garlic, other fish and meat dishes. Pool table and bar.

Mick and Craig's. Thankfully, the menu here is a lot more creative than the venue's name. Sufficiently large meals with a bit of pizzazz – pizzas, burgers, hummus etc. The restaurant also offers 'themed food nights' Sunday roast, BBQ and 'all you can eat' nights.

Endless Summer Beach Club, a block down from the roundabout. Open-air style restaurant offering some good Mexican-style food Bamboo bar. Pool tables, table soccer.

Sokha Beach

Claudes, on the hill above Sokha Beach. Claude has been running a very popular restaurant for years. French, seafood dishes. Provencal-style. Good wine list. Nice view from the restaurant.

Koh Kong *p206*

Otto's Restaurant. Big menu with western breakfasts, baguette sandwiches, schnitzels, seafood, soups, Khmer standards and lots of vegetarian options. Recommended.

There are a row of good **Thai restaurants** on stilts near the mangroves. Great food. Other than the market, which is open during the day, there are a few simple restaurants along the riverfront where you can buy well priced seafood.

Kampot and around *p208, map p209*

Molienden Restaurant, on the roof of the guesthouse of the same name. Extensive selection of pastas, spaghetti, soup and Italian seafood dishes. Fantastic food. Recommended.

Bamboo Light, River Rd, near the Old Market, T012-602661. Great little Sri Lankan restaurant with a large selection of tasty Sri Lankan dishes – korma, masala, biryani . Large choice for vegetarians. Outdoor and indoor seating. Elegantly decorated restaurant and intimate bar area. Recommended.

Phnom Kamchay, beside the bridge on the river offering an English menu, Khmer, Chinese and western dishes. Considered the best Khmer restaurant in town (free from the monotony of stand-over- beer girl tactics). Good seafood, friendly staff.

†† Rusty Key Hole Bar and Restaurant, River Rd, past **Bamboo Light**. Newest restaurant in town and a very welcome addition. Western food served. The BBQ seafood and ribs come highly recommended.

††-† Little Garden Bar, T012-994161. This is an attractive and relaxed bar and restaurant on the riverfront offering delicious Khmer and western food for reasonable prices. The rooftop bar is the place to be for the spectacular sunset descending over the Elephant Mountains.

††-† Mealey Chenda. The guesthouse has a large restaurant with a good selection of Khmer and Chinese meals. There are also a few western dishes including spaghetti bolognese and spaghetti carbonara.

Kep *p210*
See also Sleeping entries.
There are scores of seafood stalls on the beach, just before the tourist centre, that specialize in cooking freshly caught crab. At the tourist office itself there is also a row of restaurants serving crab, shrimp and fish.

Takeo and around *p211*
† Grand Café Chisor. Bakery, Khmer and western food. Very good.

☉ Bars and clubs

Sihanoukville *p202, maps p203 and p204*
Bar de la Marine, Sopheakmongkol St, T034-826104. A nice new bar run by a Frenchman. Also has some rooms.
Angkor Arms, so-called 'traditional English pub' and certainly not a bad replica. Conveniently close to the Phnom Penh bus stop.
Papagayo, Weather Station Hill. Offers pool tables, cheap cocktails, email on premises, comfy cane lounges. The US$2 tapas is exceptionally good value.
Dusk Till Dawn, near the Angkor Arms. As the name suggests this bar is open very late – hence the appeal.

✺ Entertainment

Sihanoukville *p202, maps p203 and p204*
Ru Bar has a big cinema with over 500 movies to choose from.
Sokha Beach Resort. Has a live Phillippino band perform every night from 1800.

☉ Shopping

Sihanoukville *p202, maps p203 and p204*
Casablanca, near the Golden Lions Roundabout, has a very good selection of second-hand books to cater for almost all literary tastes. There is also a small boutique at the back of the store which stocks some fashionable clothes and jewellery items. Very quick (but more expensive) email here. Petrol stations, especially **Caltex** and **Shell**, have excellent convenience stores attached wherein most little luxuries and necessaries can be bought.
Samudera Supermarket, 7 Makara St. Stocks everything and anything a person could possibly want – western foodstuffs through to toiletries.

▲▲ Activities and tours

Sihanoukville *p202, maps p203 and p204*
Diving and snorkelling
Chez Claude, was the first diving operator in Sihanoukville. These days he caters mostly to experienced divers but also offers training. US$60-125 a day. Open water US$350. Snorkelling trips are approximately half the price.
Diving and more, Victory Beach, T034-960625, www.divingandmore.com, is a relative newcomer. It markets its dives towards already certified divers. US$70 for a couple of dives.
Scuba Nation Diving Centre, Weather Station Hill, T012- 604680, scubanation@yahoo. com, www.divecambodia.com, has the best reputation in town and is the longest established PADI dive centre. It runs the complete range of PADI courses and offers PADI insurance. Prices vary depending on what you want. Open Water Course (US$350) through to dive trips ($US70). It has a custom-built dive boat. Recommended.

The Fishermen's Den, 1 block back from Ekareach St, next to the **Small Hotel**. Runs daily fishing trips for US$25 per person (can take up to 14 people out). Full day trip from 0800-1800: deep sea fishing, snorkelling, swimming and lunch. If you have caught something worth eating, the proprietor, Brian, will organize the restaurant to prepare a lovely meal from the catch (if not, there is plenty of backup seafood on hand). The boat is fully equipped with showers, toilets, life jackets etc. Can also organize charter trips (US$90-150).

Kampot and around *p208, map p209*
Tour operators
Sok Lim Tours, on the riverfront, and **Mealey Chenda Guesthouse** can organize tours to surrounding sites. A small proportion of the guides are exceptionally well-briefed but most are Fabio playboy types. Make sure you get a good guide as it really makes a difference. A scam amongst the guides is the 'bait and switch' where you arrange the tour with one of their knowledgeable guides only to have them drive round the corner and switch to an average guide/driver at the last minute.

⊖ Transport

Sihanoukville *p202, maps p203 and p204*
Sihanoukville is 230 km south of Phnom Penh on Highway 4. Getting there independently from Phnom Penh you will need to follow the airport road from town and take a right-hand turn at the main intersection between Route 3 and Route 4.

Boat
Fishermen will take visitors out to the islands (fee negotiable). The cheapest way to get out to the islands is to try and bargain with the captain from a prearranged tour from Ochheuteal Beach at around 0800. Most boats don't usually mind taking an extra passenger for US$5-10. For details on getting to **Thailand** see page 163 and below under Bus. The a/c boat from Sihanoukville to **Koh Kong** departs at 1200, US$14, 3½ hrs.

Bus
Around Khmer New Year and during the peak season you will need to book tickets the day before travel. Buses depart to **Phnom Penh** from the station on the corner of Ekareach and Sopheakmongkol sts; **Phnom Penh Public Bus Co** at 0710, 0800, 1215, 1310, 1400 and **GST** at 0715, 0815, 1230, 1315. Route 4 is quick and comfortable and the trip takes about 4 hrs, US$3.

Buses to **Koh Kong** depart from the Central Bus Station at 0700, 5-8 hrs, US$15. The Thai border is open until 2000 and buses depart until 2330 from Trat to Bangkok.

Motorbike
Motorbike rental is incredibly cheap within town, with many hiring out their bikes for US$3-4. Just be aware that the medical facilities in Sihanoukville are dire and there have been several fatalities (especially when people have been drinking and riding). **GST Bus Company** rents bikes from its office. Most guesthouses have motorbikes for hire (around US$7 per day).

Motos
Motos cost 2000 riel around town or 3000 riel from the centre to a beach. They are relentless and shout from every direction.

Shared taxi
Also from the Central Market (US$2.65-3.15/ 10,000-12,000 riel) but bear in mind there could be up to 9 people in the car. Phnom Penh hotels will also organize private taxis for around US$25. There are no longer any security risks on this route. From Sihanoukville the same arrangement works in reverse back to **Phnom Penh**. From Sihanoukville to **Kampot** shared taxi should cost no more than around 10,000 riel per person, 4 hrs. The road is good for the first 43 km on the American built Route 4. At the turn-off at Veal Renh the road becomes a muddy potholed track. It is, however, a most spectacular drive. The road hugs the narrow band of flat ground, squeezed between the coastline and the Elephant Mountains occasionally passing through riverside towns with brightly coloured boats.

Koh Kong and around *p206*
Air
The airport is west of the Independence Monument on Street 18. At the time of publication there were no flights but they may reschedule them in the near future.

Bicycle
Rental from **Otto's** and **Cheap Charlie's** for ฿50 per day.

Boat
To **Sihanoukville** leaving Koh Kong pier at 0800 returning from Sihanoukville at 1200, 4-5 hrs, US$15. Tickets available at most guesthouses.

International connections to Thailand
The border crossing is 12 km from Koh Kong, across the river (15-20 mins). The trip to the border at Cham Yem inside Cambodia costs ฿60 by moto, ฿50 by shared taxi and US$6 with own taxi. The border is open 0700-2000. There are public minibuses on the Thai side to Trat (84 km, 1¼ hrs, until 1800, ฿150. You can find private taxis after 1800 but bidding will start at ฿1000. From Trat buses run to Pattaya, Bangkok and Bangkok airport.

Ferry from Koh Kong to Thailand
Departs near the port at 1200 daily, 4hrs. A 30-day Thai visa is available at Hat Lek in Thailand. Border open 0700-1700. Some of the boats actually offer the opportunity for tourists to stopover at Koh Sdech Island en route to Koh Kong. Thereis a guesthouse.

Bus
Buses from Koh Kong Riverside Guesthouse depart for **Sihanoukville** at 0900 ฿600, 5-6 hrs. From Raksmei Bun Thaim Guesthouse at 0830, 5-6 hrs, ฿500.

Small minibuses/vans go to **Phnom Penh** leaving Koh Kong Riverside Guesthouse, 0900, ฿600, 5-6 hrs.

Motodops
About ฿10 to anywhere in town or ฿40 per hr or ฿250 per day.

Motorbike
Rental from **Otto's** and **Motobar** for ฿150-200 per day.

Shared taxi
To **Sihanoukville**, 5-6 hrs, leaves from market, US$10 person (6 per car), US$60 own car, from 0600 onwards, leaves when full.

Taxi
US$1-2 around town, about US$20 per day, 110 cc.

Kampot and around *p208, map p209*
Motos
Motos usually charge 1000 riel for short trips across town. There are usually a few gathered around the Sokimex petrol station on the way into town.

Shared taxi
From Phnom Penh, 3 hrs to Kampot. Leaving from Doeum Kor Market on Mao Tse Tung Blvd and not the central market in Phnom Penh, US$3-4, 3 hrs.
To **Phnom Penh**, vehicles leave from the truck station next to the **Total** gas station at 0700-1400, US$3.50, private taxi US$20. To **Sihanoukville**, US$4, private US$18, 2-3 hrs. To **Kep**, US$8 , return US$14-15.
There are a few early morning pickups from the market to **Kep**, US$3 or else you can hire a moto, US$2-3, US$5-6 return or car, US$14 return.

Kep *p210*
Kep is only 25 km from Kampot. The road is good and the journey can be made in 30-45 mins. A large white horse statue marks the turn-off to Kep.

Despite its tantalizing proximity it is not possible to cross into Vietnam from Kep either by land or by sea. Word on the ground in Kep is that in 2006 the border crossing at Ha Tien in Vietnam will open but this should be checked with a local operator prior to planning a trip.

Takeo and around *p211*
Bus
Buses leave Takeo market for **Phnom Penh** every hour between 0700-1600, 6000 riel, 2½ hrs.

❶ Directory

Sihanoukville *p202, maps p203 and p204*
Banks There are 4 banks in town (often shut): Acleda, **Canadia**, **Mekong Bank** and UCB. All 4 are on Ekareach St in downtown. Acleda does Western Union money transfer and **UCB** and **Canadia** do Visa/MasterCard cash advances. Cash advances are also available at **S**amudera Supermarket, in town, 5% commission. **Lucky Web**, on Weather Station Hill, charges 4% commission. The gold traders at the market are often more convenient and can offer a better exchange rate on cash than some of the banks. **Embassies and consulates** Vietnamese Consulate, 'Main Street' in town for visa business. **Internet** All tourist areas in Sihanoukville have internet within 1-2 mins' walking distance. Prices vary from 3000-8000 riel per hr. **Post office** There are 2 post offices: 1 opposite the central market and another behind the casino at Victory Beach. **Telephone** Larger hotels have IDD facilities and most major internet cafés let you make internet calls (Casablanca, **Ana**, **Lucky Web** etc.

Koh Kong and around *p206*
Banks There are no banks in town, change money at the market. **Internet** Internet Coffee, St 2, across from market, internet ฿120 per hr, overseas calls ฿10 per min.

Good coffee and some tourism info available. **Koh Kong Computer**, on road southwest from traffic circle between Ramsay Bun Thaim Guesthouse and Pailin Guesthouse, internet ฿120 per hr, overseas calls ฿10 per min, CD burning, printing, scanning. **Otto's Restaurant** has internet. **Sohka Internet**, on St 2 near riverside (intersection with St 1), internet ฿180 per hr, overseas calls. **Telephone** Calls within Cambodia can be made from the phone boxes scattered around town. **Camintel Office**, near the post office, which charges US$2 a min for international calls.

Kampot and around *p208, map p209*
Banks Acleda Bank, T033-932880, offers a Western Union Service. **Canadia Bank** is close to the Blissful Guesthouse. Cash advances on Visa and MasterCard (with no commission fee). Money changers are concentrated at the traffic circle by the market. **Internet** Recently, numerous internet cafés have cropped up around town. There is a cluster of them on the road between the river and the central roundabout, US$1 per hr. International calls can be made and vary between 600-900 riel per min. **Post office** On the river road in town. There are many print and phone shops around town where you can fax and make international phone calls.

Background

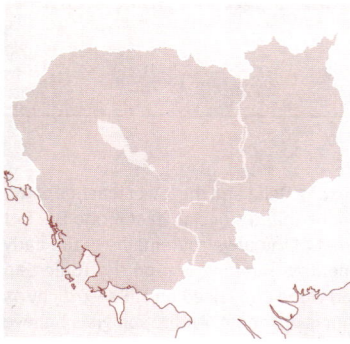

Footprint features

History

Pre-history

Archaeological evidence suggests that the Mekong Delta and the lower reaches of the river – in modern-day Cambodia – have been inhabited since at least 4,000 BC. But the wet and humid climate has destroyed most of the physical remains of the early civilizations. Excavated remains of a settlement at Samrong Sen on the Tonlé Sap show that houses were built from bamboo and wood and raised on stilts – exactly as they are today. Where these people came from is uncertain. Anthropologists believe there were two waves of migration; one from the Malay peninsula and Indonesia and a second from Tibet and China.

Rise of the Lunar and Solar Dynasties

For thousands of years Indochina was isolated from the rest of the world and was virtually unaffected by the rise and fall of the early Chinese dynasties. India and China 'discovered' Southeast Asia early in the first millennium and trade networks were quickly established. The Indian influence was particularly strong in the Mekong basin area. The Khmers adopted and adapted Indian script as well as their ideas about astrology, religion (Buddhism and Hinduism) and royalty (the cult of the semi-divine ruler). Today, several other aspects of Cambodian culture are recognizably Indian in origin – including classical literature and dance. Religious architecture also followed Indian models. These Indian cultural influences which took root in Indochina gave rise to a legend to which Cambodia traces its historical origins. An Indian Brahmin called Kaundinya, travelling in the Mekong Delta area, married Soma, daughter of the Naga (the serpent deity), or Lord of the Soil. Their union, which founded the 'Lunar Dynasty' of Funan (a pre-Angkorian Kingdom), symbolized the fertility of the kingdom and occupies a central place in Khmer cosmology. The Naga, Soma's father, helpfully drank the floodwaters of the Mekong, enabling people to cultivate the land.

Funan

The kingdom of Funan – the forerunner of Kambuja – was established on the Mekong by tribal people from South China in the middle of the third century AD and became the earliest Hindu state in Southeast Asia. Funan was known for its elaborate irrigation canals which controlled the Mekong floodwaters, irrigated the paddy fields and prevented the incursion of seawater. By the fifth century Funan had extended its influence over most of present day Cambodia, as well as Indochina and parts of the Malay Peninsula. Leadership was measured by success in battle and the ability to provide protection and in recognition of this fact, rulers from the Funan period onward incorporated the suffix 'varman' (meaning protection) into their names. Records of a third century Chinese embassy give an idea of what it was like: "There are walled villages, places and dwellings. The men ... go about naked and barefoot. ... Taxes are paid in gold, silver and perfume. There are books and libraries and they can use the alphabet." Twentieth-century excavations suggest a seafaring people engaged in extensive trade with both India and China, and elsewhere.

Chenla

The 'Solar Dynasty' of Chenla was a tributary kingdom of Funan, probably first based on the Mekong at the junction with the Mun tributary, but it rapidly grew in power. It was the immediate predecessor of Kambuja and the great Khmer Empire. According to Khmer legend, the kingdom was the result of the marriage of Kambu, an ascetic, to a celestial nymph named Mera. The people of Chenla – the Kambuja, or the sons of Kambu – lent their name to the country. Chenla was centred in the area of present day southern Laos. In AD 540 a Funan prince married a Chenla princess, uniting the Solar and Lunar dynasties. But the prince sided with his wife, turning against his own people and Funan was swallowed by Chenla. The first capital of this fusion of Chenla and Funan was at **Sambor**. King Ishanavarman (616-635) established a new capital at Sambor Prei Kuk, 30 km from modern Kompong Thom, in the centre of the country (the monuments of which are some of the best preserved of this period). His successor, Jayavarman I, moved the capital to the region of Angkor Borei near Takeo.

Quarrels in the ruling family led to the break-up of the state in the seventh century: it was divided into 'Land Chenla', a farming culture located north of the Tonlé Sap (maybe centred around Champassak in Laos), and 'Water Chenla', a trading culture based along the Mekong. Towards the end of the eighth century Water Chenla became a vassal of Java's powerful Sailendra Dynasty and members of Chenla's ruling family were taken back to the Sailendra court. This period, from the fall of Funan until the eighth century, is known as the pre-Angkorian period – it is a hazy period of Cambodian history. The Khmers remained firmly under Javanese suzerainty until Jayavarman II (802-850), who was born in central Java, returned to the land of his ancestors around AD 800 to change the course of Cambodian history.

Angkor and the god-kings

Jayavarman II, the Khmer prince who had spent most of his life at the Sailendra court, claimed independence from Java and founded the Angkor Kingdom to the north of the Tonlé Sap in 802, at about the same time as Charlemagne became Holy Roman Emperor in Europe. They were men cast in the same mould, for both were empire builders. His far-reaching conquests at Wat Phou (Laos) and Sambhupura (Sambor) won him immediate political popularity on his return and became king in 790. In 802 he declared himself a World Emperor and to consolidate and legitimize his position he arranged his coronation by a Brahmin priest, declaring himself the first Khmer devaraja, or god-king, a tradition that lasts today From then on, the reigning monarch was identified with Siva, the king of the Hindu gods. In the centuries that followed, successive devaraja strove to outdo their predecessors by building bigger and finer temples to house the royal linga, a phallic symbol which is the symbol of Siva and the devaraja. The god-kings commanded the absolute allegiance of their subjects, allowing them control of a vast pool of labour which was used to build an advanced and prosperous agricultural civilization. For many years historians and archaeologists maintained that the key to this agricultural wealth lay in a sophisticated hydraulic – that is irrigated – system of agriculture which allowed the Khmers to produce up to three harvests a year. However, this view of Angkorian agriculture has come under increasing scrutiny in recent years and now there are many who believe that flood-retreat – rather than irrigated – agriculture was the key. Jayavarman II installed himself in successive capitals north of the Tonlé Sap, secure from attack by the Sailendras, and he ruled until 850, when he died on the banks of the Great Lake at the original capital in the Roluos area. His first capital was Hariharalaya, in the Roluos region (Angkor). For reasons unknown he relocated the capital to Mount Mahendraparvata (now known as Phnom Kulen, (40 km northeast of Angkor). After several years he moved the capital back to Hariharalaya.

Jayavarman III (850-877) continued his father's traditions and ruled for the next 27 years. He expanded on his father's empire at Hariharalaya and was the original

⁝ A Chinese emissary's account of his stay at Angkor (1296-1297)

One of the most interesting documents of the great empire of Angkor is the Chinese emissary Chou Ta-kuan's short account of his stay there entitled *Notes on the customs of Cambodia*. The book was written in the late 13th or early 14th century, shortly after he had returned to China after a sojourn at Angkor between 1296 and 1297. His book describes the last days of the kingdom and his role was as male companion to the Chinese ambassador.

The book is divided into 40 short 'chapters' dealing with aspects of everyday and royal life ranging from childbirth, to justice, to clothing. The account also details aspects of the natural environment (fish and reptiles, birds), the economy of the empire (agriculture, trade, products), and technology (utensils, boats and oars). What makes the account so useful and unusual is that it describes not just the concerns and actions of great men and women, but of everyday life too. The extracts below are just a sample of the insights into everyday Cambodian life during the waning days of the Angkorian Empire. For those intending to visit the site of Angkor, the book is highly recommended. It brings to life the ruins of a city, helping the visitor to imagine a place – now so empty – full of people and life.

Cambodian dwellings Out of the [royal] palace rises a golden tower, to the top of which the ruler ascends nightly to sleep. It is common belief that in the tower dwells a genie, formed like a serpent with nine heads, which is Lord of the entire kingdom. Every night this genie appears in the shape of a woman, with whom the sovereign couples. Not even the wives of the king may enter here. At the second watch the king comes forth and is then free to sleep with his wives and his concubines. Should the genie fail to appear for a single night, it is a sign that the king's death is at hand. Straw thatch covers the dwellings of the commoners, not one of whom would dare place the smallest bit of tile on his roof.

Clothing Every man or woman, from the sovereign down, knots the hair and leaves the shoulders bare. Round the waist they wear a small strip of cloth, over which a large piece is drawn when they leave their houses. Many rules, based on rank, govern the choice of materials. Only the ruler may wear fabrics woven in an all over pattern.

The natives Generally speaking, the women, like the men, wear only a strip of cloth, bound round the waist, showing bare breasts of milky whiteness. As for the concubines and palace girls, I have heard it said that there are from three to five thousand of these, separated into various categories. When a beautiful girl is born into a family, no time is lost in sending her to the palace.

Childbirth Once a Cambodian woman's child is born, she immediately makes a poultice of hot rice and salt and applies it to her private parts. This is taken off in 24 hours, thus preventing any untoward after-effects and causing an astringency which seems to renew the young mother's virginity. When told of this for the first time, my credulity was sorely taxed. However, in the house where I lodged a girl gave birth to a child, and I was able to observe beyond peradventure that the next day she was up carrying the baby in

founder of the laterite temple at Bakong. **Indravarman (877-889),** his successor, was the first of the great temple-builders of Angkor and somewhat overshadowed the work of Jayavarman III. His means to succession are somewhat ambiguous but it is her arms and going with him to bathe in the river. This seems truly amazing!

Everyone with whom I talked said that the Cambodian women are highly sexed. One or two days after giving birth they are ready for intercourse: if a husband is not responsive he will be discarded. When a man is called away on matters of business, they endure his absence for a while; but if he is gone as much as 10 days, the wife is apt to say, "I am no ghost; how can I be expected to sleep alone?"

Slaves Wild men from the hills can be bought to serve as slaves. Families of wealth may own more than 100; those of lesser means content themselves with 10 or 20; only the very poor have none. If a slave should run away and be captured, a blue mark would be tattooed on his face; moreover, an iron collar would be fitted to his neck, or shackles to his arms or legs.

Cambodian justice Points of dispute between citizens, however trifling, are taken to the ruler. In dealing with cases of great seriousness, recourse is not had to strangulation or beheading; outside the West Gate, however, a ditch is dug into which the criminal is placed, earth and stones are thrown back and heaped high, and all is over. Lesser crimes are dealt with by cutting off feet or hands, or by amputation of the nose.

When a thief is caught red-handed, he may be imprisoned and tortured. Recourse is also had to another curious procedure. If an object is missing, and accusation brought against someone who denies the charge, oil is brought to boil in a kettle and the suspected person forced to plunge his hand into it. If he is truly guilty, the hand is cooked to shreds; if not, skin and bones are unharmed. Such is the amazing

way of these barbarians.

Products of Cambodia Many rare woods are to be found in the highlands. Unwooded regions are those where elephants and rhinoceros gather and breed. Exotic birds and strange animals abound. The most sought-after products are the feathers of the kingfisher, elephant tusks, rhinoceros horns, and beeswax.

Trade In Cambodia it is the women who take charge of trade. For this reason a Chinese arriving in the country, loses no time in getting himself a mate, for he will find her commercial instincts a great asset.

Utensils For sleeping only bamboo mats are used, laid on the wooden floors. Of late, certain families have adopted the use of low beds, which for the most part are made by the Chinese.

A prodigy Within the Walled City, near the East Gate, a Cambodian man committed fornication with his younger sister. Their skin and their flesh were fused beyond the power of separating them. After three days passed without food, both parties died. My compatriot Mr Hsieh, who spent 35 years in this country declares he has known this to happen twice. If such be the case, it shows how well the Cambodians are policed by the supernatural power of their holy Buddha.

Notes on the customs of Cambodia was originally translated from the Chinese original into French by Paul Pelliot. J Gilman d'Arcy Paul translated the French version into English, and the Siam Society in Bangkok have republished this version with colour photographs and reproductions of Delaporte's fine lithographs of the monuments. The *customs of Cambodia*, Siam Society: Bangkok, 1993.

generally agreed that he overthrew his Jayavarman III violently. Unlike his predecessor, Indravarman was not the son of a king but more than likely the nephew of Jayavarman's II Queen. He expanded and renovated the capital, building Preah Ko

Temple and developing Bakong. Indravarman is considered one of the key players in Khmer history, referred to as the "lion among kings" and "prince endowed with all the merits", his architectural work establishing many precedents that were followed by those that followed him. After Indravarman's death his sons fought for the King's title. The victor, at the end of the ninth century was **Yasovarman I (889-900)**. The battle is believed to have destroyed the palace, thus spurring a move to Angkor. He called his new capital Yasodharapura and copied the water system his father had devised at Roluos on an even larger scale, using the waters of the Tonlé Sap. After Yasovarman's death in 900 his son **Harshavarman (900-923)** took the throne, until he died 23 years later. Harshavarman was well regarded, one particular inscription saying that he "caused the joy of the universe". Upon his death, his brother **Ishanarvarman II**, assumed the regal status. In 928, **Jayavarman IV** set up a rival capital about 65 km from Angkor at Koh Ker (see page 170) and ruled for the next twenty years. After Jayavarman IV's death there was a period of upheaval as **Harsharvarman II** tried unsuccessfully to lead the empire. **Rajendravarman (944-968)** Jayarvarman's nephew, managed to take control of the empire and moved the court back to Angkor, where the Khmer kings remained. He chose to build outside of the former capital Bakheng, opting, instead, for the region south of the East Baray. Many saw him as the saviour of Angkor with one inscription reading: "He restored the holy city of Yashodharapura, long deserted, and rendered it superb and charming." Rajendravarman orchestrated a campaign of solidarity – bringing together a number of provinces and claiming back territory, previously under Yasovarman I. From the restored capital he led a successful crusade against the Champa (Vietnam). A devout Buddhist, he erected some of the first Buddhist temples in the precinct. Upon Rajendravarman's death, his son **Jayavarman V (968-1001)**, still only a child, took the royal reigns. Once again the administrative centre was moved, this time to the west, where Ta Keo was built. The capital was renamed Jayendranagari. Like his father, Jayavarman V was Buddhist but was extremely tolerant of other religions. At the start of his tenure he encountered a few clashes due to local dissidents but things settled down and he enjoyed relative peace during his rule. The next king, **Udayadityavarman I**, lasted a few months before being ousted. For the next few years Suryavarman I and Jayaviravarman battled for the King's title.

The formidable warrior **King Suryavarman I (1002-1049)** won. He may originally have come from the Malay peninsula and conquered the kingdom in the early 11th century. He was a determined leader and made all of his officials swear a blood oath to his allegiance. He undertook a series of military campaigns geared towards claiming Mon territory in central and southern Thailand and victoriously extended the Khmer empire into Lower Menam, as well as in Laos and established a Khmer capital in Louvo (modern day Lopburi in Thailand). Suryavarman holds the record for the greatest territorial expansion ever achieved in the Khmer Empire.The Royal Palace (Angkor Thom), the West Baray and the Phimeanakas pyramid temples were Suryavarman's main contributions to Angkor's architectural heritage (see page 113). He continued the royal Hindu cult but also tolerated Mahayana Buddhism. On Suryavarman's death, the Khmer Kingdom began to fragment due to internal revolt. His three successors had short, troubled reigns and the Cham (Champa was a rural kingdom based in present day Vietnam) captured, sacked and razed the capital. When the king's son, **Udayadityavarman II (1050-1066)**, assumed the throne, havoc ensued as citizens revolted against him and some of his royal appointments.

When Udayadityavarman II died, his younger brother, Harsharvarman III (1066-1080), last in the line of the dynasty, stepped in to be king. During his reign, there were reports of discord and even a defeat at the hands of the Cham.

In 1080 a new kingdom was founded by a northern provincial governor claiming aristocratic descent. He called himself **Jayavarman VI (1080-1107)** and is believed to have led a revolt against the former king. He never settled at Angkor, living instead in the northern part of the kingdom. He left monuments at Wat Phou in southern Laos and Phimai, in Thailand. There was an intermittent period where Jayavarman's IV brother, **Dharanindravarman (1107-1112)** took the throne but was overthrown by his grand-nephew **Suryavarman II (1113-1150)**, who soon became the greatest leader the Angkor Empire had ever seen. He worked prolifically across a broad range of areas and achieved some of most impressive architectural feats and political manoeuvres seen within the Angkorian period. He resumed diplomatic relations with China, the Middle Kingdom, and was held in the greatest regard by the then Chinese Emperor. He expanded the Khmer Empire as far as: Lopburi, Siam, Pagan in Myanmar, parts of Laos and into the Malay Peninsula. He attacked the Cham state relentlessly, particularly Dai Vet in Northern Vietnam. Eventually, he defeated the Cham in 1144-1145, capturing and sacking the royal capital, Vijaya. He left an incredible, monumental legacy behind, being responsible for the construction of Angkor Wat, Phnom Rung temple (Khorat) and Banteay Samre.

He was the greatest of Angkor's god-kings, during whose reign the temple of Angkor Wat was built. It was an architectural masterpiece and represented the height of the Khmer's artistic genius. A network of roads was built to connect regional capitals.

However, his success was not without its costs – his widespread construction put serious pressure on the general running of the kingdom, with major reservoirs silting up; there was an intensified discord in the provinces and his persistent battling fuelled an ongoing duel between the Cham and Khmers that was to continue (and be avenged) well-beyond his death.

Suryavarman II deposed the King of Champa in 1145 but the Cham regained their independence in 1149 and the following year, Suryavarman died after a disastrous attempt to conquer Annam (northern Vietnam). The throne was usurped by **Tribhuvanadityavarman** in 1165, who died in 1177, when the Cham seized their chance of revenge and sacked Angkor in a surprise naval attack. This was the Khmer's worst defeat recorded – the city had been completely annihilated. The 50-year-old **Jayavarman VII** – a cousin of Suryavarman – turned out to be their saviour. He battled the Cham for the next four years, driving them out of the Kingdom. In 1181 he was declared king and seriously hit back, attacking the Chams and seizing their capital, Vijaya. He expanded the Khmer Kingdom further than ever before; its suzerainty stretched from the Malay peninsula in the south to the borders of Burma in the west and the Annamite chain to the northeast.

Jayavarman's VII's first task was to plan a strong, spacious new capital – Angkor Thom; but while that work was being undertaken he set up a smaller, temporary seat of government where he and his court could live in the meantime – Preah Khan meaning 'Fortunate City of Victory' (see page 120). He also built 102 hospitals throughout his kingdom, as well as a network of roads, along which he constructed resthouses. But because they were built of wood, none of these secular structures survive; only the foundations of four larger ones have been unearthed at Angkor.

Angkor's decline

Jayavarman VII's extensive building campaign put a large amount of pressure on the kingdom's resources, rice was in short supply as labour had been completely consumed by construction.

Jayavarman VII died in 1218 and the Kambujan Empire fell into progressive decline over the next two centuries. Territorially, it was eroded by the eastern migration of the Siamese. The Khmers were unable to prevent this gradual incursion but the diversion of labour to the military from temple building and rice farming helped seal the fate of Angkor. Another reason for the decline was the introduction of Theravada Buddhism in the 13th century, which undermined the prestige of the king and the priests. There is even a view that climatic change disrupted the agricultural system and led to Kambuja's demise. After Jayavarman VII, no king seems to have been able to unify the kingdom by force of arms or personality – internal dissent increased while the king's extravagance continued to place a crippling burden on state funds. With its temples decaying and its once-magnificent agricultural system in ruins, Angkor became virtually uninhabitable. In 1431 the royal capital was finally abandoned to the Siamese, who drove the Khmers out and made Cambodia a vassal of the Thai Sukhothai Kingdom.

Explaining Angkor's decline

Why the Angkorian Empire should have declined has always fascinated scholars in the West – in the same way that the decline and fall of the Roman Empire has done. Numerous explanations have been offered, and still the debate remains unresolved. As Anthony Barnett argued in a paper in the New Left Review in 1990, perhaps the question should be "why did Angkor last so long? Inauspiciously sited, it was nonetheless a tropical imperium of 500 years' duration."

There are essentially five lines of argument in the 'Why did Angkor fall?' debate. First, it has been argued that the building programmes became simply so arduous and demanding of ordinary people that they voted with their feet and moved out, depriving Angkor of the population necessary to support a great empire. Second, some scholars present an environmental argument: the great irrigation works silted-up, undermining the empire's agricultural wealth. (This line of argument conflicts with recent work that maintains that Angkor's wealth was never based on hydraulic – or irrigated – agriculture, see pages 110 and 111.) Third, there are those who say that military defeat was the cause – but this only begs the question: why they were defeated in the first place? Fourth, historians with a rather wider view, have offered the opinion that the centres of economic activity in Southeast Asia moved from land-based to sea-based foci, and that Angkor was poorly located to adapt to this shift in patterns of trade, wealth and, hence, power. Lastly, some scholars argue that the religion which demanded such labour of Angkor's subjects became so corrupt as to corrode the empire from within.

After Angkor – running scared

The next 500 years or so, until the arrival of the French in 1863, was an undistinguished period in Cambodian history. In 1434 the royal Khmer court under Ponheayat moved to Phnom Penh, where a replica of the cosmic Mount Meru was built. There was a short-lived period of revival in the mid-15th century until the Siamese invaded and sacked the capital again in 1473. One of the sons of the captured King Suryavarman drummed up enough Khmer support to oust the invaders and there were no subsequent invasions during the 16th century. The capital was established at Lovek (between Phnom Penh and Tonlé Sap) and then moved back to the ruins at Angkor. But a Siamese invasion in 1593 sent the royal court fleeing into Laos; finally, in 1603, the Thais released a captured prince to rule over their Cambodian vassal. There were at least 22 kings between 1603 and 1848.

Politically, the Cambodian court tried to steer a course between its powerful neighbours of Siam and Vietnam, seeking one's protection against the other. King **Chey Chetta II** (1618-28), for example, declared Cambodia's independence from Siam and in order to back up his actions he asked Vietnam for help. To cement the allegiance he was forced to marry a Vietnamese princess of the Nguyen Dynasty of Annam, and then obliged to pay tribute to Vietnam. His successors – hoping to rid themselves of Vietnamese domination – sought Siamese assistance and were then forced to pay for it by acknowledging Siam's suzerainty. Then in 1642, **King Chan** converted to Islam, and encouraged Malay and Javanese migrants to settle in Cambodia. Considering him guilty of apostasy, his cousins ousted him – with

Vietnamese support. But 50 years later, the Cambodian **Ang Eng** was crowned in Bangkok. This see-saw pattern continued for years; only Siam's wars with Burma and Vietnam's internal disputes and long-running conflict with China prevented them from annexing the whole of Cambodia, although both took territorial advantage of the fragmented state.

By the early 1700s the kingdom was centred on Phnom Penh (there were periods when the king resided at Ondong). But when the Khmers lost their control over the Mekong Delta to the Vietnamese in the late 18th century, the capital's access to the sea was blocked. By 1750 the Khmer royal family had split into pro-Siamese and pro-Vietnamese factions. Between 1794-1811 and 1847-63, Siamese influence was strongest; from 1835-37 the Vietnamese dominated. In the 1840s, the Siamese and Vietnamese armies fought on Cambodian territory devastating the country. This provoked French intervention – and cost Cambodia its independence, even if it had been nominal for several centuries. On 17 April 1864 (the same day and month as the Khmer Rouge soldiers entered Phnom Penh) King Norodom agreed to French protection as he believed they would provide military assistance against the Siamese. The king was to be disappointed: France honoured Siam's claim to the western provinces of Battambang, Siem Reap and Sisophon, which Bangkok had captured in the late 1600s. And in 1884, King Norodom was persuaded by the French governor of the colony of Cochin China to sign another treaty that turned Cambodia into a French colony, along with Laos and Vietnam in the Union Indochinoise. The establishment of Cambodia as a French protectorate probably saved the country from being apportioned between Siam and Vietnam.

The French colonial period

The French did little to develop Cambodia, preferring instead for the territory to pay for itself. The French only invested income generated from tax revenue to build a communications network. In the 1920s French private-sector investors planted out rubber estates in Kompong Cham in east Cambodia. From a Cambodian perspective, the only benefit of colonial rule was that the French forestalled the total disintegration of the country, which would otherwise have been divided up between its warring neighbours. French cartographers also mapped Cambodia's borders for the first time and in so doing, the French forced the Thais to surrender the northwestern provinces of Battambang and Siem Reap.

For nearly a century the French alternately supported two branches of the royal family, the Norodoms and the Sisowaths, crowning the 18-year-old schoolboy **Prince Norodom Sihanouk** in 1941. The previous year, the Nazis had invaded and occupied France; French territories in Indochina were in turn occupied by the Japanese – although Cambodia was still formally governed and administered by the French. It was at this stage that a group of pro-independence Cambodians realized just how weak the French control of their country actually was. In 1942 two monks were arrested and accused of preaching anti-French sermons; within two days this sparked demonstrations by more than 1,000 monks in Phnom Penh. These demonstrations marked the beginning of Cambodian nationalism. In March 1945 Japanese forces ousted the colonial administration and persuaded King Norodom Sihanouk to proclaim independence. Following the Japanese surrender in August 1945, the French came back in force; Sihanouk tried to negotiate independence from France and they responded by abolishing the absolute monarchy in 1946 – although the king remained titular head of state. A new constitution was introduced allowing political activity and a National Assembly elected.

Independence and neutrality

By the early 1950s the French army had suffered several defeats in the war in Indochina. Sihanouk dissolved the National Assembly in mid-1952, which he was entitled to do under the constitution, and personally took charge of steering Cambodia towards independence from France. To publicize the cause, he travelled to Thailand, Japan and the United States, and said he would not return from self-imposed exile until his country was free. His audacity embarrassed the French into granting Cambodia independence on 9 November 1953 – and Sihanouk returned, triumphant.

The people of Cambodia did not want to return to absolute monarchy, and following his abdication· in 1955, Sihanouk became a popular political leader. But political analysts believe that despite the apparent popularity of the former king's administration, different factions began to develop at this time, a process which was the root of the conflict in the years to come. During the 1960s, for example, there was a growing rift between the Khmer majority and other groups. Even in the countryside, differences became marked between the rice-growing areas and the remoter mountain areas where people practised shifting cultivation supplementing their diet with lizards, snakes, roots and insects. As these problems intensified in the late 1960s and the economic situation deteriorated, the popular support base for the Khmer Rouge was put into place. With unchecked population growth, land ownership patterns became skewed, landlessness grew more widespread and food prices escalated.

Sihanouk managed to keep Cambodia out of the war that enveloped Laos and Vietnam during the late 1950s and 1960s by following a neutral policy – which helped attract millions of dollars of aid to Cambodia from both the West and the Eastern Bloc. But when a civil war broke out in South Vietnam in the early 1960s, Cambodia's survival – and Sihanouk's own survival – depended on its outcome. Sihanouk believed the rebels, the National Liberation Front (NLF) would win; and he openly courted and backed the NLF. It was an alliance which cost him dear. In 1965-66 the tide began to turn in South Vietnam, due to US military and economic intervention. This forced NLF troops to take refuge inside Cambodia (in 1966 half of Cambodia's rice supplies, normally sold abroad, were distributed to the NLF agents inside Cambodia). A peasant uprising in northwestern provinces in 1967 showed Sihanouk that he was sailing rather close to the wind; his forces suppressed the rebellion by massacring 10,000 peasants.

But slowly – and inevitably – he became the focus of resentment within Cambodia's political élite. He also incurred American wrath by allowing North Vietnamese forces to use Cambodian territory as an extension of the **Ho Chi Minh Trail**, ferrying arms and men into South Vietnam. This resulted in his former army Commander-in-Chief, **Marshal Lon Nol** masterminding Sihanouk's removal as Head of State while he was in Moscow in 1970. Lon Nol abolished the monarchy and proclaimed a republic. One of the most auspicious creatures in Khmer mythology is the white crocodile. The crocodile is said to appear above the surface at important times. A white crocodile was sighted near Phnom Penh just before Lon Nol took over.

The Third Indochina War and the rise of the Khmer Rouge

On 30 April 1970, following the overthrow of Prince Norodom Sihanouk, US President Richard Nixon officially announced **Washington's military intervention in Cambodia** – although in reality it had been going on for some time. The invasion aimed to deny the Vietnamese Communists the use of Sihanoukville port through which 85% of their heavy arms were reaching South Vietnam. The US Air Force had been secretly bombing Cambodia using B-52s since March 1969. In 1973, facing defeat in Vietnam, the US Air Force B-52s began carpet bombing Communist-controlled areas to enable Lon Nol's inept regime to retain control of the besieged provincial cities.

Historian David P Chandler wrote: "When the campaign was stopped by the US Congress at the end of the year, the B-52s had dropped over half a million tons of bombs on a country with which the United States was not at war – more than twice the tonnage dropped on Japan during the Second World War.

The war in Cambodia was known as 'the sideshow' by journalists covering the war in Vietnam and by American policy-makers in London. Yet the intensity of US bombing in Cambodia was greater than it ever was in Vietnam; about 500,000 soldiers and civilians were killed over the four-year period. It also caused about two million refugees to flee from the countryside to the capital."

As Henry Kamm suggested, by the beginning of 1971 the people of Cambodia had to face the terrifying realisation that nowhere in the country was safe and all hope and confidence in Cambodia's future during the war was lost. A year after the coup d'etat the country was shattered: guerrilla forces had invaded Angkor the country's primary oil refinery, Lol Non had suffered a stroke and had relocated to Hawaii for months of treatment; Lol Non's irregularly paid soldiers were pillaging stores at gunpoint and extreme corruption was endemic.

By the end of the war, the country had become totally dependent on US aid and much of the population survived on American rice rations. Confidence in the Lon Nol government collapsed as taxes rose and even children were drafted into combat units. At the same time, the **Khmer Rouge** increased its military strength dramatically and began to make inroads into areas formerly controlled by government troops. Although officially the Khmer Rouge rebels represented the Beijing-based Royal Government of National Union of Cambodia (Grunc), which was headed by the exiled Prince Sihanouk. Grunc's de facto leaders were Pol Pot, Khieu Samphan (who, after Pol Pot's demise, becamethe public face of the Khmer Rouge), Ieng Sary (later foreign minister) and Son Sen (Chief of General Staff) – all Khmer Rouge men. By the time the American bombing stopped in 1973, the guerrillas dominated about 60% of Cambodian territory, while the government clung tenuously to towns and cities. Over the next two years the Khmer Rouge whittled away Phnom Penh's defence perimeter to the point that Lon Nol's government was sustained only by American airlifts into the capital.

Some commentators have suggested that the persistent heavy bombing of Cambodia, which forced the Communist guerrillas to live in terrible conditions – was in part, responsible for the notorious savagery of the Khmer Rouge in later years. Not only were they brutalized by the conflict itself, but they became resentful that the city-dwellers had no inkling of how unpleasant their experiences really were. This, writes US political scientist Wayne Bert, "created the perception among the Khmer Rouge that the bulk of the population did not take part in the revolution, was therefore not enthusiastic about it and could not be trusted to support it. The final step in this logic was to punish or eliminate all in these categories who showed either real or imagined tendencies toward disloyalty". And that, as anyone who has watched *The Killing Fields* will know, is what happened.

The 'Pol Pot time': building year zero

On 1 April 1975 President Lon Nol fled Cambodia to escape the rapidly advancing Khmer Rouge. Just over two weeks later, on 17 April, the victorious Khmer Rouge entered Phnom Penh. The capital's population had been swollen by refugees from 600,000 to over two million. The ragged conquering troops wearing Ho Chi Minh sandals made of used rubber tyres – which were de rigueur for guerrillas in Indochina – were welcomed as heroes. None in the crowds that lined the streets appreciated the

Pol Pot – the idealistic psychopath

Prince Norodom Sihanouk once referred to Pol Pot as "a more fortunate Hitler". Unlike his erstwhile fascist counterpart, the man whose troops were responsible for the deaths of perhaps two million fellow Cambodians has managed to get away with it. He died on 15 April 1998, either of a heart attack or, possibly, at his own hands or somebody elses.

Pol Pot's real name was Saloth Sar – he adopted his nom de guerre when he became Secretary-General of the Cambodian Communist Party in 1963. He was born in 1928 into a peasant family in Kompong Thom, central Cambodia, and is believed to have lived as a novice monk for nine months when he was a child. His services to the Democrat Party won him a scholarship to study electronics in Paris. But he became a Communist in France in 1949 and spent more time at meetings of Marxist revolutionary societies than in classes. In his 1986 book *Sideshow*, William Shawcross notes that at that time the French Communist Party, which was known for its dogmatic adherence to orthodox Marxism, "taught hatred of the bourgeoisie and uncritical admiration of Stalinism, including the collectivization of agriculture". Pol Pot finally lost his scholarship in 1953.

Returning to newly independent Cambodia, Pol Pot started working as a school teacher in Phnom Penh and continued his revolutionary activities in the underground Cambodian Communist Party (which, remarkably kept its existence a secret until 1977). In 1963, he fled the capital for the countryside, fearing a crackdown of the left by Sihanouk. There he rose to become Secretary-General of the Central Committee of the Communist Party of Kampuchea. He was trained in guerrilla warfare and he became a

horrors that the victory would also bring. Cambodia was renamed Democratic Kampuchea (DK) and Pol Pot set to work establishing a radical Maoist-style agrarian society. These ideas had been first sketched out by his longstanding colleague Khieu Samphan, whose 1959 doctoral thesis – at the Sorbonne University in Paris – analysed the effects of Cambodia's colonial and neo-colonial domination. In order to secure true economic and political independence he argued that it was necessary to isolate Cambodia completely and to go back to a self-sufficient agricultural economy.

It was Prince Norodom Sihanouk who had first coined the term 'Khmer Rouge' when he faced a peasant uprising in 1967; they called themselves Angkar Loeu – 'The Higher Organization'. Within days of the occupation, the rubber sandalled revolutionaries had forcibly evacuated many of the inhabitants of Phnom Penh to the countryside, telling citizens that the American's were about to bomb the capital. A second major displacement was carried out at the end of the year, when hundreds of thousands of people from the area southeast of Phnom Penh were forced to move to the northwest. Prior to the Khmer Rouge coming to power, the Cambodian word for revolution had a conventional meaning: bambahbambor or 'uprising'. Under Pol Pot's regime, the word pativattana was used instead; it meant 'return to the past'. The Khmer Rouge did this by obliterating everything that did not subscribe to their vision of the past glories of ancient Khmer culture. Pol Pot wanted to return the country to **'Year Zero'** – he wanted to begin again. One of the many revolutionary slogans was "we will burn the old grass and new will grow"; money, modern technology, medicine, education and newspapers were outlawed. Khieu Samphan, who became the Khmer Rouge Head of State, following Prince Sihanouk's resignation in 1976, said at the time: "No, we have no machines. We do everything by mainly relying on the strength of our people. We work completely self-sufficiently. This shows the overwhelming leader of the Khmer Rouge forces, advocating armed resistance to Sihanouk and his 'feudal entourage'. In 1975 when the Khmer Rouge marched into Phnom Penh, Pol Pot was forced out of the shadows to take the role of leader, 'Brother Number One'. Although he took the title of prime minister, he ruled as a dictator and set about reshaping Cambodia with his mentor, Khieu Samphan, the head of state. Yet, during the years he was in power, hardly any Cambodians – save those in the top echelons of the Khmer Rouge – had even heard of him.

The Vietnam-backed Hun Sen government, which took over the country after the overthrow of the Khmer Rouge in December 1978, calculated that by demonizing Pol Pot as the mastermind of the genocide, it would avert the possibility of the Khmer Rouge ever making a comeback. The Hun Sen regime showed no interest in analysing the complex factors which combined to bring Pol Pot to power. Within Cambodia, he has been portrayed simply as a tyrannical bogey-man. During the 1980s, 20 May was declared National Hate Day, when everyone reaffirmed their hatred of Pol Pot.

In a review of David Chandler's biography of Pol Pot (*Brother Number One: A Political Biography of Pol Pot*, Westview Press, 1992), Peter Carey – the co-director of the British-based Cambodia Trust – was struck by what he called "the sinister disjunction between the man's evident charisma ... and the monumental suffering wrought by his regime". Carey concludes: "one is left with the image of a man consumed by his own vision, a vision of empowerment and liberation that has little anchorage in Cambodian reality".

heroism of our people. This also shows the great force of our people. Though bare-handed, they can do everything".

The Khmer Rouge, or Angkar as they touted themselves, maintained a strangle-hold on the country by dislocating families, disorientating people and sustaining a persistent fear of violence, torture and death. At the heart of their strategy was to unfurl people's strongest bonds and loyalties, those that existed between family members. The term kruosaa, which traditionally means family in Khmer, came to simply mean "spouse" under the Khmer Rouge. In Angkar, family no longer existed. Krusosaa niyum, which loosely translated to "familyism" (or pining for ones relatives) was a criminal offence punishable by death. Under heinous interrogation procedures people were intensively probed about their family members (sisters, brothers, grand-parents and in-laws) and encouraged to inform on their family. Those people who didn't turn over relatives considered adversaries (teachers, former soldiers, doctors etc.) faced odious consequences, with the fate of the whole family (immediate and extended) in danger.

Memoirs from survivors detailed in the book *Children of Cambodia's Killing Fields* repeatedly refer to the Khmer Rouge dictum "to keep you is no benefit to destroy you is no loss." People were treated as nothing more than machines. Food was scarce under Pol Pot's inefficient system of collective farming and administration was based on fear, torture and summary execution. A veil of secrecy shrouded Cambodia and, until a few desperate refugees began to trickle over the border into Thailand, the outside world was largely ignorant of what was going on. The refugees' stories of atrocities were, at first, disbelieved. Jewish refugees who escaped from Nazi occupied Poland in the 1940s had encountered a similarly disbelieving reception simply because (like the Cambodians) what they had to say was, to most people, unbelievable. Jan Karski, a

Pole, escaped from a concentration camp in 1942 and made his way to America. He described to a Supreme Court Judge the conditions he had experienced. The Judge replied "I do not believe you". Not unnaturally Karski protested. The Judge replied "I do not mean that you are lying, I simply said I cannot believe you." Some left wing academics initially viewed the revolution as an inspired and brave attempt to break the shackles of dependency and neo-colonial domination. Others, such as Noam Chomsky, dismissed the allegations as right wing press propaganda.

It was not until the Vietnamese 'liberation' of Phnom Penh in 1979 that the scale of the Khmer Rouge carnage emerged and the atrocities witnessed by the survivors became known. The stories turned the Khmer Rouge into international pariahs – but only until 1982 when, remarkably, their American and Chinese sympathizers secured them a voice at the United Nations. Wives had been encouraged to denounce their husbands; children their mothers. Anyone who had smoked an American cigarette was a CIA operative; anyone with a taste for café crème was a French collaborator. During the Khmer Rouge's 44-month reign of terror, it had hitherto been generally accepted that around a million people died. This is a horrendous figure when one considers that the population of the country in 1975 was around seven million. What is truly shocking is that the work undertaken by a team from Yale University indicates that this figure is far too low.

Although the Khmer Rouge era in Cambodia may have been a period of unprecedented economic, political and human turmoil, they still managed to keep meticulous records of what they were doing. In this regard the Khmer Rouge were rather like the Chinese during the Cultural Revolution, or the Nazis in Germany. Using Australian satellite data, the team was expecting to uncover around 200 mass graves; instead they found several thousand. The Khmer Rouge themselves have claimed that around 20,000 people died because of their 'mistakes'. The Vietnamese have traditionally put the figure at 2-3 million, although their estimates have generally been rejected as too high and politically motivated (being a means to justify their invasion of the country in 1978/79 and subsequent occupation). The real figure is more likely to be around 1.5-1.7 milion. But the Yale work seems to indicate that the Vietnamese figures may well be closer to the truth. The Documentation Center of Cambodia, involved in the heavy mapping project, said that 20,492 mass graves were uncovered containing the remains of 1,112,829 victims of execution. In addition, hundreds of thousands more died from famine and disease; frighteningly the executions are believed to only account for about 30%-40% of the total death toll.

How such a large slice of Cambodia's people died in so short a time (between 1975 and the end of 1978) staggers belief. Some were shot, strangled or suffocated; many more starved; while others died from disease – malaria was rife – and overwork. The Khmer Rouge transformed Cambodia into what the British journalist, William Shawcross, described as: "a vast and sombre work camp where toil was unending, where respite and rewards were non-existent, where families were abolished and where murder was used as a tool of social discipline... The manner of execution was often brutal. Babies were torn apart limb from limb, pregnant women were disembowelled. Men and women were buried up to their necks in sand and left to die slowly. A common form of execution was by axe handles to the back of the neck. That saved ammunition".

The crimes transcended all moral boundaries known to mankind – soldiers cooked and ate the organs of victims, removed while they were screaming alive; pregnant women were bound and eviscerated. Sydney Schanberg's forward to *Children of Cambodia's Killing Fields* says of the memoirs: "painful though it may be to contemplate these accounts of young survivors, they desperately need to be passed, whole and without softening, from generation to generation. For it is only by such bearing of witness that the rest of us are rendered unable to pretend that true evil is exceedingly rare in the world, or worse, is but a figment".

The Khmer Rouge revolution was primarily a class-based one, fed by years of growing resentment against the privileged élites. The revolution pitted the least-literate, poorest rural peasants (referred to as the "old" people) against the educated, skilled and foreign-influenced urban population (referred to as the "new people). The "new" people provided an endless flow of numbers for the regime's death lists. Through a series of terrible purges, the members of the former governing and mercantile classes were liquidated or sent to work as forced labourers. But Peter Carey, Oxford historian and Chairman of the Cambodia Trust, argues that not all Pol Pot's victims were townspeople and merchants. "Under the terms of the 1948 Genocide Convention, the Khmer Rouge stands accused of genocide," he wrote in a letter to a British newspaper in 1990. "Of 64,000 Buddhist monks, 62,000 perished; of 250,000 Islamic Chams, 100,000; of 200,000 Vietnamese still left in 1975, 100,000; of 20,000 Thai, 12,000; of 1,800 Lao, 1,000. Of 2,000 Kola, not a trace remained." American political scientist Wayne Bert noted that: "The methods and behaviour compare to that of the Nazis and Stalinists, but in the percentage of the population killed by a revolutionary movement, the Khmer Rouge holds an unchallenged record."

It is still unclear the degree to which these 'genocidal' actions were controlled by those at the centre. Many of the killings took place at the discretion of local leaders, but there were some notably cruel leaders in the upper echelons of the Khmer Rouge and none can have been ignorant of what was going on. Ta Mok, who administered the region southwest of Phnom Penh, oversaw many mass executions for example. There is also evidence that the central government was directly involved in the running of the Tuol Sleng detention centre in which at least 20,000 people died. It has now been turned into a memorial to Pol Pot's holocaust (see page 60).

In addition to the legacy left by centres such as Tuol Sleng, there is the impact of the mass killings upon the Cambodian psyche. One of which is – to western eyes – the startling openness with which Khmer people will, if asked, matter-of-factly relate their family history in detail: this usually involves telling how the Khmer Rouge era meant they lost one or several members of their family. Whereas death is talked about in hushed terms in western society, Khmers have no such reservations, perhaps because it touched, and touches them all.

The Vietnamese invasion

The first border clashes over offshore islands between Khmer Rouge forces and the Vietnamese army were reported just a month after the Khmer Rouge came to power. These erupted into a minor war in January 1977 when the Phnom Penh government accused Vietnam of seeking to incorporate Kampuchea with an Indochinese federation. Hanoi's determination to oust Pol Pot only really became apparent however, on Christmas Day 1978 when 120,000 Vietnamese troops invaded. By 7 January (the day of Phnom Penh's liberation) they had installed a puppet government which proclaimed the foundation of the People's Republic of Kampuchea (PRK): Heng Samrin, a former member of the Khmer Rouge, was appointed president. The Vietnamese compared their invasion to the liberation of Uganda from Idi Amin – but for the western world it was an unwelcome Christmas present. The new government was accorded scant recognition abroad, while the toppled government of Democratic Kampuchea retained the country's seat at the United Nations.

But the country's 'liberation' by Vietnam did not end the misery; in 1979 nearly half Cambodia's population was in transit, either searching for their former homes or fleeing across the Thai border into refugee camps. The country reverted to a state of outright war again, for the Vietnamese were not greatly loved in Cambodia – especially by the Khmer Rouge. American political scientist Wayne Bert wrote: "The Vietnamese had long seen a special role for themselves in uniting and leading a

King Norodom Sihanouk: latter day god-king

An uncomplimentary profile of Prince Norodom Sihanouk in *The Economist* in 1990 said that over the preceding 20 years, he "twisted and turned, sulked, resigned many times, [was] humiliated and imprisoned. In one thing, however, he [was] consistent: his yearning to recover the face he lost in 1970, and return to Phnom Penh in triumph". The following year, on 14 November, Prince Sihanouk did exactly that, arriving in his former royal capital to a rapturous welcome, after 13 years of exile. In November 1991, as in 1953 when he returned from exile at Independence, he represented the one symbol Cambodia had of any semblance of national unity.

Norodom Sihanouk was crowned King of Cambodia at the age of 18 in 1941. He owed his accession to the throne to a method of selection devised by the French colonial regime who hoped that the young, inexperienced Sihanouk would be a compliant puppet-king. But in the event he turned out to be something very different. Using his position to great advantage, he became a nationalist leader and crusaded for independence in 1953. But following

independence, his royal title worked against him: the 1947 constitution restricted the role the monarch could play in politics. So, he abdicated in favour of his father, Norodom Suramarit, in 1955 and, as Prince Sihanouk, was free to enter politics. He immediately founded the Sangkum Reastr Niyum – the Popular Socialist Community (PSC). The same year, the PSC won every seat in the National Assembly – as it did in subsequent elections in 1958, 1962 and 1966.

The old king died in 1960, but Sihanouk side-stepped the problem of succession by declaring himself Head of State, without ascending to the throne. Michael Leifer, a British political scientist, writes: "As Head of State, Prince Sihanouk became literally the voice of Cambodia. He articulated its hopes and fears within the country and to the outside world... He appeared as a popular figure revered especially in the rural areas as the father figure of his country." He was a populist of the first order.

Someth May, in his autobiography *Cambodian Witness*, describes Phnom Penh in the early 1960s: "Sihanouk's portrait was everywhere around town: in uniform with a sword, in a suit, in

greater Indochina Communist movement and the Cambodian Communists had seen with clarity that such a role for the Vietnamese could only be at the expense of their independence and prestige."

Under the Lon Nol and Khmer Rouge regimes, Vietnamese living in Cambodia were expelled or exterminated. Resentment had built up over the years in Hanoi – exacerbated by the apparent ingratitude of the Khmer Rouge for Vietnamese assistance in fighting Lon Nol's US-supported Khmer Republic in the early 1970s. As relations between the Khmer Rouge and the Vietnamese deteriorated, the Communist superpowers, China and the Soviet Union, polarized too – the former siding with the Khmer Rouge and the latter with Hanoi. The Vietnamese invasion had the full backing of Moscow, while the Chinese and Americans began their support for the anti-Vietnamese rebels.

Following the Vietnamese invasion, three main anti-Hanoi factions were formed. In June 1982 they banded together in an unholy and unlikely alliance of convenience to fight the PRK and called themselves the Coalition Government of Democratic Kampuchea (CGDK), which was immediately recognized by the United Nations. The three factions of the CGDK were: The Communist **Khmer Rouge**, whose field monk's robes, dressed in white with a shaved head like an achar; on posters, on notebooks; framed in every classroom above the teacher's head; in the shops and offices. In the magazine that he edited himself we saw him helping a farmer dig an irrigation canal, reviewing the troops, shooting a film (for he was also a film-maker), addressing the National Assembly, giving presents to the monks, opening the annual regatta with his wife, Monique. On the radio we heard his speeches, and one year when he had a craze for singing you could hear his songs more than 10 times a day."

Sihanouk liked to run the show single-handedly and he is said to have treated his ministers like flunkies. In *Sideshow*, William Shawcross paints him as being vain – "a petulant showman who enjoyed boasting of his sexual successes. He would not tolerate criticism or dissent... At the same time he had enormous political skill, charm, tenacity and intelligence."

With an American-backed right-wing regime in power after the coup in 1970, the former king went into exile in China, where his supporters formed an alliance with his former enemies, the Khmer Rouge: the Royal Government of National Union of Cambodia – otherwise known as the Grunc. When the Khmer Rouge marched into Phnom Penh in 1975, they restored Prince Sihanouk as Head of State.

He resigned in April 1976 as he became increasingly marginalized, and the Grunc was dissolved. Sihanouk was kept under house-arrest until a few days before the Vietnamese army occupied Phnom Penh in January 1979, whereupon he fled to Beijing. There Sihanouk and his supporters once again joined forces with the Khmer Rouge in a tripartite coalition aimed at overthrowing the Hanoi-backed government.

The peace settlement which followed the eventual Vietnamese withdrawal in 1989 paved the way for Sihanouk's return from exile. His past association with the Khmer Rouge had tarnished the prince's image, but to many Cambodians, he represented their hopes for a stable future. Following the elections of 1993, Sihanouk returned from Beijing to be crowned King on 24 September, thus reclaiming the throne he relinquished in 1955. In 2004 the King abdicated, making way for his son Sihamoni to fill his shoes.

forces had recovered to at least 18,000 by the late 1980s. Supplied with weapons by China, they were concentrated in the Cardamom Mountains in the southwest and were also in control of some of the refugee camps along the Thai border. The National United Front for an Independent Neutral Peaceful and Co-operative Cambodia (Funcinpec) – known by most people as the **Armée Nationale Sihanoukiste** (ANS). It was headed by Prince Sihanouk – although he spent most of his time exiled in Beijing; the group had fewer than 15,000 well-equipped troops – most of whom took orders from Khmer Rouge commanders. The anti-Communist **Khmer People's National Liberation Front** (KPNLF), headed by Son Sann, a former prime minister under Sihanouk. Its 5,000 troops were reportedly ill-disciplined in comparison with the Khmer Rouge and the ANS.

The three CGDK factions were ranged against the 70,000 troops loyal to the government of President Heng Samrin and Prime Minister Hun Sen (previously a Khmer Rouge cadre). They were backed by Vietnamese forces until September 1989. Within the forces of the Phnom Penh government there were reported to be problems of discipline and desertion. But the rebel guerrilla coalition was itself seriously weakened by rivalries and hatred between the different factions: in reality, the idea of a 'coalition' was fiction. Throughout most of the 1980s the war followed the progress of the seasons: during the dry season from November to April the PRK forces with their tanks and heavy arms took the offensive but during the wet season this heavy equipment was ineffective and the guerrilla resistance made advances.

The road towards peace

In the late 1980s the Association of Southeast Asian Nations (ASEAN) – for which the Cambodian conflict had almost become its raison d'être – began steps to bring the warring factions together over the negotiating table. ASEAN countries were united primarily in wanting the Vietnamese out of Cambodia. While publicly deploring the Khmer Rouge record, ASEAN tacitly supported the guerrillas. Thailand, an ASEAN member-state, which has had a centuries-long suspicion of the Vietnamese, co-operated closely with China to ensure that the Khmer Rouge guerrillas over the border were well-supplied with weapons.

After Mikhail Gorbachev had come to power in the Soviet Union, Moscow's support for the Vietnamese presence in Cambodia gradually evaporated. Gorbachev began leaning on Vietnam as early as 1987, to withdraw its troops. Despite saying their presence in Cambodia was 'irreversible', Vietnam completed its withdrawal in September 1989, ending nearly 11 years of Hanoi's direct military involvement. The withdrawal led to an immediate upsurge in political and military activity, as forces of the exiled CGDK put increased pressure on the now weakened Phnom Penh regime to begin power-sharing negotiations (see page 242).

Modern Cambodia

Until the mid-19th century, the outside world knew almost nothing of the interior of Cambodia. From the 16th and 17th centuries, rumours began to surface in Europe – based on tales from Portuguese and French missionaries – about a magnificent city, hidden somewhere in the middle of the jungle. It is usually claimed that the ruins of Angkor were 'discovered' by the French naturalist and explorer Henri Mouhot in 1861. This is a travesty of history: Southeast Asians never forgot that Angkor existed. Truth, as they say, is determined by the powerful, and in this case the west determined that a westerner should 'discover' what was already known. In a sense, Angkor is a great weight on the collective shoulders of the Cambodian people. The usual refrain from visitors is: 'How could a people who created such magnificence have also nurtured Pol Pot and the Khmer Rouge?' A simple answer might be that only despotic rule could create anything on the scale of Angkor. The totalitarianism of the Khmer Rouge echoed that of the Khmer kings, but as the kings built, so the Khmer Rouge destroyed. Nonetheless, it is easy enough to see a stark disjuncture between the glory of Angkor and the horrors of recent history. As Elizabeth Becker wrote at the beginning of 1995: "Cambodia's recent history is one of breathtaking tragedy; by comparison its immediate future looks small and venal." Today Cambodia resembles many of the striving, corrupt, developing nations trying to make up for time lost behind the iron curtain. The nation that bore the horrors of the Khmer Rouge seemed ready for a kinder if not a more prosperous transformation."

In his book *Sideshow*, the British journalist William Shawcross says the diplomats, journalists and tourists who visited Cambodia in the 1950s and 1960s described it as "an idyllic, antique land unsullied by the brutalities of the modern world". Paddy farmers laboured in their ricefields, mystical ruins lay hidden in the jungle, the capital had the charm of a French provincial town and pagodas dotted the landscape. "Such was the illusion," writes Shawcross, of "bucolic plenty, Buddhist serenity, neutralist peace". This was an illusion because for centuries Cambodia had been in a state of continuous social and political upheaval. Since the demise of the Angkorian Empire in the 15th century, the country has been at the mercy of its much larger neighbours, Siam (Thailand) and Vietnam, and of various foreign powers – China, France, the US and the former Soviet Union. This history of foreign domination is starkly overshadowed by the so-called 'Pol Pot time'. Between 1975 and 1979, Cambodians suffered one of the worst human tragedies to afflict any country since the Second World War – more than a million people died out of a total population of about seven million. If the preceding period, during America's involvement in Indochina, is also taken into account, it is possible that up to a fifth of Cambodia's population was killed.

The relics and reminders of those days are now firmly on the tourist's sightseeing agenda. These include the chilling Tuol Sleng Genocide Museum, in the former high school where the Khmer Rouge tortured and killed at least 20,000 people and Choeung Ek, a series of mass graves, the 'Killing Fields', 15 km southwest of Phnom Penh. Rather unsettling is that the government sold the rights for this memorial site to a Japanese firm in 2005.

Politics

Since the mid-1960s Cambodian politics has been chaotic, with warring and bickering factions, backed by different foreign powers and domestic cliques, and shifting alliances. The groups which battled for power following the Vietnamese invasion in 1979 are still in the political arena and although the country may have 'enjoyed' democratic elections in 1993, 1998 and 2002 civil society remains poorly developed. Gangsterism, political terrorism and extra-judicial killings remain very much part of the political landscape even after the end of the Khmer Rouge and despite the pretence of democracy. It is only the sheer horror of the Pol Pot years which gives the months and years since that ghastly episode a rosy tint. Henry Kamm, for one, gave a dismal reading of Cambodia's prospects in his short article in *The New York Review*: "No equitable rule of law or impartial justice shelters Cambodians against a mean-spirited establishment of political and economic power, a cabal, dominated by Prime Minister Hun Sen, that is blind and deaf to the crying needs of an abused people". (August 13th 1998) While elements of Kamm's depressing take on Cambodia's prospects remain just as true today, the general picture over the last seven years (through to 2005) has been one of modest, stagnated improvement.

The road to peace (of a kind), 1989-1993
In September 1989, under pressure at home and abroad, the Vietnamese withdrew from Cambodia. The immediate result of this withdrawal was an escalation of the civil war as the rebel factions – comprised of the Khmer Rouge, the Sihanoukists and Son Sann's KPNLF (see page 240) – tried to take advantage of the supposedly weakened Hun Sen regime in Phnom Penh. The government committed itself to liberalizing the economy and improving the infrastructure in order to undermine the political appeal of the rebels – particularly that of the Khmer Rouge. Peasant farmers were granted life tenancy to their land and collective farms were substituted with agricultural co-operatives. But because nepotism and bribery were rife in Phnom Penh, the popularity of the Hun Sen regime declined. The rebel position was further strengthened as the disparities between living standards in Phnom Penh and those in the rest of the country widened. In the capital, the government became alarmed; in a radio broadcast in 1991 it announced a crackdown on corruption claiming it was

Cambodia 1953-2005

1953 Cambodian independence from France.

1965 Prince Sihanouk's government cuts links with the United States following deployment of US troops in Vietnam.

1966 Right-wing beats Sihanouk in the election; Lon Nol elected prime minister.

1967 Lon Nol toppled following left-wing demonstrations.

1969 Lon Nol becomes prime minister again.

1970 Lon Nol topples Sihanouk in US-backed coup; US bombs Communist bases in Cambodia.

1972 Lon Nol becomes first president of the Khmer Republic.

1975 Lon Nol flees as Khmer Rouge seizes power; Sihanouk made head of government. December: Vietnam invades.

1976 Cambodia renamed Democratic Kampuchea; Sihanouk resigns and Khieu Samphan becomes head of state, with Pol Pot as prime minister. Government moves people from towns to labour camps in the countryside.

1981 Cambodia renamed the People's Republic of Kampuchea (PRK).

1982 Coalition government-in-exile formed by anti-Hanoi resistance comprising Sihanoukists, Khmer Rouge and KPNLF. Sihanouk appointed President; Khieu Samphan, Vice-President and Son Sann, Prime Minister. Coalition backed by China and ASEAN.

1984 Vietnam gains rebel-held territory along Thai border; Vietnamese civilians settle in Kampuchea.

1989 People's Republic of Kampuchea renamed the State of Cambodia. September: last of the Vietnamese troops leave.

1991 International Conference on Cambodia in Paris leads to peace treaty and deployment of UNTAC.

1993 In May elections were held under the auspices of the United Nations Transitional Authority in Cambodia. A coalition government was formed and Norodom Sihanouk was re-crowned King in September.

causing a "loss of confidence in our superb regime... which is tantamount to paving the way for the return of the genocidal Pol Pot regime".

With the withdrawal of Vietnamese troops, the continuing civil war followed the familiar pattern of dry season government offensives, and consolidation of guerrilla positions during the monsoon rains. Much of the fighting focused on the potholed highways – particularly Highway 6 which connects the capital with Battambang – with the Khmer Rouge blowing up most of the bridges along the road. Their strategy involved cutting the roads in order to drain the government's limited resources. Other Khmer Rouge offensives were designed to serve their own economic ends – such as their capture of the gem-rich town of Pailin.

The Khmer Rouge ran extortion rackets throughout the country, even along the strategic Highway 4 which ferried military supplies, oil and consumer goods from the port of Kompong Som (Sihanoukville) to Phnom Penh. The State of Cambodia – or the government forces, known as SOC – was pressed to deploy troops to remote areas and allot scarce resources, settling refugees in more secure parts of the country. To add to their problems, Soviet and Eastern Bloc aid began to dry up.

Throughout 1991 the four warring factions were repeatedly brought to the negotiating table in an effort to hammer out a peace deal. Much of the argument centred on the word 'genocide'. The Prime Minister, Hun Sen, insisted that the wording of any agreement should explicitly condemn the former Khmer Rouge regime's 'genocidal acts'. But the Khmer Rouge refused to be party to any power-sharing deal which

1996 Ieng Sary (Brother Number Two) splits from Khmer Rouge and is granted a royal pardon.

1997 Hun Sen's coup ousts Ranariddh and Funcinpec from government.

1998 Pol Pot dies. Elections and Hun Sen becomes sole prime minister.

1999 Cambodia joins ASEAN.

2001 Cambodian Senate approves a law to create a tribunal to bring genocide charges against Khmer Rouge leaders.

2002 First multi-party commune elections; the incumbent Cambodian People's Party wins in all but 23 out of 1,620 communes.

2003 Major diplomatic upset with Thailand in January over comments attributed to a Thai TV star that the Angkor Wat temple complex was stolen from Thailand. Angry crowds attack the Thai embassy and Thai-based businesses in Phnom Penh.

2003 Prime Minister Hun Sen's Cambodian People's Party wins the election in July but fails to secure sufficient majority to govern alone. A political deadlock arises.

2004 After nearly a year of political stalemate, Prime Minister Hun Sen is re-elected after his ruling Cambodian People's Party (CPP) forms a coalition with the royalist Funcinpec party.

2004 In August the parliament ratifies Cambodia's entry into World Trade organization (WTO).

2004 King Sihanouk abdicates in October and is succeeded by his son Norodom Sihamoni.

2005 Opposition leader Sam Rainsy flees the country after his parliamentary immunity is stripped.

labelled them in such a way. Fighting intensified as hopes for a settlement increased – all sides wanted to consolidate their territory in advance of any agreement.

Rumours emerged that China was continuing to supply arms – including tanks, reportedly delivered through Thailand – to the Khmer Rouge. There were also accusations that the Phnom Penh government was using Vietnamese combat troops to stem Khmer Rouge advances – the first such reports since their official withdrawal in 1989. But finally, in June 1991, after several attempts, Sihanouk brokered a permanent ceasefire during a meeting of the Supreme National Council (SNC) in Pattaya, South Thailand. The SNC had been proposed by the United Nations Security Council in 1990 and formed in 1991, with an equal number of representatives from the Phnom Penh government and each of the resistance factions, with Sihanouk as its chairman. The following month he was elected chairman of the SNC, and resigned his presidency of the rebel coalition government in exile. Later in the year, the four factions agreed to reduce their armed guerrillas and militias by 70%. The remainder were to be placed under the supervision of the United Nations Transitional Authority in Cambodia (UNTAC), which supervised Cambodia's transition to multi-party democracy. Heng Samrin's decided to drop his insistence that reference should be made to the former Khmer Rouge' "genocidal regime". It was also agreed that elections should be held in 1993 on the basis of proportional representation. Heng Samrin's Communist Party was promptly renamed the Cambodian People's Party, in an effort to persuade people that it sided with democracy and capitalism.

The Paris Peace Accord

On 23 October 1991, the four warring Cambodian factions signed a peace agreement in Paris which officially ended 13 years of civil war and more than two decades of warfare. The accord was co-signed by 15 other members of the International Peace Conference on Cambodia. There was an air of unreality about the whole event, which brought bitter enemies face-to-face after months of protracted negotiations. There was, however, a notable lack of enthusiasm on the part of the four warring factions. Hun Sen said that the treaty was far from perfect because it failed to contain the word 'genocide' to remind Cambodians of the atrocities of the former Khmer Rouge regime. western powers obviously agreed. But in the knowledge that it was a fragile agreement, everyone remained diplomatically quiet. US Secretary of State James Baker was quoted as saying "I don't think anyone can tell you there will for sure be lasting peace, but there is great hope."

Political analysts ascribed the successful conclusion to the months of negotiations to improved relations between China and Vietnam – there were reports that the two had held secret summits at which the Cambodia situation was discussed. China put pressure on Prince Norodom Sihanouk to take a leading role in the peace process, and Hanoi's new understanding with Beijing prompted Hun Sen's participation. The easing of tensions between China and Moscow – particularly following the Soviet Union's demise – also helped apply pressure on the different factions. Finally, the United States had shifted its position: in July 1990 it had announced that it would not support the presence of the Khmer Rouge at the UN and by September US officials were talking to Hun Sen.

On 14 November 1991, Prince Norodom Sihanouk returned to Phnom Penh to an ecstatic welcome, followed, a few days later, by Son Sen, a Khmer Rouge leader. On 27 November Khieu Samphan, who had represented the Khmer Rouge at all the peace negotiations, arrived on a flight from Bangkok. Within hours mayhem had broken out, and a lynch mob attacked him in his villa. Rumours circulated that Hun Sen had orchestrated the demonstration, and beating an undignified retreat down a ladder into a waiting armoured personnel carrier, the bloodied Khmer Rouge leader headed back to Pochentong Airport. The crowd had sent a clear signal that they, at least, were not happy to see him back. There were fears that this incident might derail the entire peace process – but in the event, the Khmer Rouge won a small public relations coup by playing the whole thing down. When the Supreme National Council (SNC) finally met in Phnom Penh at the end of December 1991, it was unanimously decided to rubberstamp the immediate deployment of UN troops to oversee the peace process in the run-up to a general election.

The UN peace-keeping mission

The UN mission "...conducted a brief, profound and very welcome social revolution [in Cambodia]" (William Shawcross, *Cambodia's new deal: a report* (1994)).

The UN mission favoured "Phnom Penh's profiteers, the Khmer Rouge utopists, the Chinese businessmen of Southeast Asia, the annexationist neighbours..." (Marie Alexandrine Martin (1994) Cambodia: a shattered society).

Yasushi Akashi, a senior Japanese official in the United Nations, was assigned the daunting task of overseeing the biggest military and logistical operation in UN history. UNTAC comprised an international team of 22,000 peacekeepers – including 16,000 soldiers from 22 countries, 6,000 officials as well as 3,500 police and 1,700 civilian employees and electoral volunteers. The first 'blue-beret' UN troops began arriving in November 1991, even before the SNC had agreed to the full complement of peacekeepers. The UN Advance Mission to Cambodia (UNAMIC) was followed four months later by the first of the main peacekeeping battalions. The odds were stacked against them. Shortly after his arrival, Akashi commented: "If one was a masochist one could not wish for more."

UNTAC's task

UNTAC's central mission was to supervise free elections in a country where most of the population had never voted and had little idea of how democracy was meant to work. The UN was also given the task of resettling 360,000 refugees from camps in Thailand and of demobilizing more than a quarter of a million soldiers and militiamen from the four main factions. In addition, it was to ensure that no further arms shipments reached these factions, whose remaining forces were to be confined to cantonments. In the run-up to the elections, UNTAC also took over the administration of the country, taking over the defence, foreign affairs, finance, public security and information portfolios as well as ensuring respect for human rights.

By early 1993, UN electoral workers had successfully registered 4.7 million of roughly nine million Cambodians – about 96% of the population above voting age. With a US$2 bn price-tag, this huge operation was the most expensive mission ever undertaken by the UN. At the time, the UN was running 12 peacekeeping operations throughout the world, but two-thirds of its peacekeeping budget was earmarked for Cambodia. Over the months a steady stream of VIPs arrived to witness the operation – they included the UN Secretary-General, Boutros-Boutros Ghali, the Chinese Foreign Minister, Qian Qichen and President François Mitterrand of France.

UNTAC's job would have been easier if the different guerrilla factions and militias had stopped fighting once the Peace Accord was signed. In the months after their arrival UN troops had to broker successive ceasefires between government forces and the Khmer Rouge. During 1992, the Khmer Rouge refused to demobilize their fighters as required by the Accord and attempted to gain a foothold in the strategic central province of Kompong Thom in advance of the full deployment of UN peacekeeping forces. This prompted further scepticism among observers as to their commitment to the peace process. The Khmer Rouge – which was by then referred to (in politically neutral parlance) as the Party of Democratic Kampuchea, or the DK – made it as difficult as possible for the UN. It refused UN soldiers, officials and volunteers access to areas under its control. On a number of occasions in the months running up to the elections, UN military patrols were held hostage after entering Khmer Rouge-held territory.

The Khmer Rouge pulls out

At the beginning of 1993 it became apparent that the Khmer Rouge had no intention of playing ball, despite its claim of a solid rural support base. The DK failed to register for the election before the expiry of the UN deadline and its forces stepped up attacks on UN personnel. In April 1993 Khieu Samphan and his entire entourage at the Khmer Rouge compound in Phnom Penh left the city. It was at this stage that UN officials finally began expressing their exasperation and anxiety over the Khmer Rouge's avowed intention to disrupt the polls. The faction was well-known to have procured fresh supplies of Chinese weapons through Thailand – although there is no evidence that these came from Beijing – as well as their having large arms caches hidden all over the country.

By the time of the elections, the group was thought to be in control of between 10% and 15% of Cambodian territory. Khmer Rouge guerrillas launched attacks in April and May 1993. Having stoked racial antagonism, they started killing ethnic Vietnamese villagers and settlers, sending up to 20,000 of them fleeing into Vietnam. In one particularly vicious attack, 33 Vietnamese fishermen and their families were killed in a village on the Tonlé Sap. The Khmer Rouge also began ambushing and killing UN soldiers and electoral volunteers.

The UN remained determined that the elections should go ahead despite the Khmer Rouge threats and mounting political intimidation and violence between other factions, notably the Cambodian People's Party and Funcinpec. But it did not take any chances: in the week before the elections, 6,000 flak jackets and helmets were flown into the country and security was tightened. In the event, however, there were remarkably few violent incidents and the feared co-ordinated effort to disrupt the voting failed to materialize. Voters took no notice of Khmer Rouge calls to boycott the election. In fact, reports came in from several provinces of large numbers of Khmer Rouge guerrillas and villagers from areas under their control, turning up at polling stations and casting their ballots.

The UN-supervised elections

The voting was by proportional representation, province by province. The election was conducted under the aegis of 1,400 International Polling Station Officers from more than 40 countries. The Cambodian people were voting for a 120-member Constituent Assembly to write a new constitution.

The days following the election saw a political farce – Cambodian style – which, as Nate Thayer wrote in the *Far Eastern Economic Review* "might have been comic if the implications were not so depressing for the country's future". In just a handful of days, the Phnom Penh-based correspondent went on, Cambodia "witnessed an abortive secession, a failed attempt to establish a provisional government, a royal family feud and the manoeuvres of a prince [Sihanouk] obsessed with avenging his removal from power in a military coup more than 20 years [previously]". The elections gave Funcinpec 45% of the vote, the CPP 38% and the BLDP, 3%. The CPP immediately claimed the results fraudulent, while Prince Norodom Chakrapong – one of Sihanouk's sons – announced the secession of the country's six eastern provinces. Fortunately, both attempts to undermine the election dissolved. The CPP agreed to join Funcinpec in a power sharing agreement while, remarkably, the Khmer Rouge were able to present themselves as defenders of democracy in the face of the CPP's claims of vote-rigging. The new Cambodian constitution was ratified in September 1993, marking the end of UNTAC's involvement in the country. Under the new constitution, Cambodia was to be a pluralistic liberal-democratic country. Seventy-year-old Sihanouk was crowned King of Cambodia, reclaiming the throne he relinquished in 1955. His son Norodom Ranariddh was appointed First Prime Minister and Hun Sen, Second Prime Minister, a situation intended to promote national unity but leading to internal bickering and dissent.

An uncivil society? 1993-1998

Almost from day one of Cambodia's rebirth as an independent state espousing the principles of democracy and the market, cracks began to appear in the rickety structure that underlay these grand ideals. Rampant corruption, infighting among the coalition partners, political intrigue, murder and intimidation all became features of the political landscape – and have remained so to this day. There are three bright spots in an otherwise pretty dismal political landscape. First of all, the Khmer Rouge – along with Pol Pot – is dead and buried. Second, while there have been coups, attempted coups, murder, torture and intimidation, the country does still have an operating political system with an opposition of sorts. And third, the trajectory of change since the last edition of this guide was published has been upwards. But, as the following account shows, politics in Cambodia makes Italy seem a model of stability and common sense.

From the elections of 1993 through to 1998 relations between the two key members of the ruling coalition, the CPP and Funcinpec, went from bad to quite appalling. At the end of 1995 Prince Norodom Sirivudh was arrested for plotting to kill Hun Sen and the prime minister ordered troops and tanks on to the streets of Phnom Penh. For a while the capital had the air of a city under siege. Sirivudh, secretary-general of Funcinpec and King Norodom Sihanouk's half brother, has been a vocal critic of corruption in the government, and a supporter of Sam Rainsy, the country's most outspoken opposition politician and the bane of Hun Sen's life. The National Assembly voted unanimously to suspend Sirivudh's immunity from prosecution. Few

Piseth Pilika

On 6 July 1999 Piseth Pilika, a classical dancer-turned-film star, was gunned down in a crowded Phnom Penh street while shopping with her sister and niece. After two days struggling to survive, Piseth died. Her niece was also shot and left with a shattered arm and a bullet lodged in her spine.

Why a woman trained in such a tranquil art should have died so violently perplexed many Cambodians. Just hours after the shooting, rumours began to circulate that she had been having an affair with a general, a senior policemen, one of Hun Sen's aides. The reality is that in Cambodia it's about US$200 for a high profile person; just US$20 for someone of no account.

Before she died in hospital, Piseth said to her sister: "What have I done wrong? I didn't make any mistakes. I did no harm to anybody. Why?"

After Piseth's death it emerged that the police seemed strangely uninterested in the case. They interviewed no one and even released a statement that they did not expect anyone to be apprehended. A few more diligent local reporters began to investigate Piseth's life and found that she owned property valued at way beyond the means of a mere classical dancer. It seemed she probably did have a rich and powerful lover. One theory was that her lover's wife might have taken out the contract on her life. But other reporters noted that she was due to leave Cambodia for a long tour to France. Perhaps she had broken off the relationship and her jilted lover had called in a hit man to satisfy his honour. Certainly, as Michael Sheridan puts in his article in *The Sunday Times* (25.7.99), her life was full of hope "until the killer came along on the corner of 182 Street and Nou Ram Street, and a dark curtain came down on Piseth's last performance".

commentators really believed that Sirivudh had plotted to kill Hun Sen. Though he had been outspoken, and occasionally rather injudicious in his public remarks, Sirivudh was not seen to be someone who would involve himself in such a serious conspiracy. The assumption, then, was that Hun Sen – a 'notorious bully' in the words of *The Economist* – was merely playing politics Cambodia-style. In the end Hun Sen did not go through with a trial. His half-brother agreed to voluntary exile.

In 1996, relations between the CPP and Funcinpec reached another low. First Prime Minister Prince Norodom Ranariddh joined his two exiled brothers – princes Chakkrapong and Sirivudh – along with Sam Rainsy, in France. Hun Sen smelled a rat and when Ranariddh threatened in May to pull out of the coalition his worries seemed to be confirmed. Only pressure from the outside prevented a meltdown. Foreign donors said that continuing aid was contingent on political harmony, and Asean sent the Malaysian foreign minister to knock a few heads together. A few months later relations became chillier still following the drive-by killing of Hun Sen's brother-in-law as he left a restaurant in Phnom Penh after eating breakfast.

Things, it seemed, couldn't get any worse – but they did. In February 1997 fighting between forces loyal to Ranariddh and Hun Sen broke out in Battambang. March saw a grenade attack on a demonstration led by opposition leader Sam Rainsy outside the National Assembly leaving 16 dead and 150 injured – and Rainsy with minor injuries. In April Hun Sen mounted what became known as the 'soft coup'. This followed a complicated series of defections from Ranariddh's Funcinpec party to the CPP which, after much to-ing and fro-ing overturned Funcinpec's small majority in the National Assembly. In May, Hun Sen's motorcade was attacked and a month later, on 16 June, fighting broke out between Hun Sen and Ranariddh's bodyguards leaving three dead.

It was this gradual decline in relations between the two leaders and their parties which laid the foundations for the coup of 1997.

In July 1997 the stage was set for Cambodia to join the Association of Southeast Asian Nations (Asean) along with Laos and Myanmar (Burma). This would have marked Cambodia's international rehabilitation. Then, just a month before the historic day, on 5-6 June, Hun Sen mounted a coup d'état and ousted Norodom Ranariddh and his party, Funcinpec, from government. It took two days for Hun Sen and his forces to gain full control of the capital. Ranariddh escaped to Thailand while the United Nations Centre for Human Rights reported that 41 senior military officers and Ranariddh loyalists were hunted down in the days following the coup, tortured and executed. In August the National Assembly voted to withdraw Ranariddh's immunity from prosecution. Five months later, in January 1998, United Nations High Commissioner for Human Rights Mary Robinson visited Cambodia and pressed for an investigation into the deaths – a request that Hun Sen rejected as unwarranted interference. Asean, long used to claiming that the Association has no role interfering in domestic affairs, found it had no choice but to defer Cambodia's accession. The coup was widely condemned and on 17 September the UN decided to keep Cambodia's seat vacant in the General Assembly.

Following the coup of 1997 there was some speculation that Hun Sen would simply ignore the need to hold elections scheduled for 26 July. In addition, opposition parties threatened to boycott the elections even if they did occur, claiming that Hun Sen and his henchmen were intent on intimidation. But despite sporadic violence in the weeks and months leading up to the elections, all parties ended up participating. It seems that intense international pressure got to Hun Sen who appreciated that without the goodwill of foreign aid donors the country would simply collapse. Of the 4.9 million votes cast – constituting an impressive 90% of the electorate – Hun Sen's Cambodian People's Party won the largest share at just over 41% while Ranariddh's Funcinpec secured 31.7% of the vote and the Sam Rainsy Party (SRP), 14.3%.

Hun Sen offered to bring Funcinpec and the SRP into a coalition government, but his advances were rejected. Instead Rainsy and Ranariddh encouraged a series of demonstrations and vigils outside the National Assembly – which quickly became known as 'Democracy Square', à la Tianamen Square. At the beginning of September 1998, following a grenade attack on Hun Sen's residence and two weeks of uncharacteristic restraint on the part of the Second Prime Minister, government forces began a crack down on the demonstrators. A week later the three protagonists – Ranariddh, Sam Rainsy and Hun Sen – agreed to talks presided over by King Sihanouk in Siem Reap. These progressed astonishingly well considering the state of relations between the three men and two days later the 122-seat National Assembly opened at Angkor Wat on 24 September. Shortly before the talks, Cambodia's Queen Monineath put forward the suggestion that the three leaders should play more golf together – believing that this might lead to greater co-operation. (Southeast Asian leaders are great believers in the diplomatic powers of golf.) In mid-November further talks (it was not made clear whether these were before, during or after any golf match) between the CPP and Funcinpec led to the formation of a coalition government. Hun Sen became sole prime minister and Ranariddh chairman of the National Assembly. While the CPP and Funcinpec took control of 12 and 11 ministries respectively, with Defence and Interior shared, the CPP got the lion's share of the key portfolios. Sam Rainsy was left on the opposition benches. Even so King Sihanouk could say, before embarking on another round of medical tests in Beijing in November 1998 that "The big political crisis in our country has been solved, the political deadlock is over". It was only after the political détente that followed the elections that Cambodia was given permission to occupy its UN seat in December 1998. At a summit meeting in Hanoi around the same time, Asean also announced that they had agreed on the admission of Cambodia to the grouping – which finally came through on 30 April 1999.

The press and the King

The years since the UN-supervised elections in 1993 have seen, in the eyes of some commentators, a gradual erosion of press freedoms as the government has become becoming increasingly authoritarian. In July 1995 a new press law gave additional powers to a state which has too often resorted to thuggery to convince its opponents. As one observer was quoted as saying in the *Far Eastern Economic Review* at the beginning of 1996, "many people's initial reactions in Cambodia are still violent". At times the sensitivity of politicians has descended into farce. In March 1995, Cambodian newspaper editor Chan Rottana was sentenced to a year in gaol for writing a 'false and defamatory statement' that First Prime Minister Prince Norodom Ranariddh was 'three times more stupid' than Second Prime Minister Hun Sen. In mid-1995 former foreign minister Sam Rainsy summed up the state of political affairs in the country when he said: "If you are satisfied with cosmetics, everything is OK, like some Americans tell me. But if you scratch a little bit below the surface, there is nothing democratic about the government. The parliament is a rubber stamp. The press is being killed ... The judiciary is far from independent."

There is no doubt that by the mid-1990s the job of being a newspaper editor with opposition leanings was becoming increasingly dangerous. In May 1995, the *Khmer Ideal* newspaper was closed down and its publisher fined; in the same month, the editor of *New Liberty* was jailed for a year for penning an editorial entitled 'Nation of thieves', alluding to corruption in government ranks; a week after this, the government began proceedings against the editor of the *Morning News* – a man who was jailed in 1994 for a previous offending article. Human Rights Watch Asia reported that this series of actions "represent one of the most serious assaults yet on freedom of expression". In January 1996 the offices of the opposition Khmer Nation Party were raided by police, and in the following month Ek Mongkol, a radio commentator and Funcinpec member, was shot and seriously injured. In May 1996 anti-government newspaper editor Thun Bunly was gunned down in Phnom Penh and later died. Human Rights Watch reported that in 2003, Chou Chetharith, the deputy editor at royalist radio station, *Ta Prohm*, was shot and killed outside his office after Hun Sen publicly warned the station to stop broadcasting insults directed at the CPP. However, local journalists today claim they have more "press freedom" or as one Khmer journalist aptly put it "the party you are aligned with protects you." Many media outlets depend on financial support from political parties. Not surprisingly, Prime Minister Hun Sen and his allies control several broadcasters. A report by USAID into corruption in 2004 indicated that the media is far from free of bias – politicians will regularly pay journalists to run certain stories and pay them to not run others. It was reported that at the Poipet border, a quagmire of trafficking, corruption and lawlessness, journalists clued up on the pay-offs, regularly gather by the border and wait for officials to come and pay them off for not reporting the terrible border stories.

Most commentators also viewed former King Norodom Sihanouk as part of the problem, simply because he was so revered. He interfered in the political process, changed his mind constantly, and exasperated government ministers. Yet the respect held for him by Cambodians meant that he could not be ignored, or easily contradicted.

Nonetheless, in 1995 the government apparently had a stab at trying to reduce his influence and role. For a start the police confiscated all copies of a booklet entitled *Only the King can save Cambodia* – reputed to call for the return of King Sihanouk to politics. But this council consists of a myriad of competing factions.

In 1996 William Shawcross returned to Cambodia and spent two hours with Sihanouk. The former King "was his usual charming and voluble self", Shawcross wrote of the meeting, "offering Tattinger champagne and chocolates". But he was also, apparently, a saddened man as he watched his country lurch from crisis to crisis. Sihanouk explained to Shawcross: "I am like a piece of ham in a sandwich, but not a delicious sandwich like those created by Lord Sandwich. I'm stuck instead between the government and the opposition. I am very miserable. Very, very miserable. I would like to conciliate. I cannot. I cannot reunite the two sides. My hope for Cambodia to become one of the world's most advanced liberal democracies is finished" (*The New York Review*, 14 November 1996).

After countless threats, on October 7, 2004, King Sihanouk abdicated; requesting by letter that all "compatriots please allow him [sic] to retire". Sihanouk's long-time battle with cancer was cited as his motivation. It is said that a fortune teller once predicted that he would not live past his 74th birthday, so he was already defying the odds. On his website the King explained: "My abdication allows me to give our country, our nation and our people a serious opportunity to avoid mortal turmoil the day after my death."

On October 14, the Cambodian Throne Council selected Prince Norodom Sihamoni to succeed Sihanouk as King. King Norodom Sihamoni officially ascended the throne in a coronation ceremony held on October 29.

Even though Cambodia's constitution, states that the king officially reigns as head of state but does not govern, Sihanouk king never stayed far from politics. Unlike his father, Sihamoni has no background in politics or appears likely to head that way. Instead, the new King is renowned for his ballet-dancing prowess, having trained as a ballet dancer in Prague in the 1970s. He later studied film in North Korea and served as Cambodia's envoy to the UNESCO in Paris.

Sihanouk, based in Beijing in 2005, continued to prove that out of sight wasn't out of mind, retaining an omnipresent voice in the Cambodian arena. Having tried his hand as author, film maker, song writer, actor, and of course king, the serial multi-tasker, Sihanouk assumed a new hobby, blogging.

A return to some kind of normality

1997 was the low point in Cambodia's stuttering return to a semblance of normality. The Asian economic crisis combined with the coup (see above) to rock the country back on its heels. On 3 February 2002 free, fair and only modestly violent local commune elections (the number killed were down from close to 400 to 'just' 20 in the latest elections) were held. The CPP won the vote by a landslide and although there is little doubt that Hun Sen's party used a bit of muscle here and there, foreign election observers decided that the result reflected the will of the 90 per cent of the electorate who voted. The CPP, despite its iron grip on power, does recognize that democracy means it has to get out there and make a case. Around one third of the CPP's more unpopular commune chiefs were replaced prior to the election. Funcinpec did badly, unable to shake off the perception that it sold out its principles to join the coalition in 1998. The opposition Sam Rainsy Party did rather better, largely for the same reason: the electorate viewed it as standing up to the might of the CPP, highlighting corruption and abuses of power.

In July 2002 Hun Sen took on the rotating chairmanship of Asean and used a round of high-profile meetings to demonstrate to the region, and the wider world, just how far the country has come. Hun Sen, who hardly has an enviable record as a touchy-feely politician, used the chairmanship of Asean to polish his own as well as his country's credentials in the arena of international public opinion. But despite the PR some Cambodians are concerned that Hun Sen is becoming a little like Burma's Ne Win. Like Ne Win, Hun Sen would seem to be obsessed with numbers. His lucky number is 9; in 2002 he brought the local elections forward by three weeks so that the digits in the date would add up to 9. Worrying for a prime minister. In 2001 Hun Sen closed down all Cambodia's karaoke bars; fine if he was closing down drug dens, but karaoke bars? With over 20 years as prime minister there is no one to touch Hun Sen and he seems to revel in his strongman reputation. Judges bow to his superior knowledge of the judicial system; kings and princes acknowledged his unparalleled role in appointing the new king; many journalists are in thrall to his power. Hun Sen once said to foreign monitors that "international standards exist only in sports". (*The Economist*, 2.5.2002). If even the most fundamental of rights are negotiable then it would seem that only Cambodia's dependence on foreign largesse constrains his wilder impulses.

Compared to its recent past, the last 10 years has been a period of relative stability for Cambodia. However, political violence and infighting between parties continues to be a major problem.

In early 2002, Cambodia was embarking on a process of political decentralization. Also, not free from political violence were Cambodia's first commune elections, held in February 2002. By international standards the elections were borderline unacceptable, however most of the major parties were reasonably satisfied with the results, which resulted in a landslide victory for Hun Sen.

The 2003 election wasn't smooth-sailing either. Prior to the June 2003 election the alleged instructions given by representatives of the CPP to government controlled election monitoring organizations were: "If we win by the law, then we win. If we lose by the law, we still must win."

Nonetheless a political deadlock arose, when the CPP won a majority of votes but not the two-thirds required under the constitution to govern alone. The incumbent CPP-led administration assumed power and took on a caretaker role, pending the creation of a coalition which would satisfy the required number of National Assembly seats to form government. Without a functioning legislature, the course of vital legislation was stalled. After almost a year-long stalemate, the National Assembly approved a controversial addendum to the constitution, which allowed a new government to be formed by vote. The vote took place on July 15, and the National Assembly approved a new coalition government, an amalgam of the CPP and FUNCINPEC, with Hun Sen at the helm as Prime Minister and Prince Norodom Ranariddh as President of the National Assembly.

The government's democratic principles came under fire once again in February 2005, when opposition leader Sam Rainsy, fled the country after losing his parliamentary immunity from prosecution. Rainsy's perceived as somewhat of a threat due to his slow, gaining audience with young urban dwellers whose growing disenchantment with the current government he feeds off. On the one hand, his keep the bastards' honest style of politics has added a new dimension of accountability into Cambodian politics, but on the other, his nationalist, racist rantings, particularly the anti-Vietnamese sentiments, could be a very bad thing for the country. In May, 2005 Hun Sen said that Sam Rainsy would have to wait until the "next life" before he would guarantee his safety.

The lingering death of the Khmer Rouge

What many outsiders found hard to understand was how the Khmer Rouge enjoyed such popular support among Cambodians – even after the massacres and torture. UN officials working in Phnom Penh in 1992 and 1993 found this disquieting. In June 1994, the retiring Australian ambassador to Cambodia, John Holloway, in a leaked account of his 2½ years in Phnom Penh wrote: "I was alarmed in a recent dialogue with about 100 students from different groups at the University of Phnom Penh to hear them espousing a return to government by the Khmer Rouge... They estimated that 60% of the student body favoured Khmer Rouge participation in government... It is necessary for outsiders to understand, that for most Cambodians, the Vietnamese are a far more traumatic issue than the Khmer Rouge."

The Khmer Rouge was not, of course, just a political force. Its political influence was backed up and reinforced by military muscle. And it has been the defeat of the Khmer Rouge as an effective fighting force which seems to have delivered the fatal blow to its political ambitions.

In mid-1994 the National Assembly outlawed the Khmer Rouge, offering a six month amnesty to rank and file guerrillas. By the time the six months was up in January

1995, 7,000 Khmer Rouge had reportedly defected to the government, leaving at that time somewhere between 5,000 and 6,000 hardcore rebels still fighting. A split in this core group can be dated to 8 August 1996 when Khmer Rouge radio announced that former 'brother number two', Ieng Sary, had betrayed the revolution by embezzling money earned from mining and timber contracts, and branded him a traitor.

This was the first evidence available to western commentators that a significant split in the Khmer Rouge had occurred. In retrospect, it seems that the split had been brewing for some years – ever since the UN-sponsored elections had revealed a division between 'conservatives' and 'moderates'. The latter, apparently, wished to co-operate with the UN, while the former group desired to boycott the elections. In 1996 the moderate faction, headed by Ieng Sary, finally broke away from the conservatives led by Pol Pot and hardman General Ta Mok. Hun Sen announced soon after the radio broadcast in August 1996 that two Khmer Rouge commanders, Ei Chhien and Sok Pheap had defected to the government. At the end of September Ieng Sary held a press conference to declare his defection. He told an incredulous audience that he "had nothing to do with ordering the execution of anyone, or even the suggestion of it". On 14 September King Norodom Sihanouk granted Ieng Sary a royal pardon.

The Cambodian government's conciliatory line towards Ieng Sary seemed perplexing given the man's past. Although he cast himself in the mould of 'misguided and ignorant revolutionary', there are few who doubt that he was fully cognizant of what the Khmer Rouge under Pol Pot were doing even if, as Michael Vickery argues, he was not Brother Number Two, just Brother Number Four or Five. Indeed he has admitted as much in the past. Not only is he, as a man, thoroughly unpleasant – or so those who know him have said – but he was also a key figure in the leadership and was sentenced to death in absentia by the Phnom Penh government. Stephen Heder of London's School of Oriental & African Studies was quoted as saying after the September press conference: "It's totally implausible that Ieng Sary was unaware that people were being murdered [by the Khmer Rouge]". This was confirmed in October 1996 when Laurence Piq, formerly married to Suong Sikoeun an aide to Ieng Sary, wrote: "As in The Little Red Riding Hood, the hand he [Ieng Sary] extends for photographs is the better to grab you with. The jovial demeanour he affixes to his mouth is the better to bite you with. The red carpet is laid out. Abominable crimes are being erased. All shame is swallowed. The world's nations accept this under the pretext of peace. What kind of peace? A peace à la Khmer Rouge, dripping with the blood of genocide." The split in the Khmer Rouge and the defection of Ieng Sary deprived the Khmer Rouge of 3,000-5,000 men – halving its fighting force – and also denied the group important revenues from key gem mining areas around Pailin and many of the richest forest concessions.

The disintegration of the Khmer Rouge continued in 1997 after a complicated deal involving Pol Pot, Khieu Samphan, Son Sen and Ta Mok, as well as members of Funcinpec, collapsed. In early June Khieu Samphan, the nominal leader of the Khmer Rouge, was thought to be on the verge of brokering an agreement with Funcinpec that would give Pol Pot and two of his henchmen (Son Sen and Ta Mok) immunity from prosecution. This would then provide the means by which Khieu Samphan might enter mainstream Cambodian politics. It seems that Hun Sen, horrified at the idea of an alliance between Khieu Samphan and Funcinpec, mounted the coup of June 1997 to prevent the deal coming to fruition (see above). Pol Pot was also, apparently, less than satisfied with the terms of the agreement and pulled out – killing Son Sen in the process. But before Pol Pot could flee, Ta Mok captured his erstwhile leader on June 19th at the Khmer Rouge stronghold of Anlong Veng.

A little more than a month later the 'Trial of the Century' began in this remote jungle hideout. It was a show trial more like a Cultural Revolution lynching. A crowd of a few hundred people were on hand to shout slogans like 'Crush, crush, crush Pol Pot and his clique'. Pol Pot offered the usual Khmer Rouge defence: the revolution made mistakes, but its leaders were inexperienced. And, in any case, they saved Cambodia

from annexation by Vietnam. (There is an argument purveyed by some academics
that the Khmer Rouge was essentially involved in a programme of ethnic cleansing aimed at ridding Cambodia of all Vietnamese and Vietnamese influences.) Show trial or not, few people had any sympathy for Pol Pot as he was sentenced by the Khmer Rouge 'people's' court to life imprisonment for the murder of Son Sen. A Khmer Rouge radio station broadcast that with Pol Pot's arrest and sentencing, a 'dark cloud' had been lifted from the Cambodian people.

Confirmation of this bizarre turn of events emerged in mid-October when journalist Nate Thayer of the *Far Eastern Economic Review* became the first journalist to interview Pol Pot since 1979. He reported that the former Khmer Rouge leader was "very ill and perhaps close to death". Even more incredibly than Ieng Sary's defence, Pol Pot denied that the Cambodian genocide had ever occurred and told Nate Thayer that his 'conscience was clear'. "I came to carry out the struggle, not to kill people", he said, adding "Even now, and you can look at me, am I a savage person?".

In March 1998 reports filtered out of the jungle near the Thai border that the Khmer Rouge was finally disintegrating in mutinous conflict. The end game was at hand. The government's amnesty encouraged the great bulk of the Khmer Rouge's remaining fighters to lay down their arms and in December 1998 the last remnants of the rebel army surrendered to government forces, leaving just a handful of men under hardman 'The Butcher' Ta Mok still at large. But even Ta Mok's days of freedom were numbered. In March 1999 he was captured near the Thai border and taken back to Phnom Penh.

The death of Pol Pot

On 15 April 1998 unconfirmed reports stated that Pol Pot – a man who ranks with Hitler, Stalin and Mao in his ability to kill – had died in a remote jungle hideout in the north of Cambodia. Given that Pol Pot's death had been announced several times before, the natural inclination among journalists and commentators was to treat these reports with scepticism. But it was already known that Pol Pot was weak and frail and his death was confirmed when journalists were invited to view his body the following day. Pol Pot was reported to have died from a heart attack. He was 73.

Amnesty and the long-awaited trial?

The question of what to do with Ieng Sary (see above) was the start of a long debate over how Cambodia – and the international community – should deal with former members of the Khmer Rouge. The pragmatic, realist line is that if lasting peace is to come to Cambodia, then it may be necessary to allow some people to get away with – well – murder. As one western diplomat pondered: "Do you owe fealty to the dead for the living?" This would seem to be Hun Sen's preferred position.

By late 1998, with the apparent end of the Khmer Rouge as a fighting force, the government seemed happy to welcome back the rank and file into mainstream Cambodian life – and even into the armed forces – while putting on trial key characters in the Khmer Rouge like Ta Mok, Khieu Samphan and Nuon Chea. While the government was considering what to do, former leaders of the Khmer Rouge were busy trying to rehabilitate their muddied reputations. Khieu Samphan, 67 years old in 1998, when he was asked at a news conference whether he had any regrets replied "Yes", adding that he was "sorry, very sorry". Nuon Chea, 71 years old in 1998, also offered an apology at the same press conference, but in his case for the death of animals rather than people when he said that "they died because we wanted to win the war". Khieu Samphan suggested "Let bygones be bygones". Other apologists for the Khmer Rouge offered the argument that the group had tried to protect Cambodia against invasion by the Vietnamese.

Most of the key figures in the Khmer Rouge, if they are not dead, are either abroad or living – openly – pretty comfortable lives around the country, particularly Pailin, which was given amnesty. Take Ieng Sary, for example, former Khmer Rouge foreign minister and deputy prime minister. He lives in a reasonably large house in Pailin, where his son is governor. His side-kicks Nuon Chea, Brother Number Two and Khieu Samphan, who held several senior positions including that of PM and party president, also live in comfortable cottage style houses outside of Pailin, with mod cons like washing machines.

A funny sort of justice. While Hun Sen might have desired to sidestep a messy trial, the international community and, more significantly, the mass of the Cambodian people have always thought otherwise. Public opinion in Cambodia, it seems, was firmly against letting the remaining Khmer Rouge leaders off the hook after they had played such an important part in the deaths of perhaps two million Cambodians. Particularly galling was the manner in which Hun Sen seemed to welcome Samphan and Chea back to Phnom Penh, more as visiting dignitaries than mass murderers.

In March 1999, the UN released the report of legal experts appointed to consider the issue. Their original advice: appoint an international tribunal, sitting outside Cambodia, to try the 20-30 most senior Khmer Rouge leaders. They recommended a trial outside Cambodia because, as they put it, "Cambodia still lacks a culture of respect for an impartial criminal justice system". But the government rejected any idea of a trial in another country.

It was not until July 2001 that Cambodia's politicians finally passed legislation in the National Assembly that – in theory – would lead to a tribunal being set up to try the Khmer Rouge leaders. The legal text agreed between Cambodia and the UN states that the Tribunal is expected 'to bring to trial senior leaders of Democratic Kampuchea and those who were most responsible for the serious crimes and violations of Cambodian penal law, international humanitarian law and custom, and international conventions recognised by Cambodia that were committed during the period' from April 17 1975 to January 6 1979.' The legislation was signed into law by the king in August. The tribunal will be held in Cambodia but, as the key foreign players have always insisted, it will also cooperate with the UN. UN-appointed as well as Cambodian judges will preside over the court. This critical element in the make-up of the court was the main sticking point, holding proceedings back. After years of negotiations, the UN and Cambodian Government came to an agreement. The compromise is far from satisfactory. In particular critics highlight the lack of experience of Cambodian judges. The tribunal is to be made up of Cambodian and foreign prosecutors and judges, with Cambodians in the majority. Decisions will require a vote of a majority plus one. One source of comfort, however, is the stipulation that in any majority ruling there must be at least one international judge.

The long-awaited tribunal is nigh. It is seven years since Cambodia formally requested assistance to trial the Khmer Rouge leaders. (The ratification of the agreement between the UN and the government to create the tribunal was in October 2004.) The commencement of the tribunal has been fraught with all kinds of obstacles and political stalling. Under a veil of secrecy, in May 2005, the government selected a shortlist of 31 judges for the Khmer Rouge tribunal. As per usual, this was laden with cronyism, many critics complaining that the majority of judges were politically biased – one was described as part of Hun Sen's "iron fist"; another ordered the eviction of hundreds of families in Poipet, resulting in the death of five, and many others, simply had no training.

Another hurdle was encountered when the cost of proceedings, tipped at $US56.3 million, to be shared jointly by the UN and the Cambodian government, fell short when the government reneged on its agreement to contribute US$13.3 million, claiming it could only meet $US1.5 million of its agreed amount. At the time of publication, in June 2005, Deputy Prime Minister, Sok An was appealing to the international community to cover the gap. In 2005, the tribunal was mired until the government's share of the funding was met.

Journalist, James Pringle, one of the first journalists to visit Cambodia after the Khmer Rouge's demise in 1979 wrote in the *Cambodia Daily* in 2005 that the Khmer Rouge tribunal could possibly be influenced "by the current Hun Sen regime and its ruling Cambodian People's Party, a number of whose leaders - like 54-year-old Hun Sen himself - are former Khmer Rouge. The CPP Party President, Chea Sim, one of Cambodia's most powerful men, was an eastern zone district party secretary in the Khmer Rouge and some analysts say such officials were key figures in killings throughout the country." The tribunal was scheduled to start in 2005 but will more than likely be stalled until 2006. It is expected to run for three years.

There are a number of inherent problems at hand, firstly, the fear, is that those to be trialled might die before the proceedings begin, the most senior, Nuon Chea, Brother No. 2, was believed to have been the most powerful official after Pol Pot and is in reasonably poor health. Secondly, the tribunal will only trial seven - eight pivotal players, while those responsible for the thousands of executions will be living freely amongst the families of their victims. Understandably, it is impossible (and unfair) to trial all involved, but still many Cambodian's may, personally, feel like justice hasn't been served, when they are living amongst murderers.

The tribunal is an undoubtedly a good thing. If nothing else, it will serve to educate people about the history of what happened. The level of awareness and comprehensive understanding, amongst young people today, is surprisingly low. Many parents do not discuss the Khmer Rouge period with their children and the period is not taught as part of the school curriculum. One 20-something worker, upon being told that they Khmer Rouge weren't Vietnamese but actually Khmer, responded poignantly "I don't believe that the Khmer Rouge were Cambodian. I know that Cambodians would never, ever do that to one another. Why would Cambodians do that to that to each other? Never."

Cambodia became the first Southeast Asian country to ratify the Rome Statute of the International Criminal Court in 2002. In June 2003, Prime Minister Hun Sen agreed to a bilateral immunity agreement with the U.S. that exempts U.S. citizens from the authority of the court, which is expected to be approved by National Assembly.

At the beginning of January 2002 the Prime Minister said that the time for justice had arrived – in 2005 the victims of the Khmer Rouge were still patiently waiting.

Economy

A briefing on Cambodia's economy published in mid-1999 in the *Far Eastern Economic Review* offered the view that "for Cambodia, it's deemed progress simply when things aren't falling apart". But looking back on the period since 1993 and the UN-supervised elections, this might seem rather too downbeat. On paper at least the economy has been fairly buoyant – except, that is, for 1998. Between 1995 and 1998 the economy grew by around 5.6% per year –a very reasonable response when one considers the political turmoil the country was experiencing. This changed following the coup in 1997. Foreign donors cut off assistance and in 1998 economic growth was zero. (The Asian economic crisis also played a role.) Furthermore, even while the economy was growing many people were suffering. Henry Kamm in an article in *The New York Review* entitled 'The Cambodian Calamity' provided a tellingly different picture from the one painted by economists: "Today's Cambodia is a basket case. It is a country that hardly nourishes and barely teaches its ever-increasing population, nor does it bind its multiple wounds or cure its many ills. In large measure its workers are exploited, its women ill-used, its children unprotected, its soil studded with treacherous land mines primed to kill."

But like Kamm's view of Cambodian politics there is more than a grain of truth in this dismal picture. In total, life for Cambodians has been slowly improving. In the late

90s economic growth picked up again, GDP growing on average 6.8% between 1999 and 2002. Many economists credit this growth to significant aid flows and a bilateral trade agreement with the US in 1996. However, everything is not rosy on the horizon. Following the country's economic peak of 10.8% GDP growth in 1999, the economic indicators have started to fall. GDP expanded by 5% in 2000, 5.3% in 2001 and 5.2% in 2003. Thankfully the World Bank reforecast its figures in late 2005, saying the country's growth will probably be more like 6.1%. Another issue in the country's economic development is tax collection and revenue generation. In 2004 the revenue to GDP ratio of 12.0%, with tax revenues accounting for only 8.4% of GDP, was noted by the IMF, as among the lowest in the world. Inequality and poverty remain very much part of Cambodia's human development landscape.

Unfortunately, there is no evidence that this tortured country is going to emerge from the chrysalis as Asia's next tiger economy. The challenges facing the Cambodian government as it tries to improve the lot of one of the world's most abused populations are manifold. Floods in 2000 and 2001 undermined agricultural production; in 2004-2005 the country suffered from a drought which severely affected crop production, in particular rice yields, foreign investment remains desultory as the country struggles to compete with its Asian neighbours, tax revenues are stunted because so many of the wealthy and well-connected can simply by-pass the authorities; and the country remains overly dependent on foreign assistance.

Economic progress, of sorts

1989 was a turning point for Cambodia. When the Vietnamese troops pulled out in September, the economy was in a sorry state. Hanoi had done what it could to restore some semblance of order after the mess left by the Khmer Rouge in 1979. But, with the collapse of the Soviet Union, aid from Moscow and its erstwhile Eastern Bloc allies dried up. This deprived Phnom Penh of about US$100mn a year. The Hun Sen government also faced a total aid and trade boycott from the west, while the civil war against the resistance factions further sapped the regime's scant resources. But the Phnom Penh regime gradually shifted away from orthodox Communist ideology and central planning towards market economics. At first this was nothing more than paper policy, but deregulation and reform began to spark an upsurge in business activity.

Before, during and immediately after the elections of 1993, the economy was in dire straits. The value of the riel collapsed against the US dollar, inflation reached 340%, provincial towns were crowded with people subsisting by recycling rubbish or begging, and foreign investors were shying away from a country so wracked by manifold problems. This situation began to improve during 1993. Inflation declined from 100% in 1993 to 20% by the end of 1994 and had reached 4-5% by mid-1996. Today it is stable. Furthermore, foreign investors began to pluck up courage and put their money in the country. Malaysian, Singaporean, Thai, Taiwanese and other Asian companies were in the vanguard of this investment modest tide.

The government's intention has been to try and entice labour intensive manufacturing enterprises to set up shop in Cambodia. In August 1994 the National Assembly passed a new investment law to make the country enticing to foreign business interests, including tax exemption on profits for eight years and allowing foreign investors to hold 100% equity. The real success story on the manufacturing side was Cambodia's garment industry (although anti-globalization activists would not see it as such). The garment sector in 2000 contributed 70% of the country's exports and continued to absorb the lion's share of manufacturing investment upto 2005. However to date most investment has been concentrated in the service sector. There has been property speculation, and hotels, bars and restaurants have been going up at the rate of knots around Phnom Penh, Sihanoukville and in Siem Reap. The increasing value of property has helped spur on one of the government's favourite games, the "great land grab" government but they aren't the only ones gravitating to the dollar. At the beginning of the country's emergence as a destination for foreign investment Grant Evans, writing in *The Far Eastern Economic Review* noted that businessmen "have descended on the country like locusts in the atmosphere of frontier, tax-free capitalism. A few dollars trickle down to the Khmer."

In 2004, Cambodia joined Nepal as the first developing states to be admitted as members to the World Trade Organization.

Speed humps bar the high road

By 2005 the country's progress was not looking good. The amount of people living below the international dollar-a-day poverty line had risen, from 36% (2002) to 40% (2004). Infant mortality had increased since 1991, as had the adult illiteracy rate. Income disparity between rich and poor had widened to a gaping chasm.

Over half of Cambodian children are underweight. UNICEF reporting that 45% of Cambodian children are malnourished; 66% do not have access to safe water, and less than half the girls who enter primary school finish sixth grade. Though, they warned, the statistics were gathered from visits to district hospitals and clinics, so only represent the one third of the population with access to the medical system. Sadly, the clichéd images from the aid agencies advertisements - the children with distended tummies, flies festering around their mouths, scampering around for a cup of questionable water - are still unfortunately a large reality in Cambodia.

Cambodia ranked 130 out of 177 countries in the 2004 UNDP human development index. The country's public health indicators are rated among the worst in the world, and well below regional standards. The average Cambodian will only live to 57 years, about 13 years less than the Southeast Asian average. The country's infrastructure is still in dire straights. The electrification rate is one of the lowest outside sub-Saharan Africa; 1.9% of Cambodians have access to a telephone and the roads, are possibly the least developed in the region.

In April, 2005, Peter Leuprecht, Special Representative of the Secretary-General for human rights, stated to the 61st Session of the Commission on Human Rights stated: "For the majority of Cambodians poverty has not been reduced. Most of the population is clustered around the poverty line. A growing number of people who have nothing to lose are a leaven of unrest in any society".

And the forecast isn't good. The National Institute of Statistics (NIS) suggested that the inflation rate may further increase (between 2003 and 2004 it rose by 4.1%) and economic growth was forecast to slump to between 1.9-2.4%, from the strong growth of 6% it had enjoyed since 2003. Though a more optimistic forecast was delivered in late 2005 to around 6.1%

This depressing economic prediction is largely due to the elimination of the quota system in January 2005, which protected the Cambodian garment industry from foreign competition. At the time, the garment sector was the country's largest export market accounting for 80% of all exports. The industry employed some 230,000 -300,000 workers officially (possibly double unofficially) and generated $US1.5 billion income annually. In January-February 2005, the *Phnom Penh Post* reported that, 12 garment factories closed and a further 24 suspended operations, causing more than 20,000 job losses. The pressure on the garment factories has had a trickle-down effect and those workers not rendered unemployed bore the brunt of cost-cutting as either their 'piece work' rate was reduced (the income paid for each item produced) or work conditions and rights were diminished. The unions, somewhat sympathetic with the plight of the factories and sensing an imminent crisis, requested the workers remain compliant and not protest, to ensure stability prevailed in the factories and no other buyers were frightened off. Many remain optimistic that even though larger markets, such as the US, may opt out, others will stick with the Cambodian garment industry on an ethical "best practices" basis as opposed to supporting the slave-like labour, of a cheaper counterpart i.e. China.

Cambodia – the biggest minefield in the world

Thanks to free-flowing supplies of military hardware to rebel factions throughout the 1980s, Cambodia became the most heavily mined war zone in the world. When UNTAC supervised Cambodia's elections in 1993 there were thought to be around 10 million mines, mostly concentrated in the northwest province of Battambang (a Khmer Rouge stronghold) as well as countless thousands more planted close to the main roads. But statistics on the likely number of mines are irrelevant. Far more meaningful is the total area of land which cannot be used for anything because of the threat of mines. The Cambodian Mine Action Center reported in 2004 that 3,073 distinct areas, totalling over 4,500 square kilometres were contaminated with mines and unexploded ordinance (UXO). This far-reaching problem is believed to affect over 42% of Cambodian villages, depriving 22% of the affected population of agricultural land, 15% of housing land and 12% of access to a water resource. It is not unusual to see little red landmine flags a hop, skip and jump away from villagers' homes and local authorities estimate that 5,186,770 Cambodians are at risk.

In 2003, one in every 236 Cambodians (more than 40,000 people) was an amputee, compared to one in 22,000 in the US, the highest proportion of any country in the world. Between 1979 and 2005, the Cambodia Red Cross and Handicap International registered over 60,000 mine/UXO casualties. Every month, more people are added to the list of victims. In 1993, an Australian Red Cross doctor said Cambodia's most obvious characteristic of national identity is the one-legged man.

A number of charities have been set up, where Cambodian craftsmen are trained to make cheap and simple prostheses, and many amputees have now been fitted with artificial limbs. UN troops, as well as private companies – such as the British-based charity, the Halo Trust – have been involved in delicate mine-clearance operations since 1990. At the beginning of 1995 the first Mine Awareness Day was declared. The most common mine in Cambodia is the Soviet-made PMN-2 mine, which mine clearance experts say guarantees above-the-knee amputation if triggered. Initially, it was thought that ridding

The massive job losses anticipated from the garment sector aside, the Cambodian government has a larger unemployment crisis looming. Cambodia's current population of over 13 million is comprised of more than 50% who are under the age of 20. Each year, between 250,000- 300,000 people leave school or reach the age to look for a job. Considering that approximately 35,000 new jobs are created annually, many of which were in the garment sector, this presents a major problem. The Economic Institute of Cambodia (EIC) estimates that more than half a million young people will migrate from rural to urban areas during the next four years. It said: "one must question the ability of Cambodia's economy to absorb the new entrants into the labour market and hence get prepared to see an additional 1 million unemployed or underemployed people". Even at best case scenario, where 40,000 jobs-per-year are created from anticipated growth in the tourism and service industries, there will still be a shortfall of jobs by over 75-80%. This level of unemployment, potentially, has huge implications for the society as a whole, and could fuel a whole array of already existing social problems. One must wonder, considering there is no imminent threat to Cambodia, if the government's introduction of conscription law in September 2004, was a way to ease the burden?

Cambodia of land mines would take a century. In an attempt to speed up the de-mining process new technologies were introduced. The MV1O3C, for example, is a US$1 mn Swedish-built, 45-tonne monster which rumbles a carbide steel roller along in front of it, gouging out mines in its path. Cheaper and nimbler are the dogs trained to respond to the vapour that explosives give off, dropping prone to the ground with their noses – in theory – a foot or two away from the offending hardware. Though dogs are cheap, and unlike metal detectors don't get side-tracked by bits of scrap metal, de-miners worry what would happen if an animal loses concentration on the job or just gets out on the wrong side of its basket. Nonetheless, experts now believe that de-mining Cambodia will 'only' take 20-30 years. While there were thought to be 10 million mines in 1993 the figure being quoted at the end of 1998 was 5-6 million.

Of course since the high-profile involvement of Princess Diana, mines have become front page news. In 1997 the Ottawa Convention banned its signatories (120 at the end of 2001, and growing) from the use, production, stockpiling, sale and purchase of landmines but, to their shame, the US, Russia and China have not signed up to the convention. Between them these three countries are sitting on a stock of 186 million land mines. The total figure for the world is estimated by the International Campaign to Ban Landmines (ICBL) at 240 million. This may seem a stunningly large figure, but it is coming down as new signatories to the convention destroy their stockpiles. Even so, the ICBL estimates that 15,000 people still become victims of land mines each year in about 90 countries. More than a few of these are in Cambodia.

Ba Bun Ra, a 29year-old amputee and victim of a mine blast, is well aware of the challenges that face him: "I forgot my early dreams... I no longer have the capacity..." he was quoted as saying in 1994. Mines are the perfect weapon in a long war of attrition. They are designed not to kill, but to maim and thereby consume enemy resources in the evacuation, first aid, rehabilitation and then support of the man, woman, girl or boy affected. Mines create dependants and, in turn, tend to create poverty.

The law states that all males between 18-30 years of age must undertake compulsory military service for 18 months.

On the lighter side, the tourism sector has good prospects, with progressive growth and continual expansion; 1 million international tourists visited Cambodia in 2004 representing a 41% growth on the previous year. As a result, the service sector increased by 9.2% in 2004 and is expected to continue growing.

The Economist begged the question (17/2/2005) – "How can Cambodia have so little to show for over a decade of reconstruction and development, costing roughly $400m a year in international aid?" One of the explanations offered is bad governance. Governance, a buzz word of the development world, is seen to underpin all efforts geared towards poverty alleviation and the Cambodian government still has a long way to come in its pursuit of good governance.

Corruption in Cambodia is old hat. These days one would only be shocked to read that the government hadn't been misappropriating funds and budget allocation was kosher. The perpetual rhetoric of donors, slating the government graft and mostly, empty threats of repercussion, has become nothing more than dull background noise, both to the wider audience and, one imagines, to the Cambodian government.

To a certain degree, endemic corruption is now part of the cultural fabric. Citizens are exposed to corruption from a very early age, with reports that 53% of total bribes are paid to schools to ensure children get a good education (or at least falsified documents that say that they have). Low paid government officials will whack on a bribe, similar to tax, for the wide array of services offered. Most of the police or fire department will negotiate their bribes at the scene of an emergency before taking action, as will many doctors and nurses before administering treatment. It is estimated that the average Cambodian is required to pay around 2% of their income in bribes.

The graft, permeating every sector of society, has never really been sustainable but by 2005 had reached such epic proportions that most of the government and donor's broader development goals, including most of the Millenium Development Goals, looked like an impossible dream. In 2004, 80% of businesses reported paying bribes, accounting for an average 5.2% of their gross revenue. This is double the figures of Bangladesh, Pakistan, or China, all notorious for corruption. According to Private Sector Forum, about US$120 million is paid under-the-table from the manufacturing and service industries.

The corruption goes from being outright wrong to ridiculously obscene. In 2004, USAID estimated the annual diversions due to corruption to be between US$300-500 million, well over 50% of the overall aid budget. The incessant stealing from the poor to give to the rich makes taking candy from a baby look tender. In one such case in 2003-2004, the government stole and sold 400 metric tonnes of rice, worth an estimated $US2 million dollars, from the World Food Programme, the largest supplier of food aid in Cambodia. As a result the organization, charged with distributing food rations to the poor, suspended its operations for a year until the government agreed to pay back, in part, the money for the provisions they pilfered. James Wolfensohn, former president of the World Bank, said the Cambodian government's top three priorities should be "fighting corruption, fighting corruption, fighting corruption".

At a foundation level, government corruption in Cambodia is spurred on by large levels of impunity and a poor legal system. An epithet frequently used to describe Cambodia is lawless. Laws exist, in theory, but rule of law and access to justice is routinely denied. The judicial system lacks independence and is rotten to the core with corruption. Cambodia's legal system is considered one of the most corrupt in the region, primarily because the judiciary is so closely controlled by the executive. Over 80% of the firms interviewed in a World Bank survey in 2004, perceived the judiciary negatively stating it was either "never" fair or "seldom" fair.

In March 2005, the *Phnom Penh Post* reported that on the same day, in the same court, Hun Sen's nephew received an 18-month jail sentence (under the watchful eye of the international community) for his role in the shooting of two people (and the death of another), while a poor labourer, who stole just over US$0.50 was given four years in jail. This is all only unusual in the sense that more often than not the rich get off scot free. The poor are highly discriminated against in the legal system, in part, because the average Cambodian can't afford to pay the judge's standard kickback of US$357.50.

Even the Cambodian Bar Association, an organization normally considered the cornerstone of any fair judicial system, was not free from government tampering. Prior to the Bar Association election in November 2004, Prime Minister Hun Sen and his CPP crony posse, none of whom were trained lawyers, were admitted to the Bar. The election resulted in a legal aid lawyer fairly elected as president, only to have the Appeals Court overturn the results and order, a CPP supporter, to assume the position until another election could be held.

It is a sad, but understandable indictment of affairs, when the average Cambodian has absolutely no faith in country's police or judicial system, with many now preferring to take justice into their own hands. Vigilantism is rife and it's not uncommon for thieves to be bludgeoned to death by disgruntled citizens fed up with the escalating crime rate and lack of justice.

Cambodia's recent human rights record doesn't look particularly promising either. In April, 2005 Peter Leuprecht, Special Representative of the Secretary-General for human rights in Cambodia, stated to the 61st Session of the Commission on Human Rights: "We all prefer to convey and to receive good rather than bad news...Sometimes I felt there was some light at the end of the Cambodian tunnel, and I reported accordingly. I regret to say that this time I have little good news to report." Free-wielding government officials widely use violence and intimidation as a tool to censor public demonstrations, citizens and politicians critical of or non compliant with the government. Between 1999 and 2005 it was reported that 30 opposition Sam Rainsy Party members had been killed.

It's more than a little hypocritical that the self-professed democratic government effectively outlawed public demonstrations in January 2003. Human Rights Watch reported that during 2004, authorities banned, dispersed, or intervened during at least 16 public demonstrations in Phnom Penh, sometimes using excessive or disproportionate force.

Due to the government's policy of granting large-spread land concessions, the frightening issue of land-grabbing has also spread like wildfire across the country – from the northeastern province of Ratanakiri through to the coastline of Sihanoukville. In March 2005, plans to build a new casino in Poipet required the bloody eviction of hundreds of families in order to secure the land. Five people were killed and many more arrested and tortured. The *Cambodia Daily* interviewed Ieng Saroueun, who had been imprisoned and tortured after being evicted from his home. He said: "I don't know why they (the police and military police) arrested me....They said to me I exploited human rights, but I don't understand." Unfortunately this black irony is no laughing matter in Cambodia.

The land-grabbing is due, largely, to the widespread practice of privatization, where chunk by chunk, the government is selling what isn't nailed down, without whisper or word to its citizens. This is a country where everything is for sale - women, children, weapons, drugs. And now public and private property - is sold without consent. Perhaps, no one was overly surprised that the government sold the rights to Cambodia's crown jewels, the Angkor complex, to petroleum company, Sokimex. Nor were there waves of shock and disbelief when the government brokered further deals with Sokimex for the country's other major temple sites in 2004-2005. Again, when the Traffic Police Headquarters was sold to a private company, the public weren't particularly flabbergasted. More galling and entirely unforgivable though, was when the government, in April 2005, sold the rights to the Chouek Ek, the Killing Fields, a national memorial for Khmer Rouge victims, to a Japanese firm, J.C.Royal, for 30 years. Equally as heinous is that the deal was sealed, as per usual, without public consent and that senior cabinet minister, Chea Vandeth, who was involved in brokering the arrangement, was reported to have business ties with J.C. Royal. Neang Say, the manager of the site said to the *Cambodia Daily*: "I want the world to know that Cambodia has become a place where they use the bones of the dead to make business." And the market price for a mass grave site today? $US15,000 per year, apparently.

The government also came under fire from human rights groups due to their handling of hundreds of Vietnamese asylum seekers from the Central Highlands (Montagnards) who were forcibly returned to Vietnam, despite evidence of ill-treatment amounting to torture and long prison sentences after unfair trials upon their return.

Cambodia's future, to a considerable extent, rests in the hands of the international aid community, especially the IMF, UNDP and the World Bank. In 2001 foreign assistance covered the entire budget deficit and external aid, as a proportion of GDP, increased from under 12% in 1993 to over 16% (in 2000). Without continuing generosity the country would collapse – as occurred in 1998 in the wake of the coup.

On average, Cambodia receives more than half of its annual budget from foreign aid these days, over 500 donor programmes and projects were operating across the country. The major donors include Japan, France, the United States, South Korea, Australia and Singapore; China is playing an increasingly influential role in the country, both as a donor and investor. In 2005, for their part, the donors pledged 504 million U.S dollars to support Cambodia's development programmes in 2005.

Many critics level at least a portion of the blame for the country's stagnant development on the donor community. In May 2005, the watchdog ActionAid tabled a scathing report about the world aid situation. They stated that approximately half of all Cambodia aid is spent on "technical assistance" (TA), or in non-development-jargon, foreign workers. ActionAid says 1.2 billion dollars was spent on TA between 1999 and 2003 and that the total cost of just 740 top-paid international advisors in Cambodia is estimated to be around - $US50-$70 million, almost equal to the wages of the entire Cambodian civil service of 160,000 people. In many of Cambodia's government ministries, the pay of foreign advisers is more than the annual budget (over twice the budget of the agricultural ministry and four times that of the justice ministry).

Brad Adams of Human Rights Watch said in an interview with John Pilger: "In the 1980s, there was a popular T-shirt satirising US army recruitment commercials with the slogan, 'Join the army. Travel to exotic, distant lands. Meet exciting, unusual people. And kill them'. In the new millennium, it could be rephrased, 'Join the aid community. Travel to exotic, distant lands. Meet exciting, unusual people. And make a killing'.

However the criticism doesn't stop at inflated foreign workers' wages. The effectiveness in application of donor funds is also questionable. When dealing with a government widely known for inherent corruptions the highest forms of monitoring and evaluation, as well as measurable result-orientated goals, are required. In 2004, the World Bank knocked donors for failing to tie results to handouts. Others criticize the propensity for multiple donors to overlap. *The Economist* (2005) further criticized by noting that the donors had neglected agriculture, the livelihood of most Cambodians.

ActionAid believe that governments are inflating the value of already minimal aid to poor countries by a third. As John Pilger (May, 2005) explained : "Britain frequently exaggerates its aid figures (by including debt relief) and America binds its aid to trade and ideology and its "interests". In fact, real aid accounts for just 0.1% of rich countries' combined national income. Set against the UN's minimum "target" of 0.7 per cent, this is barely a crumb. Cambodia is a prime example." The Economic Institute of Cambodia claims that while foreign assistance is helping reduce budget deficit, there could by dire implications for the country later on. In 2005, loans represented about 21% of total foreign aid disbursed during the last twelve years, with an increasing share over that period. At the end of 2004 Cambodia's outstanding foreign debt was estimated to be at US$ 1.2 billion. Therein lies the problem. Should growth of loan disbursement remain strong over the next 10 years, and if crucial reforms aren't established to improve tax collection, Cambodia will inevitably face a debt crisis.

Despite continual threats of withdrawal and aid reduction, the donors are here to stay. Cambodia is highly dependent on aid and the donor community plays an exceptionally important role in the country's development. If aid was withdrawn, the economy, particularly the way it stood in 2005, would surely collapse. There are signs that their patience is wearing thin though. The main areas of concern are corruption, lack of 'transparency' in public finances, the size of the military, the poor state of the legal system and poor fiscal performance. Donors are demanding that the size of Cambodia's army be cut. The *Phnom Penh Post* reported that although Cambodia faces no imminent external threats, the government spends approximately 25% of its tiny budget on a bloated army of around 110,000. In addition, the army is augmented by around 32,000 dead or fictitious "ghost soldiers", whose names are maintained on the payroll so that commanders can line their pockets with extra salaries. In 1999 the military budget was consuming 50% of government expenditure – health, just 2%. In 2004 the Asian Development Bank registered reduced spending again in the priority sectors of health, education, rural development, and agriculture. At a wider level, donors are keeping an eye on political stability in the country. In 2005, the US was constructing one of their largest embassies in the world in Phnom Penh, to what end, one can't be sure, considering, domestic security looked reasonably stable at the time of publication.

Few people believe that the international community is getting a good return from its aid investment. Such vast quantities of money are siphoned off by the powerful and well-connected that, in developmental terms, Cambodia is not getting many bangs for its bucks. It is for all these reasons that the Consultative Group (which links the main aid agencies involved in Cambodia) have made an explicit link between continued funding and reform. Conditionality has become the name of the game and donors would seem to be less sympathetic to Cambodia's appalling history in mapping out the future. It would seem that Prime Minister Hun Sen would like to be remembered as a reformist prime minister – rather than as a thug. In 2001 the National Assembly, under pressure from foreign donors, passed yet more reformist legislation including new audit and land laws, and in 2002 a revised investment law was also passed. In 2004-2005 anti-corruption legislation was said to be a priority for the government.

For multilateral organizations such as the Asian Development Bank, Cambodia needs to base its future development on foreign investment, particularly tourism and service industries. But foreign investors are scared away by the poor physical infrastructure, the lack of a transparent legal system, a corrupt bureaucracy, and the absence of skilled workers – not to mention the country's poor image abroad. Of these, corruption is probably the most serious problem because it reaches into every nook and cranny of public life from the highest politicians to the lowliest bureaucrat. Thailand – the regional economic superpower – is beginning to dominate Cambodia just like it has in another neighbouring country, Laos. During the Khmer Rouge period the control, particularly of the timber and gem-mining sectors, was clandestine and therefore hidden. Now it is open. The new era of economic imperialism began with Thailand flooding the country with consumer goods. Now it is the service sector, from telephones, to air travel, banking and tourism. Really it is not that surprising; Cambodia isn't really in a position to develop itself.

Tensions between the two countries surfaces from time-to-time. In January 2003 there was a serious diplomatic upset with Thailand when a Thai TV star was misquoted as saying that the Angkor Wat temple complex was stolen from Thailand. Chaos ensued and the Khmer's ransacked Phnom Penh's businesses, razed the Thai embassy and 500 Thai nationals were evacuated by military aircraft. Many apologies were offered by the Cambodian government, who negotiated an airspace deal with the Thais as some form of compensation. (Preah Vihear temple, on the Cambodian border with Thailand, has been a source of ongoing contention between the two countries for years and as recent as May 2005, hostility boiled to the surface, resulting in the closure of the border and armed border troops deployed from both sides.)

There is no getting away from the fact that Cambodia is not just poor, but one of the world's least developed nations. Not only are the country's human resources in poor shape but roads are potholed, bridges destroyed, power cuts are commonplace and there is a shortage of skilled managers to oversee reconstruction of the war-shattered economy. Paddy fields are littered with land mines and marketing and distribution systems continue to be hampered by the civil war. In the district of Rattanak Mondal in the west of Battambang province, comprising some of the country's richest farmland, one adult male in seven was killed or maimed by a mine between 1984 and 1994. In short, there is a considerable gap between the macro-economic view from the windows of the finance ministry and that from the paddy field. (It needs to be remembered that 85% of the population still work on the land, and manufacturing accounts for less than 17% of GDP.)

The constraints on Cambodia's development do not begin and end with things like roads, education and health. Cambodians also have to live with the legacy of years of violence. There are 250,000 firearms in the hands of civilians – of which fewer than one in 25 are registered. In 2005 it was possible to buy an AK-47 in Phnom Penh for less than US$1000.

In the past, resentment due to the huge discrepancies in wealth between city and countryside has been responsible for much of the political upheaval. Rampant corruption and the creation of private monopolies of national resources – particularly timber, rubber and gemstones – made a few people very wealthy. One senior UN official described Cambodia's economy to William Shawcross in 1996 as being a 'casino culture' with 200 very rich families and four million very poor people. If historical precedent is anything to go by, future governments are unlikely to learn from past governments' mistakes. As in many Southeast Asian countries, politics is a sure way of getting rich quick. Gemstones and timber both offer Cambodia's most lucrative possibilities.

Bert Hoak of Bert's Books, formerly one of Phnom Penh's top bookshops, finally gave up following the 1997 coup. He saw no end to the problems which he eloquently summarized: "The reality is the donors have given $5bn in the past five years and every dollar they've put in has freed up money for Cambodia's élite to buy more Cognac or another Mercedes. We build roads so people can get to market and those roads are destroyed by logging trucks."

Criticizing Cambodia's political system and the politicians and bureaucrats who are meant to be guiding it towards a bright new future is like shooting fish in a bucket. There is so much corruption, waste, intimidation and inefficiency that there's no fun in it. When foreign observers come to the country on fact-finding missions and are overtly critical this tends to get rejected as 'unhelpful' or 'unconstructive'. The leadership falls back on the excuse that having experienced such horrors it will take time for the country to right itself. There is also no doubt that Cambodia and its people are in a better state today than at any time since 1975. In mid-1999 Sok Chenda, the head of the Council for Development for Cambodia explained of the state of the country's economy: "It's not ideal yet, it's not yet paradise. But compared to before it's much better".

People and society

Before 1975, Cambodia had a population of about 7.2 million; within four years this had dropped to around six million (some were the victims of genocide, others became refugees). The population topped 10 million in 1995 and in 2005 stood at around 13,607,069. The Khmers are the dominant group and there are significant Chinese and Vietnamese minorities as well as a small percentage of tribal groups – most of whom suffered badly during the Pol Pot years.

Khmers
The Khmers are believed to have lived in the region from about the second century AD but there is some argument as to where they migrated from. They may constitute a fusion of Mongul and Melanesian elements. The Khmers now constitute 85% of the population. They have been mainly influenced over the centuries by the powerful Indian and Javanese kingdoms.

Khmer Loeu

The Khmer Loeu, or Upland Khmer (divided into the Saoch, Pear, Brao and Kui), are one of the main tribal groups and live in the forested mountain zones, mainly in the northeast. The Saoch live in the Elephant Mountains to the southwest; the Pear occupy the Cardamom Mountains to the west; while the Brao are settled along the Lao border to the northeast. Traditionally the Khmer Loeu were semi-nomadic and practised slash and burn agriculture. Like many tribal groups in Southeast Asia they were also mainly animist. In recent years, however, increasing numbers have turned to settled agriculture and adopted many of the customs of the lowland Khmers.

Chinese

In the 18th and 19th centuries large numbers of ethnic Chinese migrated to Southeast Asia, where most became involved in commerce. The Chinese settled in the countryside as well as in cities and towns. Until the Khmer Rouge take-over in 1975, the Chinese played a central role in the economy, controlling trade, banking and transport. As in neighbouring Thailand, they assimilated to a greater degree than in other parts of Southeast Asia. In recent decades, most of Cambodia's urban and governing élite has had at least some Chinese blood – Lon Nol, for example had a Chinese grandparent. The Chinese started leaving the country when civil war broke out in 1970 – and many of those who did not get out before 1975 were killed during the Pol Pot years. The few who survived the Khmer Rouge era emigrated during the first months of the pro-Vietnam PRK rule. Officially, the Chinese population of Cambodia today (1995) is 50,000, although some unofficial sources put the number as high as 400,000.

Vietnamese

The southern part of Cambodia, particularly along the Mekong, has always had many inhabitants of Vietnamese descent as well as the area around Phnom Penh. The Vietnamese live very separate lives to the Cambodians due to centuries of mistrust and animosity between the two groups. They are known by the Khmers as 'youn', a derogatory term meaning 'people from the north'. The Cambodian Vietnamese can be distinguished from the Khmers by their typical two-piece pyjama suits and archetypal conical hats. Many of the Vietnamese population left following the takeover of the Khmer Rouge as they were a target of special persecution. A large percentage returned after 1979 with the Vietnamese military presence in the country. As in neighbouring Laos, the Hanoi government encouraged an active resettlement programme for Vietnamese in Cambodia. Most estimates currently put Cambodia's Vietnamese population at 6% of the total. Many Vietnamese have traditionally been businessmen and money changers; some work in skilled jobs and are tailors, mechanics and electricians but those living around the Tonlé Sap are mainly fishermen.

It is the Vietnamese in Cambodia who have suffered most in recent years, and who are most at risk. There are thought to be about 600,000 Vietnamese in the country, and some sources put the figure as high as one million. However officially the Vietnamese population is less than 100,000 (see table). Not only have they been specifically targeted by the Khmer Rouge, but it is hard to find a single Cambodian who has anything positive to say about Vietnamese settlers in the country – it is not uncommon to hear myths that the Vietnamese are responsible for the country's social problems, such as, drugs, rape and theft. Some Khmers will even go so far to state that the Khmer Rouge were actually the Vietnamese thinly disguised as Khmers. One human rights official was quoted as saying "Given a choice, a lot of people in this country would expel every single Vietnamese". And if the nationalistic fervour of Sam Rainsy ever comes into power, this could potentially happen. This dislike of the Vietnamese stems partly from historical fears – Vietnam absorbed large areas of the former Cambodian Empire in the

18th and 19th centuries; partly from Vietnam's role in Cambodia between 1979 and 1989; and partly from the sheer size of Vietnam – some 70 million inhabitants – when set against Cambodia's population of 10 million. As a result anti-Vietnamese sentiment is mainstream politics in the country. Inventing fanciful stories about Vietnamese commandos infiltrating the country, or Vietnamese control of the economy, is never likely to do harm to a budding populist politician. Many Vietnamese (and Cham) live in floating villages due to the foreign ownership laws relating to property.

Cham-Malays

There are about 200,000 Cham-Malays, descended from the Cham of the royal kingdom of Champa based in present day central Vietnam. They now constitute the single largest ethnic minority in the country. In the 15th century the Vietnamese moving south drove many of the Cham living in the lower Mekong area into Cambodia. They now mainly live along the Mekong, north of Phnom Penh. The Chams were badly persecuted during the Pol Pot years and their population more than halved, from about 800,000 during the rule of King Norodom Sihanouk to 350,000 by the end of the Khmer Rouge period. They are Muslim and their spiritual centre is Chur-Changvra near Phnom Penh. They adopted their faith and script from Malays who settled in Kampot and interior regions on the invitation of the Muslim Khmer King Chan in 1642, after he had converted to Islam. The Cham are traditionally cattle traders, silk weavers and butchers – Theravada Buddhism forbids the Khmer to slaughter animals. Their batik sarongs are very similar to those found in Malaysia.

Although the Cham are now free to pursue their faith largely free from persecution, they still suffer from the stigma of being viewed, by many Cambodians, as second class citizens. Strangely perhaps, there is a close affinity between Christians and Muslims in Cambodia – in the face of an overwhelmingly dominant Buddhist faith.

Other groups

There are also a small number of Shans, Thai and Lao, most who live near Battambang, the descendants of miners and jewellers who came to work the ruby mines of Pailin during the French colonial era.

Women in Cambodia

Many academics have heralded the fact that a large proportion of Cambodian women control the finances at home as a measure of equality. And yes, on many fronts Khmer women are equal, it is not uncommon to see female labourers constructing new buildings, nor is it odd to see women heaving around big boulders to build the country's roads. In total, it is believed that Khmer women account for 65% of agricultural labour and 80% of food production.

However, like most undeveloped countries it's women and children that carry the biggest burden of poverty. Oxfam reports that 80% of males are literate yet only 22% of Cambodia women could read a newspaper or write a simple letter in 2003. Many Cambodian families, particularly in rural areas still arrange marriages for their daughters - most of the time trading them off to the highest bidder. The Cambodian League for the Promotion and Defence of Human Rights (LICADHO), www.licadho.org/ reported that even the upper echelons of society are perpetuating this practice, where public figures have arranged the marriages of their children.

On almost every social indicator front, Cambodian women rank worse-off than males but perhaps most alarming, is the amount of violence targeted at females. On a similar scale to developed countries, domestic violence is rife: the Cambodian NGO committee on CEDAW (Convention on the Elimination of All Forms of Discrimination Against Women) reported that 17% of married women aged between 15-49 have experienced physical and sexual violence. Most incidents of rape go unreported, particularly those involving loss of virginity, due to the shame involved. Of those reported to LICADHO in 2003, only 2.3% resulted in conviction. Of these, 38% of rape victims were minors and over 40% of these under the age of 12. LICADHO reported that government employees accounted for 29.5% of rape perpetrators. In 2005 there was a general consensus amongst NGOs and the government that the incidence of rape was increasing. A particularly disturbing report, *Princelings and Paupers by Gender and Development Cambodia*, tabled in 2003, brought to light the insidious spread of gang-rape across Cambodia's urban areas. Referred to as bauk, which means "plus".

Prostitution

In 2003, a survey put the number of prostitutes in the country as a whole at 55,000 prostitutes. Of those 35% are children under the age of 16.

Many of the women and girls working in these establishments are from poor farming families and it seems that most intend to return home with their savings, some to set up small businesses. Many are also Vietnamese.

In 2004 research indicated that 64.45% of prostitutes had been forced into this work; including 52.9% who were duped by the prospect of a good job, and 11.04% who were sold.

Trafficking is a huge problem in Cambodia with the number of trafficked women and children in country estimated to be between 2,000 (Steinfett, 2003) and 100,000 (Human Development Report of the Ministry of Planning, 2000). Inter-country trafficking is also an issue. It is estimated that 88,000 Cambodian bonded workers (not necessarily sex slaves) are in Thailand at any given time. Hundreds of these people are deported every month, half of which are children. Many are then retrafficked back to Thailand and the cycle is repeated.

On paper at least, the prostitution industry in Phnom Penh should now be history: in August 1994 the Mayor of Phnom Penh banned brothels from operating in the city, threatening a fine of one million riel (US$250) to any brothel owners discovered ignoring the ban. However this edict did little to stop prostitution, and many commentators saw it as just a wheeze so that the police could extort money from brothel owners, sex workers, and their clients. There were numerous reports of plainclothes policemen entering brothels, having sex, and then whipping out their police ID cards before demanding a payment. Other stories tell of prostitutes being arrested by the police for illegally plying their trade, and then being 'sold' to another brothel. According to LICADHO's *Project Against Torture* report, "The flesh trade is lucrative business and, like most lucrative businesses in Cambodia, is controlled by people with weapons and influence. Police, military police, army and other state personnel are deeply enmeshed in the trade, actively running or protecting trafficking rings and brothels."

Child prostitution is also rife and more than one half of commercial prostitutes are thought to be underage. In one village, young girls who have been sold into prostitution for as little as US$300 by their destitute parents are paraded for clients from the Cambodian military and government, and for European and American paedophiles. In 2002 it was reported that underage virgins were being sold to foreign visitors for US$1,000 – and after their ordeal, tattooed with a butterfly to indicate their loss of virginity before being sent to brothels. Gary Haugen, a former United Nations investigator described to Forbes magazine Cambodia's child sex industry: "Nothing compares to the deadness in the eyes of a kid in a brothel. In Rwanda, the dead were already gone. In the brothels of Cambodia, they are the living dead." (12.4.2004) An article in the *Phnom Penh Post* in mid-1997 claimed that tourist buses from the state-owned Phnom Penh Tourism had been seen in villages which specialize in child prostitution.

Child sex tourism is flourishing in Cambodia – a result, in part, of the number of abandoned children in the country. This, in turn, can be linked back to the corrosive effects that the KR period had on family structures. Until late 2000 the government did little to stamp out child sex tourism. But even now it is firmly on the government agenda, the problem is proving to be an intractable one. Not only is there a large pool of vulnerable children who can be tempted into the industry, but corruption in the police force means that many paedophiles can buy their way out of trouble. The authorities now have the power to deport or deny entry to anyone suspected of being a paedophile. In April 2002 ageing British rock star Garry Glitter, who is on the UK's sex offenders register, was deported from Cambodia after his arrival in the country (under his real name, Paul Francis Gadd) was reported to the authorities.

The problems that have led to a flourishing child prostitution industry are also seen reflected in another area: the **adoption racket**. Until 2000 when the laws were tightened, Cambodia was possibly the easiest place to adopt a child. The infamous baby brokering by Lauryn Galindo, between 1997-2001, is believed to have been responsible for the 'sale' of over 700 Cambodian children. (Galindo was an Hawaiian baby trafficker. She took children from families and then represented them as orphans needing to be adopted with people paying big fees for the adoption - up to US$3500 per child.) The *Cambodia Daily* suggested that government officials, the major profiteers of the racquet, netted themselves up to $US2.45 million from her business alone.

Many children put up for adoption, like many of those sold into prostitution, come from families so mired in poverty that they see no option but to sell their babies. Foreigners pay US$5,000-15,000 to officials to grease the process of adoption while poor villagers, it has been said, sell their babies to orphanages for as little as US$100. A fallacy often reported, which spurs on the business, is that Cambodia has over half a million orphans. These figures are largely sensationalized; the *Cambodia Daily* said in April 2005 that of these 670,000, 85% have at least one parent. In 2005, it was estimated that there were 12,000 orphans in institutionalized care. Kek Galabru, representative from human rights organization, LICADHO believes: "not all the children in orphanages are orphans. Some of them are there because their parents are too poor to look after them. Others are victims of trafficking and are waiting to be sold".

HIV and AIDS

Like some other countries of Southeast Asia, Cambodia is thought to be in the midst – of an AIDS epidemic. Although the first AIDS case was only diagnosed in 1993 and even by September 1996 there were just 240 reported cases, the scale of HIV infection is growing very rapidly. A study conducted in 1992 found that 9% of sex workers were HIV infected, 3.5% of blood donors and 4% of those treated for other sexually transmitted diseases. At the end of 1994 another study found that the rate of infection among sex workers had risen to 69%. At the end of 1996 it was thought that between 70,000 and 120,000 people were HIV positive. A UN study released in 1997 stated that Cambodia had the highest HIV infection rate among commercial sex workers of any country in Asia. Perhaps a glimmer of hope and a pat on the back for the government and donors is that the exponentially escalating AIDS epidemic has been somewhat curbed, for now at least. In 2005 donors believed that the proportion of Cambodian adults (15-49 years) living with HIV/AIDS had fallen to 2% (sources vary between 1.9% and 4.4%). UNAIDS reported that access to antiretroviral therapy had increased tenfold since 2003, and since 1998 there has been a significant reduction of HIV infection among brothel-based sex workers from 42.6% to 28.8%. Despite all cumulative efforts the country, for its size, Cambodia still has the highest rate of infection in Asia.

AIDS has a corrosive, widespread effect on countries, extending from social implications to economic, and as UN Secretary-General Kofi Annan emphasizes: "AIDS unleashes a chain of events that threatens to cause entire societies to unravel." Reflecting this is the new face of AIDS in Cambodia – married women. In

2005, this group represented over 50% of new HIV infections, a sharp increase from 1999, when they accounted for only 10%. This is largely due to the double-edged sword where married men frequent brothels yet wives don't have the bargaining power to negotiate safe sex. This has led to an increased incidence of mother-to-child HIV transmission and like Africa, if not properly handled, this could lead to a crisis where care of orphans and wide-spread care becomes another side-effect of the epidemic, burdening an already poverty-stricken society. UNICEF believe that the country could be left to look after an estimated 30,000 AIDS orphans below 15 years of age. UNAIDS and the Asian Development Bank estimate that AIDS will slow the rate of poverty reduction in Cambodia by an average of 60% until 2015.

Most AIDS researchers believe that Cambodia is likely to follow the path that Thailand has already forged – towards an AIDS epidemic of increasingly serious proportions. (The Cambodia-Thailand border is porous and the employment of Cambodian women in Thai brothels is helping Thailand 'export' its problem to Cambodia.) Past claims that two million Cambodians could die of AIDS seem highly excessive on current evidence and projections but sexual culture in Cambodia provides a fertile environment for rapid spread. A study undertaken by the Cambodian AIDS Social Research Project revealed that 80% of young men have had sex with a prostitute and 10% with other men. Another survey, undertaken in 2000, revealed that almost half of men who had had anal sex with other men in the month prior to the survey had also had sex with women during the same period. In other words, and this also extends to the intravenous drug-using population, unlike in the West in Cambodia many of those men who engage in homosexual anal sex also have sex with women and a significant proportion also take drugs intravenously. They are far from being discrete populations.

The UN study noted above tried to put a price tag on Cambodia's AIDS problem: between US$1.97bn and US$2.82bn by 2006, or between four and six times the country's total annual aid budget in 1996. The challenge facing Cambodia is the need to inform people of the dangers of unprotected sex and multiple partners particularly between husbands and wives when education levels and facilities are poor and resources comparatively paltry. Thailand offered an insight into the AIDS problem, where an innovative and broad-based AIDS education programme increased the number of prostitutes using condoms from virtually zero a few years back to more than 90% in 1998. This model of how to deal with the epidemic was adopted by Cambodia and largely facilitated by the mega Number One condom campaign, run by Population Services International. The campaign was so successful that "number one" has become a household phrase and the majority of sex workers are now practicing safe sex. The hope is that just as Cambodia has tracked Thailand's trajectory of increase in the use of condoms, it will also mirror that country's continued stabilization.

Religion

The god-kings of Angkor

Until the 14th century Buddhism and Hinduism existed side-by-side in Kambuja. In the pre-Angkor era, the Hindu gods Siva and Vishnu were worshipped as a single deity, Harihara. The statue of Harihara from Phnom Da (eighth century) is divided in half: the 'stern' right half is Siva (with wild curly hair) and the 'sublime' left half, Vishnu (who wears a mitre). The first city at Angkor, built by Jayavarman II in the early ninth century, was called Hariharalaya after this god. Early Angkor kings promoted various Hindu sects, mainly dedicated to Siva and Vishnu. During the Angkor period, Siva was the most favoured deity but by the 12th century Vishnu replaced him. Jayavarman VII introduced Mahayana Buddhism as the official court religion at the

The Cambodian Ramayana: the *Reamker*

The *Reamker* – 'The Story of Rama' – is an adaptation of the Indian Hindu classic, the *Ramayana*, which was written by the poet Valmiki about 2,000 years ago. This 48,000 line epic odyssey – often likened to the works of Homer – was introduced into mainland Southeast Asia in the early centuries of the first millennium. The heroes were simply transposed into a mythical, ancient, Southeast Asian landscape.

In Cambodia, the *Reamker* quickly became highly influential. The scenes carved in stone at Angkor, many of the murals painted on monastery walls, and the tales enacted in shadow theatre (*nang sbaek*) all derive inspiration from the *Reamker*. The Cambodian *Ramayana* dates back to the Angkor period, although the earliest existing written work only dates back to 1620. In the first part of the story, Rama – who in the Cambodian version is depicted as the Buddha – renounces his throne following a long and convoluted court intrigue, and flees into exile. With his wife Sita and trusted companion Hanuman (the monkey god), they undertake a long and arduous journey. In the second part, his wife Sita is abducted by the evil king Ravana, forcing Rama to wage battle against the demons of Langka Island (Sri Lanka). He defeats the demons with the help of Hanuman and his monkey army, and recovers his wife. In the third and final part of the story – and here it diverges sharply from the Indian original – Sita and Rama are reunited and reconciled with the help of the gods (in the Indian version there is no such reconciliation). Another difference to the Indian version is the significant role played by Hanuman – here an amorous adventurer who dominates much of the third part of the epic.

There are also numerous sub-plots which are original to the *Reamker*, many building upon events in Cambodian history and local myth and folklore. In tone and issues of morality, the Cambodian version is less puritanical than the Indian original. There are also, of course, differences in dress, ecology, location and custom.

Hanuman
Adapted from Hallet, Holt (1890)
A Thousand miles on an elephant in the Shan States, William Blackwood: Edinburgh

end of the 12th century. The constant chopping, changing and refining of state religion helped sustain the power of the absolute monarch – each change ushered in a new style of rule and historians believe refinements and changes of religion were deliberately imported to consolidate the power of the kings.

One reason the Khmer Empire was so powerful was its basis on the Hindu concept of the god-king or devaraja. Jayavarman II (802-850) crowned himself as a reincarnation of Siva and erected a Siva lingam (a phallic monument to the god) at Phnom Kulen, the source of power for the Khmer Dynasty. Siva-worship was not originally introduced by Jayavarman II however – it had been previously practised in

the old kingdom of Funan. The investiture of power was always performed by a
Brahmin priest who also bestowed divinity on the king as a gift from Siva. This
ceremony became an essential rite of kingship which was observed continuously –
right into the 20th century. The king's spirit was said to reside in the lingam, which
was enshrined in the centre of a monumental religious complex, representing the
spiritual axis of the kingdom. Here, the people believed, their divinely ordained king
communicated with the gods. Succeeding monarchs followed Jayavarman II's
example and continued to install themselves as god-kings, evoking the loyalty of
their subjects.

Very few of the statues of Vishnu and Siva and other gods left by the Khmer
Empire were traditional representations of the deities. The great majority of the
images were portraits of kings and princes and high dignitaries, each represented as
the god into whom he would be absorbed at the end of his earthly existence. That the
names given to the statues were usually a composite of the names of the man and the
god, indicates that men were worshipped as gods.

The installation of the devaraja cult by Jayavarman II took place on the summit of
Phnom Kulen. Under subsequent kings, it was transferred, in turn, to Bakong, Phnom
Bakheng, Koh Ker and Phimeanakas. At the end of the 11th century, the Baphuon was
constructed to house the golden lingam. The tradition of the god-king cult was so
deeply rooted in the court that even Theravada Buddhism introduced in the 14th
century bowed to its influence. Following the adoption of Buddhism in the second
half of the 12th century, the god-king left his lingam to enter the statue of the Buddha.
Jayavarman VII built the Bayon to shelter the statue of the Buddha-king in the centre
of the city of Angkor.

Temple-mountains were built as microcosms of the universe, with Mount Meru,
the home of the gods, at the centre, surrounded by oceans (followed most perfectly at
Angkor Wat, see page 101). This concept was not invented by the Khmers but was part
of an inherited tradition from India. At the summit of the cosmic mountain, located at
the centre of the city, the king, embodied by his own sacred image, entered into
contact with the world of gods. Each temple was the personal temple of an individual
king, erected by him during his life. When, after his death, his ashes or remains were
deposited there (to animate the statue and give the cult a living image), the temple
became his mausoleum. His successor always built another sanctuary to house the
image of the god-king. During the Angkor period the Khmers did not seem to question
this system. It ordered their lives, regulating everything from agriculture to birth and
death rites. But the temples were not the products of a popular faith, like Christian
cathedrals – they were strictly the domain of royalty and high priests and were
reserved for the worship of kings and members of the entourage deified in the form of
one of the Hindu or Buddhist gods.

Theravada Buddhism

Despite the powerful devaraja cult, most Khmers also practised an amalgam of
ancestor worship and animism. As Theravada Buddhism swept through Southeast
Asia (well after the adoption of Mahayana Buddhism), propagated by missionary
monks, its message of simplicity, austerity and humility began to undermine the cult
of the god-king. As a popular religion, it held great attractions to a population which
for so many centuries had been denied access to the élitist and extravagant devaraja
cult. By the 15th century Theravada Buddhism was the dominant religion in Cambodia
– and across mainland Southeast Asia.

Buddhism shares the belief, in common with Hinduism, in rebirth. A person goes
through countless lives and the experience of one life is conditioned by the acts in a
previous one. This is the Law of Karma (act or deed, from Pali kamma), the law of
cause and effect. But, it is not, as commonly thought in the West, equivalent to fate.

Background Religion

❢ In Siddhartha's footsteps: a short history of Buddhism

Buddhism was founded by Siddhartha Gautama, a prince of the Sakya tribe of Nepal, who probably lived between 563 and 483 BC. He achieved enlightenment and the word buddha means 'fully enlightened one', or 'one who has woken up'.

Siddhartha Gautama is known by a number of titles. In the west, he is usually referred to as The Buddha, ie the historic Buddha (but not just Buddha); more common in Southeast Asia is the title Sakyamuni, or Sage of the Sakyas (referring to his tribal origins).

Over the centuries, the Buddha's life has become part legend, and the Jataka tales which recount his various lives are colourful and convoluted. But, central to any Buddhist's belief is that he was born under a sal tree, he achieved enlightenment under a bodhi tree in the Bodh Gaya Gardens, he preached the First Sermon at Sarnath, and he died at Kusinagara (all in India or Nepal).

The Buddda was born at Lumbini (in present-day Nepal), as Queen Maya was on her way to her parents' home. She had had a very auspicious dream before the child's birth of being impregnated by an elephant, whereupon a sage prophesied that Siddhartha would become either a great king or a great spiritual leader.

His father, being keen that the first option of the prophecy be fulfilled, brought him up in all the princely skills – at which Siddhartha excelled – and ensured he only saw beautiful things, not the harsher elements of life.

Despite his father's efforts Siddhartha saw four things while travelling between palaces – a helpless old man, a very sick man, a corpse being carried by lamenting relatives, and an ascetic, calm and serene as he begged for food. The young prince renounced his princely origins and left home to study under a series of spiritual teachers. He finally discovered the path to enlightenment at the Bodh Gaya Gardens in India. He then proclaimed his thoughts to a small group of disciples at Sarnath, near Benares, and continued to preach and attract followers until he died at the age of 81 at Kusinagara.

For most people, nirvana is a distant goal, and they merely aim to accumulate merit by living good lives and performing good deeds such as giving alms to monks. In this way the layman embarks on the Path to Heaven. It is also common for a layman to become ordained, at some point in his life (usually as a young man), for a three month period during the Buddhist Rains Retreat.

Monks should endeavour to lead stringently ascetic lives. They must refrain from murder, theft, sexual intercourse, untruths, eating after noon, alcohol, entertainment, ornament, comfortable beds and wealth. They are allowed to own only a begging bowl, three pieces of clothing, a razor, needle, belt and water filter. They can only eat food that they have received through begging. Anyone who is male, over 20, and not a criminal can become a monk.

The 'Way of the Elders', is believed to be closest to Buddhism as it originally developed in India. It is often referred to by the term 'Hinayana' (Lesser Vehicle), a disparaging name foisted onto Theravadans by Mahayanists. This form of Buddhism is the dominant contemporary religion in the mainland Southeast Asian countries of Thailand, Cambodia, Laos and Burma.

In Theravadan Buddhism, the historic Buddha, Sakyamuni, is revered above all else and most images of the Buddha are of Sakyamuni. Importantly, and unlike Mahayana Buddhism, the Buddha image is only meant to serve as a meditation aid. In theory, it does not embody supernatural powers, and it is not supposed to be worshipped. But the popular need for objects of veneration has meant that most

In the First Sermon at the deer park in Sarnath, the Buddha preached the Four Truths, which are still considered the root of Buddhist belief and practical experience: suffering exists; there is a cause of suffering; suffering can be ended; and to end suffering it is necessary to follow the 'Noble Eightfold Path' – namely, right speech, livelihood, action, effort, mindfulness, concentration, opinion and intention.

Soon after the Buddha began preaching, a monastic order – the Sangha – was established. As the monkhood evolved in India, it also began to fragment into different sects. An important change was the belief that the Buddha was transcendent: he had never been born, nor had he died; he had always existed and his life on earth had been mere illusion. The emergence of these new concepts helped to turn what up until then was an ethical code of conduct, into a religion. It eventually led to the appearance of a new Buddhist movement, Mahayana Buddhism which split from the more traditional Theravada 'sect'.

Despite the division of Buddhism into two sects, the central tenets of the religion are common to both. Specifically, the principles pertaining to the Four Noble Truths, the Noble Eightfold Path, the Dependent Origination, the Law of Karma, and nirvana. In addition, the principles of non-violence and tolerance are also embraced by both sects. In essence, the differences between the two are of emphasis and interpretation. Theravada Buddhism is strictly based on the original Pali Canon, while the Mahayana tradition stems from later Sanskrit texts. Mahayana Buddhism also allows a broader and more varied interpretation of the doctrine. Other important differences are that while the Thervada tradition is more 'intellectual' and self-obsessed, with an emphasis upon the attaining of wisdom and insight for oneself, Mahayana Buddhism stresses devotion and compassion towards others.

images are worshipped. Pilgrims bring flowers and incense, and prostrate themselves in front of the image. This is a Mahayanist influence which has been embraced by Theravadans.

Buddhism in Cambodia

The Cambodian Buddhist clergy divide into two groups: the Mahanikay and Thommayuth (or Dhammayuttikanikay) orders. The latter was not introduced from Thailand until 1864, and was a reformist order with strong royal patronage. Theravada Buddhism remained the dominant and unchallenged faith until 1975.

It was a demonstration by Buddhist monks in Phnom Penh which first kindled Cambodian nationalism in the wake of World War II (see page 231). According to historians, one of the reasons for this was the intensifying of the relationship between the king and the people, due to the founding of the Buddhist Institute in Phnom Penh in 1930. The Institute was under the joint patronage of the kings of Laos and Cambodia as well as the French. It began printing and disseminating Buddhist texts – in Pali and Khmer. Historian David P Chandler wrote: "As the Institute's reputation grew, enhanced by frequent conferences, it became a rallying point for an emerging intelligentsia." The institute's librarian founded a Khmer-language newspaper (Nagaravatta – or 'Angkor Wat') in 1936, which played a critical role in articulating and spreading the nationalist message.

Before 1975 and the arrival of the Khmer Rouge, there were 3,000 monasteries and 64,000 monks (bonzes) – many of these were young men who had become ordained to escape conscription – in Cambodia and rural life was centred around the wat (Buddhist monastery). Under Pol Pot, all monks were 'defrocked' and, according to some sources, as many as 62,000 were executed or died in the ricefields. Monasteries were torn down or converted to other uses, Pali – the language of Theravada Buddhism – was banned, and former monks were forced to marry. Ironically, Saloth Sar (Pol Pot) himself spent several years as a novice when he was a child. Buddhism was revived in 1979 with the ordination of monks by a visiting delegation of Buddhists from Vietnam; at the same time, many of the wats – which were defiled by the Khmer Rouge – were restored and reconsecrated. The two orders of Theravada Buddhism – the Thommayuth (aristocratic) and Mahanikay (common) – previously practised in Cambodia have now merged. The Hun Sen government softened the position on Buddhism to the degree that it was reintroduced as the national religion in 1989 and young men were allowed to be ordained (previously restricted to men over 45 that were no longer able to serve in the army).

Today 90% of Cambodian citizens are Buddhist. In 2004, the country had almost 59,500 monks spread across the country's 3980 wats. Cambodian Buddhism is an easy-going faith and tolerates ancestor and territorial spirit worship, which is widely practised. The grounds usually consist of a Vihara (Buddhist temple), Sala Thoama Saphea (the hall where Dharma is taught) and kods (the quarters where the monks live). Traditionally, the Vihara and the Buddha statues contain within them will face east in order to express gratitude to Lord Buddha for enlightenment and guide others toward the path of enlightenment. There are often small rustic altars to the guardian spirits or neak ta in the corner of pagodas. Cambodians often wear katha – or charms – which are believed to control external magical forces. Many Khmer communities have achars, who share in the spiritual guidance of people but do not compete with the monks. Most important ceremonies – weddings, funerals, coming of age – have both Buddhist and animist elements. Wats play an important role in education and it is fairly common to find schools built inside or beside wats.

Other religions

There are around 60,000 Roman Catholics in Cambodia, mainly Vietnamese, and about 2,000 Protestants. Islam, of the Sunni sect, is practised by many of the 200,000 (some commentators would say 500,000) Cham. During the Khmer Rouge period it was reported that Cham were forced to eat pork while most Cham mosques were destroyed, and only now are they being slowly rebuilt. A new International Mosque in Phnom Penh, built with Saudi money, was opened in 1994. Almost all the Chinese in Cambodia are Taoist/Confucianist.

Culture

Language and literature

The Khmer language

The Khmer language belongs to the Mon-Khmer family, enriched by the Indian Pali and Sanskrit languages and peppered with Thai and French influences. The use of Sanskrit in royal texts became more widespread after the introduction of Mahayana Buddhism in the 12th century (although there are inscriptions dating from the sixth century) and the Pali language spread into Cambodia via Siam with Theravada Buddhism. Khmer is related to languages spoken by hill tribe people of Laos, Vietnam and even Malaysia – but is very different to Thai or Lao. Khmer has no tones, no tenses, and words attached to the masculine or feminine genders. But Khmer does have 23 vowel-sounds and 33 consonants; it is also a very specific language – for instance, there are 100 different words for types of rice. The Khmer language is written from left to right with often no separation between words. ⟩⟩ *For a list of Khmer words and phrases, see page 290.*

French was widely spoken by the intelligentsia before 1975 and is still spoken by a few elderly Cambodians. Today however, everyone seems to want to learn English, and there are informal pavement English schools setting up on Phnom Penh's streets. This has led to some Franco-Anglophone friction. Understandably, the French government – one of Cambodia's largest aid donors – would like to see the French language sustained, perhaps even developed. In 1995 this led to the strange spectacle of language riots on the campus of Phnom Penh's Cambodian University of Technology as students burnt French text books in protest at being forced to learn a language which, they said, 'got them nowhere'.

Cambodian literature

Religious literature comprises works of religious instruction, derived from the Sanskrit and Pali texts of the Theravada Buddhist canon, the Tripitaka. The Jataka tales are well known in Cambodia and several modern adaptations have been made from these texts. The Jatakas recount the former lives of the historic Buddha and were probably first introduced to Cambodia from Laos. Most of the stories tell of how the Buddha – then a prince – managed to overcome some defect by the use of magic or the assistance of some god, enabling him to be born higher up the scale of birth and re-birth on his long road to nirvana. The two Khmer epics are the poem of Angkor Wat and the Reamker (or Ramakerti), derived from the Indian Ramayana. Traditionally the literature was recorded by incising palm leaf manuscripts with a sharp stylus, the incisions then being blackened to make them easily visible. Such manuscripts, if stored in favourable conditions, can last for over 100 years.

From around the 17th century, **chap** poetry, an import from Thailand, became popular. The poetry took root in monasteries as a means by which monks could more easily teach the laity the lessons of the Buddhist texts. However, over time, they also took on a secular guise and became a means by which more everyday homilies were communicated.

Most of the early literature has been destroyed but there are surviving Sanskrit inscriptions on stone monuments dating from the sixth century and some early palm leaf manuscripts. Many of these are contained in the Bibliothèque Nationale in Paris – the Khmer Rouge managed to destroy most of those housed in monasteries and museums in Cambodia itself. Historical literature consists largely of inscriptions from Angkor Wat as well as the Cambodian royal chronicles. Fictional literature is diverse in Cambodia and includes the Ipaen folk stories written in prose. French literature has had a profound influence on modern Cambodian literature. The first modern Cambodian novel was Sophat published in 1938. It, and the novels and short stories that followed it, represented a break with the past. The authors wrote of ordinary people, used natural conversation, and wrote in prose, not poetry. Most of the recent Cambodian novels have been written by Cambodians living abroad – most writers and journalists were either killed by the Khmer Rouge or fled the country.

Arts and architecture

Indian origins

The art of modern Cambodia is almost completely overshadowed by its past. The influence of the Khmers at the height of the empire spread as far as the Malay peninsula in the south, to the Burmese border in the west and the Vietnamese frontier

Mudras and the Buddha image

An artist producing an image of the Buddha does not try to create an original piece of art; he is trying to be faithful to a tradition which can be traced back over centuries. It is important to appreciate that the Buddha image is not merely a work of art but an object of and for, worship. Sanskrit poetry even sets down the characteristics of the Buddha – albeit in rather unlikely terms: legs like a deer, arms like an elephant's trunk, a chin like a mango stone and hair like the stings of scorpions. The Pali texts of Theravada Buddhism add the 108 auspicious signs, long toes and fingers of equal length, body like a banyan tree and eyelashes like a cow's. The Buddha can be represented either sitting, lying (indicating paranirvana), or standing, and (in Thailand) occasionally walking. He is often represented standing on an open lotus flower: the Buddha was born into an impure world, and likewise the lotus germinates in mud but rises above the filth to flower. Each image will be represented in a particular mudra or 'attitude', of which there are 40. The most common are:

Abhayamudra – dispelling fear or giving protection; right hand (sometimes both hands) raised, palm outwards, usually with the Buddha in a standing position.

Varamudra – giving blessing or charity; the right hand pointing downwards, the palm facing outwards, with the Buddha either seated or standing.

Vitarkamudra – preaching mudra; the ends of the thumb and index finger of the right hand touch to form a circle, symbolizing the Wheel of Law. The Buddha can either be seated or standing.

Dharmacakramudra – 'spinning the Wheel of Law'; a preaching mudra symbolizing the teaching of the first sermon. The hands are held in front of the chest, thumbs and index fingers of both joined, one facing inwards and one outwards.

Bhumisparcamudra – 'calling the earth goddess to witness' or 'touching the earth'; the right hand rests on the right knee with the tips of the fingers 'touching ground', thus calling the earth goddess Dharani/Thoranee to witness his enlightenment and victory over Mara, the king of demons. The Buddha is always seated.

Dhyanamudra – meditation; both hands resting open, palms upwards, in the lap, right over left.

Other points of note:
Vajrasana – yogic posture of meditation; cross-legged, both soles of the feet visible.

Virasana – yogic posture of meditation; cross-legged, but with the right leg on top of the left, covering the left foot (also known as paryankasana).

Buddha under Naga – the Buddha is shown in an attitude of meditation with a cobra rearing up over his head. This refers to an episode in the Buddha's life when he was meditating; a rain storm broke and Nagaraja, the king of the nagas (snakes), curled up under the Buddha (seven coils) and then used his seven-headed hood to protect the Holy One from the falling rain.

Buddha calling for rain – the Buddha is depicted standing, both arms held stiffly at the side of the body, fingers pointing downwards.

Bhumisparcamudra – calling the earth goddess to witness. Sukhothai period, 13th-14th century.

Dhyanamudra – meditation. Sukhothai period, 13th-14th century.

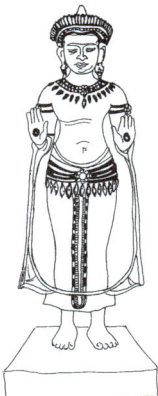

Abhayamudra – dispelling fear or giving protection. Lopburi Buddha, Khmer style 12th century.

Vitarkamudra – preaching, "spinning the Wheel of Law". Dvaravati Buddha, 7th-8th century, seated in the "European" manner.

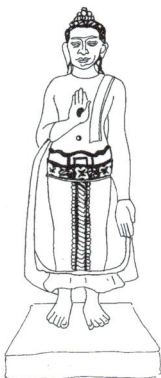

Abhayamudra – dispelling fear or giving protection; subduing Mara position. Lopburi Buddha, Khmer style 13th century.

The Buddha 'Calling for rain'.

Background Culture

in the north and east. But ancient Khmer culture was itself inherited. Indian influence was particularly strong in the Mekong basin area and the Khmers accepted Indian ideas about astrology, religion and royalty – including the cult of the god-king (deva-raja). Other elements of Cambodian culture which are recognizably Indian in origin include classical literature and dance, as well as religious architecture. Hindu deities inspired the iconography in much of Cambodian art and Sanskrit gave the Khmers access to a whole new world of ideas. Cambodian influence is very strong in Thai culture as Siam's capture of a large part of the Khmer Empire in the 15th century resulted in many of Cambodia's best scholars, artists and craftsmen being transported to Siam (Thailand).

Artistic revival

The richness of their culture remains a great source of pride for the Khmer people and in the past it has helped forge a sense of national identity. There has been an artistic revival since 1979 and the government has devoted resources to the restoration of monuments and pagodas. (Many local wats have been repaired by local subscription; it is estimated that one-fifth of rural disposable income is given to the upkeep of wats.) The resurgence of Buddhism has been paralleled in recent years by a revival of traditional Khmer culture, which was actively undermined during the Pol Pot years. Today Phnom Penh's two Fine Arts Schools are flourishing again; one teaches music and dance, the other specializes in architecture and archaeology. There is a surprisingly good collection of artefacts in the National Museum of Arts even though huge quantities of treasure and antiques have been stolen and much of the remainder destroyed by the Khmer Rouge.

Angkor period

The height of Khmer art and architecture dates from the Angkor period spanning the 8th to 13th centuries. All the surviving monuments are built of stone or brick, and all are religious buildings. The culture and art of the early kingdoms of **Funan** and **Chenla** were central to the evolution of Angkorian art and architecture. Art historian Philip Rawson wrote that these two kingdoms were the foundation of Khmer art, "just as archaic Greek sculpture was the foundation of later classical Greek art". Funan's centre was to the southwest of the Mekong Delta but extended into present day Cambodia. The only remains that definitely came from the early kingdom of Funan are limited to four Sanskrit inscriptions and a few sculptures. The earliest surviving statues from Funan are at Angkor Borei and date from the sixth century; but by then Funan was a vassal of Chenla. The kingdom of Chenla – based at Sambor and later at Sambor Prei Kuk – expanded at the expense of Funan. It refined and developed Funan's earlier artistic styles.

Relics of the **pre-Angkorian periods** have been found all over South Cambodia and between the Mekong and the Tonlé Sap. The principal monuments are brick towers with square ground plans, false doors and mounting storeys of decreasing size. They were characterized by strong sculptural work, based on Indian ideas but carved in a unique style. Many of the statues from this era are in the National Museum of Arts at Phnom Penh (see page 57). Most of the art from the pre-Angkorian kingdoms is Hindu but it seems that Mahayana Buddhism was briefly introduced into the country as a number of images of Bodhisattvas have been found. In the late eighth century, the Chenla Kingdom collapsed and Jayavarman II, who had lived most of his life in the Sailendra court in Java, returned to declare himself devaraja in 802.

During the Angkor period, Javanese and neighbouring Champa architectural influences were incorporated into Khmer designs. The architecture and its decoration were governed by a series of mystical and religious beliefs. Temples were designed to represent the cosmic Mount Meru, surrounded by oceans. For a detailed account of the typical design features and evolution of Angkor temple architecture, as well as the development of Khmer sculpture, see page 95.

Textiles

Cambodia is not well known for the quality and range of its textiles, especially when compared with the industry in neighbouring Thailand and Laos. In Chou Ta-kuan's account of life at Angkor written in 1296-1297, he claimed that "Not only do the Khmer women lack skill with needle and thread for mending and sewing, they only know how to weave fabrics of cotton, not of silk". However by the time the French arrived in the second half of the 19th century, weaving in silk and cotton was well-established. The Cambodian royal court had a large retinue of weavers producing sumptuous, richly patterned and coloured silk cloth. Even as recently as the 1940s, weaving was still a craft practised in just about every village, and every woman worth her salt was expected to be able to weave. Then, in the 1950s, cheap imported silk and cotton cloth began to undermine the local product and people began to turn to other occupations. One elderly silk weaver, Liv Sa Em, explained in 1995, "you could earn more selling cakes in two days than you could earn weaving in five months". But it was the Khmer Rouge period which finally sealed the fate of Cambodia's textile industry. Apart from producing the familiar checked cloth used as a head scarf, or kramar, weaving virtually died out between 1975 and 1979. Many of the most skilled weavers, especially those associated with the Cambodian court, were either murdered or fled the country.

Now the government and many NGOs see a bright future for silk weaving and resources are being directed towards its revitalization. Many women find weaving attractive: it can be built around the demands of housework and childcare; it can be done at home; and it can provide an important supplementary source of income. However, because the domestic industry was so withered after years of neglect, NGOs are finding it necessary to bring in foreign weaving experts from Thailand, Laos, Vietnam and China to teach people anew how to raise silkworms and train women in more advanced weaving techniques.

The Cambodian national dress is the samphot, a long rectangle of cloth (about twice as long as a sarong length) which is wrapped around the body and then taken up between the legs to be tucked in at the waist. Traditionally women wore this with a simple breast cloth and men with a jacket. Samphot are woven in rich, warm colours. Sometimes the warp and weft are different colours giving the finished cloth a shimmering appearance. Weft ikat is used to produce the well-known samphot hol and it is thought that this process influenced Thai designs after Siam conquered Angkor in the mid-15th century taking many of the most skilled weavers back to the capital, Ayutthaya, as booty.

Dance, drama and music

There is a strong tradition of dance in Cambodia which has its origins in the sacred dances of the apsaras, the mythological seductresses of ancient Cambodia. Classical dance reached its height during the Angkor period; it was based on interpretations of the Indian epics, particularly the Ramayana. Dance also became a religious tradition, designed to bring the king and his people divine blessing. Dancers, nearly all of whom were well born, were central to the royal court and were protected as a separate part of the king's harem; only the god-king could touch them. The dancers became legendary even outside Cambodia: when Thailand invaded, the Khmer classical ballet dancers were part of their war booty and were taken to the Thai court. The decline of Angkor brought the decline of classical dance, although it continued to survive as an art form through the patronage of the royal Thai court. When the French colonialists revived Khmer ballet in the 20th century they initially imported dancers from Thailand.

The dances are very symbolic. Court dances are subject to a precise order, a strict form and a prescribed language of movements and gestures. Most of the dancers are women and the male and female roles are distinguished by costume. All the dancers are barefoot as the unimpeded movement of the feet is very important. The national dance is called the lamthon which is characterized by slow graceful movements of the hands and arms. The most highly trained lamthon dancers wear elaborate, tight-fitting costumes of silk and velvet that have to be sewn onto them before each performance.

Due to their close association with the royal family (they were based at the royal palace right up to 1970 and danced regularly for Prince Sihanouk), the once-famous and flourishing National Dance Group was a prime target for the Khmer Rouge regime of the mid-1970s. Many dancers were killed; others fled into exile. Em Tiay was one of the few to survive the killing fields. She began dancing at the age of six in 1937 and the only reason she survived the Pol Pot years was because the headman of the village where she lived was so captivated by her dancing that he protected her. Her two sisters were not so lucky. With the fall of the Khmer Rouge she returned to dancing and became a full-time classical dance teacher at the Bassac Theatre in Phnom Penh. In 1981 the School of Fine Arts was reopened to train new recruits, 80% of whom were orphans. Today the National Dance Group performs for some tour groups and made its first tour to the wSest in 1990.

The government, with the help of overseas cultural groups, has been trying to resurrect Cambodia's classical dance tradition. By 1997 about 50% of the classical Khmer dance repertoire had been recovered. Support has come in from sources as diverse as the Japanese city of Fukuoka and UNESCO. Some 80 elderly Khmer who managed to survive the Khmer Rouge holocaust are being interviewed and their knowledge committed to paper while 4,000 dance gestures and positions have been recorded on video. Nonetheless the effort is proving difficult. The National Theatre's dancers are paid just US$15-20 per month and in 1994 the Bassac Theatre, the country's premier dance venue, was burnt down. In early 1999 it had still not been rebuilt.

Folk dancing has managed to survive the 1970s intact, although as a form of regular village entertainment, it has been undermined by the arrival of radios, televisions and videos. Unlike the court dances, folk dances are less structured, with dancers responding to the rhythm of drums. The dancers act out tales from Cambodian folk stories; folk dancing can often be seen at local festivals.

Folk plays and **shadow plays** (nang sbaek) are also a popular form of entertainment in the countryside. The latter are based on stories from the Ramayana, embroidered with local legends. The characters are cut out of leather and often painted. Wandering shadow puppeteers perform at local festivals.

Because of the importance of dance to the ancient royal Khmer court, **music** – which always accompanied dance routines – was also central to Cambodian court and religious life. Singers and musicians were often attached to specific temples. Cambodian music has evolved from Indian and Indonesian influences and, more recently, Thai. The traditional orchestra consists of three xylophones, khom thom (a horseshoe-shaped arrangement with 16 flat gongs), violins, wind instruments including flutes, flageolets and a Khmer version of bagpipes, as well as drums of different shapes and sizes. There are three types of drum: the hand drum, the cha ayam drum and the yike drum. The drummer has the most important role in folk music as he sets the rhythm. In 1938 a musical scholar estimated that only 3,000 melodies were ever employed in Khmer music. There is no system of written notation so the tunes are transmitted orally from generation to generation. There are five tones (compared to seven in western music) and no real harmony – the melodies are always simple.

Land and environment

Geography

Cambodia is all that remains of the once mighty Khmer Empire. Covering a land area of 181,035 sq km – about the size of England and Wales combined – the country is squeezed in between Thailand to the west, Vietnam to the east and Laos to the north. Cambodia holds many features of international conservation significance. The country has one of the highest proportions of land as natural habitat (forest and wetlands) in the world, and one of the least disturbed coastlines in continental Asia. The coastline stretches along the Gulf of Thailand for 435 km, supports 64 islands and extensive mangroves and coral reefs. The **Mekong** is as central to life in Cambodia as the Nile is to life in Egypt. The river runs through Cambodia for about 500 km, bisecting the east lowlands, north to south. It is navigable by cargo ships from the delta in Vietnam, right up to Phnom Penh and beyond. Near the centre of the country is the **Tonlé Sap** – the 'Great Lake' – the largest freshwater lake in Southeast Asia. It is connected to the Mekong via the short channel-like Tonlé Sap River. The Tonlé Sap basin includes all or part of 8 of Cambodia's 24 provinces and covers 80,000 square kilometers (44% of Cambodia's total area) and is estimated to be home to 3.6 million, one third of Cambodia's total population.When the Mekong floods between June and October – sometimes these floods can be devastating, as they were in 1991 – the Tonlé Sap River reverses its flow and the floodwaters fill the Great Lake, which doubles in size, covering the surrounding countryside (see page 129).

North of Phnom Penh, the Mekong is known as the Upper Mekong – or just the Mekong; downriver from the capital it divides into the Lower Mekong and the Bassac rivers. These two tributaries then swing to the southeast across the fertile alluvial plain, towards the sprawling delta and the sea. The broad valley of the Mekong is a centuries-old trade route and its fertile central flood-plain is densely populated. The alluvial soils are irrigated but have an even greater potential for agricultural production than is presently being realized. Throughout most of its course in Cambodia the river averages more than 1.6 km in width. There are viscous rapids at Kratie, northeast of Phnom Penh, and a succession of dramatic waterfalls – Li Phi and Khong Phapheng Falls – on the border with Laos.

The **central lowlands** are surrounded by savannah; in south Cambodia these plains run all the way to the Vietnamese border. But to the north, east and west, Cambodia is enclosed by mountain chains: the Cardamom Mountains and Elephant Range to the west and southwest, while the sandstone escarpment of the Dangrek Range forms a natural border with Thailand. The **Cardamom Mountains** (named after the spice) run in a gentle curve from just south of Battambang towards Phnom Penh. Phnom Aoral, in the Cardamoms, is Cambodia's highest peak at 1,813 metres and in 2004 Global Witness detected a large amount of illegal logging in the area. The **Elephant Mountains** run along the south coastline. All these mountains are densely forested and sparsely inhabited, making them perfect operational bases for Cambodia's rebel guerrilla factions, who fought the Phnom Penh government throughout the 1980s. On the south coast around Kompong Som is a lowland area cut off from the rest of the country by mountains. Because the Mekong was a major thoroughfare, the **coastal region** never developed into a centre of trade until a road was built with American aid from Kompong Som to Phnom Penh in the 1960s.

Climate

The monsoons determine rainfall and temperature patterns in Cambodia. The southwest monsoon, from May to October, brings heavy rain throughout the country. This period accounts for between 75% and 80% of the total annual rainfall. The northeast monsoon blows from October to April and ushers in the dry season. In the mountain areas the temperature is markedly cooler and the dry season only lasts three months. Between the heat and rains there are transitional periods and the best time to visit the country is between November and January, before it gets too hot. Rainfall varies considerably from region to region. The Cardamom Mountains are the wettest. The mean temperature for Cambodia is 27.5°C. It is cooler – around 24°C – from November to January and hotter – around 32°C – between February and April. Humidity is generally high.

Flora and fauna

The central plains are a predominantly agricultural area and are sparsely wooded but most of the rest of Cambodia – until recently – was still forested. In 1970, 73% of Cambodia's land area was thought to be forested; the figure in 1995 was less than 40%, and a paper published at the end of 1998 put the area at 30%. So the trend is rapidly down.

The reasons for the alarming decline in Cambodia's forests are pretty clear – illegal logging. In the southwest, around the Cardamom and Elephant Mountains, there are still large tracts of primary forest where teak predominates. There are also tracts of virgin rainforest in the west and the northeast. At higher elevations in these mountains there are areas of pine forest and in the north and east highlands, temperate forest.

Cambodia has a wide variety of fauna and, before war broke out in the 1970s, was on the international game-hunters' circuit; there were tigers (now an endangered species), buffalo, elephants, wild oxen, majestic birds, clouded leopards (also endangered) and bears including Malaysian sun bears. Today, there are 630 types of protected wildlife, including 122 mammal species, 537 bird species, 114 are rodents from the rodent family, 40 are aquatic animals and 300 are insects and butterflies.

Even after all the fighting, game is still said to be abundant in forested areas, particularly in north-eastern provinces of Mondulkiri and Ratanakiri. Smaller animals include monkeys, squirrels, tree rats and shrews, flying foxes and numerous species of reptile, including several varieties of poisonous snake, the most common being Russell's viper, the banded krait, cobra and king cobra. The kouprey (meaning 'jungle cow') is Cambodia's most famous animal and a symbol of the Worldwide Fund for Nature. A wild ox, it was first identified in 1939 but is now virtually extinct worldwide. In 1963, King Sihanouk declared the animal Cambodia's national animal. Small numbers are thought to inhabit the more remote areas of the country, although some experts fear that the last specimens were either killed by guerrillas for meat or are being fatally maimed after treading on anti-personnel mines laid by the Khmer Rouge. An effort to capture and breed the kouprey is underway in Vietnam.

Even around Phnom Penh one can see herons, cranes, grouse, pheasant, wild duck, pelicans, cormorants and egrets. The Tonlé Sap area is particularly rich in fish-eating waterfowl.

The Tonlé Sap is also rich in marine life, and supports possibly the largest inland fisheries industry in the world. The lake is the lifeline for about 40% of the Cambodian population and provides almost 60% of the country's protein. In 1997 the government applied to UNESCO seeking the nomination of the Great Lake as a Biosphere Reserve - for a reserve covering 300,000 ha including both the lake and its surrounding shores. 1.36 million Khmer's are estimated to be wholly dependent on inland waterways for transport.

The lower reaches of the Mekong, marking the border between Cambodia and Laos, is also the last place in Indochina where the rare Irrawaddy dolphin (Orcaella brevirostris) is to be found. Unfortunately, fishermen in the area took to fishing using dynamite and this threatens the survival of the mammal. Explosives historically have been widely available, and evidently this method of fishing is quick and effective. It is also indiscriminate and wasteful, killing juvenile as well as mature fish, and animals like the dolphin which were hitherto left unharmed. Countless numbers were also killed under the Khmer Rouge regime. It was also once found in Thailand's Chao Phraya River, but pollution put paid to that population years ago.

The poverty of most of Cambodia's population has made the trade in exotic fauna an attractive proposition. By 1997 the trade in wildlife had become 'rampant', according to the environmental NGO Global Witness. A case in point is the plight of the Malayan sun bear (*Helarctos malayanus*), which has been protected in Cambodia since 1992. But its paws and gall bladder are treasured by many Chinese and bear bile is said to command a price of US$100 per gramme in China due to its perceived medicinal properties. The animals are captured and caged and the bile siphoned off through a steel tube inserted into the gall bladder. There is also documentary footage of animals having their paws amputated while still alive. Once again, the failure to protect the sun bear, and many other wild animals, is not due to an absence of environmental legislation but due a lack of commitment to its implementation. Giant ibis and black-necked storks are sold for US$400-500 a pair, rewards are put out for black cranes, turtles and pythons are sold to Chinese and Korean restaurants, and the eggs and chicks of water birds are collected for sale in markets. Cambodia's fauna is being caught, sold and slaughtered on a truly grand scale.

Timber tragedy

In 1995 the Cambodian government, to much fanfare, introduced a new environment law. This was heralded as the first step in the sustainable exploitation of Cambodia's forests and other natural resources. The introduction of the law was accompanied by other legislation, including a new Environmental Impact Assessment Law. At the end of 1996 the government seemed to go one step further when they outlawed the export of whole logs. But even in 1995 experts were sceptical about the ability of the Cambodian government to deliver on its environmental promises. The lack of transparency in many of the regulations, and the ease with which companies and individuals with political and economic power could – and can – circumvent those regulations, makes environmental protection difficult to achieve in any systematic sense.

This scepticism was borne out later, in 1998, when the UK-based environmental group Global Witness claimed that, unless the rate of logging was reduced substantially, Cambodia was "heading toward deforestation of all saleable timber within three to five years". Patrick Alley, who has done much to highlight the plight of Cambodia's wild areas, claimed at a press conference that "the logging situation is out of control". Although Cambodia still has forests, it is believed 40-50% of the country's forests have been logged.

The problem is that apparently just about everyone from senior government ministers through to senior army officers and foreign governments or their representatives are involved in illegal logging activities.

With foreign donors becoming increasingly frustrated at the Cambodian government's lack of commitment to protecting the environment, Prime Minister Hun Sen ordered a crack-down on illegal loggers in March 1999. The fact that some donors were moving towards making further aid dispersal contingent on forestry reform no doubt concentrated the mind of the Prime Minister. The difficulty for one of the poorest countries in the world is that forestry is one of Cambodia's major industries, accounting for 43% of foreign trade and contributing 15% of GDP in 1997. But even more important than the fact that forestry is important to the nation is that timber is valuable to individuals.

The army and politicians are making a killing. As Ly Thuch, Under-Secretary for State for the Environment, told a meeting at the Foreign Correspondents Club in Phnom Penh, "the main destroyers of the environment are the Khmer Rouge and the rich and powerful". It is doubtful that even Cambodia's aid donors can make a difference. In mid-1996 international aid donors had become so worried about the failure of the Cambodian government to control logging that the IMF suspended a US$20 mn budget-support payment. But Cambodia's two prime ministers continued to sign logging contracts – without cabinet discussion and in contravention of their own environmental laws.

In early 2000, Hun Sen vouched: "If I cannot put an end to the illegal cutting of trees, I will resign from my position of prime minister in the first quarter of 2001." True to his word? No. Needless to say the Cambodian government was still entering into illegal logging concessions in 2004-2005 breaking an international moratorium on logging that was due to expire in late 2005. Furthermore, those critical of the government's illegal activities have been threatened and hassled. In April 2002, a senior official with the independent forestry monitor Global Witness was beaten near her office. The next day she was sent an e-mail instructing her to quit. The forestry monitor, Global Witness was later sacked by Hun Sen.

In 1970, about 70% of the country was covered by primary forest with sources suggesting that half has been logged, the majority of this, in the past 10 years. There are major ecological side effects of deforestation, particularly in a country where 80% of the population rely on subsistence agriculture. The ongoing rice crop failure and siltation of the waterways, effecting the valuable fisheries can largely be contributed to the rampant deforestation.

In an interview published in November 1996, William Shawcross suggested that illegal logging was "perhaps the most serious crisis of corruption in the regime". Nothing much has changed in the intervening years.

National parks

Cambodia was the first country in Southeast Asia to establish protected areas, with the forests surrounding the Angkor temples declared a national park in 1925. By 1969, six wildlife sanctuaries had been established covering 2.2 million hectares or 12% of the country for the protection of wildlife, in particular large mammals. Towards the end of 1993, King Sihanouk signed a decree to create 23 protected areas, now covering over 21% of the country. Cambodia has one of the highest percentages of national territory within protected areas in the world and had the goal to increase that area to 25% by the end of 2005.

It may be rather ironic, but the dislocations caused by Cambodia's long-running civil war have probably helped to protect the environment, rather than destroy it. Although larger animals like the kouprey may have suffered from the profusion of land mines that dot the countryside, other animals have benefited from the lack of development that has occurred. Unlike Thailand and Vietnam forest has not been cleared for agriculture and many regions became 'no-go' areas to all except for the foolhardy and the well-armed. This created conditions in which wildlife could survive largely undisturbed by the forces of 'development'. Now wildlife experts and environmentalists are arguing that Cambodia has a unique asset that should be preserved at all costs – and not just because it might be the morally 'right' thing to do. In addition, the growth in eco-tourism world wide could create a considerable money-spinner for the country.

Books

Southeast Asia

Cambridge History of Southeast Asia. (Cambridge: Cambridge University Press, 1992). Two-volume edited study, long and expensive with contributions from most of the leading historians of the region. A thematic and regional approach is taken, not a country one, although the history is fairly conventional.

Dumarçay, Jacques *The Palaces of South-East Asia: architecture and customs.* (Singapore: OUP, 1991). A broad summary of palace art and architecture in both.

Fenton, James *All the Wrong Places: adrift in the politics of Asia.* (London: Penguin, 1988). British journalist James Fenton skilfully and entertainingly recounts his experiences.

Fraser-Lu, Sylvia *Handwoven Textiles of South-East Asia.* (Singapore: OUP, 1988). Well-illustrated, large-format book with informative text.

Higham, Charles *The Archaeology of Mainland Southeast Asia from 10,000 BC to the Fall of Angkor.* (Cambridge: Cambridge University Press, 1989). Best summary of changing views of the archaeology of the mainland.

King, Ben F and Dickinson, EC *A Field Guide to the Birds of South-East Asia.* (London: Collins, 1975). Best regional guide to the birds of the region.

Osborne, Milton *Southeast Asia: an introductory history.* (Sydney: Allen & Unwin, 1979). Good introductory history, clearly written, published in a portable paperback edition.

Rawson, Philip *The Art of Southeast Asia.* (London: Thames & Hudson, 1967). Portable general art history of Cambodia, Vietnam, Thailand, Laos, Burma, Java and Bali; by necessity, rather superficial.

Reid, Anthony *Southeast Asia in the Age of Commerce 1450-1680: the lands below the winds.* (New Haven: Yale University Press, 1988). Perhaps the best history of everyday life in Southeast Asia, looking at such themes as physical well-being, material culture and social organization.

Reid, Anthony *Southeast Asia in the age of commerce 1450-1680: expansion and crisis.* (Yale University Press: New Haven. Volume 2, 1993).

Sesser, Stan *The Lands of Charm and Cruelty: travels in Southeast Asia.* (Basingstoke: Picador, 1993). A series of collected narratives first published in the New Yorker including essays on Singapore, Laos, Cambodia, Burma and Borneo. Finely observed and thoughtful, the book is an excellent travel companion.

Steinberg, DJ *et al In Search of Southeast Asia: a modern history.* (Honolulu: University of Hawaii Press, 1987). The best standard history of the region; it skilfully examines and assesses general processes of change and their impacts from the arrival of the Europeans in the region.

Novels

See also Cambodian literature, page 275.

Cixous, Helene *The Terrible but Unfinished Story of Norodom Sihanouk, King of Cambodia.* (University of Nebraska Press, 1994). Avant-garde 20th-century literature associated with recent political history.

Drabble, Margaret *The Gates of Ivory.* (London: Penguin, 1992). The third part of a trilogy which deals with Cambodia during the period of the civil war while the Vietnamese 'occupied' Phnom Penh and the Khmer Rouge controlled much of the countryside.

Documentation Centre of Cambodia *The Khmer Rouge – From Victory to Destruction.* The compilation of reports, orders and chronological details helps to give an insight into how the Khmer Rouge operated during this period.

Ho, Minfong *Brother Rabbit: A Cambodian Tale.* (Lothrop, Lee and Shepard Books, 1997). Traditional legend translated into English along with a discussion on the place of folklore in Cambodia, relating themes to Cambodian history.

Koch, Christopher *Highways to War.* (Minerva, 1996). New novel about wartime Cambodia and Vietnam – part thriller, part mystery, part heroic epic by the author of The Year of Living Dangerously.

Dith Pran *Children of Cambodia's Killing Fields.* (Yale University Press, 1998). Eyewitness accounts of the Khmer Rouge regime by Cambodian survivors.

Ngor, Haing S *Surviving the Killing Fields*. One of the best, first-hand accounts of this terrible period. Recommended.

Ryan, Paul Ryder *Khmer Rouge End Game*. (Munewata Press, 1999). Work of 'faction' relating the kidnapping of six foreigners by the one-legged guerrilla leader Ta Mok.

History

Chou Ta-kuan *The Customs of Cambodia*. (Bangkok: Siam Society, 1993). Written in 1296-97 by Chou Ta-kuan, a Chinese emissary to the kingdom of Angkor. It is a potted, first hand account of life and livelihoods in the 13th century. Widely available in Bangkok.

Chandler, David P *The Tragedy of Cambodian History: politics, war and revolution since 1945*. (Yale University Press: New Haven, 1993).

Chandler, David P *Brother Number One: a political biography of Pol Pot*. (Colorado: Westview Press, 1992). Chandler is considered one of the most authoritative academics in the field of Cambodian history.

Chandler, David P *Voices from S-21: terror and history in Pol Pot's secret prison*. (University of California Press, 2000).

Chanda, Nayan *Brother Enemy: the war after the war*. (New York: Macmillan, 1986). Exhaustive and engrossing account of 'the third Indochina war' puts Cambodian conflict into regional perspective: vivid journalistic style.

Criddle, Joan & Butt Mam, *To Destroy You Is No Loss: the odyssey of a Cambodian family*. (Doubleday, 1987).

Jackson, K (edit) *Cambodia 1975-1978: rendezvous with death*. (Princeton University Press, 1989).

May, Someth *Cambodian Witness*. (London: Faber and Faber, 1986). A chilling personal account of the Pol Pot period. Of Someth May's family of 14 only four survived the terrible years of the Khmer Rouge.

Osborne, Milton *Sihanouk*. (Allen and Unwin, 1996). A biography of the controversial Asian leader chronicling his evolution from a dilettante king to rigorous and ruthless politician.

Pin Yathay *Stay alive my father*. (Touchstone Books, 1998).

Ponchaud, Francois *Cambodia Year Zero* (translation from French). (London: Penguin, 1978).

Shawcross, William *Sideshow: Kissinger, Nixon and the destruction of Cambodia*. (London: Chatto & Windus, 1979, revised 1986). Excellent, balanced and very readable investigative work on American involvement in the Cambodian 'sideshow'; it runs through to cover the Pol Pot period.

Shawcross, William *The Quality of Mercy: Cambodia, holocaust and the modern conscience*. (London: Fontana, 1984).

Shawcross, William *Cambodia's New Deal* (1994). A book by Shawcross examining the UN-brokered peace deal and the country's progress since the elections.

Swain, Jon *River of Time*. (London: Minerva, 1995). Jon Swain was a journalist in Indochina during the Vietnam War and then stayed on to be one of the few foreigners to witness the fall of Phnom Penh to the Khmer Rouge. The chapters on Cambodia are excellent and Swain's account of Indochina during this traumatic period is enthralling.

Szymusiak, Moldya *The stones cry out: a Cambodian childhood*. (London: Jonathan Cape, 1986). A book recounting the recent tragedy of Cambodia from the perspective of one person.

Ung, Loung *First They Killed My Father: A Daughter Of Cambodia Remembers* (Harper Perennial, 2001) The devastatingly sad and true story of what Loung and her family experienced during the Khmer Rouge period.

General

Gilboa, Amit *Off the rails in Phnom Penh: into the Dark Heart of Guns, Girls and Ganja, Bangkok*. Slightly breathless account of some of Phnom Penh's well known vices (1997).

Livingston, Carol *Gecko Tails*. (Orion Paperbacks, 1997). A humorous chronicle of the new wave of tourism that followed the demise of the Khmer Rouge.

Oeur, U. Sam *Sacred Vows*. (Coffee House Press 1998). Collection of poems recalling the horror of the author and his family's spell in six different concentration camps.

Jacob, Judith M. *The Traditional Literature of Cambodia: A Preliminary Guide*. (OUP 1996). Comprehensive survey of ancient Cambodian writing.

Page, Tim *Derailed in Uncle Ho's Victory Garden*. (Scribner Paperback 1999). Page's odyssey, 20 years after the liberation of

Vietnam, through the land that dominated his life as a wartime photographer.

Venn, Savat and Downie, Sue *Down Highway One: Journeys Through Vietnam and Cambodia*. (Allen and Unwin, 1993). Highway One is one of the longest and most historic roads in Asia. This recounts the author's travels there.

Travel, geography and guides

Hoskins, John *The Mekong*. (Bangkok: Post Publishing, 1991). A large format coffee table book with good photographs and a modest text. Widely available in Bangkok.

Jacobson, Matt *Adventure Cambodia*. Silkworm Books. A good guide for people interested in motorcycling through Cambodia.

Jensen, Carsten and Haveland Barbara *I Have Seen the World Begin*. (Harvill Press, 2000). Collection of travel writings with insights into local households, lives and personal points of view.

Lewis, Norman *A Dragon Apparent: travels in Indochina*. (London: Jonathan Cape, 1951). Republished by Eland Books. Possibly Norman Lewis' best known travel book. Witty and perceptive, about a fifth is based on his travels in Cambodia. Gives a good feel of Cambodia 'before the fall'.

Economics, politics, society and development

Elizabeth Becker *When the War Was Over*. (New York: Simon & Schuster, 1988).

Brady, Christopher *United States Foreign Policy towards Cambodia, 1977-1992*. (Macmillan Press Ltd, 1999). A study of US foreign policy that delves into decision making theory and foreign policy analysis. Widely considered one of the best accounts of this historical period. Recommended.

Chandler, David P *Revolution and Its Aftermath in Kampuchea: Eight Essays*. (Yale University. SE Asia Studies, 1983).

Curtis, Grant *Cambodia Reborn? The transition to Democracy and Development*. (Brookings Institution Press, 1998). This book examines Cambodia's uneasy renaissance from years of conflict, isolation and authoritarian rule following the UN-sponsored elections of 1993.

Findlay, Trevor *Cambodia (Macmillan Press, 1997)*. This is an account and analysis of the United Nations peacekeeping operation mounted in Cambodia between 1991 and 1993.

Heininger, Janet E *Peacekeeping in Transition: The United Nations in Cambodia*. (Brookings Institution Press, 1994). This book investigates the United Nations Transitional Administration in Cambodia's experiences in their entirety arguing that they can make future UN peace-keeping efforts more effective.

Art and architecture

le Bonheur, Albert *Of Gods, Kings, and Men: Bas-reliefs of Angkor Wat and Bayon*. (Serindia Publications 1995).

Dumarcay, Jaques and Smithies, Michael *Cultural Sites of Burma, Thailand and Cambodia*. (OUP SE Asia, 1996). An investigation of the most important historic sites in these countries.

Dumarcay, Jaques and Smithies, Michael *The Site of Angkor*. (OUP SE Asia, 1998). An introduction to this amazing complex's history and construction.

Giteau, Madeleine and **Gueret, Danielle** and **Renaut, Thomas** and **Keo, Pich** *L'Art Khmer/Khmer Art*. (ASA Editions, 1998). A representation of more than a millennium of Cambodian art.

Ibbitson Jessup, Helen *Sculpture of Angkor and Ancient Cambodia: Millennium of Glory*. (Thames and Hudson, 1997). 1,000-year artistic legacy of Cambodia displayed in an extensively illustrated volume.

Jaques, Claude and Freeman, Michael *Ancient Angkor*. (Thames and Hudson, 2000).

Mannikka, Eleanor *Angkor Wat: Time, Space and Kingship*. (University of Hawaii Press, 1996). An attempt to understand the temple in terms of the measurement systems used by its original builders and uncovering a sophisticated system of philosophical and religious principles within them.

Miyamato, R *Angkor*. (Art Data, 1994).

Roveda, Vittorio *Khmer Mythology*. (Thames and Hudson, 1997). The thousands of temples and shrines erected by the Khmer people were carved with stone reliefs. This volume studies these 'stories in stone'.

288 **Werly, Richard, Renaut, Thomas** and **Lacouture, Jean** *Eternal Phnom Penh*. (ASA Editions, 1998). Photographs and descriptions of Phnom Penh of today.

Zephir, Thierry *Khmer*. (Thames and Hudson, 1998). The Khmer Empire's art and architecture, its influences, rise and fall explained.

Footnotes

Useful Khmer words and phrases

There are a number of sounds in Khmer, or Cambodian, which have no equivalent in English. The transcription given here is only an approximation of the sound in Khmer and is taken from David Smyth and Tran Kien's (1991) Courtesy and Survival in Cambodia, School of Oriental and African Studies: London.

Consonants

bp	is a sharp 'p' somewhere between 'p' & 'b' in English
ch	as in 'chase'
dt	is a sharp 't', somewhere between 't' & 'd'
j	as in 'jump'
g	as in 'get'
kh	a 'k' as in 'kettle'
ng	as in 'ring'
ph	a 'p' sound as in 'pill', not an 'f' sound as in 'phone'

Vowels

a	as in 'ago'
ah	as in 'car'
ai	as in 'Thai'
ao	as in 'Lao'
ay	as in 'pay'
ee	as in 'see'
eu	as in 'uugh'
i	as in 'fin'
o	as in 'long'
oh	as in 'loan'
oo	as in 'boot'
OO	more of a 'u' sound as in 'cook'
u	as in 'run'

Useful words and phrases

Yes	*baht* (male speakers)
	Jah (female speakers)
no	*(ot) dtay*
Please	*suom mehta*
thank you (very much)	*or-gOOn (j'run)*
Hello	*jOOm ree-up soo-a*
Goodbye	*lee-a hai*
see you later	*juab k'nea ta'ngay krai*
how are you?	*Tau neak sok sapbay jea teh?*
good morning	*arun suor sdei*
good afternoon	*tiveah suor sdei*
good evening	*sa-yoanh suor sdei*
good night	*reah-trey suor sdei*
excuse me/sorry!...	*...som dta(h)*
where's the...?	*...noev ai nah?*

how much is...?	...t'lai bpon-mahn?
it doesn't matter	mun ay dtay
never mind/that's alright	dop bprum moo-ay
I don't understand	mun yoo-ul dtay
I want a...	k'nyom jang baan
what is your name?	Neak ch'muah ei?
my name is...	k'nyom tch much

Basic vocabulary

Bank	ta-nee-a-gee-a
Doctor	bpairt
Hospital	mOOn-dti-bpairt
Khmer Rouge	k-mai gra-horm
Market	p'sah
post office	brai-sa-nee-ya-than
Toilet	borng-goo-un
Water	dteuk

Food

Bread	nOOm bpung
Chicken	moan
Delicious	ch'ngun
Fish	dt'ray
Food	m'hohp
Meat	saich
Restaurant	hanng bai
Rice	bai
Tea	dtai
Water	dteuk

Travel

is it far?	Ch'ngai dtay?
turn left/right	bot dtoh kahng ch'wayng/s'dum
go straight	ondtoh dtrong
where is the...?	noev eah nah?
Bus	laan ch'nuol
Boat	dtook
train station	ra dteah plerng
Cyclo	see kloa
will you go for...riel?...	ree-ul bahn dtay?
that's expensive	t'lai na(h)

Time/date

Morning	bpreuk
Midday	dtrong
Night	yOOp
Today	t'ngai ni(h)
Day	t'ngai

Tomorrow	*sa-aik*
Yesterday	*m'seri mern*
Midnight	*aa-tree-at*
Sunday	*t'ngai aa-dteut*
Monday	*t'ngai jan*
Tuesday	*t'ngai ong-gee-a*
Wednesday	*t'ngai bpoot*
Thursday	*t'ngai bpra-hoa-a*
Friday	*t'ngai sok*
Saturday	*t'ngai sao*
Month	*khaeh*
Year	*ch'nam*
last year	*ch'nam moon*
new year	*ch'nam thmey*
next year	*ch'nam groy*
January	*ma ga raa*
February	*kompheak*
March	*mee nah*
April	*meh sah*
May	*oo sa phea*
June	*mi thok nah*
July	*ka kada*
August	*say haa*
September	*kan'ya*
October	*dto laa*
November	*wech a gaa*
December	*t'noo*

Numbers

1	*moo-ay*	20	*m'pay*
2	*bpee*	30	*sahm seup*
3	*bay*	40	*sai seup*
4	*boo-un*	50	*hah seup*
5	*bprum*	60	*hok seup*
6	*bprum moo-ay*	70	*jert seup*
7	*bprum bpee* or *bprum*	80	*bpait seup*
	bpeul	90	*gao seup*
8	*bprum bay*	100	*moo-ay roy*
9	*bprum boo-un*	1,000	*moo-ay bpohn*
10	*dop*	10,000	*moo-ay meun*
11	*dop moo-ay*	100,000	*moo-ay sain*
12	*dop bpee… etc*	1,000,000	*moo-ay lee-un*
16	*dop bprum moo-ay*	10,000,000	*dahp lee-un*

Index

Map index

Advertisers' index

Credits

Footprint credits

Text editor: Claire Boobbyer
Map editor: Sarah Sorensen
Picture editor: Robert Lunn
Proofreader: Stephanie Lambe

Publisher: Patrick Dawson
Editorial: Alan Murphy, Sophie Blacksell,
Sarah Thorowgood, Felicity Laughton,
Nicola Jones
Cartography: Robert Lunn, Claire Benison,
Kevin Feeney
Series development: Rachel Fielding
Design: Mytton Williams and Rosemary
Dawson (brand)
Sales and marketing: Andy Riddle
Advertising: Debbie Wylde
Finance and administration:
Sharon Hughes, Elizabeth Taylor

Photography credits

Front cover: Alamy (Angkor Wat, Buddhist
stone sculpture)
Back cover: Alamy (colourful fishing boats at
Sihanoukville)
Inside colour section: Alamy, Claire
Boobbyer, Aleta Moriarty, Photolibrary,
Superstock

Print

Manufactured in India by Nutech
Photolithographers, Delhi. Pulp from
sustainable forests

Footprint feedback

We try as hard as we can to make each
Footprint guide as up to date as possible
but, of course, things always change. If you
want to let us know about your experiences
– good, bad or ugly – then don't delay, go
to www.footprintbooks.com and send in
your comments.

Publishing information

Footprint Cambodia
4th edition
© Footprint Handbooks Ltd
April 2006

ISBN 1 904 777 51 1
CIP DATA: A catalogue record for this book is
available from the British Library

® Footprint Handbooks and the Footprint
mark are a registered trademark of
Footprint Handbooks Ltd

Published by Footprint

6 Riverside Court
Lower Bristol Road
Bath BA2 3DZ, UK
T +44 (0)1225 469141
F +44 (0)1225 469461
discover@footprintbooks.com
www.footprintbooks.com

Distributed in the USA by

Publishers Group West

Neither the black and white nor colour
maps are intended to have any political
significance.

Every effort has been made to ensure that
the facts in this guidebook are accurate.
However, travellers should still obtain advice
from consulates, airlines etc about travel and
visa requirements before travelling. The
authors and publishers cannot accept
responsibility for any loss, injury or
inconvenience however caused.

Acknowledgements

A great many people have helped in the preparation of this new edition of *Footprint Cambodia*, so thanks to everyone, particularly the Cambodian people who helped me understand their country.

Thanks to all the Phnom Penhoites, especially my best friend in Cambodia, photographer, Martin Flitman; to Bruce Lasky for the "refuge" and Srean, Vuthy and particularly the "can-do-anything man", Suon Kong; to the lakesiders – Neil (enormous gratitude), Don Juan, Wency, Vin, Dan and James and to Hurley, Derek, Wendy and Al for great conversation and insights into the country; to Steven Briggs for giving PP the once over and introducing the wonders of North Korean food; to Nick for empathy and his mate, with the lotus telephone, who made me laugh hard when I needed it most.

In the provinces thanks to Angela and trusty side-kick, Elvis, plus Christian of the *Rusty Key Hole* in Kampot; to Nicolas, of *Champey Inn*, and the gang from *Verandah* in Kep. Infinite gratitude to Alan, in Siem Reap, for endless support and for flagging Laos in the UK. Thanks to Gordon, of *Two Dragons,* and Sheila, of *Hidden Cambodia*, in Siem Reap for their invaluable tips and advice. Thanks is also due to Little Fezworth for being a ray of sunshine in Sihanoukville, to Jim Algae up north and to Mr Pou of Battambang for being the best driver/guide/insect capturer/travel companion in the country; and to Hak Sophal in Kompong Chhnang for his overwhelming enthusiasm for the area and to Charles in Kratie.

A zillion thank yous to Justin Armstrong. You are the best, supporting me through hell and high water, unconditionally and patiently, even though you probably wanted to throttle me. The memory of being stuck on the worst sandy roads in the world at midnight, with a broken bike, surrounded by mines, while the skies opened upon us, will stay with me forever. And, we could still laugh about it.

At Footprint HQ, a multitude of gratitude to Claire Boobbyer for her devotion and ability to buy time, to Alan Murphy for getting me the job and to those involved with deciphering my maps. And in Oz, thanks to David Scott, Woodslane, who planted the seed and to Eva and Kevster for constantly being there. Previous editions of this guide were researched and written by John Colet and Joshua Eliot.

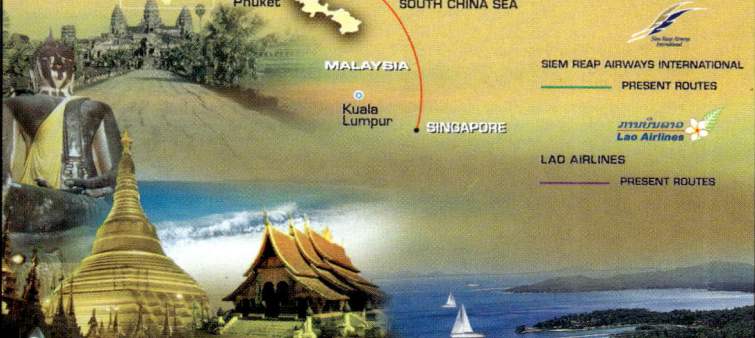

Trails of Asia

Journey through lost kingdoms and
hidden history of Southeast Asia
and let Asian Trails be your guide!

asian TRAILS
Blazing new paths in travel

Choose Asian Trails, the specialists in Southeast Asia.
We will organise your holiday, hotels, flights and tours to the region's
most fascinating and undiscovered tourist destinations.
Contact us for our brochure or log into
www.asiantrails.net or www.asiantrails.com

CAMBODIA
No. 33, Street 240, P.O. Box 621, Phnom Penh
Tel: (855 23) 216 555, Fax: (855 23) 216 591, E-mail: res@asiantrails.com.kh

INDONESIA
JL. By Pass Ngurah Rai No. 260, Sanur, Denpasar 80228, Bali
Tel: (62 361) 285 771, Fax: (62 361) 281 515, E-mail: renato@asiantrailsbali.com

LAO P.D.R.
Unit 1, Ban Hai Sok, P.O.Box 815, Chanthabouly Dis., Vientiane,
Lao P.D.R.Tel: (856 21) 263 936 Mobile: (856 205) 211 950
Fax: (856 21) 262 956, E-mail: vte@asiantrails.laopdr.com

MALAYSIA
11-2-B Jalan Manau off Jalan Kg. Attap 50460 Kuala Lumpur, Malaysia
Tel: (60 3) 2274 9488, Fax: (60 3) 2274 9588, E-mail: res@asiantrails.com.my

MYANMAR
73 Pyay Road, Dagon Township, Yangon, Myanmar
Tel: (95 1) 211 212,223 262, Fax: (95 1) 211670, E-mail: res@asiantrails.com.mm

THAILAND
9th floor SG Tower, 161/1 Soi Mahadlek Luang 3, Rajdamri Road,
Lumpini, Pathumwan, Bangkok 10330, Thailand
Tel: (66 2) 626 2000, Fax: (66 2) 651 8111, E-mail: res@asiantrails.org

VIETNAM
Unit 712 7/F Saigon Trade Center
37 Ton Duc Thang St., D. 1, Ho Chi Minh City
Tel: (84 8) 9 10 28 71-3 Fax: (84 8) 9 10 28 74, E-mail: asiantrails@hcm.vnn.vn

Map symbols

Administration

- ☐ Capital city
- ○ Other city/town
- International border
- Regional border
- Disputed border

Roads and travel

- Motorway
- Main road (National highway)
- Minor road
- Track
- Footpath
- Railway with station
- ✈ Airport
- 🚌 Bus station
- Ⓜ Metro station
- Cable car
- Funicular
- 🚢 Ferry

Water features

- River, canal
- Lake, ocean
- Seasonal marshland
- Beach, sandbank
- Waterfall

Topographical features

- Contours (approx)
- Mountain
- Volcano
- Mountain pass
- Escarpment
- Gorge
- Glacier
- Salt flat
- Rocks

Cities and towns

- Main through route
- Main street

- Minor street
- Pedestrianized street
- Tunnel
- One way-street
- Steps
- Bridge
- Fortified wall
- Park, garden, stadium
- Sleeping
- Eating
- Bars & clubs
- Building
- Sight
- Cathedral, church
- Chinese temple
- Hindu temple
- Meru
- Mosque
- Stupa
- Synagogue
- Tourist office
- Museum
- Post office
- Police
- Bank
- Internet
- Telephone
- Market
- Medical services
- Parking
- Petrol
- Golf
- A Detail map
- A Related map

Other symbols

- Archaeological site
- National park, wildlife reserve
- Viewing point
- Campsite
- Refuge, lodge
- Castle
- Diving
- Deciduous/coniferous/palm trees
- Hide
- Vineyard
- Distillery
- Shipwreck
- Historic battlefield

Cambodia

THAILAND

Chong Jom
O Smach
Preah Vihear
Dangrek Mountains
Samrong
Anlong Veng
Choam Ksant
Banteay Chhmar
SIEM REAP-ODDAR MEANCHEY
Thma Pok
Koh Ker
Kulen
T'Beng Meanchey
Srah Chhuk
PREAH VIHEAR
Poipet
Mongkol Borei
Thkov
Phnum Liep
Phnom Kulen
Sisophon
6
BANTEAY MEANCHEY
Banteay Srei
Beng Mealea
Kouk Kduoch
Siem Reap
Angkor
Bakong
Preah Khan
Ta Seng
12
Knach Roméas
Phnom Krom
Roluos
Prek Toal Bird Sanctuary
Chong Khneas
Dam Dek
Kamping Poy
Battambang
Sambor Prei Kuk
Reang Kesei
5
Tonlé Sap
Daun Lem
Pruhm
Pailin
10
BATTAMBANG
Moung Roessei
Stoeng
Kompong Thom
Phnom Santuk
Pursat
Kompong Luong
PURSAT
Kompong Chhnang
Cardamom Mountains
Phnom Aural (1,813m)
KOMPONG CHHNANG
Skon
Phnom Knang Trapeang (1,210m)
5
Tonlé Sap
Oudong
Hat Lek
Cham Yem
26
5
Koh Dach
Kie Sva
Koh Kong
KOH KONG
KOMPONG SPEU
Kompong Speu
PHNOM PENH
KANDA
Kirirom National Park
Choeung Ek
Tonlé Bati
Koh Kong
4
Phnom Tamao
Phnom Chisor
Sre Ambel
18
3
Takeo
25
Angkor Borei
Koh Rong
Elephant Mountains
KAMPOT
16
TAKEO
4
Chhuk
3
Sihanoukville (Kompong Som)
Bokor Mountain National Park
Phnom Bokor
Kampot
2
3
Kep
16
Kompong Trach
Caves
17
Preah Sihanouk 'Ream' National Park
Koh Prins
Koh Tang

Gulf of Thailand

The Great Escape

Little time, sensible budget, **big** adventure

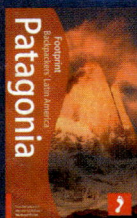